How to Think About Weird Things

How to Think About Weird Things

Critical Thinking for a New Age

EIGHTH EDITION

Theodore Schick Jr.
Muhlenberg College

Lewis Vaughn

Foreword by Martin Gardner

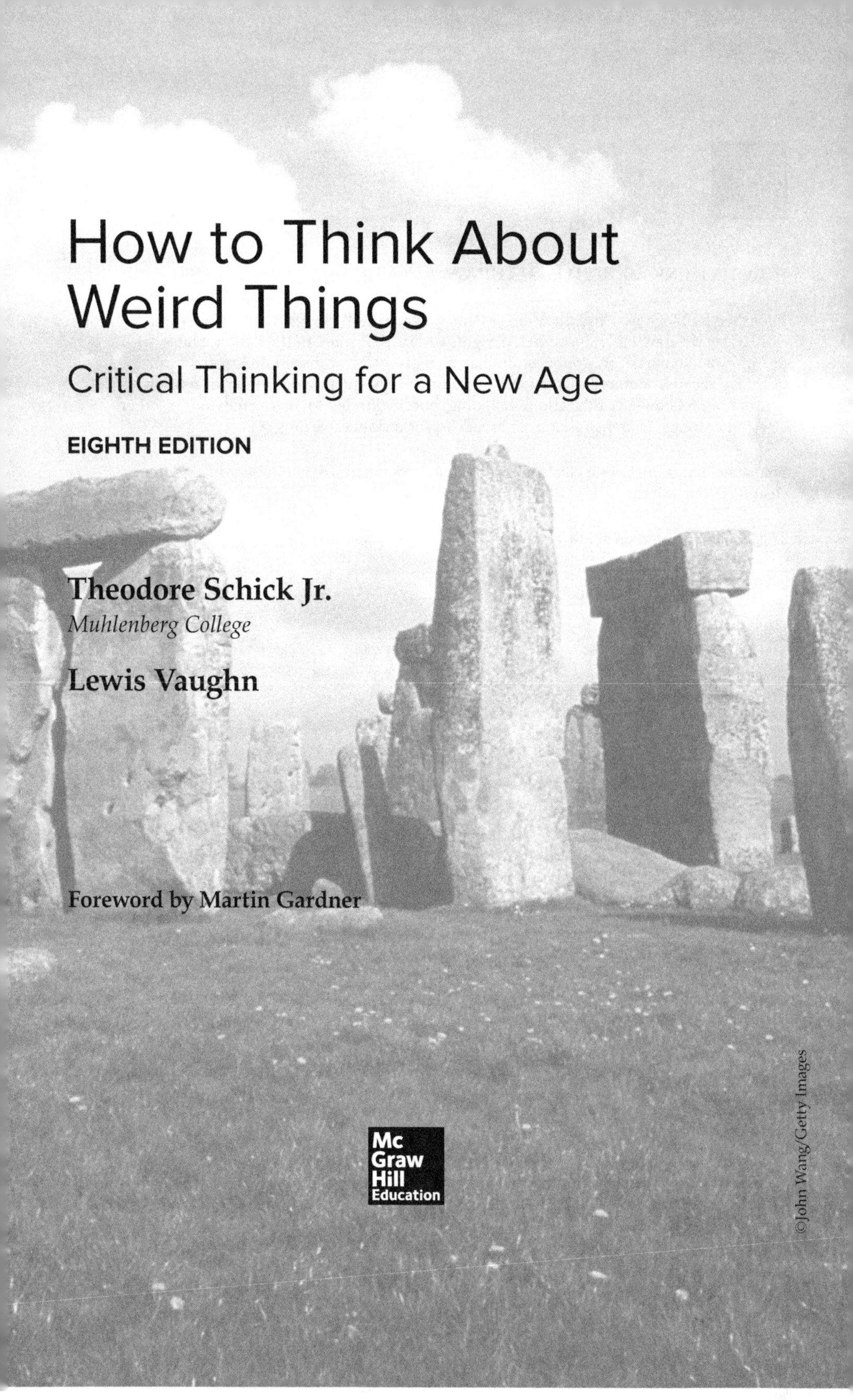

©John Wang/Getty Images

McGraw Hill Education

Mc
Graw
Hill
Education

HOW TO THINK ABOUT WEIRD THINGS

Published by McGraw-Hill Education, 2 Penn Plaza, New York, NY 10121.

This book is printed on acid-free paper.

2 3 4 5 6 7 8 9 BRP 21 20

ISBN 978-1-260-54807-5
MHID 1-260-54807-4

Cover Image: ©*Mediaparts/Shutterstock*

mheducation.com/highered

To Erin, Kathy, Katie, Marci, Patrick, and T. J.

Foreword

Every year, in English-speaking countries alone, more than a hundred books that promote the wildest forms of bogus science and the paranormal are published. The percentage of Americans today who take astrology seriously is larger than the percentage of people who did so in the early Middle Ages, when leading church theologians—Saint Augustine, for example—gave excellent reasons for considering astrology nonsense. We pride ourselves on our advanced scientific technology, yet public education in science has sunk so low that one-fourth of Americans and 55 percent of teenagers, not to mention a recent president of the nation and his first lady, believe in astrology!

Now and then a courageous publisher, more concerned with enlightening the public than with profits, will issue a book that honestly assesses pseudoscience and the paranormal. Works of this sort now in print can be counted on your fingers. It is always an occasion for rejoicing when such a book appears, and there are several ways in which *How to Think about Weird Things* is superior to most books designed to teach readers how to tell good science from bad.

First of all, this book covers an enormous range of bogus sciences and extraordinary claims that currently enjoy large followings in America. Second, unlike most similar books, the authors heavily stress principles that help you critically evaluate outlandish claims—and tell you *why* these principles are so important. Third, the book's discussions are readable, precise, and straightforward.

I am particularly pleased by the book's clearheaded assessment of scientific realism at a time when it has become fashionable in New Age circles to think of the laws of science as not "out there," but somehow a projection of our minds and cultures. Yes, quantum mechanics has its subjective tinge. There is a sense in which an electron's properties are not definite until it is measured, but this technical aspect of quantum theory has no relevance on the macroscopic level of everyday life. In no way does the mathematical formalism of quantum mechanics imply, as some physicists smitten by Eastern religions claim, that the moon is not there unless someone looks at it. As Einstein liked to ask, Will a mouse's observation make the moon real?

The authors give clear, accurate explanations of puzzling physical theories. Quantum theory indeed swarms with mind-boggling experiments that are only dimly understood. None of them justify thinking that $E = mc^2$ is a cultural artifact, or that E might equal mc^3 in

Afghanistan or on a distant planet. Extraterrestrials would of course express Einstein's formula with different symbols, but the law itself is as mind-independent as Mars.

As the authors say simply: "There is a way that the world is." It is the task of science to learn as much as it can about how this universe, not made by us, behaves. The awesome achievements of technology are irrefutable evidence that science keeps getting closer and closer to objective truth.

As the authors tell us, there are two distinct kinds of knowledge: logical and mathematical truth (statements that are certain within a given formal system), and scientific truth, never absolutely certain, but which can be accepted with a degree of probability that in many instances is practically indistinguishable from certainty. It takes a bizarre kind of mind to imagine that two plus two could be anything but four, or that, as the authors put it, cows can jump over the moon or rabbits lay multicolored eggs.

The authors are to be especially cheered for their coverage of unsubstantiated alternative treatments, some of them weird beyond imagining. Preposterous medical claims can cause untold harm to gullible persons who rely on them to the exclusion of treatment by mainstream physicians.

The authors are also to be commended for finding colorful and apt quotations from other writers. Bertrand Russell, for instance, gave three simple rules for curbing one's tendency to accept what he called "intellectual rubbish"[1]:

1. When the experts are agreed, the opposite opinion cannot be held to be certain.
2. When they are not agreed, no opinion can be regarded as certain by a nonexpert.
3. When they all hold that no sufficient grounds for a positive opinion exist, the ordinary person would do well to suspend judgment.

"These propositions seem mild," Russell added, "yet, if accepted, they would absolutely revolutionize human life."

I am under no illusions about how effective this book will be in persuading readers to adopt Russell's three maxims. I *can* say that to the extent it does, it will have performed a service that our technologically advanced but scientifically retarded nation desperately needs.

—Martin Gardner

[1]Bertrand Russell, *Sceptical Essays* (Psychology Press, 2004), p. 225.

Preface

Few claims seem to arouse more interest, evoke more emotion, and create more confusion than those dealing with the paranormal, the supernatural, or the mysterious—what in this book we call "weird things." Although many such claims are unbelievable, many people believe them, and their belief often has a profound effect on their lives. Billions of dollars are spent each year on people and products claiming supernatural powers. Channelers claim to communicate with aliens from outer space, psychics and astrologers claim to foretell the future, and healers claim to cure everything from AIDS to warts. Who are we to believe? How do we decide which claims are credible? What distinguishes rational from irrational claims? This book is designed to help you answer such questions.

Why do you believe in any given claim? Do you believe for any of the following reasons?

- You had an extraordinary personal experience.
- You embrace the idea that anything is possible—including weird things.
- You have an especially strong feeling that the claim is true or false.
- You have made a leap of faith that compels you to accept the claim.
- You believe in inner, mystical ways of knowing that support the claim.
- You know that no one has ever disproved the claim.
- You have empirical evidence that the claim is true.
- You believe that any claim is true for you if you believe it to be true.

This list of reasons for belief could go on and on. But which reasons are *good* reasons? Clearly, some are better than others; some can help us decide which claims are most likely to be true, and some can't. If we care whether any claim is actually true, whether our beliefs are well founded (and not merely comfortable or convenient), we must be able to distinguish good reasons from bad. We must understand how and when our beliefs are justified, how and when we can say that we *know* that something is true or believable.

The central premise of this book is that such an understanding is possible, useful, and empowering. Being able to distinguish good reasons from bad will not only improve your decision-making ability; it will also give you a powerful weapon against all forms of hucksterism. This volume shows you step-by-step how to sort out reasons, how to evaluate evidence, and how to tell when a claim (no matter how strange) is likely to be true. It's a course in critical thinking as applied to claims and phenomena that many people think are immune to critical thinking.

The emphasis, then, is neither on debunking nor on advocating specific claims, but on explaining principles of critical thinking that enable you to evaluate any claim for yourself. To illustrate how to apply these principles, we supply analyses of many extraordinary claims, including conclusions regarding their likely truth or falsity. But the focus is on carefully wielding the principles, not on whether a given claim goes unscathed or is cut down.

Often in the realm of the weird, such principles themselves are precisely what's at issue. Arguments about weird things are frequently about *how people know* and *if people know*—the main concerns of the branch of philosophy called *epistemology*. Thinking about weird things, then, brings us face-to-face with some of the most fundamental issues in human thought. So we concentrate on clearly explaining these issues, showing why the principles themselves in this book are valid, and demonstrating why many alternatives to them are unfounded. We explore alleged sources of knowledge such as faith, intuition, mysticism, perception, introspection, memory, reason, and science. We ask: Do any of these factors give us knowledge? Why or why not?

Since we show how these principles can be used in specific cases, this book is essentially a work of *applied epistemology*. Whether you're a believer or nonbeliever in weird things, and whether or not you're aware of it, you have an epistemology, a theory of knowledge. If you ever hope to discern whether a weird claim (or any other kind of claim) is true, your epistemology had better be a good one.

The principles discussed in this book can help you evaluate any claim—not just those dealing with weird phenomena. We believe that if you can successfully use these principles to assess the most bizarre, most unexpected claims, you're well prepared to tackle anything run-of-the-mill.

NEW EDITION, NEW MATERIAL

For this eighth edition, we have added new sections, new boxes, and new practice questions, revised or updated several existing sections, and included new discussions of topics that now draw a great deal of popular interest. These changes include:

- New sections on evaluating sources of information, identifying fake news, and detecting cognitive errors
- New boxes on recognizing bias, the flat Earth hypothesis, the Advanced Aviation Threat Identification Program, and paranormal monetary awards
- New practice questions to help students hone their critical thinking skills
- Updated or revised material on near-death experiences, creationism, parapsychology, and psychic predictions

IMPORTANT CONTINUING FEATURES

This volume also includes the following:

- Explanations of over thirty principles of knowledge, reasoning, and evidence that you can use to enhance your problem-solving skills and sharpen your judgment.
- Discussions of over sixty paranormal, supernatural, or mysterious phenomena, including astrology, ghosts, fairies, ESP, psychokinesis, UFO abductions, channeling, dowsing, near-death experiences, prophetic dreams, demon possession, time travel, parapsychology, and creationism.
- Details of a step-by-step procedure for evaluating any extraordinary claim. We call it the SEARCH formula and give several examples showing how it can be applied to some popular weird claims.
- Numerous boxes offering details on various offbeat beliefs, assessments by both true believers and skeptics of extraordinary claims, and reports of relevant scientific research. We think this material can stimulate discussion or serve as examples that can be assessed using the principles of critical thinking.
- A comprehensive treatment of different views about the nature of truth, including several forms of relativism and subjectivism.
- A detailed discussion of the characteristics, methodology, and limitations of science, illustrated with analyses of the claims of parapsychology and creationism. This discussion includes a complete treatment of science's criteria of adequacy and how those criteria should be used to evaluate extraordinary claims.

ACKNOWLEDGMENTS

The authors shared equally in the work of writing this book and thus share equally in responsibility for any of its shortcomings. But we are not alone in the project. We're grateful to Muhlenberg College for the research funds and library resources made available to us, to the Muhlenberg Scholars who participated in the course based on this book, and to the many people who helped us by reviewing the manuscript for accuracy, giving expert advice, and offering insightful commentary.

For the eighth edition, these included the following people:

Richard Beno, Wilmington University
Joy Branch, Southern Union State Community College
Martin C. Fowler, Elon University
Courtney Heinle, Wilmington University
Gene Kleppinger, Eastern Kentucky University
Keith Korcz, University of Louisiana at Lafayette
Ryan M. Lozano, Alamo Colleges–Central Texas Technology Center
Lucia Nemeth, Wilmington University
Erin Rowe, Wilmington University

And we continue to thank the reviewers of the sixth and seventh editions, who include:

H. E. Baber, University of San Diego
Anne Berre, Schreiner University
Tim Black, California State University, Northridge
James Blackmon, San Francisco State University
Douglas E. Hill, California State University, Fullerton
William Holly, Modesto Junior College
Michael Jackson, St. Bonaventure University
Don Merrell, Arkansas State University
Rebekah Ross-Fountain, Texas State University–San Marcos
Tadd Ruetenik, St. Ambrose University
Dennis Shaw, Lower Columbia College
Weimin Sun, California State University at Northridge
Mark C. Vopat, Youngstown State University
Helen Woodman, Ferris State University

R STUDENTS

ctive, efficient studying.

ect helps you be more productive with
study time and get better grades using
like SmartBook, which highlights key
epts and creates a personalized study
Connect sets you up for success, so
alk into class with confidence and
out with better grades.

really liked this app—it
le it easy to study when
u don't have your text-
ook in front of you.”

- Jordan Cunningham,
Eastern Washington University

surprises.

onnect Calendar
eports tools keep
n track with the work
eed to get done and
ssignment scores.
ts busy; Connect
elp you keep
g through it all.

©Shutterstock/wavebreakmedia

Study anytime, anywhere.

Download the free ReadAnywhere app and access your online eBook when it's convenient, even if you're offline. And since the app automatically syncs with your eBook in Connect, all of your notes are available every time you open it. Find out more at **www.mheducation.com/readanywhere**

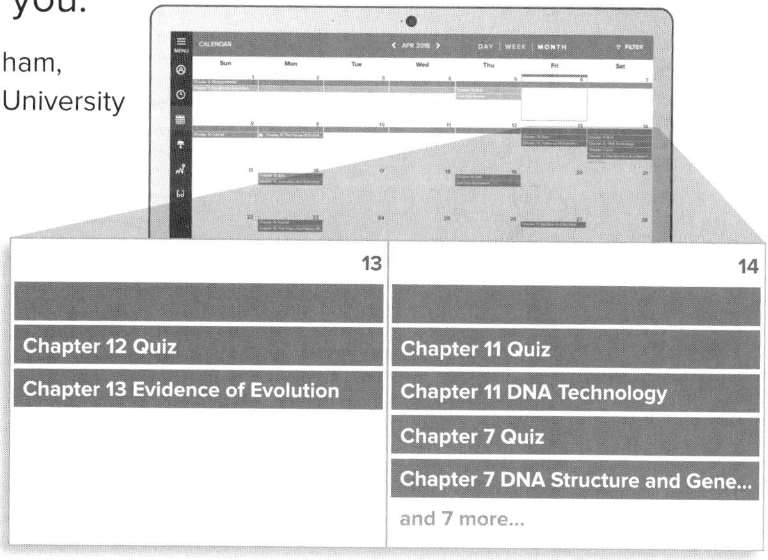

Learning for everyone.

McGraw-Hill works directly with Accessibility Services Departments and faculty to meet the learning needs of all students. Please contact your Accessibility Services office and ask them to email accessibility@mheducation.com, or visit **www.mheducation.com/about/accessibility.html** for more information.

Contents

ONE

Introduction: Close Encounters with the Strange

THIS BOOK IS FOR you who have stared into the night sky or the dark recesses of a room, hairs raised on the back of your neck, eyes wide, faced with an experience you couldn't explain but about which you have never stopped wondering, "Was it real?" It's for you who have read and heard about UFOs, psychic phenomena, time travel, out-of-body experiences, ghosts, monsters, astrology, reincarnation, mysticism, acupuncture, iridology, incredible experiments in quantum physics, and a thousand other extraordinary things, and asked, "Is it true?" Most of all, it's for you who believe, as Einstein did, that the most beautiful experience we can have is the mysterious—and who yet, like him, have the courage to ask tough questions until the mystery yields answers.

Wonder is the feeling of a philosopher, and philosophy begins in wonder.

—PLATO

But this is not primarily a book of such answers, though several will be offered. This book is about *how to find the answers for yourself*—how to test the truth or reality of some of the most influential, mysterious, provocative, bewildering puzzles we can ever experience. It's about how to think clearly and critically about what we authors have dubbed *weird things*—all the unusual, awesome, wonderful, bizarre, and antic happenings, real or alleged, that bubble up out of science, pseudoscience, the occult, the paranormal, the mystic, and the miraculous.

THE IMPORTANCE OF WHY

> *Skeptical habits of thought are essential for nothing less than our survival—because baloney, bamboozles, bunk, careless thinking, flimflam and wishes disguised as facts are not restricted to parlor magic and ambiguous advice on matters of the heart.*
>
> —CARL SAGAN

Pick up almost any book or magazine on such subjects. It will tell you that some extraordinary phenomenon is real or illusory, that some strange claim is true or false, probable or improbable. Plenty of people around you will gladly offer you their beliefs (often unshakable) about the most amazing things. In this blizzard of assertions, you hear a lot of *whats,* but seldom any good *whys.* That is, you hear the beliefs, but seldom any solid reasons behind them—nothing substantial enough to justify your sharing the beliefs; nothing reliable enough to indicate that these assertions are likely to be *true.* You may hear naiveté, passionate advocacy, fierce denunciation, one-sided sifting of evidence, defense of the party line, leaps of faith, jumps to false conclusions, plunges into wishful thinking, and courageous stands on the shaky ground of subjective certainty. But the good reasons are missing. Even if you do hear good reasons, you may end up forming a firm opinion on one extraordinary claim, but fail to learn any principle that would help you with a similar case. Or you hear good reasons, but no one bothers to explain why they're so good, why they're most likely to lead to the truth. Or no one may dare to answer the ultimate why—why good reasons are necessary to begin with.

Without good whys, humans have no hope of understanding all that we fondly call *weird*—or anything else, for that matter. Without good whys, our beliefs are simply arbitrary, with no more claim to knowledge than the random choice of a playing card. Without good whys to guide us, our beliefs lose their value in a world where beliefs are already a dime a dozen.

We especially need good whys when faced with weirdness. For statements about weird things are almost always cloaked in swirling mists of confusion, misconception, misperception, and our own yearning to disbelieve or believe. Our task of judging the reality of these weird things isn't made any easier by one fact that humbles and inspires every scientist: Sometimes the weirdest phenomena are absolutely real; sometimes the strangest claims turn out to be true. The best scientists and thinkers can never forget that sometimes wondrous discoveries are made out there on the fringe of experience, where anomalies prowl.

Space aliens are abducting your neighbors. Psychic detectives solve crimes. You were a medieval stable boy in a former life. Nostradamus predicted JFK's assassination. Herbs can cure AIDS. Levitation is possible. Reading tarot cards reveals character. Science proves the wisdom of Eastern mysticism. The moon landing was a hoax. Magnet therapy works. Near-death experiences prove there's life after death. Crystals heal. Bigfoot stalks. Elvis lives.

Do you believe any of these claims? Do you believe that some or all of them deserve a good horselaugh, that they're the kind of hooey that only a moron could take seriously? The big question then is *why?* Why do you believe or disbelieve? Belief alone—without good whys—can't help us get one inch closer to the truth. A hasty rejection or acceptance of a claim can't help us tell the difference between what's actually likely to be true (or false) and what we merely want to be true (or false). Beliefs that do not stand on our best reasons and evidence simply dangle in thin air, signifying nothing except our transient feelings or personal preferences.

What we offer here is a compendium of good whys. As clearly as we can, we explain and illustrate principles of rational inquiry for assessing all manner of weirdness. We give you the essential guides for weighing evidence and drawing well-founded conclusions. Most of these principles are simply commonplace, wielded by philosophers, scientists, and anyone else interested in discovering the facts. Many are fundamental to scientific explorations of all kinds. We show why these principles are so powerful, how anyone can put them to use, and *why they're good whys to begin with*—why they're more reliable guides for discovering what's true and real than any alternatives.

Call him wise whose actions, words, and steps are all a clear "because" to a clear "why."

—JOHANN KASPAR LAVATER

We think this latter kind of explanation is sorely needed. You may hear that there's no reliable scientific evidence to prove the reality of psychokinesis (moving physical objects with mind power alone). But you may never hear a careful explanation of why scientific evidence is necessary in the first place. Most scientists would say that the common experience of thinking of a friend and then suddenly getting a phone call from that person doesn't prove telepathy (communication between minds without the use of five senses). But why not? Only a few scientists and a handful of others bother to explain why. Say 100 people have independently tried eating a certain herb and now swear that it has cured them of cancer. Scientists would say that these 100 stories constitute anecdotal evidence that doesn't prove the effectiveness of the herb at all. But why not? There is indeed a good answer, but it's tough to come by.

A man is a small thing, and the night is very large and full of wonders.
—LORD DUNSANY

The answer is to be found in the principles that distinguish good reasons from bad ones. You needn't take these principles (or any other statements) on faith. Through your own careful use of reason, you can verify their validity for yourself.

Nor should you assume that these guides are infallible and unchangeable. They're simply the best we have until someone presents sound, rational reasons for discarding them.

These guides shouldn't be a surprise to anyone. Yet, to many, the principles will seem like a bolt from the blue, a detailed map to a country they thought was uncharted. Even those of us who are unsurprised by these principles must admit that we probably violate at least one of them daily—and so run off into a ditch of wrong conclusions.

BEYOND WEIRD TO THE ABSURD

I really think we are all creating our own reality. I think I'm creating you right here. Therefore I created the medium, therefore I created the entity, because I'm creating everything.
—SHIRLEY MACLAINE

To these pages, we cordially invite all those who sincerely believe that this book is a gigantic waste of time—who think that it's impossible or pointless to use rational principles to assess the objective truth of weird claims. To this increasingly prevalent attitude, in all its forms, we offer a direct challenge. We do the impossible, or at least what some regard as impossible. We show that there are good reasons for believing that the following claims are, in fact, false:

- There's no such thing as objective truth. We make our own truth.
- There's no such thing as objective reality. We make our own reality.
- There are spiritual, mystical, or inner ways of knowing that are superior to our ordinary ways of knowing.
- If an experience seems real, it is real.
- If an idea feels right to you, it is right.
- We are incapable of acquiring knowledge of the true nature of reality.
- Science itself is irrational or mystical. It's just another faith or belief system or myth, with no more justification than any other.
- It doesn't matter whether beliefs are true or not, as long as they're meaningful to you.

We discuss these ideas because they're unavoidable. If you want to evaluate weird things, sooner or later you'll bump into notions that challenge your most fundamental assumptions. Weirdness by definition is out of the norm, so it often calls into question our normal ways of knowing. It invites many to believe that in the arena of extraordinary things, extraordinary ways of knowing must prevail. It leads many to conclude that reason just doesn't apply, that rationality has shown up at the wrong party.

You can learn a lot by seriously examining such challenges to basic assumptions about what we know (or think we know) and how we know it. In fact, in this volume you learn three important lessons about the above ideas:

1. If some of these ideas *are* true, knowing anything about anything (including weird stuff) is *impossible.*
2. If you honestly believe any of these ideas, you cut your chances of ever discovering what's real or true.
3. Rejecting these notions is liberating and empowering.

The essence of the independent mind lies not in what it thinks but in how it thinks.

—CHRISTOPHER HITCHINS

The first lesson, for example, comes through clearly when we examine the idea that there's no such thing as objective truth. This notion means that reality is literally whatever each of us believes it to be. Reality doesn't exist apart from a person's beliefs about it. So truth isn't objective, it's subjective. The idea is embodied in the popular line "It may not be true for you, but it's true for me." The problem is, if there's no objective truth, then *no* statement is objectively true, including the statement "There's no such thing as objective truth." The statement refutes itself. If true, it means that the statement and *all* statements—ours, yours, or anybody else's—aren't worthy of belief or commitment. Every viewpoint becomes arbitrary, with nothing to recommend it except the fact that someone likes it. There could be no such thing as knowledge, for if nothing is true, there can be nothing to know. The distinction between asserting and denying something would be meaningless. There could be no difference between sense and nonsense, reasonable belief and illusion. For several reasons, which we'll discuss later, people would be faced with some intolerable absurdities. For one thing, it would be impossible to agree or disagree with someone. In fact, it would be impossible to communicate, to learn a language, to compare each other's ideas, even to think.

Light—more light.

—JOHANN WOLFGANG VON GOETHE

The point of the third lesson is that if such outrageous notions shackle us, rejecting them sets us free. To reject them is to say that we *can* know things about the world—and that our ability to reason and weigh evidence is what helps us gain that knowledge. In part, the purpose of much that follows is to demonstrate just how potent this ability is. Human reason empowers us, like nothing else, to distinguish between fact and fiction, understand significant issues, penetrate deep mysteries, and answer large questions.

A WEIRDNESS SAMPLER

People everywhere enjoy believing things that they know are not true. It spares them the ordeal of thinking for themselves and taking responsibility for what they know.
—BROOKS ATKINSON

How many people actually care about weird things? Plenty. Book sales, coverage in magazines and on television, movies, and opinion polls suggest that there's widespread interest in things psychic, paranormal, occult, ghostly, and otherworldly. A Gallup poll published in 2005, for example, shows that:

- 55 percent of Americans believe in psychic or spiritual healing or the power of the human mind to heal the body.
- 41 percent believe in ESP (extrasensory perception).
- 42 percent believe that people on Earth are sometimes possessed by the devil.
- 32 percent believe that ghosts or the spirits of dead people can come back in certain places and situations.
- 31 percent believe in telepathy, or communication between minds without using the traditional five senses.
- 24 percent believe that extraterrestrial beings have visited Earth at some time in the past.
- 26 percent believe in clairvoyance, or the power of the mind to know the past and predict the future.
- 21 percent believe that people can hear from or communicate mentally with someone who has died.
- 25 percent believe in astrology, or that the position of the stars and planets can affect people's lives.
- 21 percent believe in witches.
- 20 percent believe in reincarnation, that is, the rebirth of the soul in a new body after death.

There are many, many more extraordinary things that thousands of people experience, believe in, and change their lives because of. Several will be discussed in this book. Here's a sampling:

- Hundreds of people who were near death but did not die have told of blissful experiences in the beyond. Their reports vary, but certain details keep recurring: While they were at death's door, a feeling of peace overcame them. They watched as they floated above their own bodies. They traveled through a long, dark tunnel. They entered a bright, golden light and glimpsed another world of unspeakable beauty. They saw long-dead relatives and a being of light that comforted them. Then they returned to their own bodies, awoke, and were transformed by their incredible experience. In each case, the experience seemed nothing like a dream or a fantasy; it seemed vividly *real.* Such episodes are known as near-death experiences (NDEs).

Pseudoteachers

Two social scientists—sociologist Ray Eve and anthropologist Dana Dunn of the University of Texas at Arlington—tried to find out where pseudoscientific beliefs might come from. They theorized that teachers might be passing such ideas on in school.

To test their theory, they surveyed a national sample of 190 high-school biology and life-science teachers. Their findings: 43 percent thought that the story of the Flood and Noah's ark was definitely or probably true; 20 percent believed in communication with the dead; 19 percent felt that dinosaurs and humans lived at the same time; 20 percent believed in black magic; and 16 percent believed in Atlantis. What's more, 30 percent wanted to teach creation science; 26 percent felt that some races were more intelligent than others; and 22 percent believed in ghosts.

Although 30 to 40 percent of the teachers were doing a good job, says Eve, "it boils down to the observation that a large number of the teachers are either football coaches or home-economics teachers who have been asked to cover biology."

Is there hope for change? "Much like the Department of Defense," says Eve, "the education bureaucracy has become so intractable that even when you know something is wrong, the chances of fixing it are not great."[1]

Many who have had such experiences say that their NDEs give undeniable proof of life after death.

- Some people report the often chilling experience known as a precognitive dream, a dream that seems to foretell the future. Here's an example: "I dreamed I was walking along a steep ridge with my father. He was stepping too close to the edge, making the dirt cascade to the rocks far below. I turned to grab his arm, but the ridge fell away under his feet, leaving him to dangle from my hands. I pulled as hard as I could, but he grew larger and heavier. He fell, in slow motion, crying out to me but making no sound. Then I woke up screaming. Three weeks later my father fell to his death from a second-story window while he was painting the windowsill. I was in the room with him at the time but wasn't able to reach him fast enough to prevent his fall. I rarely remember any dreams, and I had never before dreamed about someone falling." Such dreams can have a profound emotional impact on the dreamer and may spark a firm belief in the paranormal.

- There are probably hundreds of people claiming that they once lived very different lives in very different places—long before they were born. Tales of these past lives surface when people are "regressed" during hypnosis back to their alleged long-hidden selves. It all started in 1952 when Virginia Tighe, an American homemaker, was apparently hypnotically regressed back to a previous life in nineteenth-century Ireland. Speaking in an uncharacteristic Irish brogue, she related an astounding account of her former life. Many others during hypnosis have related impressively detailed past lives in early Rome, medieval France, sixteenth-century Spain, ancient Greece or Egypt, Atlantis, and more, all the while speaking in what often sound like authentic languages or accents. A lot of famous people claim that they too have been hypnotically regressed to discover earlier existences. Shirley MacLaine, for example, has said that she's been a pirate with a wooden leg, a Buddhist monk, a court jester for Louis XV, a Mongolian nomad, and assorted prostitutes. Many believe that such cases are proof of the doctrine of reincarnation.

Colt Born with Human Face—just like his father!

—WEEKLY WORLD NEWS

- Some U.S. military officers have expressed strong interest in an astonishing psychic phenomenon called *remote viewing*. It's the alleged ability to accurately perceive information about distant geographical locations without using any known sense. The officers claimed that the former Soviet Union was way ahead of the United States in developing such powers. Remote viewing is said to be available to anyone, as it needs no special training or talents. Experiments have been conducted on the phenomenon, and some people have said that these tests prove that remote viewing is real.

- A lot of people look to psychics, astrologers, and tarot card readers to obtain a precious commodity: predictions about the future. You can get this commodity through websites, newspapers, magazines, TV talk shows, and hotlines. Predictions may concern the fate of movie stars, momentous events on the world stage, or the ups and downs of your personal life. Everywhere, there's word that some startling, unlikely prediction has come true. Here's an example: On April 2, 1981, four days after the assassination attempt on President Reagan, the world was told that a Los Angeles psychic *had predicted the whole thing weeks earlier.* On that April morning, NBC's *Today* show, ABC's *Good Morning America,* and Cable News Network aired a tape showing the psychic, Tamara Rand, offering a detailed prediction of the assassination attempt. The tape was said to have been made on January 6, 1981. She foresaw that Reagan would be shot by a sandy-haired young man with the initials "J. H.," that Reagan would be wounded in the chest, that there would be a "hail of bullets," and that the fateful day would occur in the last week of March or first week of April.

- Something strange is going on in physics, something so strange, in fact, that some people who've bothered to think about the strangeness now declare that physics is looking more and more like Eastern mysticism. This weirdness is taking place in the branch of physics known as quantum mechanics, which studies subatomic particles, the tiny bits that make up everything in the universe. The notorious weirdness is this: In the quantum realm, particles don't acquire some of their characteristics *until they're observed by someone.* They seem not to exist in a definite form until scientists measure them. This spooky fact didn't sit well with Einstein, but it has been confirmed repeatedly in rigorous tests. It has caused some people to speculate that reality is subjective, that we as observers create the universe ourselves—that the universe is a product of our imagination. This quantum freakiness has prompted some people, even a physicist or two, seriously to ask, "Is a tree really there when no one's looking?"

- In 1894 the Society for Psychical Research published the first survey of personal encounters with ghostly phenomena. There were hundreds of firsthand accounts by people who claimed to have seen real apparitions. A recent scholarly history of apparitions documents an unsurprising fact: People have been reporting such encounters for centuries. Today, things haven't changed much. You're likely to hear at least one firsthand account yourself from somebody you know—somebody who says it's not a ghost *story* at all, but fact. Research suggests that the experiences can happen to perfectly sane persons, appear vividly real, and have a powerful emotional impact. There are also reports of people feeling a "sense of presence," as though another person, invisible, is close by. There's no end to the stories of more famous apparitions, told and retold, with eerie details that raise bumps on the skin. And you don't have to read a tabloid newspaper (more reputable newspapers will do) to discover that when someone wonders "Who ya gonna call?" there are real ghostbusters ready to handle a haunting.

Fat Woman's Bra Snaps—13 Injured!

—WEEKLY WORLD NEWS

- *The Exorcist* dramatized it. *The Amityville Horror* reinforced awareness of it. The Catholic Church endorses it. The news media eagerly report it. It is the idea of demon possession—that people and places can be haunted, harmed, and controlled by supernatural entities of immense evil. A typical case: On August 18, 1986, the Associated Press reported that demons were said to be haunting a house in West Pittston, Pennsylvania. Jack and Janet Smurl lived there with their four children and claimed that the demons were terrorizing them. According to the report: "The Smurls said they have smelled the stench of smoke and rotten meat, heard pig grunts, hoofbeats, and bloodcurdling screams and moans. Doors have opened and shut, lights have gone on and off, formless ghostly glows have traveled before them, and the television set has shot across the room. Even the

Oh God, how did I get into this room with all these weird people?
—STEWART BRAND

family dog, a 75-pound German shepherd, has been slammed against the wall while [Jack] Smurl said he stood nearby."[2] Later, Jack Smurl was quoted in the *New York Daily News* as saying that "at least a dozen times [a female demon, or succubus] has had intercourse with me in bed. I was awake, but I was immobile." The Smurls invited demonologist Ed Warren, who had been involved in the Amityville case, to investigate. Warren declared that several demons did indeed inhabit the house.

• Long ago, Earth was visited by extraterrestrial beings who imparted advanced technology and learning to primitive humans. So say many people, who ask, How else do you explain the stunning engineering of the pyramids in Egypt and the New World? The ancient designs cut into the Nazca plain in Peru that look like airfield markings meant for approaching spacecraft? The highly accurate Piri Reis map of 1513 that must have been created by some kind of aerial photography? The facts possessed by the primitive Dogon tribe of Africa about a star that no one can see with the naked eye and wasn't even discovered by astronomers until the nineteenth century? In myths and legends, they say, our ancestors told of the visitation of these "gods." This theme is sounded by many, most notably Erich von Däniken in his books *Chariots of the Gods, Gods from Outer Space,* and *Von Däniken's Proof.* Sparks still fly when somebody asserts that somebody else's ancestors were too primitive to have managed certain engineering feats without alien help.

• Many people have turned to a method of disease treatment shunned by mainstream medicine and at odds with modern science: homeopathy. Around since the 1700s, it now has several hundred practitioners in the United States and is built on two main doctrines. One is that "like cures like"—symptoms of a sick person can be cured by substances that actually produce the same symptoms in healthy people. The other doctrine is that the smaller the dose of this substance, the mightier the healing effect. Homeopathic drugs are diluted for maximum power—and are often so watered down that not one molecule of the original substance remains. That such dilutions could possibly heal anything flies in the face of the laws of chemistry. Yet in recent years there's been an increase in homeopathic remedies offered in drugstores and health-food stores. And growing numbers of people believe in them (including members of the British Royal Family).

• The story of a strange, miraculous event has been circulating for a number of years. It was first told by author Lyall Watson, who, in his 1979 book *Lifetide,* said he gleaned it from scientists, and it's

Paranormal Profile

Where do you stand on these issues? Indicate your views by writing the appropriate number in the space provided at the end of each question. Use the following scale: 5 = true; 4 = probably true; 3 = neither probable nor improbable; 2 = probably false; and 1 = false. After you've finished the book, you might want to take the survey again to see if your views have changed.

1. People can read other people's minds. ______
2. People can see into the future. ______
3. People can move external objects solely with the power of their minds. ______
4. Poltergeists can move physical objects. ______
5. Alien spacecraft have landed on Earth. ______
6. People have been abducted by aliens from other planets. ______
7. People have been possessed by demons. ______
8. In addition to physical bodies, people have nonphysical astral bodies. ______
9. People can project their astral bodies out of their physical bodies and travel to distant places. ______
10. After the physical body dies, a person can reincarnate in another physical body. ______
11. People can talk to the spirits of the dead. ______
12. The positions of the sun, stars, and planets at birth can affect a person's body, character, and destiny. ______
13. Angels exist. ______
14. People can be cured by faith healers. ______
15. People can be cured by homeopathic treatments. ______

been repeated by countless other writers. Watson reported that in the 1950s some wild Japanese monkeys on the island of Koshima were given raw sweet potatoes for the first time. One of the monkeys, Imo, learned to wash the potatoes in a stream to remove the sand and grit. Over the years, Imo taught this skill to other monkeys in the colony. Then one day, when a certain number of monkeys, say 100, had learned the washing trick, the impossible happened. Suddenly almost all the other monkeys knew how to do it, too. "Not only that," says Watson, "but the habit seems to have jumped natural barriers and to have appeared spontaneously, like glycerin crystals in sealed laboratory jars, in colonies on other islands."[3] With the hundredth monkey, a kind of "critical mass" had been reached, he says, forcing a kind of group mind. This, then, is the hundredth-monkey phenomenon. Some believe that it's a fact story and that the phenomenon is at work in all of humanity. If so, we're faced with an astounding implication: When enough people believe something is true, it becomes true for everyone. Others say that it's pointless to ask whether the story is factual—it's a metaphor or myth and, as such, is

What we need is not the will to believe, but the will to find out.

—BERTRAND RUSSELL

as true as science. Still, we stubbornly ask, Did the incident actually happen? And does it really matter after all?

The trouble with most people is that they think with their hopes or fears or wishes rather than with their minds.
—WILL DURANT

Aliens, spirits, miracle cures, mind over matter, life after death: wonders all. The world would be a more wonderful place, if these things existed. We wouldn't be alone in the universe, we would have more control over our lives, and we would be immortal. Our desire to live in such a world undoubtedly plays a role in the widespread belief in these things. But the fact that we would like something to be true is no reason to believe that it is. To get to the truth of the matter we must go beyond wishful thinking to critical thinking. We must learn to set aside our prejudices and preconceptions and examine the evidence fairly and impartially. Only then can we hope to distinguish reality from fantasy.

But, you may object, what's wrong with a little fantasy? If someone finds a belief comforting, does it matter whether it's true or not? Yes it does, because our actions are based on our beliefs. If our beliefs are mistaken, our actions are unlikely to succeed. Nowhere is this more obvious than in the case of alternative medicine. Each year, Americans spend billions of dollars on bogus remedies, and often end up paying for them with their lives. As attorney John W. Miner reveals, "Quackery kills more people than those who die from all crimes of violence put together."[4]

Not only can irrational beliefs cost us our lives; they can threaten our livelihood as well. To take but one example: Tarot card readers and psychics of every stripe are only a phone call—or a mouse click—away, and their services are not free. Psychic hotlines have charged as much as $3.99 a minute. That comes to $240 an hour, more than most psychoanalysts get paid. Psychic phone calling used to be a multi-million-dollar industry, with one group—the Psychic Readers Network—making over $300 million in phone service charges in 2002. But exposés of the industry revealed that most psychic hotlines are staffed by unemployed homemakers.[5] They were not tested for psychic ability, and they were not given any psychic instruction. Their only training consisted of being told how to keep people on the line.

Psychic services have since multiplied and now seem to do most of their work on websites, chat lines, and Skype—and their readings are still pricey. Many psychics offer dollar-a-minute readings, but prices vary, with the higher-end psychics charging hundreds of dollars.

Tim Farley has been collecting data about the harm caused by irrational beliefs for many years. His website—http://www.whatstheharm.net/—has identified over 670,000 cases in which people were injured either physically or financially because they believed things they were not justified in believing. This lack of critical thinking, in the cases he's studied, has resulted in 368,379 deaths, 306,379 injuries, and over $2,815,931,000 in economic damages. The failure of the victims to ground their beliefs in reality ultimately cost them their lives or, in many cases, their life savings.[6]

In addition to threatening our individual well-being, irrational beliefs also threaten our social well-being. A democratic society depends on the ability of its members to make rational choices. But rational choices must be based on rational beliefs. If we can't tell the difference between reasonable and unreasonable claims, we become susceptible to the claims of charlatans, scoundrels, and mountebanks. As Stephen J. Gould observes, "When people learn no tools of judgment and merely follow their hopes, the seeds of political manipulations are sown."[7] Political opportunists like to play upon people's fears, hopes, and desires. If we lack the ability to distinguish credible claims from incredible ones, we may end up sacrificing more than our good sense—we may forfeit our freedom as well.

Irrationally held truths may be more harmful than reasoned errors.

—Thomas Henry Huxley

No one wants to be duped, conned, or fleeced. Unfortunately, our educational system spends much more time teaching people what to think rather than how to think. As a result, many people are unaware of the principles and procedures that should be used to minimize error and maximize understanding. This book is designed to acquaint you with those principles and procedures and to explain why any attempt to get at the truth should employ them. Understanding their justification should make you more adept at wielding them in unfamiliar situations.

The quality of your life is determined by the quality of your decisions, and the quality of your decisions is determined by the quality of your thinking. By helping improve the quality of your thinking, we hope we can, in some small measure, improve the quality of your life.

NOTES

1. Paul McCarthy, "Pseudoteachers," *Omni,* July 1989, p. 74.
2. Associated Press, August 18, 1986.
3. Lyall Watson, *Lifetide: The Biology of the Unconscious* (Simon and Schuster, 1979), p. 148.
4. W. E. Schaller & C. R. Carrol, *Health, Quackery, and the Consumer* (Philadelphia: Saunders, 1976), p. 169.
5. Frederick Woodruff, *Secrets of a Telephone Psychic* (Hillsboro, OR: Beyond Words, 1998).
6. Thomas Farley, http://www.whatstheharm.net/.
7. Stephen J. Gould, *An Urchin in the Storm: Essays about Books and Ideas* (Collins Harvill, 1987), p. 245.

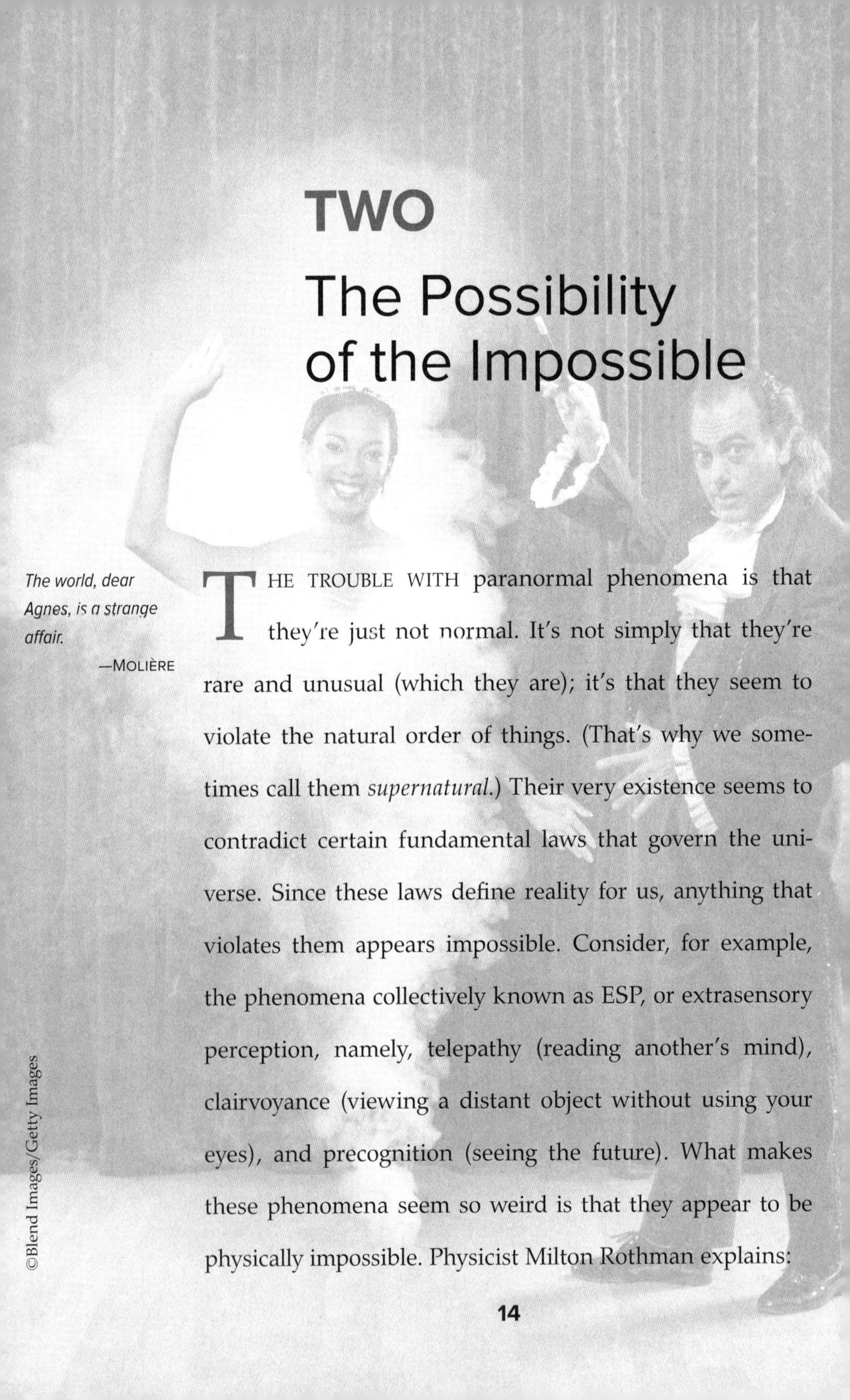

©Blend Images/Getty Images

TWO
The Possibility of the Impossible

> *The world, dear Agnes, is a strange affair.*
>
> —Molière

THE TROUBLE WITH paranormal phenomena is that they're just not normal. It's not simply that they're rare and unusual (which they are); it's that they seem to violate the natural order of things. (That's why we sometimes call them *supernatural.*) Their very existence seems to contradict certain fundamental laws that govern the universe. Since these laws define reality for us, anything that violates them appears impossible. Consider, for example, the phenomena collectively known as ESP, or extrasensory perception, namely, telepathy (reading another's mind), clairvoyance (viewing a distant object without using your eyes), and precognition (seeing the future). What makes these phenomena seem so weird is that they appear to be physically impossible. Physicist Milton Rothman explains:

> Transmission of information through space requires transfer of energy from one place to another. Telepathy requires transmission of an energy-carrying signal directly from one mind to another. All descriptions of ESP imply violations of conservation of energy [the principle that mass-energy can be neither created nor destroyed] in one way or another, as well as violations of all the principles of information theory and even of the principle of causality [the principle that an effect cannot precede its cause]. Strict application of physical principles requires us to say that ESP is impossible.[1]

According to Rothman, anything that violates physical principles is impossible. Because ESP violates these principles, it is impossible.

PARADIGMS AND THE PARANORMAL

When nothing is sure, everything is possible.

—MARGARET DRABBLE

But according to the true believers (those who accept the reality of the paranormal), nothing is impossible. As Erich von Däniken, author of *Chariots of the Gods,* puts it, "*nothing* is incredible any longer. The word 'impossible' should have become literally impossible for the modern scientist. Anyone who does not accept this today will be crushed by the reality tomorrow."[2] What von Däniken is referring to here is the fact that many things that scientists once considered impossible are now considered real. The most notorious example is meteorites. For many years, the scientific community dismissed meteorites as impossible. The great chemist Lavoisier, for example, argued that stones couldn't fall from the sky because there were none up there. No less a freethinker than Thomas Jefferson, after reading a report by two Harvard professors claiming to have observed meteorites, remarked, "I could more easily believe that two Yankee professors would lie than that stones would fall down from heaven."[3] The true believers hold that Lavoisier and Jefferson were blinded by science. There was no place in their worldview for stones that fell from the sky, so they refused to accept the reality of meteorites. Many of today's scientists, say the true believers, suffer from a similar myopia. They're unable to see beyond the narrow confines of their pet theories.

This defect is a potentially serious one, for it can block scientific development. The historian Thomas Kuhn, in his seminal work, *The Structure of Scientific Revolutions,* has shown that science advances only by recognizing and dealing with *anomalies* (phenomena that don't seem to obey known laws). According to Kuhn, all scientific investigations take place within a *paradigm,* or theoretical framework, that determines what questions are worth asking and what methods should be used to answer them. From time to time, however, certain phenomena are discovered that don't fit into the established paradigm; that is, they can't be explained

Difficult things take a long time; the impossible takes a little longer.
—CHAIM WEIZMANN

by the current theory. At first, as in the case of meteorites, the scientific community tries to dismiss or explain away these phenomena. But if no satisfactory account of them is forthcoming, the scientific community is forced to abandon the old paradigm and adopt a new one. In such a case, the scientific community is said to have undergone a *paradigm shift.*

There have been many paradigm shifts in the past. Galileo's discovery of the moons of Jupiter and the phases of Venus led to a shift from a geocentric (Earth-centered) view of the solar system to a heliocentric (sun-centered) one. Darwin's discovery of the strange creatures of the Galápagos Islands led to the shift from creationism to evolution. The failure to detect the "luminiferous ether" (the medium in which light waves were supposed to travel) led to a shift from Newtonian physics to Einsteinian physics. Similarly, say the true believers, paranormal phenomena may lead to another paradigm shift. The resulting worldview may be as different from ours as ours is from the aborigines. We may have to give up many of our most cherished beliefs about the nature of reality and knowledge. But it's happened before, and, they claim, there's no reason to think it won't happen again. As Shakespeare so eloquently put it, "There are more things in heaven and earth, Horatio, than are dreamt of in your philosophy."

So whom are we to believe? Should we follow the scientist who dismisses paranormal phenomena on the grounds that they contradict fundamental physical principles or the true believer who sees paranormal phenomena as a harbinger of a new age? To evaluate the relative merits of these positions, we'll have to take a closer look at the notions of possibility, plausibility, and reality.

LOGICAL POSSIBILITY VERSUS PHYSICAL IMPOSSIBILITY

One can't believe impossible things.
—ALICE, IN *THROUGH THE LOOKING GLASS*

Although it's fashionable to claim that anything is possible, such a claim is mistaken, for there are some things that can't possibly be false, and others that can't possibly be true. The former—such as "2 + 2 = 4," "All bachelors are unmarried," and "Red is a color"—are called *necessary truths,* because there are no situations in which they would be false. The latter—such as "2 + 2 = 5," "All bachelors are married," and "Red is not a color" are called *necessary falsehoods* because there are no situations in which they would be true.[4] The Greek philosopher Aristotle (Plato's pupil) was the first to systematize our knowledge of necessary truths. The most fundamental of them—the ones upon which all other truths rest—are often called the *laws of thought.* They are:

> *The law of noncontradiction:* Nothing can both have a property and lack it at the same time. (For example, nothing can be both round and not-round at the same time.)

The law of identity: Everything is identical to itself. (For example, every round thing is a round thing and not something else.)

The law of excluded middle: For any particular property, everything either has it or lacks it. (For example, everything is either round or not-round.)

These principles are called the laws of thought because without them thought—as well as communication—would be impossible. In order to think or communicate, our thoughts and sentences must have a specific content; they must be about one thing rather than another. If the law of noncontradiction didn't hold, there would be no way to distinguish one thought or sentence from another. Whatever was true of one would be true of the other. Every claim would be equally true (and false). Thus, those who deny the law of noncontradiction can't claim that their position is superior to that of those who accept that law.

One of the most effective techniques of refuting a position is known as *reductio ad absurdum:* reduction to absurdity. If you can show that a position has absurd consequences, you've provided a powerful reason for rejecting it. The consequences of denying the law of noncontradiction are about as absurd as they get. Any position that makes thought and communication theoretically impossible is, to say the least, suspect. Aristotle, in Book IV of the *Metaphysics,* put the point this way:

> If all are alike both wrong and right, one who is in this condition will not be able either to speak or to say anything intelligible; for he says at the same time both "yes" and "no." And if he makes no judgment but "thinks" and "does not think," indifferently, what difference will there be between him and a vegetable?[5]

What difference indeed. Without the law of noncontradiction, we can't believe things to be one way rather than another. But if we can't believe things to be one way rather than another, we can't think at all.

Logic is the study of correct thinking. As a result, the laws of thought are often referred to as the laws of logic. Anything that violates these laws is said to be *logically impossible,* and whatever is logically impossible can't exist. We know, for example, that there are no round squares, no married bachelors, and no largest number because such things violate the law of noncontradiction—they attribute both a property and its negation to a thing and are thus *self-contradictory.* The laws of thought, then, not only determine the bounds of the rational; they also determine the bounds of the real. Whatever is real must obey the law of noncontradiction. That is why the great German logician Gottlob Frege called logic "the study of the laws of the laws of science." The laws of science must obey the laws of logic.

Why, sometimes before breakfast I've believed as many as six impossible things.

—THE WHITE QUEEN, IN *THROUGH THE LOOKING GLASS*

Aristotle on Demonstrating the Laws of Thought

Since the laws of thought are the basis for all logical proofs, they can't be proven by means of a logical demonstration. But, says Aristotle, they can nevertheless be demonstrated negatively:

> There are some who, as we said, both themselves assert that it is possible for the same thing to be and not to be, and say that people can judge this to be the case. And among others many writers about nature use this language. But we have now posited that it is impossible for anything at the same time to be and not to be, and by this means have shown that this is the most indisputable of all principles. Some indeed demand that even this shall be demonstrated, but this they do through want of education, for not to know of what things one should demand demonstration, and of what one should not, argues want of education. For it is impossible that there should be demonstration of absolutely everything (there would be an infinite regress, so that there would still be no demonstration); but if there are things of which one should not demand demonstration, these persons could not say what principle they maintain to be more self-evident than the present one.
>
> We can, however, demonstrate negatively even that this view is impossible. . . . The starting point for all such proofs is that our opponent shall say something which is *significant* both for himself and for another; for this is necessary, if he really is to say anything. For, if he means nothing, such a man will not be capable of reasoning, either with himself or with another. But if any one says something that is significant, demonstration will be possible; for we shall already have something definite. The person responsible for the proof, however, is not he who demonstrates but he who listens; for while disowning reason he listens to reason. And again he who admits this has admitted that something is true apart from demonstration.[6]

In other words, the law of noncontradiction can't be demonstrated to someone who won't say something definite, for demonstration requires that our words mean one thing rather than another. On the other hand, the law of noncontradiction need not be demonstrated to someone who will say something definite, for in saying something definite he or she has already assumed its truth.

Source: Aristotle, *Metaphysics*, Book IV.

Thus, von Däniken is mistaken. Some things are logically impossible, and whatever is logically impossible cannot exist.

Rothman claims that ESP is impossible. Now if he means that ESP is logically impossible, then, provided he's right, we can dismiss it out of hand, for in that case, it can't exist. But ESP isn't logically impossible. The notions of reading another's mind, viewing distant objects, and even knowing the future are not self-contradictory in the way that married bachelors or round squares are. Neither are such paranormal phenomena as alien abduction, out-of-body experiences, or communicating with the dead. What, if anything, these phenomena violate are not the laws of logic, but the laws of physics or, more generally, the laws of science. If they violate those laws, they're *physically impossible.*

Science attempts to understand the world by identifying the laws that govern it. These laws tell us how various physical properties are related to one another. For example, Newton's second law of motion, $f = ma$, tells us that the force of a projectile is equal to its mass times its acceleration. Einstein's law, $E = mc^2$, tells us that the energy of an object is equal to its mass times the velocity of light squared. Knowing these laws not only helps us understand why things happen as they do but also allows us to predict and control what happens. Newton's laws of motion, for example, allow us to predict the positions of the planets and control the trajectory of missiles.

We have to live today by what truth we can get today, and be ready tomorrow to call it falsehood.

—WILLIAM JAMES

Anything that's inconsistent with the laws of nature is physically impossible. A cow jumping over the moon, for example, is physically impossible because such a feat would violate the laws governing cow physiology and gravity. The muscles of a cow simply cannot produce enough force to accelerate the cow to the speed required to escape the Earth's gravity. But a cow jumping over the moon is not logically impossible. There is no contradiction involved in the notion of a moon-jumping cow. Similarly, there is no contradiction involved in the notion of a bunny that lays multicolored eggs. So physical possibility is a more limited notion than logical possibility; whatever is physically possible is logically possible, but not everything that's logically possible is physically possible.

There is yet another type of possibility that is useful to know about: *technological possibility*. Something is technologically impossible if it is (currently) beyond our capabilities to accomplish. Manned intergalactic space travel, for example, is technologically impossible because we do not currently have the capability of storing enough food and energy to travel to another galaxy. It's not physically impossible, however, because making such a trip does not involve breaking any laws of nature. We simply lack the technology to perform such a feat.

What makes a thing weird or a claim extraordinary is that it seems to be impossible. Time travel, psychokinesis, and ancient astronauts, for example, are weird things—and the claims that they exist, extraordinary—because they seem to run afoul of one or more of the types of possibility discussed above.

Time travel seems to be logically impossible because it implies that an event both did and did not happen. Suppose you travel back in time to a place you've never been before. History records that you were not present at that place and time, but now you are. You cannot both be and not be at a place and time, however. So time travel seems to violate the law of noncontradiction. That is why sophisticated time

The Impossibility of Magic

Magicians regularly appear to do things that violate natural laws. They don't actually violate them, of course, but they create the illusion of violating them. Most magicians admit that what they're doing is sleight of hand. There are those, however, who maintain that what they're doing is real; that they're performing supernatural feats. One such is Uri Geller. In the 1970s, as a result of national TV appearances, he convinced millions of Americans that he could bend metal and fix broken watches with his mind. He would take a key or a spoon, for example, and without any apparent use of physical force, bend it. On numerous shows he invited viewers at home to take a stopped watch and place it on their TV set. Through an intense act of will, he claimed he would make them work again. Remarkably, many of them did start working again. Jewelers claimed, however, that the repair had less to do with Geller's psychic ability than with the fact that many watches stop working because their lubricating oil becomes too thick. Putting a watch on a hot TV set thins the oil and thus frees the frozen gears.

A story is told of one young woman who was convinced of Geller's powers. It appears that she got pregnant while watching Uri Geller on television. The woman was using an IUD (intrauterine device) for birth control at the time. She claimed that her IUD failed because Uri Geller's mind energy unwound its coils. Needless to say, she did not receive any compensation from Geller.

Geller's metal-bending feats have been duplicated by many magicians. That doesn't prove that he can't bend metal with his mind, but if that's what he's doing, he's doing it the hard way. Even trained observers can be taken in by magicians' sleight of hand. This is why paranormal investigators such as the Amazing Randi and Martin Gardner suggest that magicians be present when investigating purveyors of the paranormal. Because magicians know even better than scientists how we can be misled by misdirection, they are in a better position to evaluate the veracity of such claims.

travel tales, like Michael Crichton's *Timeline,* have their travelers go to parallel universes rather than their own. Science writer Martin Gardner explains: "The basic idea is as simple as it is fantastic. Persons can travel to any point in the future of their universe, with no complications, but the moment they enter the past, the universe splits into two parallel worlds, each with its own time track. Along one track rolls the world as if no looping had occurred. Along the other track spins the newly created universe, its history permanently altered."[7] If the universe splits when you travel backward in time, there will be no contradiction because in neither universe will something both be and not be the case.

Psychokinesis, the ability to move external objects with the power of one's mind, seems to be physically impossible because it seems to imply the existence of an unknown force. Science has identified only two forces whose effects can be felt over long distances: electromagnetism and gravity. The brain, however, is not capable of producing enough of either of these forces to directly affect objects outside of the body. So psychokinesis seems to violate the laws of science.

The notion that we have been visited by ancient astronauts or aliens from outer space seems technologically impossible because the amount of energy needed to travel to the stars is astronomical. Marc Mills, project manager for NASA's Breakthrough Propulsion Physics Project, has calculated the fuel requirements for interstellar travel using various types of propulsion systems, and invariably they seem beyond our reach. For example, suppose we wanted to deliver a space shuttle–sized payload to our nearest star in 900 years. If we used conventional (chemical) rocket fuel, the amount of fuel needed would be greater than the mass of the entire universe. If we used fission to power our rocket ship (fission is the process that creates atomic bombs), we would need a billion supertanker-sized propellant tanks.[8] If we used fusion (fusion is the process that creates hydrogen bombs and powers the sun), we would need a thousand such tanks. If we used anti-matter (the most efficient energy source known), we would still need ten railway car–sized propellant tanks.[8] And these are just the requirements for a one-way trip. They would have to be doubled for a return journey and multiplied many times over if we wanted to make the trip in less time. Interstellar travel, then, looks to be beyond our technological capabilities for many years to come, if not forever.

Contrary to what von Däniken would have us believe, it is possible to apply the word *impossible* to things. Some things are logically impossible, others are physically impossible, and still others are technologically impossible. And as Krauss's example of interstellar travel shows, even if something is physically possible, it doesn't necessarily follow that it will ever become actual. The principle that should guide our thinking in these matters, then, is this:

I have learned to use the word "impossible" with the greatest caution.

—Werner von Braun

Just because something is logically or physically possible doesn't mean that it is, or ever will be, actual.

If logical or physical possibility were grounds for eventual actuality, we could look forward to a world containing moon-jumping cows or egg-laying bunnies. To determine whether something is actual, we have to examine the evidence in its favor.

There are those, however, who measure the credibility of a claim not in terms of the evidence for it, but in terms of the lack of evidence against it. They argue that since there is no evidence refuting their position, it must be true. Although such arguments have great psychological appeal, they are logically fallacious. Their conclusions don't follow from their premises because a lack of evidence is no evidence at all. Arguments of this type are said to commit the fallacy of *appeal to ignorance*. Here are some examples:

> *No one has shown that Jones was lying. Therefore he must be telling the truth.*
> *No one has shown that there are no ghosts. Therefore they must exist.*
> *No one has shown that ESP is impossible. Therefore it must be possible.*

All a lack of evidence shows is our own ignorance; it doesn't provide a reason for believing anything.

If a lack of evidence against a claim actually constituted evidence for it, all sorts of weird claims would be well founded. For example, the existence of mermaids, unicorns, and centaurs—not to mention Bigfoot, the Loch Ness monster, and the abominable snowman—would be beyond question. Unfortunately, substantiating a claim is not that easy. The principle here is this:

Just because a claim hasn't been conclusively refuted doesn't mean that it's true.

A claim's truth is established by the amount of evidence in its favor, not by the lack of evidence against it.

You could claim that anything's real if the only basis for believing in it is that nobody's proved it doesn't exist.
—JOANNE ROWLING

In addition, the strategy of placing the burden of proof on the non-believer is unfair insofar as it asks him to do what is often impossible, namely, prove a universal negative. A universal negative is a claim to the effect that nothing of a certain sort exists. For example, the claim "There is no such thing as ghosts" is a universal negative. Now if you could prove that the notion of a ghost is self-contradictory—like the notion of a married bachelor—then you could prove that there is no such thing as ghosts. (Remember, anything that involves a logical contradiction cannot exist.) But in the absence of such a proof, the only way to prove a universal negative would be to investigate all of time and space and fail to find what you're looking for, and that's clearly impossible. So it's unreasonable to demand it of anybody. Whenever someone proposes something novel—whether it be a policy, a fact, or a theory—the burden of proof is on her to provide reasons for accepting it.

It's not only true believers who commit the fallacy of appeal to ignorance, however. Skeptics often argue like this: No one has proven that ESP exists; therefore it doesn't. Again, this is fallacious reasoning; it's an attempt to get something for nothing. The operative principle here is the converse of the one cited above:

Just because a claim hasn't been conclusively proven doesn't mean that it's false.

Even if no one has yet found a proof of ESP, we can't conclude that none ever will be found. Someone could find one tomorrow. So even if there is no good evidence for ESP, we can't claim that it doesn't exist. We can claim, however, that there is no compelling reason for thinking that it does exist.

THE POSSIBILITY OF ESP

What about Rothman's claim that ESP is physically impossible? Is it? If so, is investigating it really worth our while? Let's tackle the second question first. Even if our best scientific theories seem to indicate that ESP is physically impossible, investigating it still has some value, for our best scientific theories may be wrong. The only way we can tell whether or not they're wrong is to test them, and investigating ESP constitutes one such test. Failure to come up with any credible examples of ESP (or other paranormal phenomena) serves to confirm our current theories. But if we were to find good evidence for ESP—if, for example, someone were consistently to score well above the score predicted by chance on ESP tests for a number of years under conditions that ruled out any possibility of fraud—we would have to rethink our current scientific theories.

Certainly nothing is unnatural that is not physically impossible.

—Richard Brinsley Sheridan

But we still wouldn't necessarily have to reject them. For what at first appears to be a contradiction may, upon further examination, turn out not to be. Meteorites provide a case in point. As we've seen, the scientific establishment of the seventeenth and eighteenth centuries refused to admit the existence of meteorites because they seemed to conflict with the accepted model of reality. But once their existence was verified and scientists took seriously the task of explaining them, it was found that they violated no physical laws. None of Newton's laws had to be rejected in order to accommodate them. In fact, as scientists came to understand the physics of planetary development, they found that Newton's laws actually *predicted* the existence of meteorites.

Anyone with an active mind lives on tentatives rather than tenets.

—Robert Frost

This point is particularly applicable to the study of miracles. A miracle is commonly considered to be a violation of natural (physical) law. Because only something supernatural can violate natural law, miracles are often taken as evidence of the existence of God. But in light of the preceding principle, it's difficult to see how we could ever be justified in believing that a miracle occurred, for an event's seeming impossibility may simply be due to our ignorance of the operative forces or principles. As the Roman Catholic theologian Saint Augustine noted, "A miracle is not contrary to nature but contrary to our knowledge of nature."[9] The scientific ignorance of the ancient Jews and early Christians may explain why they reported so many miraculous occurrences.

Nature never breaks her own laws.

—Leonardo da Vinci

Consider, for example, the miracle of the parting of the Red Sea. The Bible tells us that "the Lord caused the sea to go back by a strong east wind all the night, and made the sea dry land, and the waters were divided" (Exodus 14:21).[10] Two oceanographers have recently shown that, because of the geological structure of the Red Sea, a strong east wind could make the sea dry land. They write in the abstract of their article:

> [Suppose that a] uniform wind is allowed to blow over the entire gulf for a period of about a day. . . . It is shown that, in a similar fashion to the familiar wind setup in a long and narrow lake, the water at the edge of the gulf slowly recedes away from its original prewind position. . . . It is found that, even for moderate storms . . . a receding distance of more than one kilometer and a sea level drop of more than 2.5 meters are obtained.[11]

The parting of the Red Sea, then, need not be considered a miracle because it may not violate any physical laws. The same goes for Jesus's walking on water. Nof has recently shown that such a feat could have been the result of a natural phenomena: springs ice (ice from underground springs).[12] In both cases, there is no need to invoke a supernatural cause, because the event can be explained in purely natural terms. What this example shows is that:

Just because you can't explain something doesn't mean that it's supernatural.

Your inability to explain something may simply be due to your ignorance of the operative forces or principles. When faced with something you don't understand, then, the most rational course of action is to seek a natural explanation.

THEORIES AND THINGS

How many things, too, are looked upon as quite impossible until they have been actually effected?
—PLINY THE ELDER

Skeptics who wish to maintain that paranormal phenomena are physically impossible often write as if the phenomena themselves contradict physical law, but a phenomenon can't contradict a law any more than a tree can get married. Since marriage is a relation between people, only people can get married. Similarly, since contradiction is a relation between propositions, only propositions can contradict one another. It isn't the phenomena themselves that contradict physical law, but rather our theories about them. Since these theories may be mistaken, we must approach claims of physical impossibility with extreme caution.

The philosopher C. J. Ducasse notes that, 200 years ago, making one's voice heard all the way across the Atlantic would have seemed physically impossible.[13] People of that time would have assumed that the only way to do so would be to use air as a means of transmission, and air can't carry a message that far. But if you use a telephone wire or radio waves, you can make yourself heard across the Atlantic fairly easily. The seeming impossibility of the feat, then, was based on a particular theory of what was involved. By changing the theory, the impossibility disappears. Similarly, the seeming impossibility of ESP is based on a particular theory of what is involved. If that theory is mistaken, so may be the claim that ESP is physically impossible.

Rothman's claim that ESP is impossible is based on the theory that ESP is a transmission of information from one object to another and that the information transfer has features (like the failure to degrade over distance) that violate physical law. If his theory is correct, his claim is justified. If not, it's unfounded.

Adrian Dobbs, a parapsychologist, argues that there's no good reason for believing that ESP signals actually do violate physical law. In the first place, according to Dobbs, there's no evidence that ESP signals don't degrade over distance. "We have," he tells us, "no systematically compiled data to test whether it has happened as frequently over long distances as over short distances, taking into account the number of occasions when it has been tried experimentally."[14] Second, even electromagnetic signals don't always get weaker the farther they travel. "Every experienced operator of radio transmitters," he explains, "knows that 'breakthrough' conditions occur sporadically when signals are picked up 'loud and clear' over distances far in excess of those their transmitters are designed to reach under normal working conditions."[15] Perhaps the purported cases of long-distance ESP are caused by some such special conditions. Third, even if a signal is picked up over a great distance, it doesn't mean that it has not attenuated, "for modern radio technology has shown that it is practicable for a receiver to detect exceedingly weak electromagnetic signals; and by using systems of Automatic Gain Control, to amplify incoming signals . . . in such a way that both strong and weak signals appear at the output stage of the loudspeaker with subjectively equal audible strengths."[16] Perhaps there's some sort of "automatic gain control" at work in ESP so that both weak and strong signals are output at the same level. In any case, contrary to what Rothman would have us believe, the evidence available concerning ESP doesn't rule out a physical explanation. ESP may well be physically possible.

I've gone into hundreds of [fortune-teller's parlors], and have been told thousands of things, but nobody ever told me I was a policewoman getting ready to arrest her.

—New York City Detective

ON KNOWING THE FUTURE

Precognition is even more puzzling than telepathy—because it not only seems to be physically impossible, it also seems to be logically impossible. To precognize an event is to know what will happen before

Tachyons and Precognition

According to relativity theory, anything that travels faster than the speed of light must go backward in time. Furthermore, no ordinary object (having a rest mass greater than zero) can go faster than the speed of light for, at that speed, it would have infinite mass. By plugging different numbers into the variables for mass in Einstein's equations, however, physicist Gerald Feinberg found that if something had imaginary mass (mass represented by an imaginary number), it would be physically possible for it to travel faster than the speed of light. Such particles he dubbed *tachyons.*[17]

If tachyons exist, they must travel backward in time because they travel faster than light. Consequently, some have thought that tachyons might be able to explain precognition. Prescient individuals may simply have especially sensitive tachyon receptors. (This is the theory of precognition employed in the movie *Watchman*. Doctor Manhattan was unable to see the future because Adrian Veidt jammed his tachyon receptors with tachyon emissions.) Electrical engineer Laurence Beynam explains the tachyonic theory of precognition this way:

> The fact that precognition involves information transfer in the reverse time direction necessitates, due to the theory of relativity, the adoption of faster-than-light (superluminal or supraluminal) processes as a possible explanatory cause allowed for by the laws of physics. . . . Physicist Gerald Feinberg and mathematician Adrian Dobbs . . . have theorized superluminal particles of (mathematically) imaginary mass. . . . Tachyons can be viewed either as carrying negative energy backwards in time or positive energy forwards in time. This interchangeability allows us to view a tachyon as a bidirectional discontinuous field line, microminiature "warp," "wormhole," or short-circuit that carries information across space-time regardless of direction, somewhat as light photons carry information within ordinary space-time.[18]

Although tachyons are physically possible, to date no one has detected one. In fact, G. A. Benford, D. L. Book, and W. A. Newcomb argue in "The Tachyonic Antitelephone" that no one ever will, because tachyonic communication involves a logical contradiction.[19] Martin Gardner explains:

> Suppose physicist Jones on the Earth is in communication by tachyonic antitelephones with physicist Alpha in another galaxy. They make the following agreement. When Alpha receives a message from Jones, he will reply immediately. Jones promises to send a message to Alpha at three o'clock Earth time, if and only if he has not received a message from Alpha by one o'clock. Do you see the difficulty? Both messages go back in time. If Jones sends his message at three, Alpha's reply could reach him before one. "Then," as [Benford, Book, and Newcomb] put it, "the exchange of messages will take place if and only if it does not take place . . . a genuine . . . causal contradiction."[20]

it actually does. Precognition, then, is a form of fortune-telling–it's seeing into the future. Such an ability certainly appears physically impossible, for it seems to be at odds with the principle of causality, which states that an effect cannot precede its cause. But more important, it also appears logically impossible, for it seems to suggest that the future exists now, and that's a contradiction in terms. We can

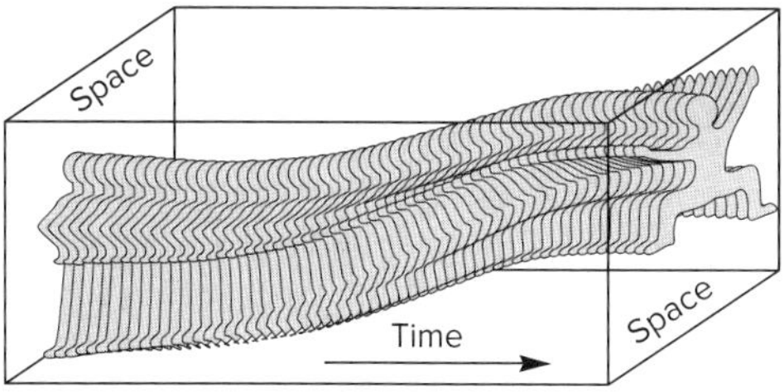

perceive only that which currently exists. If we perceive the future, the future must currently exist, but the future, by definition, doesn't currently exist. It will exist, when the time comes, but does not exist now. So precognition seems to commit us to an existing nonexistent, which is a logical impossibility.

The problem with this view is that there are models of physical reality, consistent with all known physical laws, in which the future does exist now. Such models draw their inspiration from Hermann Minkowski's interpretation of Einstein's special theory of relativity.

In his special theory of relativity, published in 1905, Einstein showed that space and time are much more intimately related than anyone had previously thought. He showed, for example, that the faster you travel, the slower you age. At the speed of light, you don't age at all; time stands still, so to speak. If you were to go faster than the speed of light, you would go backward in time.[21] But if you went backward in time, you could get into all sorts of trouble. You could, for example, kill your father before he met your mother. What, then, would happen to you? In Einstein's theory, we don't have to worry about such things, for nothing can travel faster than the speed of light.

It is easy to see, hard to foresee.

—Benjamin Franklin

Einstein's discovery that space and time are related is often expressed by saying that time is a fourth dimension. What this means is that time is as much a direction of travel as are the directions up-down, right-left, and forward-backward. Objects travel through both space and time.

The entire history of an object can be represented on a graph where one axis stands for the three dimensions of space and another for time. On such a graph, you would appear as a curved bar extending from the time you were born to the time that you die. (See above figure.) Each slice of the bar would represent a moment of your life. From a fourth-dimensional point of view, then, all the moments of your life exist simultaneously.

People like us, who believe in physics, know that the distinction between past, present and future is only a stubborn, persistent illusion.

—Albert Einstein

Einstein's theory of relativity provides a way of looking at the universe that makes it both logically and physically possible for the future to exist now. This view of the universe has come to be known as the "block universe" view because it takes the universe to be a static, unchanging "block." But the universe doesn't seem static.

Failed Psychic Predictions

Every year, psychics make predictions about the year to come. And every year, most of them fail to come true. Here's an annotated list of many of the failures for 2017, compiled by the writers at relativelyinteresting.com:

Psychic Lyndsay Edwards

- Prediction: Donald Trump will be assassinated. *Didn't happen.*
- Prediction: Donald Trump sacrifices hostages' lives. *Didn't happen.*
- Prediction: NASA Rocket will be hit by Russian missile. *Didn't happen.*

Psychic Nikki

- Prediction: A worldwide pasta shortage. *Didn't happen. Italy will be fine.*
- Prediction: The moon will turn green. *Didn't happen.*
- Prediction: An earthquake in Niagara Falls. *Didn't happen.*
- Prediction: A meteor hitting San Francisco. *Didn't happen.*
- Prediction: Doctors find cures for many diseases in a manuscript that was buried in a cavern in England near the druids. *Didn't happen.*
- Prediction: A robot will break into the White House. *Didn't happen.*
- Prediction: A UFO lands in Lake Erie. *No, but that would have been awesome.*
- Prediction: A terror attack at a Trump hotel. *Didn't happen.*
- Prediction: All of North America will be in the dark with a power blackout. *Didn't happen.*
- Prediction: Spaceship landing. *Didn't happen.*
- Prediction: Statue of Liberty under water. *Didn't happen.*
- Prediction: A magician will bring a woman back from the dead. *Didn't happen.*

Psychic Sidney Friedman

- Prediction: Surprisingly, and to the delight of liberal-leaning folks, the White House proposes to Congress some form

So what creates the illusion of change? Some believe it is created by the interaction between our consciousness and our four-dimensional selves.

Movie reels can create the illusion of change by being projected onto the screen of the theater one frame at a time. Similarly, it has been claimed, four-dimensional objects can create the illusion of change by being projected onto the screen of consciousness one slice at a time. Ordinarily, each slice is projected in sequence. In the case of precognition, however, slices are taken out of order. The mind skips ahead, so to speak. As a result, we are aware of something "before" it happens.[22] So even precognition may be physically possible.

But as we've seen, just because something is possible doesn't mean that it's real. To determine whether it is, we have to examine the reasons behind it. If the reasons are good ones, we have good reason for believing in it. If not, belief in it is irrational.

of tuition-free college, an idea initially talked about by Bernie Sanders during the primaries. *Didn't happen.*

- Prediction: Chicago has one of the hottest summers on record. *Didn't happen.*
- Prediction: Stock markets will be strong but we see volatility later in the year. We see a major stock market correction. *Nope, no major correction. Should have quit while you were ahead!*

And here are some major 2017 events that psychics *failed* to predict:

- Harvey Weinstein and exposure of **sexual harassment** and misconduct in the entertainment industry, politics, and more. This has been an ongoing story for months and has impacted many victims and big-name celebrities—none of which were predicted.
- The Las Vegas shooting that claimed 58 lives and injured more than 500 people. It was the **deadliest mass shooting in modern U.S. history.**
- The death of Linkin Park frontman Chester Bennington (41), Soundgarden's Chris Cornell (52), and Tom Petty (66). They were all relatively young, making their deaths predictably difficult.
- Hurricane Harvey, its torrential rain, flooding, and impact on Houston.
- Hurricane Maria, which struck the Caribbean and destroyed much of Puerto Rico.
- Hurricane Irma, the **strongest recorded storm ever to exist in the Atlantic**, which claimed more than one hundred lives.
- The **surge in Bitcoin's price to over $17,000**. Some psychics could have been millionaires, if only they were able to predict this.
- Emmanuel Macron's presidential win in France, which, at 39, made him the youngest leader France has had since Napoleon Bonaparte.
- The assassination of North Korean leader Kim Jong-un's half brother, Kim Jong-nam.
- The **resignation of Robert Mugabe** in Zimbabwe.
- And so much more![23]

Logic is the study of good reasoning. It does not tell us how people, in fact, reason. Instead, it tells us how people should reason if they want to avoid error and falsehood. In the next chapter, we'll explore the nature of good reasoning in more detail.

SUMMARY

It is not the case that anything is possible, as some people claim. Anything that violates the laws of logic is said to be logically impossible, and whatever is logically impossible can't exist. Such things as round squares and married bachelors are logically impossible, for they attribute both a property and its negation to a thing and are therefore self-contradictory. Many extraordinary things such as ESP, alien abduction, and out-of-body experiences are logically possible—they are not self-contradictory. But if they violate the laws of science, they are physically impossible. Anything that is inconsistent with the laws of science, or nature, is physically impossible. Something can also be technologically impossible—currently beyond our capabilities to accomplish. Time travel seems to be logically impossible; psychokinesis, the ability to move external objects with the mind, seems to be physically impossible; and visitation by aliens from outer space seems to be technologically impossible. The principle to keep in mind about such things is that just because something is logically or physically possible doesn't mean that it is, or ever will be, actual.

We must approach claims of physical impossibility with caution, for it isn't phenomena themselves that contradict physical law, but rather our theories about them—and our theories may be mistaken. Precognition, for example, seems both physically and logically impossible. But there are models of physical reality, consistent with all known physical laws, in which the future does now exist.

STUDY QUESTIONS

1. What is the difference between logical possibility and physical possibility?
2. Is ESP logically impossible?
3. Is ESP physically impossible?
4. Consider this argument: No one can explain how it happened. Therefore it must be a miracle. Is this argument a good one? Why or why not?
5. Consider this argument: You can't prove that aliens haven't visited Earth. Therefore it's reasonable to believe that they have. Is this argument a good one? Why or why not?

EVALUATE THESE CLAIMS. ARE THEY REASONABLE? WHY OR WHY NOT?

1. Scientists have no evidence of intelligent life on other planets. So Earth must contain the only intelligent life in the universe.
2. The Egyptians couldn't have built the pyramids because the precision with which the stones are cut is far beyond their primitive capabilities. Therefore the pyramids must have been built by extraterrestrials.
3. Ever since we moved into the house, the lights have occasionally flickered and gone dim. We've checked the wiring and found no problems at all. So the house must be haunted.
4. There's nothing on record to indicate that Madame Zelda, the palm reader, is a fake. Therefore she must be genuine.
5. You shouldn't be skeptical of ESP because scientists have never proven that it doesn't exist.

DISCUSSION QUESTIONS

1. Is it logically possible to travel backward in time and live in a former era? Why or why not?
2. Is it logically possible to make a robot (a mechanical device composed of inorganic materials) that can think, feel, and act like we do? Is it physically possible? Why or why not?

3. In his book, *The Bible and UFOs*, Larry Downing claims that the miraculous events recounted in the Bible were actually caused by space aliens. Is his claim as reasonable or more reasonable than the claim that God caused them? Why or why not?
4. When are we justified in believing (i) that a law of logic has been violated? (ii) that a law of nature has been violated?

FIELD PROBLEM

Predictions by the nation's top psychics are a mainstay of tabloids. They are usually published close to the beginning of a new year in which the predictions are to be fulfilled. Few people ever bother to check whether any of the predictions are accurate. Tabloid psychics forecast the following events for the 1990s:

- Soviet cosmonauts will be shocked to discover an abandoned alien space station with the bodies of several extraterrestrials aboard.
- The first successful human brain transplant will be performed.
- Public water supplies will be treated with chemicals that will prevent AIDS.

Assignment 1: Determine whether any of these predictions came true. If you are not sure, check the archives of some major news sites on the Internet.

Some psychic predictions are so vague that they can easily appear to be accurate. For example, consider "The pope will become ill and could die."

Assignment 2: List at least ten events that could be considered a fulfillment of this prediction. For example, "The pope catches a cold but does not die" or "The pope falls and breaks his hip."

CRITICAL READING AND WRITING

I. Read the passage below and answer the following questions:
   1. What kind of argument is the writer using in this passage?
   2. Do you find the argument convincing? Why or why not?
   3. Does the writer place the burden of proof on the Bigfoot skeptics or on the believers?
   4. Who should properly bear the burden of proof on this issue?
   5. Would you accept the argument if the writer had argued that Bigfoot is not real because no one has conclusively proven that he exists? Why or why not?

II. Write a 200-word paper critiquing the argument in the passage. Explain what kinds of reasons would give stronger support to the conclusion.

Passage 1

After attending the conference on the Bigfoot phenomenon—the possible existence of a giant ape-man in North America—I am struck by how my beliefs have changed. I no longer dismiss the possibility of Bigfoot out of hand. I don't know exactly what is going on in the forests of western United States and Canada, but I believe that it is mysterious and strange. I was struck by the fact that no one has offered any proof that Bigfoot does not exist. There are tantalizing bits of evidence suggesting that Bigfoot might be real, but there are no knock-down arguments or volumes of evidence showing that he definitely does *not* exist. No one has shown me a scientific survey of all of North America in which Bigfoot was searched for but not detected anywhere. There is only one conclusion that I can draw from this: However unlikely it might seem, Bigfoot exists—and he likely exists exactly where eyewitnesses say he exists, in the wilderness of the West.

NOTES

1. Milton A. Rothman, *A Physicist's Guide to Skepticism* (Buffalo: Prometheus Books, 1988), p. 193.
2. Erich von Däniken, *Chariots of the Gods* (New York: Bantam Books, 1970), p. 30.
3. Saul-Paul Sirag, "The Skeptics," in *Future Science,* ed. John White and Stanley Krippner (Garden City, NJ: Doubleday, 1977), p. 535.
4. For a more in-depth examination of necessity, see Raymond Bradley and Norman Swartz, *Possible Worlds* (Indianapolis: Hackett, 1979).
5. Aristotle, *Metaphysics,* Book IV, 1008b, trans. Richard McKeon (New York: Random House, 1941), p. 742.
6. Ibid., Book IV, 1006a, p. 737.
7. Martin Gardner, *Time Travel and Other Mathematical Bewilderments* (New York: WH Freeman, 1988), p. 4.
8. Marc Mills, "Warp Drive When? A Look at the Scaling," accessed May 14, 2018, https://cdn.preterhuman.net/texts/science_and_technology/physics/Warp_Drive_When_1.txt.
9. Saint Augustine, *The City of God,* XXI, p. 8.
10. *The Holy Bible* (English Revised Version, 1885).
11. Doron Nof and Nathan Paldor, "Are There Oceanographic Explanations for the Israelites' Crossing of the Red Sea?" *Bulletin of the American Meteorological Society* 73, no. 3 (March 1992): 304–14.
12. Doron Nof et al., "Is There a Paleolimnological Explanation for 'Walking on Water' in the Sea of Galilee?" *Journal of Paleolimnology* 35 (2006): 417–39.
13. C. J. Ducasse, "Some Questions Concerning Psychical Phenomena," *The Journal of the American Society for Psychical Research* 48 (1954): p. 5.
14. John Raymond Smythies, *Science and ESP* (Routledge & Kegan Paul, 1967), p. 230.
15. Ibid., pp. 230–31.
16. Ibid., p. 234.
17. Gerald Feinberg, "Particles That Go Faster Than Light," *Scientific American,* February 1970, pp. 69–77.
18. Laurence M. Beynam, "Quantum Physics and Paranormal Events," in *Future Science* (White and Krippner, 1977), pp. 317–18.

19. G. A. Benford, D. L. Book, and W. A. Newcomb, "The Tachyonic Antitelephone," *Physical Review D,* 3d ser., 2 (1970): 63–65.
20. Martin Gardner, *Time Travel and Other Mathematical Bewilderments* (New York: W. H. Freeman, 1988), p. 4.
21. George Gamow, *One, Two, Three . . . Infinity* (New York: Bantam Books, 1979), p. 104.
22. Lee F. Werth, "Normalizing the Paranormal," *American Philosophical Quarterly* 15 (1978): 47–56.
23. "2017 Failed and Forgotten Psychic Predictions," *Relatively Interesting,* December 19, 2017, accessed April 8, 2018, http://www.relativelyinteresting.com/2017-failed-forgotten-psychic-predictions/.

THREE

Arguments Good, Bad, and Weird

THE CENTRAL FOCUS of critical thinking is the formulation and evaluation of arguments—and this is true whether the subject matter is ordinary or as weird as can be. Usually when we are doing critical thinking, we are trying either to devise arguments or to assess them. We are trying either (1) to *demonstrate* that a claim, or proposition, is true or (2) to *determine* whether in fact a claim is true. In either case, if we are successful, we are likely to increase our knowledge and expand our understanding—which is, after all, the main reason we use critical thinking in the first place.

So in this chapter, we discuss the skills you need to make sense of arguments—to identify arguments in different contexts, to distinguish arguments from nonarguments, to evaluate the worth of arguments, and to avoid the entanglements of bad arguments.

CLAIMS AND ARGUMENTS

As noted earlier, we are entitled to believe a claim when we have good reasons to believe it. The reasons for accepting a claim are themselves stated as claims. This combination of claims—a claim (or claims) supposedly giving reasons for accepting another claim—is known as an *argument.* Or to put it another way, when claims (reasons) provide support for another claim, we have an argument.

> *Logical consequences are the scarecrows of fools and the beacons of wise men.*
>
> —THOMAS HENRY HUXLEY

People sometimes use the word *argument* to refer to a quarrel or verbal fight. But this meaning has little to do with critical thinking. In critical thinking, an argument is as defined above—reasons supporting a claim.

To be more precise, claims (or reasons) intended to support another claim are known as *premises.* The claim that the premises are intended to support is known as the *conclusion.* Take a look at these simple arguments:

1. *My instructor says that ghosts are real. Therefore, ghosts are real.*
2. *Because the former tenants ran out of the house screaming, and they begged a priest to perform an exorcism on the property, the house is obviously possessed.*
3. *When Julio reads about weird things, he always gets the shakes. Since he's reading about weird things now, he will get the shakes.*
4. *All men are mortal. Socrates is a man. Therefore, Socrates is mortal.*
5. *Fifty percent of the students in this class are Republicans. Therefore, 50 percent of all students at this college are Republicans.*

In each of these five arguments, can you distinguish the premises from the conclusion? Try picking out the conclusions of each one, then look for the premises. Here are the arguments again with their parts labeled:

1. [Premise] *My instructor says that ghosts are real.* [Conclusion] *Therefore, ghosts are real.*
2. [Premise] *Because the former tenants ran out of the house screaming, and* [Premise] *they begged a priest to perform an exorcism on the property,* [Conclusion] *the house is obviously possessed.*
3. [Premise] *When Julio reads about weird things, he always gets the shakes.* [Premise] *Since he's reading about weird things now,* [Conclusion] *he will get the shakes.*

4. [Premise] *All men are mortal.* [Premise] *Socrates is a man.* [Conclusion] *Therefore, Socrates is mortal.*
5. [Premise] *Fifty percent of the students in this class are Republicans.* [Conclusion] *Therefore, 50 percent of all students at this college are Republicans.*

Now consider this passage:

> *The house has been there for a hundred years, and it's pretty spooky. Some people claim that they've seen someone or something moving about inside the house at night. John said that he would never go in there.*

Can you find an argument in this passage? We hope not because there is no argument there. The passage consists of three descriptive claims, but they are not supporting a conclusion. With a little tinkering, though, we can turn this passage into an argument. For example:

> *There is no doubt that the house is haunted because it has been there for a hundred years, it's really spooky, and even John—who is normally very brave—refuses to go anywhere near the house.*

Logic is logic. That's all I say.
—Oliver Wendell Holmes

Now we have an argument. The conclusion is "There is no doubt that the house is haunted," and there are three premises: (1) "[the house] has been there for a hundred years," (2) "it's really spooky," and (3) "John—who is normally very brave—refuses to go anywhere near the house."

Some people think that if they simply state their views on an issue, they have presented an argument. But a string of statements asserting or clarifying their views does not an argument make. Consider this passage:

> *I think that abortion is wrong. I have always believed that and always will. Those who favor abortion on demand are just plain wrong. In fact, those who favor any kind of abortion for any reason are wrong. They may be sincere in their beliefs, and they may have the Supreme Court on their side, but they're still advocating an immoral act.*

This is not an argument. It is merely a collection of unsupported claims. It offers no reasons for believing that abortion is wrong. It is, however, typical of the expression of views that shows up in what many people call "arguments," which often consist of verbal sparring and pointless cycles of claim and counterclaim. Such exchanges may reveal something about the participants, but they say nothing about the grounds for believing something.

You should also keep in mind the distinction between argument and persuasion: They are not the same thing. Through various persuasive ploys—fancy rhetoric, emotional appeals, deception, coercion, and more—you may be able to influence people to accept a conclusion. But if you do, you will not have shown that the conclusion is worthy of acceptance, that there are good reasons for believing it. Of course, a good argument, in addition to presenting solid grounds for accepting a claim, can also be psychologically forceful. But these two approaches to claims should not be confused.

Unfortunately, there is no 100-percent-reliable formula for distinguishing arguments from nonarguments. There are, however, some ways to make the job easier. One technique is to look for *indicator words*—terms that often accompany arguments and signal that a conclusion or premise is nearby. For example, in the haunted house argument above, notice that the word *because* alerts us to the presence of the premises that follow. In arguments 1, 4, and 5 above, the word *therefore* indicates that a conclusion follows.

Here are some common conclusion indicator words:

thus	hence
so	therefore
consequently	as a result
it follows that	we can conclude that
which means that	which implies that

And here are some common premise indicator words:

since	because
the reason being	in view of the fact
assuming that	given that
for the reason that	as indicated by
for	due to the fact that

Keep in mind that indicator words do not *invariably* point to conclusions or premises. Sometimes indicator words are used when no argument is present. For example: "Julio has been working *since* nine o'clock." Or, "Naomi works here *because* she wants to." Also, occasionally arguments can be stated without the use of any indicator words:

> *Look, there is no doubt that the house is haunted. It has been there for a hundred years, it's really spooky, and even John—who is normally very brave—refuses to go anywhere near the house.*

The minimum requirement for an argument is at least one premise and a conclusion. This simple structure, though, can have many configurations. First, an argument can have one premise or many.

If the world were a logical place, men would ride side saddle.

—RITA MAE BROWN

The haunted house argument has three premises, but it could have four, or seven, or more. Second, the conclusion of an argument can appear after the premises (as in arguments 1 through 5) or before the premises (as in the haunted house argument). Third, an argument can be buried in a cluster of other statements that are not part of the argument. These other statements may be questions, exclamations, descriptions, explanations, background information, or something else. The trick is to find the argument that's embedded in the extraneous material.

The easiest way to identify an argument is to *find the conclusion first.* If you first find the conclusion, locating the premises becomes much easier. To find the conclusion, ask yourself, "What claim is the writer or speaker trying to get me to accept?" or "For what claim is the writer or speaker providing reasons?"

An argument can be either good or bad. A good argument demonstrates that the conclusion is worthy of acceptance. A bad argument fails to demonstrate that a conclusion is worthy of acceptance.

There are also different kinds of arguments. Arguments can be either *deductive* or *inductive.* Deductive arguments are intended to provide conclusive support for their conclusions. Inductive arguments are intended to provide probable support for their conclusions. A deductive argument that succeeds in providing conclusive support is said to be *valid.* A deductive argument that fails to provide such support is said to be *invalid.* A valid deductive argument has this characteristic: If its premises are true, its conclusion *must* be true. In other words, it is impossible for a deductively valid argument to have true premises and a false conclusion. Notice that the term *valid* as used here is not a synonym for *true. Valid* refers to a deductive argument's logical structure—it refers to an argument structure that *guarantees* the truth of the conclusion *if* the premises are true. If an argument is valid, we say that the *conclusion follows from the premises.* Because a deductively valid argument guarantees the truth of the conclusion if the premises are true, it is said to be *truth-preserving.*

What danger can ever come from ingenious reasoning and inquiry? The worst speculative skeptic ever I knew was a much better man than the best superstitious devotee and bigot.
—DUGALD STEWART

Here's a classic deductively valid argument:

All men are mortal.
Socrates is a man.
Therefore, Socrates is mortal.

And here's another one:

If you have scars on your body, then you have been abducted by space aliens. You obviously do have scars on your body. Therefore, you have been abducted by space aliens.

Notice that in each of these, if the premises are true, the conclusion *must* be true. If the premises are true, the conclusion cannot possibly be false. This would be the case regardless of the order of the premises and regardless of whether the conclusion came first or last.

Now here are deductively invalid versions of these arguments:

If Socrates is a dog, he is mortal.
Socrates is not a dog.
Therefore, Socrates is not mortal.

If you have scars on your body, then you have been abducted by space aliens. You have been abducted by space aliens. Therefore, you have scars on your body.

These arguments are invalid. In each, the conclusion does not follow from the premises.

An inductive argument that succeeds in giving probable support to its conclusion is said to be *strong*. An inductive argument that fails to do this is said to be *weak*. In an inductively strong argument, if the premises are true, the conclusion is probably or likely to be true. The logical structure of an inductively strong argument can only render the conclusion probably true if the premises are true. Unlike a deductively valid argument, an inductively strong argument cannot guarantee the truth of the conclusion if the premises are true. The best that an inductively strong argument can do is show that the conclusion is very likely to be true. So inductive arguments are not truth-preserving.

Here are two inductively strong arguments:

All humans have lived less than 200 years.
Socrates is a human.
Therefore, Socrates will probably live less than 200 years.

Mysterious scars on one's body almost always indicate an alien abduction.
You have mysterious scars on your body.
So you have probably been the victim of an alien abduction.

Look at the first inductive argument. Notice that it's possible for the premises to be true and the conclusion false. After all, the first premise says that there is no guarantee that Socrates is mortal just because he's a man. He's only *likely* to be mortal. Also in the second argument, there is no guarantee that you have been abducted by space aliens if you have mysterious scars on your body. If you have mysterious scars on your body, there's still a chance that you have *not* been abducted.

Good arguments must be valid or strong—but they also must have true premises. A good argument is one that has the proper logical structure *and* true premises. Consider this argument:

All dogs can lay eggs.
The prime minister is a dog.
Therefore, the prime minister can lay eggs.

This is a valid argument, but the premises are false. The conclusion follows logically from the premises—even though the premises are false. So the argument is not a good one. A deductively valid argument with true premises is said to be *sound.* A sound argument is a good argument. A good argument gives you good reasons for accepting the conclusion. Likewise, a good inductive argument must be logically strong and have true premises. An inductively strong argument with true premises is said to be *cogent.* A cogent argument is a good argument, which provides good reasons for accepting the conclusion.

DEDUCTIVE ARGUMENTS

Our reason must be considered as a kind of cause, of which truth is the natural effect.
—David Hume

Whether a deductive argument is valid depends on its form or structure. We can see the form most easily if we represent it by using letters to substitute for the argument's statements. Consider this deductive argument:

1. If the soul is immortal, then thinking doesn't depend on brain activity.
2. The soul is immortal.
3. Therefore, thinking doesn't depend on brain activity.

By using letters to represent each statement, we can symbolize the argument like this:

If p then q.
p.
Therefore, q.

The first line is a compound statement consisting of two constituent statements, each of which is assigned a letter: *p* or *q*. Such a compound statement is known as a *conditional,* or if-then, *statement.* The statement following the *if* is called the *antecedent,* and the statement after *then* is called the *consequent.* The whole argument is referred to as a conditional argument because it contains at least one conditional statement (If *p* then *q*.).

Conditional arguments are common. In fact, many conditional argument patterns are so common that they have been given names.

These prevalent forms are worth getting to know because they can help you quickly judge the validity of arguments you encounter. Since the validity of an argument depends on its form, if you know that a particular common form is always valid (or invalid), then you know that any argument having that same form must also be valid (or invalid).

For example, the argument we just examined is cast in the common form known as *affirming the antecedent,* or *modus ponens.* Any argument in this form is always valid. We may drop whatever statements we please into this form, and the argument will remain unshakably valid—whether or not the premises are true. Now consider this *modus ponens* argument:

1. If one human is made of tin, then every human is made of tin.
2. One human is made of tin.
3. Therefore, every human is made of tin.

The premises and conclusion of this argument are false. Nevertheless, this argument is valid because if the premises were true, then the conclusion would have to be true. A valid argument can have false premises and a false conclusion, false premises and a true conclusion, or true premises and a true conclusion. The one thing it cannot have is true premises and a false conclusion.

Here is another frequently occurring, conditional form:

If p then q.
Not q.
Therefore, not p.

For example:

1. If the soul is immortal, then thinking doesn't depend on brain activity.
2. Thinking does depend on brain activity.
3. Therefore, the soul is not immortal.

This form is known as *denying the consequent,* or *modus tollens.* Any argument patterned in this way—regardless of the topic or truth of the premises—is valid.

A valid, hypothetical form that people often employ to think critically about a series of events is known as *hypothetical syllogism.* (*Hypothetical* is a synonym for *conditional;* a syllogism is simply a deductive argument consisting of two premises and a conclusion.) In this form, every statement is conditional. See:

If p then q.
If q then r.
Therefore, if p then r.

For example:

1. If the floor creaks, someone is standing in the hallway.
2. If someone is standing in the hallway, there's a burglar in the house.
3. Therefore, if the floor creaks, there's a burglar in the house.

As you might expect, some very common argument forms are invalid. This one is known as *denying the antecedent:*

If p then q.
Not p.
Therefore, not q.

1. If Joe is a bachelor, then Joe is a male.
2. Joe is not a bachelor.
3. Therefore, Joe is not a male.

The invalidity of this argument seems obvious. But consider this specimen in the same form:

1. If scientists can prove the existence of ghosts, then ghosts are real.
2. But scientists cannot prove the existence of ghosts.
3. Therefore, ghosts are not real.

The dead giveaway of invalidity here is that it's possible for both premises to be true and the conclusion false. Even if scientists cannot prove the existence of ghosts, that doesn't show that ghosts are not real. Perhaps ghosts exist despite the failure of science to prove it.

Another popular invalid form is *affirming the consequent:*

If p then q.
q.
Therefore, p.

1. If Chicago is the capital of Illinois, then Chicago is in Illinois.
2. Chicago is in Illinois.
3. Therefore, Chicago is the capital of Illinois.

Logic is the armory of reason, furnished with all offensive and defensive weapons.
—THOMAS FULLER

We can see immediately that this argument is invalid because, you will recall, it's impossible for a valid argument to have true premises and a false conclusion—and this argument clearly does have true premises and a false conclusion.

Of course, not all common deductive arguments are conditional. Here's a nonconditional valid form known as *disjunctive syllogism:*

Either p or q.
Not p.
Therefore, q.

1. Either Jill faked the UFO landing or Jack did.
2. Jill did not fake the UFO landing.
3. Therefore, Jack faked the UFO landing.

A statement in the *p*-or-*q* format of premise 1 is called a *disjunction*, and each statement in a disjunction (*p* or *q*) is called a disjunct. In a disjunctive syllogism, either one of the disjuncts can be denied, and the conclusion is that the undenied disjunct must be true.

Being familiar with these six argument forms can come in handy when you're trying to quickly determine the validity of an argument. If you come across an argument whose structure matches one of the valid forms just discussed, then you know the argument is valid. If the argument has a structure matching one of the invalid forms, then you know it's invalid. Memorizing these common forms can help make your comparison of argument patterns more efficient.

Another technique for assessing the validity of deductive arguments is known as the *counterexample method.* This approach is based on the aforementioned impossibility of a valid argument having true premises and a false conclusion. So to determine the validity of an argument (called the test argument), you try to construct a corresponding argument having *the same form as the test argument* but with unquestionably *true premises and a false conclusion.* Successfully constructing such an argument shows that the test argument is not valid.

Suppose this is your test argument:

1. If Ester could bend spoons with her mind, then she would be an extraordinary person.
2. Ester cannot bend spoons with her mind.
3. Therefore, Ester is not an extraordinary person.

To check for validity, you invent this corresponding argument:

1. If dogs could lay eggs, then they would be useful to humans.
2. Dogs cannot lay eggs.
3. Therefore, dogs are not useful to humans.

This argument and the test argument have exactly the same form (which you probably already see is denying the antecedent). This one, however, has true premises and a false conclusion. Thus it's invalid, and so is the test argument.

INDUCTIVE ARGUMENTS

Even though inductive arguments are not valid, they can still give us good reasons for believing their conclusions provided that certain conditions are met. To get a better idea of what constitutes a strong inductive argument, let's examine some common forms of induction.

Enumerative Induction

Enumerative induction is the sort of reasoning we use when we arrive at a generalization about a group of things after observing only some members of that group. The premise of a typical enumerative induction is a statement reporting what percentage of the observed members of a group have a particular property. The conclusion is a statement claiming that a certain percentage of the members of the whole group have that property.

In enumerative induction, we might reason that

> Most of the meals you've had down at Joe's Diner have been terrible. So all the meals served at Joe's are probably terrible.
>
> Sixty percent of the apples from the barrel have been tasty. Therefore, 60 percent of all the apples in the barrel are tasty.
>
> Half of the people you've met at the convention are Lutherans, so probably half of all the people at the convention are Lutherans.

Thus, enumerative induction has the following form:

> *X percent of the observed members of group A have property P.*
> *Therefore, X percent of all the members of group A have property P.*

Some technical terms will help here. The group under study—the entire class of individuals we're interested in—is known as the *target group.* The observed members of the target group are the *sample,* and the characteristic we're studying is the *relevant property.* In enumerative induction, then, we draw a conclusion about the relevant property (or properties) in the target group from observations of the relevant property in the sample. In the example about apples, the target group is the apples in the barrel, the sample is the observed apples, and the relevant property is tastiness.

As with any kind of induction, an enumerative inductive argument is good only if it is strong and its premises are true. To be strong, it must score well on two counts: (1) sample size and (2) sample representativeness. Consider this example:

> *Three of the four students Julio encountered in the quad were Democrats. Therefore, three-fourths of the students at this college are probably Democrats.*

This argument is, of course, weak. We cannot draw a reliable conclusion about the political affiliation of all the students at the college (which we may assume has hundreds or thousands of students) based solely on a fact about four of them. With a sample of four students, we may reasonably conclude that *some* students at the college are Democrats, but that's as far as we can go.

Using an inadequate sample size to draw a conclusion about a target group is a common mistake, a fallacy called *hasty generalization* (discussed later in the chapter). You would commit this error if you claimed that Chevrolets are rotten cars because you used to own one that was a lemon, or if you decided that all biology majors are boring because the last three you met were, or if you concluded that members of a race different from your own were dishonest because you saw two of them cheat on a test.

But how large a sample is large enough? Generally, the larger the sample, the more reliably it signifies the nature of the target group. But sometimes even small samples can be telling. One guiding principle is that the more homogeneous a target group is in characteristics relevant to the property being studied, the smaller the sample needs to be. We would require, for example, a very small sample of mallard ducks to determine whether they all have bills, because the physical properties of mallard ducks vary little throughout the species. But if we want to know the buying habits of Canadians, we would need to survey a much larger sample—hundreds or thousands of Canadians. People differ dramatically in their social or psychological properties, so surveying a handful of them to generalize about thousands or millions is usually pointless.

Samples must not only be the right size but also representative—that is, they must be like the target group in all the relevant ways. A sample that is not properly representative of the target group is known as a *biased sample.* Biased samples make weak arguments. To reliably generalize about the paranormal beliefs of New Yorkers, we should not have our sample consist entirely of members of the local occult club. The members' views on the paranormal are not likely to be representative of those of New Yorkers generally. To draw a trustworthy conclusion about water pollution in Lake X, we should not draw all the water samples from the part of the lake polluted by the factory. That area is not representative of the lake as a whole.

A sample is properly representative of the target group if it possesses the same relevant characteristics in the same proportions exhibited by the target group. A characteristic is relevant if it can affect the relevant property. Suppose you want to conduct a survey to find out whether adult Hispanics believe in ghosts. Characteristics that might affect adult Hispanics' belief in ghosts include religion, income, occupation, and education level. These relevant characteristics therefore should be included in your sample, and they should be present in the same proportions found in the target group, adult Hispanics. This means, for example, that if 60 percent of Hispanics are college graduates, then your sample should reflect that—60 percent of the sample should be college graduates.

As you may have guessed, enumerative inductions are the basis for opinion polls, those ubiquitous surveys that describe public attitudes about elections, political issues, moral debates, and consumer preferences. Like any enumerative induction, opinion polls reckon from samples to general conclusions about target groups. To be credible, they must use properly sized samples representative of the target group in all relevant respects. Good opinion polls must also be well conducted so they generate accurate data—numbers that truthfully describe what they claim to describe. They can fail to generate accurate data because of mathematical errors, poorly phrased questions, faulty survey design, sampling errors, and other problems. All of which means that an opinion poll can work from a properly sized, representative sample and still be a weak inductive argument.

National polling organizations have perfected techniques for generating representative samples of large target groups—all American adults, for example. Because of modern sampling procedures, these samples can contain fewer than 2,000 individuals (representing about 200 million people). Such small representative samples are possible through *random sampling.* This technique is based on the fact that the best way to devise a genuinely representative sample is to select the sample from the target group randomly. Random selection is ensured if every member of the target group has an equal chance of being chosen for the sample. Selecting sample members nonrandomly produces a biased sample.

We are frequently exposed to polls created through nonrandom sampling. Many are nonrandom because they use *self-selecting samples.* Suppose a website or TV show asks people to respond to a simple question—for example, "Do you believe that concealed weapons should be banned from college campuses?" In this case, pollsters would not randomly select the respondents; respondents would nonrandomly select themselves for all sorts of irrelevant reasons. The sample would be biased in favor of, say, people who have political views encouraged by the website or program, who like expressing their opinions on particular issues (or any issue), or who just happen to be online or watching TV when the question is posed. These organizations will often admit that their self-selecting surveys are unreliable, declaring (sometimes in small print) that the polls are "unscientific."

Even the best of opinion polls cannot guarantee 100 percent reliability—that their random, properly sized sample will precisely reflect the views of the larger target group. No matter how careful pollsters are, their sampling can only approach the values they would get if they surveyed every member of the target group. This discrepancy between the poll results and the ideal results is known as the *margin of error.* An honest poll is explicit about its margin of error—stating, for example, that the proportion of adult Americans who favor gun control is 77 percent, plus or minus 4 points (typically expressed as 77 percent $\pm$ 4). This translates as "the percentage of adult Americans who favor gun control is between 73 and 81 percent." Because of the margin of error, small differences between two poll numbers (for example, percentages of people who intend to vote for a particular presidential candidate) mean little. So if the margin of error is $\pm$ 3 points, there is no notable difference between candidate A with 43 percent of the vote and candidate B with 45 percent—though political commentators may want us to believe that candidate B is winning.

Opinion polls can be unreliable and misleading because of how the polling questions are phrased, who asks them, or how they are asked. Question phrasing is especially important. Think how easy it would be to get a large percentage of people in a sample to answer no to a question like "Are you in favor of negating the constitutional right of citizens to bear arms by passing gun-control laws?" Or "Are you in favor of destroying innocent human life by funding stem-cell research?" Such questions are not designed to objectively gauge opinions on an issue—they're meant to prod the respondent to give a particular answer. Good pollsters try to use more neutral wording that will accurately and fairly measure attitudes. Pollsters bent on advocacy will ask their questions accordingly. Sometimes pollsters create biased questions accidentally, but probably more often the slanting is deliberate.

Analogical Induction

When we show how one thing is similar to another, we draw an analogy between them. When we claim that two things that are similar in some respects are similar in some further respect, we make an analogical induction. For example, before the various missions to Mars, NASA scientists may have argued as follows: The Earth has air, water, and life. Mars is like the Earth in that it has air and water. Therefore, it's probable that Mars has life. The form of such analogical inductions can be represented as follows:

Object A has properties F, G, H, etc., as well as the property Z.
Object B has properties F, G, H, etc.
Therefore, object B probably has property Z.

Like all inductive arguments, analogical inductions can only establish their conclusions with a certain degree of probability. The more similarities between the two objects, the more probable the conclusion. The fewer similarities, the less probable the conclusion.

The dissimilarities between the Earth and Mars are significant. The Martian atmosphere is very thin and contains very little oxygen, and the water on Mars is trapped in ice caps at the poles. So the probability of finding life on Mars is not very high. Mars was more like the Earth in the past, however. So the probability of finding evidence of past life on Mars is greater.

Logic is the art of convincing us of some truth.
—JEAN DE LA BRUYÈRE

Scientists are not the only ones who make analogical inductions. This kind of reasoning is used in many other fields, including medical research and law. Whenever medical researchers test a new drug on laboratory animals, they are making an analogical induction. Essentially they are arguing that if this drug has a certain effect on the animals, then it's probable that the drug will have the same sort of effect on human beings. The strength of such arguments depends on the biological similarities between the animals and humans. Rats, rabbits, and guinea pigs are often used in these kinds of experiments. Although they are all mammals, their biology is by no means identical to ours. So we cannot be certain that any particular drug will affect us in the same way that it affects them.

The American legal system is based on precedents. A precedent is a case that has already been decided. Lawyers often try to convince judges of the merits of their case by citing precedents. They argue that the case before the court is similar to one that has been decided in the past, and since the court decided one way in that case, it should decide the same way in this case. The opposing attorney will try to undermine that reasoning by highlighting the differences between the case cited and the current case. Who wins such court cases is often determined by the strength of the analogical arguments presented.

Hypothetical Induction (Abduction, or Inference to the Best Explanation)

Science when well digested is nothing more than good sense and reason.
—STANISŁAW LESZCZYŃSKI

We attempt to understand the world by constructing explanations of it. Not all explanations are equally good, however. So even though we may have arrived at an explanation of something, it doesn't mean that we're justified in believing it. If other explanations are better, then we're not justified in believing it.

Inference to the best explanation has the following form:

Phenomena p.
Hypothesis h explains p.

No other hypothesis explains p as well as h.
Therefore, it's probable that h is true.

The great American philosopher Charles Sanders Peirce was the first to codify this kind of inference, and he dubbed it *abduction* to distinguish it from other forms of induction.

Inference to the best explanation may be the most widely used form of inference. Doctors, auto mechanics, and detectives—as well as the rest of us—use it almost daily. Anyone who tries to figure out why something happened uses inference to the best explanation. Sherlock Holmes was a master of inference to the best explanation. Here's Holmes at work in *A Study in Scarlet:*

> I knew you came from Afghanistan. From long habit the train of thoughts ran so swiftly through my mind that I arrived at the conclusion without being conscious of intermediate steps. There were such steps, however. The train of reasoning ran, "Here is a gentleman of a medical type, but with the air of a military man. Clearly an army doctor, then. He has just come from the tropics, for his face is dark, and that is not the natural tint of his skin, for his wrists are fair. He has undergone hardship and sickness, as his haggard face says clearly. His left arm has been injured. He holds it in a stiff and unnatural manner. Where in the tropics would an English army doctor have seen much hardship and got his arm wounded? Clearly in Afghanistan." The whole train of thought did not occupy a second. I then remarked that you came from Afghanistan, and you were astonished.[1]

Although this passage appears in a chapter titled "The Science of Deduction," Holmes is not using deduction here because the truth of the premises does not guarantee the truth of the conclusion. From the fact that Watson has a deep tan and a wounded arm, it doesn't necessarily follow that he has been in Afghanistan. He could have been in California and cut himself surfing. Properly speaking, Holmes is using abduction, or inference to the best explanation, because he arrives at his conclusion by citing a number of facts and coming up with the hypothesis that best explains them.

Often what makes inference to the best explanation difficult is not that no explanation can be found, but that too many explanations can be found. The trick is to identify which among all the possible explanations is the best. The goodness of an explanation is determined by the amount of understanding it produces, and the amount of understanding produced by an explanation is determined by how well it systematizes and unifies our knowledge. We begin to understand something when we see it as part of a pattern, and the more that pattern encompasses, the more understanding it produces. The extent to which a hypothesis systematizes and unifies our knowledge can be measured by various criteria of adequacy, such as simplicity, the number of assumptions made by a hypothesis; scope, the amount of diverse phenomena explained by the hypothesis; conservatism, how well the hypothesis fits with what we already know; and fruitfulness, the ability of a hypothesis to successfully predict novel phenomena. In Chapter 6 we will see how these criteria are used to distinguish reasonable explanations from unreasonable ones.

INFORMAL FALLACIES

We can easily forgive a child who is afraid of the dark; the real tragedy of life is when men are afraid of the light.

—PLATO

A fallacious argument is a bogus one, for it fails to do what it purports to do, namely, provide a good reason for accepting a claim. Unfortunately, logically fallacious arguments can be psychologically compelling. Since most people have never learned the difference between a good argument and a fallacious one, they are often persuaded to believe things for no good reason. To avoid holding irrational beliefs, then, it is important to understand the many ways in which an argument can fail.

An argument is fallacious if it contains (1) unacceptable premises, (2) irrelevant premises, or (3) insufficient premises.[2] Premises are *unacceptable* if they are at least as dubious as the claim they are supposed to support. In a good argument, you see, the premises provide a firm basis for accepting the conclusion. If the premises are shaky, the argument is inconclusive. Premises are *irrelevant* if they have no bearing on the truth of the conclusion. In a good argument, the conclusion follows from the premises. If the premises are logically unrelated to the conclusion, they provide no reason to accept it. Premises are *insufficient* if they do not establish the conclusion beyond a reasonable doubt. In a good argument, the premises eliminate reasonable grounds for doubt. If they fail to do this, they don't justify the conclusion.

So when someone gives you an argument, you should ask yourself: Are the premises acceptable? Are they relevant? Are they sufficient? If the answer to any of these questions is no, then the argument is not logically compelling.

Unacceptable Premises

Begging the Question An argument begs the question—or argues in a circle—when its conclusion is used as one of its premises. For example, some people claim that one should believe that God exists because the Bible says so. But when asked why we should believe the Bible, they answer that we should believe it because God wrote it. Such people are begging the question, for they are assuming what they are trying to prove, namely that God exists. Here's another example: "Jane has telepathy," says Susan. "How do you know?" asks Ami. "Because she can read my mind," replies Susan. Since telepathy is, by definition, the ability to read someone's mind, all Susan has told us is that she believes that Jane can read her mind because she believes that Jane can read her mind. Her reason merely reiterates her claim in different words. Consequently, her reason provides no additional justification for her claim.

False Dilemma An argument proposes a false dilemma when it presumes that only two alternatives exist when in actuality there are more than two. For example: "Either science can explain how she was cured or it was a miracle. Science can't explain how she was cured. So it must be a miracle." These two alternatives do not exhaust all the possibilities. It's possible, for example, that she was cured by some natural cause that scientists don't yet understand. Because the argument doesn't take this possibility into account, it's fallacious. Again: "Either have your horoscope charted by an astrologer or continue to stumble through life without knowing where you're going. You certainly don't want to continue your wayward ways. So you should have your horoscope charted by an astrologer." If someone is concerned about the direction his or her life is taking, there are other things he or she can do about it than consult an astrologer. Since there are other options, the argument is fallacious.

Irrelevant Premises

Equivocation Equivocation occurs when a word is used in two different senses in an argument. For example, consider this argument: "(i) Only man is rational. (ii) No woman is a man. (iii) Therefore no woman is rational." The word *man* is used in two different senses here: In the first premise it means human being while in the second it means male. As a result, the conclusion doesn't follow from the premises. Here's another example: "It's the duty of the press to publish news that's in the public interest. There is great public interest in UFOs. Therefore the press fails in its duty if it does not publish articles on UFOs." In the first premise, the phrase *the public interest* means the public welfare, but in the second, it means what the public is interested in. The switch in meaning invalidates the argument.

The cure for a fallacious argument is a better argument, not the suppression of ideas.

—Carl Sagan

Composition An argument may claim that what is true of the parts is also true of the whole; this is the fallacy of composition. For example, consider this argument: "Subatomic particles are lifeless. Therefore anything made out of them is lifeless." This argument is fallacious because a whole may be greater than the sum of its parts; that is, it may have properties not possessed by its parts. A property had by a whole but not by its parts is called an *emergent* property. Wetness, for example, is an emergent property. No individual water molecule is wet, but get enough of them together and wetness emerges.

Just as what's true of a part may not be true of the whole, what's true of a member of a group may not be true of the group itself. For example: "Belief in the supernatural makes Joe happy. Therefore, universal belief in the supernatural would make the nation happy." This argument doesn't follow because everybody's believing in the supernatural could have effects quite different from one person's believing in it. Not all arguments from part to whole are fallacious, for there are some properties that parts and wholes share. The fallacy lies in *assuming* that what's true of the parts is true of the whole.

Division The fallacy of division is the converse of the fallacy of composition. It occurs when one assumes that what is true of a whole is also true of its parts. For example: "We are alive and we are made out of subatomic particles. So they must be alive too." To argue in this way is to ignore the very real difference between parts and wholes. Here's another example: "Society's interest in the occult is growing. Therefore Joe's interest in the occult is growing." Since groups can have properties that their members do not have, such an argument is fallacious.

Appeal to the Person When someone tries to rebut an argument by criticizing or denigrating its presenter rather than by dealing with the argument itself, that person is guilty of the fallacy of appeal to the person. This fallacy is referred to as *ad hominem,* or "to the man." For example: "This theory has been proposed by a believer in the occult. Why should we take it seriously?" Or: "You can't believe Dr. Jones's claim that there is no evidence for life after death. After all, he's an atheist." The flaw in these arguments is obvious: An argument stands or falls on its own merits; who proposes it is irrelevant to its soundness. Crazy people can come up with perfectly sound arguments, and sane people can talk nonsense.

Genetic Fallacy To argue that a claim is true or false on the basis of its origin is to commit the genetic fallacy. For example: "Juan's idea is the result of a mystical experience, so it must be false (or true)." Or: "Jane got that message from a Ouija board, so it must be false (or true)." These arguments are fallacious because the origin of a claim is irrelevant to its truth or falsity. Some of our greatest advances have originated in unusual ways. For example, the chemist August Kekulé discovered the benzene ring while staring at a fire and seeing the image of a serpent biting its tail. The theory of evolution came to British naturalist Alfred Russell Wallace while in a delirium. Archimedes supposedly arrived at the principle of displacement while taking a bath, from which he leapt shouting, "Eureka!" The truth or falsity of an idea is determined not by where it came from, but by the evidence supporting it.

Appeal to Authority We often try to support our views by citing experts. This sort of appeal to authority is perfectly legitimate—provided that the person cited really is an expert in the field in question. If not, it is fallacious. Celebrity endorsements, for example, often involve fallacious appeals to authority, because being famous doesn't necessarily give you any special expertise. The fact that Dionne Warwick is a great singer, for example, doesn't make her an expert on the efficacy of psychic hotlines. Similarly, the fact that Linus Pauling is a Nobel Prize winner doesn't make him an expert on the efficacy of vitamin C. Pauling claimed that taking massive doses of vitamin C would help prevent colds and increase the life expectancy of people suffering from cancer. That may be the case, but the fact that he said it doesn't justify our believing it. Only rigorous clinical studies confirming these claims can do that.

Appeal to the Masses A remarkably common but fallacious form of reasoning is, "It must be true (or good) because everybody believes it (or does it)." Mothers understand that this argument is a fallacy; they often counter it by asking, "If everyone else jumped off a cliff, would you do it, too?" Of course you wouldn't. What this response shows is that just because a lot of people believe something or like something doesn't mean that it's true or good. A lot of people used to believe that the Earth was flat, but that certainly didn't make it so. Similarly, a lot of people used to believe that women should not have the right to vote. Popularity is not a reliable indication of either reality or value.

In questions of science, the authority of a thousand is not worth the humble reasoning of a single individual.

—Galileo Galilei

Appeal to Tradition We appeal to tradition when we argue that something must be true (or good) because it is part of an established tradition. For example: "Astrology has been around for ages, so there must be something to it." Or: "Mothers have always used chicken soup to fight colds, so it must be good for you." These arguments are fallacious because traditions can be wrong. This error becomes obvious when you consider that slavery was once an established tradition. The fact that people have always done or believed something is no reason for thinking that we should continue to do or believe something.

Appeal to Ignorance The appeal to ignorance comes in two varieties: Using an opponent's inability to disprove a conclusion as proof of the conclusion's correctness, and using an opponent's inability to prove a conclusion as proof of its incorrectness. In the first case, the claim is that since there is no proof that something is true, it must be false. For example: "There is no proof that the parapsychology experiments were fraudulent, so I'm sure they weren't." In the second case, the claim is that since there is no proof that something is false, it must be true. For example: "Bigfoot must exist because no one has been able to prove that he doesn't." The problem with these arguments is that they take a lack of evidence for one thing to be good evidence for another. A lack of evidence, however, proves nothing. In logic, as in life, you can't get something for nothing.

Appeal to Fear To use the threat of harm to advance one's position is to commit the fallacy of the appeal to fear. It is also known as swinging the big stick. For example: "If you do not convict this criminal, one of you may be her next victim." This argument is fallacious because what a defendant might do in the future is irrelevant to determining whether she is responsible for a crime committed in the past. Or: "You should believe in God because if you don't you'll go to hell." Such an argument is fallacious because it gives us no reason for believing that God exists. Threats extort; they do not help us arrive at the truth.

Straw Man You indulge in the straw man fallacy when you misrepresent someone's claim to make it easier to dismiss or reject. Instead of addressing the actual claim presented, you concoct a weak one to assault—a fake, or straw, man that can be easily struck down. Suppose Senator Brown asserts that she favors strong gun-control measures, and against her view you argue this way: "Senator Brown says she wants to outlaw guns, an extreme position that flies in the face of the Second Amendment right to bear arms. But we should absolutely oppose any move to gut the Constitution." Your argument, however, would distort the senator's view. She says she wants the possession of firearms to be controlled, not outlawed altogether. You could, of course, use the straw man fallacy just as easily on the other side of this issue, arguing that someone opposed to strict gun control wants to put guns in the hands of every citizen. Another distortion. Either way, your argument would be fallacious—and irrelevant to the real issue.

Insufficient Premises

Hasty Generalization You are guilty of hasty generalization, or jumping to conclusions, when you draw a general conclusion about all things of a certain type on the basis of evidence concerning only a few things of that type. For example: "Every medium that's been investigated has turned out to be a fraud. You can't trust any of them." Or: "I know one of those psychics. They're all a bunch of phonies." You can't make a valid generalization about an entire class of things from observing only one—or even a number of them. An inference from a sample of a group to the whole group is legitimate only if the sample is representative—that is, only if the sample is sufficiently large and every member of the group has an equal chance to be part of the sample.

Faulty Analogy An argument from analogy claims that things that resemble one another in certain respects resemble one another in further respects. Recall our previous example: "The Earth has air, water, and living organisms. Mars has air and water. Therefore Mars has living organisms." The success of such arguments depends on the nature and extent of the similarities between the two objects. The greater their dissimilarities, the less convincing the argument will be. For example, consider this argument: "Astronauts wear helmets and fly in spaceships. The figure in this Mayan carving seems to be wearing a helmet and flying in a spaceship. Therefore it is a carving of an ancient astronaut." Although features of the carving may bear a resemblance to a helmet and spaceship, they may bear a greater resemblance to a ceremonial mask and fire. The problem is that any two things have some features in common. Consequently an argument from analogy can be successful only if the dissimilarities between the things being compared are insignificant.

False Cause The fallacy of false cause consists of supposing that two events are causally connected when they are not. People often claim, for example, that because something occurred after something else it was caused by it. Latin scholars dubbed this argument the fallacy of *post hoc, ergo propter hoc,* which means "After this, therefore because of this." Such reasoning is fallacious, because from the fact that two events are constantly conjoined, it doesn't follow that they are causally related. Night follows day, but that doesn't mean that day causes night. Suppose that ever since you wore crystals around your neck you haven't caught a cold. From this action you can't conclude that the crystals caused you to stay healthy, because any number of other factors could be involved. Only if it has been established beyond a reasonable doubt that other factors were not involved—through a controlled study, for example—can you justifiably claim that there is a causal connection between the two events.

Slippery Slope Sometimes people argue that performing a specific action will inexorably lead to an additional bad action (or actions), so you should not perform that first action. An initial wrong step starts an inevitable slide toward an unpleasant result that could have been avoided if only the first step had never been taken. This way of arguing is legitimate if there is good reason to believe that the chain of actions must happen as alleged. If not, it is an example of the fallacy of slippery slope. For example: "Teaching evolution in schools leads to loss of faith in God, and loss of faith leads to the weakening of moral values, which causes increases in crime and social disorder. Therefore, evolution should not be taught in schools." This argument is fallacious because there are no good reasons to believe that the sequence of calamities would happen as described. If there were good reasons, then the argument—though molded in the slippery-slope pattern—would not be fallacious.

STATISTICAL FALLACIES

Statistical fallacies are misleading statements or arguments expressed with numbers. Statistics can present us with good evidence for a claim or be part of a plausible chain of reasoning. But they are frequently used to deceive us, to get us to accept a conclusion that we should reject or question. Here are a few examples:

Misleading Averages

In statistics, there are three kinds of averages—mean, median, and mode. A *mean* is what most people refer to as an average. The mean of the five numbers 2, 3, 5, 8, and 12 is 6 ($2 + 3 + 5 + 8 + 12 = 30$ divided by $5 = 6$). The *median* is the middle value in a sequence of numbers (the median of our five numbers is 5). The *mode* is the most frequently appearing value in a series.

Trouble comes when people don't specify which kind of average they are using, or they employ the kind that will make their weak case look strong. Imagine that the president promises a huge tax cut for the whole country, amounting to a mean tax savings of $10,000. But the mean has been driven upward by a few very rich people whose tax savings will be $1,000,000 or more. Ninety-five percent of taxpayers (who make less than $20,000 a year) will see a tax savings of less than $400. The president's boast of a mean tax savings of $10,000 is technically accurate—but deceiving. More truth can be told to the taxpayers by the median, which is $300, or even the mode of $250.

Missing Values

Much mischief can occur when people fail to distinguish between relative and absolute statistical values. Suppose you read that in the last year there has been a 75 percent increase in the number of muggings in your town. This sounds serious. But the 75 percent is the *relative* increase over the number of muggings last year. What you need to know to make sense of this statistic is the *absolute* number that the percentage is based on. Were there 400 muggings last year—or just 4? If 400, the increase brings us to a shocking 700 incidents. If 4, we are now facing only 7 muggings per year.

Sorting out relative and absolute numbers is critical in statistics on disease risk. Suppose researchers report that daily coffee consumption doubles the risk of pancreatitis in men 25 to 45 years old. Should men in this age group worry about this? Should they stop drinking coffee? You can't tell until you know the absolute risk involved. Let's say the absolute risk of pancreatitis for these men is extremely low—1 chance in 100,000. If daily coffee drinking doubles the risk, we get 2 chances in 100,000—still a miniscule chance of being affected and a very poor reason to give up coffee.

Hazy Comparisons

People use statistics legitimately to make comparisons, but they also use them deceptively or recklessly when the comparisons are vague or incomplete. Consider these advertising claims:

1. Super Pain Eraser reduces headaches 50 percent faster.
2. Fast-Energy Protein drinks can boost your performance by 30 percent.
3. Get twice the mileage with Exxon Hi-Grade gasoline.

In Claim 1, we need more information. What does "50% faster" mean? Fifty percent faster than the drug used to work? Fifty percent faster than other pain relievers? If the comparison is with other medicines, which ones? The least effective one? The best-selling one? If the assertion is 50 percent faster than the medicine used to work, how fast is that? After taking the drug, does your headache go away in 20 minutes or 20 hours? Claim 2 is equally vague. What does "performance" refer to? Speed? Stamina? Strength? And how are such things measured? The notion of performance is so fuzzy, and it can be defined in so many ways, that an advertiser can contrive almost any statistic to sell the product. Claim 3 has the same problems that Claim 1 does, with the additional concern that the claim of doubling gas mileage is not credible.

Good reasoning requires good evidence. Even if your logic is impeccable, your conclusions can be mistaken if your evidence is weak. In the next chapter, we examine the difference between good evidence and bad evidence in an attempt to distinguish real knowledge from false knowledge.

EVALUATING SOURCES: FAKE NEWS

If we want to know more about a subject, including weird things, we can get information and arguments from a billion sources online and off—social media, websites, blogs, newspapers, magazines, books, and other conventional media. But uncovering the hard facts nowadays is harder than you might think. We must now contend with an unprecedented outbreak of news and information sources that are *deliberately* misleading, false, or fraudulent, while they pretend to be legitimate. This is the phenomenon of *fake news*. (Satirical articles like those offered by *The Onion* and other satire sites are also sometimes called *fake news*.) It consists of unrelenting tsunamis of lies, hoaxes, fallacies, propaganda, and disinformation that clog social media feeds, blogs, and websites. The mission of the perpetrators is to make money, push political agendas, stir up hate, provoke netizens, or promote unconventional theories, including many weird and unscientific ones. And at a time when fake news is rampant, research shows that a large proportion of high school and college students are not very good at assessing the credibility of online information. They have great difficulty distinguishing advertisements (sponsored content) from noncommercial articles, fake news from the real thing, mainstream sources from fringe sources, and advocacy or activist writing from material intended to be neutral or nonpartisan.

Here's a tiny sampling of fake news that you may have already seen in your social media feeds:

- Students who survived the Parkland, Florida, school shooting are "crisis actors."
- McDonald's has been using human meat.
- Scientists found a "crystal pyramid" on the ocean's floor beneath the Bermuda Triangle.

- In 1998, NASA intercepted an intergalactic distress call.
- In 2016, Pope Francis endorsed Donald Trump for president.
- In 2016, Pope Francis endorsed Hillary Clinton for president.
- The FDA has determined that the popular candy Skittles is laced with cocaine.
- Staring at a BBQ fire while wearing contact lenses can melt the lenses and cause permanent blindness.
- The late atheist scientist Stephen Hawking converted to Christianity after he was blessed by Pope Francis.
- The nationwide anti-gun protests known as March for Our Lives were backed by violent radicals.
- In a recent seven-year period, criminal immigrants committed over 600,000 crimes against Texans.
- Electronic cigarettes (e-cigarettes) cause a horrible disease called "popcorn lung."
- Bacon is better for you than tilapia, which can cause cancer or Alzheimer's disease.
- In New South Wales, Australian authorities have discovered a feral boy living with a group of kangaroos.

A lot of fake news is simply harmless and silly, but much of it is dangerous. Websites touting cures for cancer and miracle remedies for all sorts of ailments (including some very serious diseases) abound on the internet. Typically the alleged cures and treatments are unproven, or they have been scientifically disproven, or they are harmful. As a result of fake news, some innocent people have been falsely accused of crimes; some have been condemned or threatened; and some have been mercilessly trolled by complete strangers. The infamous example of fake news that prompted violence is what is now called "Pizzagate." In 2016, a tweet from a white supremacist account falsely claimed that a Washington, DC, pizzeria was actually a front for a child sex-trafficking ring that was somehow nefariously connected to Democratic presidential candidate Hillary Clinton. The tweet was nonsense, but it circulated among other news feeds, many people believed what they read, and some took to harassing those who worked at the pizzeria. One man even went to the restaurant armed with an assault rifle to "investigate." He found no evidence of sex trafficking but fired off his weapon inside, terrifying customers, and was arrested.

Some observers worry that fake news can cause much more far-reaching effects than individual wrongful acts. They argue that fake news is a threat to democracy, which can be sustained only with a well-informed citizenry.

Fake news can go viral in a surprisingly short time, spreading to hundreds, maybe even millions of people. How is such astonishing proliferation possible? One major factor of course is internet technology, which has made the sharing of information (and misinformation) extremely easy. One click on Facebook, Twitter, or Google can send a dubious, unread story to all your friends, some of whom may believe every word. These friends will likely share it with their friends and so on. Soon this bit of fakery spreads around the globe. The technology allows this sharing to happen in minutes, if not seconds. The algorithms built into social media platforms may contribute to the problem by curating stories that are likely to go viral but that may or may not be factual. Hundreds of completely made-up stories concocted by "fake news factories" can hit your news feeds so fast that you can't possibly evaluate them all, and even full-time fact-checkers can't keep up. So fake news goes viral while factual news stories get much less attention and are themselves routinely labeled "fake news" by partisans of all stripes. But, of course, a story's going viral is no sign that it is true anymore than Google's search rankings are a sign of a site's reliability.

Another huge factor is the way our brains are wired. Some of the same cognitive errors detailed in Chapter 5 can lead us to accept fake news wholeheartedly and share it with the world.

Confirmation Bias This common error—the tendency to look for and recognize only what confirms our views—affects all of us in countless situations. When fake news arrives in our news feeds, we may construe it as supporting our beliefs, even though it does no such thing. If our bias is strong enough, we may interpret every fact we encounter as proof that we have been right all along.

Confirmation bias can be dramatically augmented by using the filters built into social media feeds. You can ensure that you see only what you want to see—only the articles you agree with and none that you don't like; only the posts and websites that reinforce your existing beliefs and none that contradict them. Search engines can help this process along by showing you search results that align with your past searches.

Denial of Contrary Evidence This cognitive error consists of refusing to accept evidence that is contrary to your existing beliefs. When confronted with evidence that calls your own views into question, you simply dismiss it, ignore it, give it less weight than it deserves, or construe it as actually supporting your views.

When you combine confirmation bias and the rejection of contrary evidence, you get an *echo chamber*—a situation in which you are exposed only to sources and people you agree with and never have to consider contrary views or disquieting information. You state your opinions and hear them echoed back to you from like-minded friends, followers, and members of your own political faction.

Let's not underestimate the appeal of echo chambers. Many people jump inside them because the reverberating noise is comfortable, reassuring, and easy. But because echo chambers distort evidence and veil the facts, they can short-circuit critical thinking and undermine the acquisition of knowledge. They can become not places of enlightenment but holding cells for the ignorant. To avoid falling into one and to ensure that you're fully informed and not missing any important news, you should read both the sources that agree with you and those that don't.

Availability Error This cognitive predisposition is relying on evidence not because it's reliable or trustworthy, but because it's vivid or memorable. This bias is operating when we remember our first encounter with fake news better than any contrary evidence or arguments that follow. For some people, it's easier to remember (and believe) that the moon landing was a hoax than that a dozen scientific reports have thoroughly debunked the idea.

Social Reinforcement Humans are social animals, so it should not be surprising that we are more likely to believe fake news sent by a friend than the same fake news sent by strangers. We might insist that our friends would not send us misinformation, but our friends can be misled or deceived just as we can, and they may pass on fake news unintentionally. The problem is compounded by our tendency to pass on stories without reading them. We may like the headline but be unaware that the body of the story is filled with lies, half-truths, or completely irrelevant information. Such mismatches between headline and story are common.

Credibility by Repetition It's common to see the same headline or story in news feeds again and again. It's also common for people to accept a claim merely because they've seen it repeatedly. Beware: Repetition can render fake news believable in the absence of any supporting evidence.

The problem of fake news is not just that it's widespread, that it's almost impossible to avoid, that internet technology works against us, and that armies of fake news creators work overtime trying to fool us. The main problem is that we are so susceptible to it for all the reasons just mentioned (and a few more). Ultimately, counteracting our cognitive vulnerabilities and avoiding the traps that fake news sets for us are challenges that we can surmount only through critical thinking skills. And the attitude that sustains these skills is one of *reasonable skepticism*—a perspective emphasized in this book and that for many people would be a drastic change in the way they view news and information online. This attitude would have you assess information sources of all kinds guided by these simple truths (some of which are versions of principles discussed in Chapters 4, 5, and 8):

- Not everything you read is true (false statements and bogus news are especially widespread online).
- Just because a source seems legitimate doesn't mean that it is. (Many sources and persons online are not what they appear to be.)
- It is unreasonable (and risky) to believe a claim without good reasons (that is, without evidence or support that increases the likelihood of the claim's truth).

Reasonable skepticism should be our default attitude whenever we encounter new claims from any online source—ads, news, speeches, advocacy blogs, political websites, editorials, and more. Adopting the default attitude means there will be many claims that you will not accept (for lack of evidence); some that you will accept (because there are good reasons for doing so); many that you will reserve judgment on; and some that you will want to research further. You will, in other words, consider claims doubtful unless you have reason to believe otherwise.

Here are some specific guidelines for implementing this approach:

- **Evaluate the legitimacy and reliability of the website.** First determine the purpose or mission of the site—is it partisan politics, advocacy, news reporting, satire, humor, marketing? Be suspicious if there is no information about the mission (check the "About" section), staff, source of income, or physical location. Be wary if the site seems strongly biased, prejudicial, or strident in its defense of a political, moral, or social view or in its promotion of a product or service. Fake news often shows up on sites that are engineered to look like real news websites. Sometimes even their URLs resemble the domain names of legitimate news organizations. Here's an example from FactCheck.org, a reliable fact-checking site:

  > In recent months, we've fact-checked fake news from abcnews.com.co (not the actual URL for ABC News), WTOE 5 News (whose "about"

page says it's "a fantasy news website"), and the Boston Tribune (whose "contact us" page lists only a gmail address). Earlier this year, we debunked the claim that the Obamas were buying a vacation home in Dubai, a made-up missive that came from WhatDoesItMean.com, which describes itself as "One Of The Top Ranked Websites In The World for New World Order, Conspiracy Theories and Alternative News" and further says on its site that most of what it publishes is fiction.[3]

Fortunately, Snopes.com, one of the oldest and most respected fact-checking websites, maintains a roster of some of the more infamous fake news websites. Here are few of them: National Report, World News Daily Report, Huzlers, Empire News, Stuppid, News Examiner, Newswatch28, The Stately Harold, NewsBuzzDaily, Now8News, Associated Media Coverage, and abcnews-us.com.

- **Investigate the authors.** As with the internet generally, the bylines of articles are often not what they seem. According to FactCheck.org:

> Another tell-tale sign of a fake story is often the byline. The pledge of allegiance story on abcnews.com.co was supposedly written by "Jimmy Rustling." Who is he? Well, his author page claims he is a "doctor" who won "fourteen Peabody awards and a handful of Pulitzer Prizes." Pretty impressive, if true. But it's not. No one by the name of "Rustling" has won a Pulitzer or Peabody award. The photo accompanying Rustling's bio is also displayed on another bogus story on a different site, but this time under the byline "Darius Rubics." The Dubai story was written by "Sorcha Faal, and as reported to her Western Subscribers." The Pope Francis story has no byline at all.[4]

- **Examine the claims.** An essential part of evaluating the reliability of a website is sizing up its claims. Ask: Is this claim plausible on its face? That is, does it sound too good, too wild, or too outrageous to be true? If so, it is at least questionable and probably false. Does it conflict with other claims you have good reason to believe? If so, you have reason to doubt it. Signs that claims are bogus include emotional or sensational wording ("Hillary Clinton Adopts Space Alien Baby!"), misspellings, ALL CAPS, insistence that "this is not a hoax," and suggestions that there's a conspiracy against the view expressed.
- **Check the supporting evidence.** If you doubt a factual claim in an article or website, check to see if it is supported by references to trustworthy research, websites, or experts. Do an internet search to try to verify the claim with other sources you trust. You may find that the claim has already been debunked (or

Taking Bias into Account

Some news sources are more biased than others, and it's good to have some idea of the bias in the sources you use. The website Media Bias/Fact Check (https://mediabiasfactcheck.com/) is a trusted, independent media outlet that has evaluated bias, deception, and accuracy in over 2,300 news sources, from mainstream to offbeat to extreme. It mostly examines political bias but also checks for skewed reporting in pseudoscience and conspiracy sources. Its most important mission is to call out fake news and try to measure bias objectively. It verifies whether a source (1) uses biased wording or headlines, (2) reports factually and supports claims with evidence, and (3) reports news in a one-sided, slanted way. It also gives a rough estimate of how strongly the source endorses a particular political ideology. But notice: Some websites do highly factual reporting but express a moderate to strong bias through selection of stories, biased wording, and slanted headlines.

At Media Bias/Fact Check, political bias is rated on a scale:

On the left—from Least Biased to Left-Center to Left to Extreme.

On the right—from Least Biased to Right-Center to Right to Extreme.

Here are some ratings and comments for a few diverse sources (not all of them necessarily political):

CNN—Left Bias
"CNN has a left bias in reporting and sometimes uses sensational headlines. CNN typically sources its news sources. Do not confuse CNN's talk shows with actual reporting of news. Further, they have failed numerous fact checks from PolitiFact." Factual Reporting: Mixed.[5]

Fox News—Right Bias
"Fox News Channel has been accused of biased reporting and promoting the Republican Party and has been deemed the least accurate cable news source according to PolitiFact." Factual Reporting: Mixed.[6]

New York Times—Left-Center Bias
"The New York Times has won 117 Pulitzer Prizes, more than any other news organization. NYT is well sourced and factual in reporting. The paper has a pretty strong left wing

confirmed) elsewhere. Chances are, if the claim or story has gone viral, at least one of the major fact-checking sites has already examined it. These professional fact-checkers are deemed trustworthy because their methodology is sound; their credentials and funding are publicly known; they are nonpartisan; and their track record for reliability, accuracy, and objectivity is excellent. They include Snopes.com, FactCheck.org, *Washington Post*'s Fact Checker, PolitiFact.com, TruthorFiction.com, and Hoax-Slayer.com.

- **Distinguish advertising and news.** A recent study of thousands of middle school, high school, and college students found that a shocking number of them had trouble distinguishing ads from news articles. The difference should be clear: ads are designed to sell products and services or to editorial bias, but is considered one of the most reliable sources for information." Factual Reporting: High.[7]

Institute for Creation Research (ICR)
"The Institute for Creation Research (ICR) is a young-Earth creationist faux-research organization that produces voluminous quote mines and logical fallacies in pursuit of debunking evolution and an old earth." Factual Reporting: Low.[8]

PolitiFact—Least Biased
"PolitiFact uses minimal loaded language in their articles and headlines. All information is well sourced to credible media and or direct statements from experts in the field or the politicians themselves. Fact Check selection leans slightly left as more right wing politicians are currently fact checked. This may be due to bias or the fact that Republicans currently control all branches of government and hence there is more to check. Overall, this update reveals a slight leftward shift in PolitiFact's fact checking selection, but not enough to move them from the least biased category." Factual Reporting: High.[9]

Conspiracy Daily Update
"Conspiracy Daily Update is an extreme right wing Conspiracy and Pseudoscience website. Essentially, they republish snippets of news from conspiracy websites such as Alex Jones and the Common Sense Show. Further, they promote anti-vaccine propaganda. Overall, the only thing accurate on this website is its name. It is indeed the Conspiracy Daily Updater." Factual Reporting: Low.[10]

Skeptical Inquirer
"Skeptical Inquirer is a bimonthly American magazine published by the Committee for Skeptical Inquiry (CSI) with the subtitle: The Magazine for Science and Reason." *Factual Reporting: Very High.*[11]

The Controversial Files
"The Controversial Files is a combination of both conspiracy and pseudoscience with a strong right wing bias. The topics covered on this website are aliens, paranormal, spiritual, the supernatural and much, much more." Factual Reporting: Low.[12]

promote causes and candidates. Imparting accurate, useful information is not their main objective, although some ads do inform if it suits their purpose. Because of these facts, we generally have good reason to doubt advertising claims, unless we have good reason not to. Online, ads may show up on websites or social media and be readily identifiable for what they are. But often they appear on websites looking very much like the surrounding news articles. These are called *native ads*, and they can vary in how closely they resemble the non-ad material. In some cases, they are labeled "sponsored content" or "ad," but frequently readers are left to figure out for themselves what's a disguised sales pitch and what's news. To determine which is which, ask: Is this information here to inform me—or to sell me something?

SUMMARY

The combination of a claim (or claims) supposedly giving reasons for accepting another claim is known as an argument. Arguments can be either deductive or inductive. Deductive arguments are intended to provide conclusive support for their conclusions. An inductive argument is intended to provide probable support for its conclusion. A deductive argument that succeeds in providing conclusive support is said to be valid; one that fails to do this is said to be invalid. An inductive argument that succeeds in giving probable support to its conclusion is said to be strong; one that fails in this is said to be weak. A valid argument with true premises is sound; a strong argument with true premises is cogent.

There are several common deductive argument forms. Some are valid: *modus ponens*, *modus tollens*, hypothetical syllogism, and disjunctive syllogism. Some are invalid: denying the antecedent and affirming the consequent. Being familiar with these forms can help you quickly determine the validity of an argument. The counterexample method can also help.

Some common inductive argument forms are enumerative induction, analogical induction, and hypothetical induction (inference to the best explanation). Enumerative induction is the kind of reasoning we use when we arrive at a generalization about a group of things after observing only some of them. The group of things—the entire class of individuals we're interested in—is known as the target group. The observed members of the target group are the sample, and the characteristic we're studying is the relevant property. An enumerative induction is strong only if the sample is large enough and properly representative. Using an inadequate sample size to draw a conclusion about a target group is a common mistake, a fallacy called hasty generalization.

An impediment to researching weird things (or anything else) is the phenomenon of fake news—news and information sources that are deliberately misleading, false, or fraudulent while pretending to be legitimate. A lot of fake news is just harmless or silly, but much of it is dangerous. Among the most harmful are claims touting cures for serious diseases and lies that can provoke violence or harassment of innocent people. Some observers fear that fake news will undermine democracy. The cognitive errors that lead people to accept and share fake news include confirmation bias, denial of contrary evidence, and the availability error. The best defense against online fake news is a reasonable skepticism in which you consider claims doubtful unless you have reason to believe otherwise.

STUDY QUESTIONS

1. What is an argument?
2. What are three common conclusion indicator words? What are three common premise indicator words?
3. What is the difference between a deductive argument and an inductive argument?

4. What is a valid deductive argument? A sound deductive argument?
5. What is a strong inductive argument? A cogent inductive argument?
6. What is the logical form of affirming the antecedent (*modus ponens*)?
7. What is the logical form of denying the consequent (*modus tollens*)?
8. What is enumerative induction?
9. What is analogical induction?
10. What is the logical form of inference to the best explanation?
11. What is the argument form known as *modus ponens? modus tollens?*
12. How is the counterexample method used to check for validity?
13. In enumerative induction, what is the target group? the sample? the relevant property?
14. Why is a self-selecting sample a biased sample?
15. What is the fallacy of false dilemma? appeal to ignorance? straw man?
16. What is fake news?
17. Why is fake news not always just harmless and silly?
18. What cognitive errors can lead people to accept and share fake news?

EVALUATE THESE CLAIMS. ARE THEY REASONABLE? WHY OR WHY NOT?

1. Objects were moving in the house. Either someone was moving them by psychokinesis or it was ghosts. It wasn't psychokinesis. So it must have been ghosts.
2. A psychic healer cheated my sister. I'm never going to a psychic. They are all con artists.
3. Jones began taking powdered rhinoceros horn and in no time was enjoying great sex. It must be an effective aphrodisiac.
4. Is the following argument strong? Every day that you've lived has been followed by another day that you've been alive. Therefore, every day you ever will live will be followed by another day that you will be alive.
5. Is the following argument strong? Every day that you've lived has been a day before tomorrow. Therefore, every day you ever will live will be a day before tomorrow.
6. Is the following argument valid? If the alien spaceship landed, there should be a large circular depression in the field. There is a large circular depression in the field. So the alien spaceship must have landed.
7. Is the following argument valid? If God created the universe, we should live in the best of all possible worlds. But we do not live in the best of all possible worlds. So God must not have created the universe.
8. Is the following conclusion a cogent inference to the best explanation? All over the country have been found mutilated cows whose body parts were removed by means of smooth cauterized incisions. Aliens must be using the cows for some sort of experiments.
9. Is the following conclusion a cogent inference to the best explanation? Cases of spontaneous human combustion have been reported from around the world. People burst into flame, and most of their body and clothing is reduced to ash, but often a limb or appendage is not burned,

and the fire does not affect objects near the victim. No natural fire could burn in such a way, so it must be a form of divine punishment.

10. Is the following conclusion a cogent analogical argument? The ancient Greek philosopher Plato described the lost continent of Atlantis in two of his dialogues: *Timaeus* and *Critias*. The Atlanteans were very advanced, both horticulturally and mechanically, and their civilization was destroyed when Atlantis sank under the ocean. Plato must have been talking about the Minoan island of Thera because the civilization of Thera was very advanced, and a volcanic explosion destroyed the civilization very quickly.

FACT-CHECKING FAKE NEWS

Evaluate the following claims using the fact-checking sites Snopes.com and FactCheck.org.

1. In 2017, a ghost was caught on camera in the hallways of an Irish school in Cork, Ireland.
2. Posted on Facebook in July 2016, a photograph of a fatal motorcycle crash shows either an angel or the victim's ghost.
3. In 2018, a notorious pedophile was killed by a mother who blew off his head with a shotgun when he tried to rape her 12-year-old child.
4. According to President Donald Trump, China and India are the "world's leading polluters" in carbon emissions.
5. The globe's ice caps are at "record" high levels, as claimed by President Donald Trump.
6. "There is a faceless, semi-human monster called Slenderman who stands eight feet tall, has tentacles for arms, stalks and eats small children, and communicates telepathically with his human servants, called 'proxies.'"
7. "A student mistook examples of unsolved statistics problems for a homework assignment and solved them." One of the problems "was an example of an equation that mathematicians since Einstein have been trying to solve without success."
8. The official portrait of former President Barack Obama contains secretly placed images of sperm cells, including one on his forehead.

DISCUSSION QUESTIONS

1. Read the following passage and answer these questions: (1) Does the passage contain an argument? (2) If so, is the argument deductive or inductive? (3) If it is deductive, does it have a familiar logical form? If yes, what form? (4) If it is an argument, is it a good one?

   Is there archaeological evidence for the [biblical] Flood? If a universal Flood occurred between five and six thousand years ago, killing all humans except the eight on board the Ark, it would be abundantly clear in the archaeological record. Human history would be marked by an absolute break. We would see the devastation wrought by the catastrophe in terms of the destroyed physical remains of pre-Flood human settlements. . . . Unfortunately for the Flood enthusiasts, the destruction of all but eight of the world's people left no mark on the archaeology of human cultural evolution.

—KENNETH L. FEDER, *Frauds, Myths, and Mysteries*

2. In the following argument, each statement is numbered. Read the argument and indicate the role that each statement plays—for example, premise, conclusion, question, example or illustration, background information, or reiteration of a premise or the conclusion.

   [1] Is global warming a real threat? [2] Or is it hype propagated by tree-hugging, daft environmentalists? [3] President George W. Bush apparently thinks that the idea of global climate change is bunk. [4] But recently his own administration gave the lie to his bunk theory. [5] His own administration issued a report on global warming called the *U.S. Climate Action Report 2002*. [6] It gave no support to the idea that global warming doesn't happen and we should all go back to sleep. [7] Instead, it asserted that global warming was definitely real and that it could have catastrophic consequences if ignored. [8] For example, global climate change could cause heat waves, extreme weather, and water shortages right here in the United States. [9] The report is also backed by many other reports, including a very influential one from the United Nations. [10] Yes, George, global warming is real. [11] It is as real as typhoons and ice storms.

3. Consider the following two analogical arguments. Which one is stronger? Why? (1) The universe is like a watch with its purposeful arrangement of parts and curious adaptation of means to ends. Every watch has a designer. So the universe must have a designer. (2) The universe is like a living thing because there is a constant circulation of matter and each part operates to preserve itself as well as the whole. Living things originate through natural reproduction. So the universe must have arisen through natural reproduction.

FIELD PROBLEM

From the "letters to the editor" section of your college newspaper or literary magazine, select a letter that contains at least one argument. Locate the conclusion and each premise. Next go through the letters again to find one that contains no argument at all. Rewrite the letter so that it contains at least one argument. Try to preserve as much of the original letter as possible. Stay on the same topic.

CRITICAL READING AND WRITING

I. Read the passage below and answer the following questions:
   1. What is the claim (conclusion) being argued for in this passage?
   2. What premise or premises are used to support the conclusion?

3. Is the argument inductive or deductive?
4. Assuming that the premise or premises are true, is the argument a good one?
5. Do you believe that reverse speech exists? Why or why not?

II. In a 200-word paper, answer this question: What evidence would persuade you to accept the proposition that reverse speech is a real phenomenon and that it can be useful as a lie detector in courts of law? Explain in detail why the evidence would justify your acceptance of the proposition.

Passage 2

In the past several years, a researcher named David Oates has been advocating his discovery of a most interesting phenomenon. Oates claims that backward messages are hidden unintentionally in all human speech. The messages can be understood by recording normal speech and playing it in reverse. This phenomena, reverse speech, has been discussed by Oates in a number of books (Oates 1996), magazines, newspapers, and radio programs, and even on television with Larry King and Geraldo Rivera. His company, Reverse Speech Enterprises, is dedicated to profiting from his discovery. . . .

We argue that there is no scientific evidence for the phenomena of reverse speech; and that the use of reverse speech as lie detection in courts of law or any other forum, as advocated by Oates, is entirely invalid and unjust. . . .

The burden of proof for any phenomenon lies upon the shoulders of those claiming its existence. To our knowledge there is not one empirical investigation of reverse speech in any peer-reviewed journal. If reverse speech did exist it would be, at the very least, a noteworthy scientific discovery. However, there are no data to support the existence of reverse speech or Oates's theories about its implications. Although descriptions of "research papers" are available on the Reverse Speech website, there is no good indication that Oates has conducted any scholarly or empirical investigation. (Tom Byrne and Matthew Normand, "The Demon-Haunted Sentence: A Skeptical Analysis of Reverse Speech," *Skeptical Inquirer,* March/April 2000.)

NOTES

1. Arthur Conan Doyle, *A Study in Scarlet* (New York: P. F. Collier and Son, 1906), pp. 29–30.
2. Ludwig F. Schlecht, "Classifying Fallacies Logically," *Teaching Philosophy* 14, no. 1 (1991): 53–64.
3. Eugene Kiely and Lori Robertson, "How to Spot Fake News," *FactCheck,* November 18, 2016, accessed March 30, 2018, https://www.factcheck.org/2016/11/how-tospot-fake-news/.
4. Ibid.
5. CNN-Left Bias, Media Bias/Fact Check.
6. Fox News-Right Bias, Media Bias/Fact Check.
7. New York Times-Left-Center Bias, Media Bias/Fact Check.

8. Institute for Creation Research (ICR)-Conspiracy-Pseudoscience, Media Bias/Fact Check.
9. PolitiFact–Least Biased, Media Bias/Fact Check.
10. Conspiracy Daily Update-Conspiracy-Pseudoscience, Media Bias/Fact Check.
11. Skeptical Inquirer-Pro-Science, Media Bias/Fact Check.
12. The Controversial Files-Conspiracy-Pseudoscience, Media Bias/Fact Check.

FOUR

Knowledge, Belief, and Evidence

There exists a passion for comprehension as much as a passion for music.
—ALBERT EINSTEIN

IT IS WRITTEN in the Scriptures, proclaimed by Francis Bacon, and enshrined in common sense: Knowledge is power.[1] Those in the know are more likely to get their way than those who aren't, because their views are based on reality—not on fantasy, illusion, or wishful thinking. Their projects have a greater chance of success, because their knowledge gives them the ability to foresee obstacles and devise ways of overcoming those obstacles. Prediction and control are keys to survival, and knowledge makes prediction and control possible.

But knowledge is valuable not only for what we can do with it; it is also valuable for its own sake. We all would like to know why things are as they are. Our desire for this knowledge, however, is not motivated by purely practical considerations. We often seek such understanding simply for the sake of understanding—because understanding, like virtue, is its own reward. Solving a mystery, discovering the truth, and acquiring insight are among the most exhilarating experiences we can have.

Since knowledge is needed to help us attain our goals and to make sense of the world, it's in our best interest to be clear about what knowledge is and how to acquire it.

BABYLONIAN KNOWLEDGE-ACQUISITION TECHNIQUES

I don't believe in astrology. I'm a Sagittarius and we're skeptical.

—ARTHUR C. CLARKE

Our thirst for knowledge, especially of the future, has inspired many strange techniques for acquiring it. Among the earliest and most elaborate are those of the Babylonians, the inventors of astrology. But astrology was not the Babylonians' first or even preferred method of prophecy. Those distinctions belong to *hepatoscopy*—divination through inspection of the liver.[2] Having realized that blood is essential to life, the Babylonians apparently concluded that the organ richest in blood—the liver—is where the life force is located. By offering this valuable organ (usually taken from sheep) in sacrifice, they presumably believed that the gods would reward their generosity by revealing the future. Why they thought the gods would choose this particular means of showing their gratitude is unclear. Nevertheless, the Babylonians were convinced that every feature of a sacrificed liver—its shape, its blood vessels, its lobes, and so on—disclosed something about the future. All manner of problems, from agricultural to military, were settled by consulting this organ.

Prediction is very difficult, especially about the future.

—NIELS BOHR

In Mesopotamia, hepatoscopy was considered to be such an effective knowledge-acquisition technique that only kings and nobles were allowed to use it. The inspection of a sheep's liver by a seer was considered a solemn act of state.[3] The seer's interpretation of a liver, however, was not a purely subjective matter. Particular features of the liver were thought to correspond to particular kinds of events. The Babylonians systematized this knowledge in the form of stenciled clay models of sheeps' livers, which were used to teach aspiring hepatoscopists their trade. Though more than 700 tablets containing hepatoscopic prophecies have come down to us, none explains how the correspondences between liver features and human affairs were established.[4]

Hepatoscopy is no longer big business, but that other form of divination pioneered by the Babylonians—astrology—still is. There are more than 10,000 professional astrologers in the United States alone. What does astrology have that hepatoscopy doesn't? Well, for one thing, it's less messy. For another, dates and places of birth are easier to come by than sheeps' livers. Astrology differs from hepatoscopy in another way, too. Astrology claims a causal relationship between the prophetic sign (the stars and planets) and the events to which they correspond that hepatoscopy doesn't. In hepatoscopy, the liver isn't the *cause* of the events it foretells; it is merely a record of them. In astrology, on the other hand, the stars and planets supposedly help to bring about the events they portend.

The Babylonians' view of how heavenly bodies acted upon humans, however, is not one many would accept today. According to the Babylonians, each of the seven "planets" that influence our lives—the sun, the moon, Mercury, Venus, Mars, Saturn, and Jupiter—is the seat of a different god, and each of these gods has a different effect on us.[5] Nowadays, astrologers want to explain the effects of heavenly bodies in more scientific terms, by appeal to such forces as gravity or electromagnetism. But neither the ancient nor the modern astrologers explain how the purported cause-and-effect relationships between heavenly bodies and human affairs were established. Are we to suppose that the Babylonians did a statistical survey correlating personal characteristics with star positions? If not—if it is not based on any reliable evidence—why take it seriously? If it is just the fantasy of some Babylonian priest (as hepatoscopy arguably is), can it really be considered a source of knowledge? To answer these questions, we'll first have to examine what knowledge involves.

PROPOSITIONAL KNOWLEDGE

We know many different types of things. We know, for example, who raised us, which pair of shoes is our favorite, what pain feels like, how to read, and that ducks quack. In each case, the object of our knowledge (what our knowledge is about) is different. In the first case, our knowledge is about a person; in the second, a physical object; in the third, an experience; in the fourth, an activity; and in the fifth, a fact. Our concern will be with the fifth, for we are interested in how we come to know the facts.

A fact, in the sense we are using it here, is a true proposition. Thus, factual knowledge is often referred to as *propositional knowledge*. One of the first and foremost attempts to characterize propositional knowledge can be found in the works of Plato. In his dialogue, *Meno,* Socrates remarks, "It is not, I am sure, a mere guess to say that right opinion and knowledge are different. There are few things that I should claim to know, but that at least is among them, whatever else is."[6] The point that Plato is trying to make here is that while having right opinions (true beliefs) may be a necessary condition for knowledge, it is not sufficient—there must be something more to having knowledge than just having true beliefs.

True belief is necessary for knowledge because we can't know something that's false, and if we know something, we can't believe that it's false. For example, we can't know that 2 + 2 equals 5 because 2 + 2 does not equal 5. In other words, we can't know what isn't so. Similarly, if we know that 2 + 2 equals 4, we can't believe that it doesn't. To know that something is true is to believe that it's true.[7]

True belief is not sufficient for knowledge because we can have true belief and yet not have knowledge. To see this, consider the following situation. Suppose you believe that it's raining in Hong Kong right now, and suppose that it is. Does this mean that you *know* that it's raining in Hong Kong right now? Not if you have no good reason for believing so, for, in that case, your belief is nothing more than a lucky guess. Having knowledge, then, would seem to require having good reasons for what you believe. Plato agrees. "True opinions," Socrates tells Meno, "are a fine thing and do all sorts of good so long as they stay in their place, but they will not stay long. They run away from a man's mind; so they are not worth much until you tether them by working out the reason. . . . Once they are tied down, they become knowledge."[8] For Plato, then, knowledge is true belief that is grounded in reality. What grounds our beliefs in reality are the reasons we have for them.

The word knowledge, strictly employed, implies three things: truth, proof, and conviction.

—RICHARD WHATELY

Not all reasons provide equally good grounds for belief, however. Circumstantial evidence, for example, is not as good as eyewitness testimony. So how good must our reasons be to adequately ground our beliefs? To answer this question we'll have to examine the evidential role of reasons.

REASONS AND EVIDENCE

Reasons confer probability on propositions. The better the reasons, the more likely it is that the proposition they support is true. But having reasons that make a proposition only somewhat more likely than its denial is not enough to justify our claim to know it. Suppose a geologist discovered a rock formation indicating that it was somewhat more likely than not that there was gold in the nearby hills. Could he legitimately claim to know that there is gold in the hills? No, for even if there is gold there, his claim would be little more than a guess—an educated guess, perhaps, but a guess nonetheless. And guesses, whether lucky or educated, don't constitute knowledge.

To doubt everything or to believe everything are two equally convenient solutions; both dispense with the necessity of reflection.

—JULES HENRI POINCARÉ

Does knowledge require certainty then? To know a proposition, must we have reasons that establish it beyond a shadow of a doubt?

Some people think so. Suppose, for example, that you and a million other people each purchased one lottery ticket. In such a case, your chance of winning is one in a million, or .000001 percent. As a result, you have a very good reason for believing that you will lose. But do you *know* that you will lose? It wouldn't seem so.

If knowledge requires certainty, however, there is little that we know, for precious few propositions are absolutely indubitable. You might object that you know many things for certain, such as that you are reading a book right now. But do you? Isn't it possible that you are dreaming at this moment? Haven't you, during dreams, been just as convinced as you are right now that what you're perceiving is real? If so, there's not much you can be certain of (except, as Descartes pointed out, that you're thinking).

There are many possibilities that, because they can't be ruled out, undermine our certainty. It's possible, for example, that you're living in a computer-generated dream world of the sort portrayed in the movie *The Matrix.* Or it's possible that you've just swallowed a pill that's making the neurons in your brain fire in exactly the same pattern that they would have fired if you were reading a book. Or it's possible that you're under the control of a superbeing that is telepathically projecting thoughts directly into your mind. If any of these possibilities are actual, then you're not really reading a book right now. To demand that a proposition be certain in order to be known, then, would severely restrict the extent of our knowledge, perhaps to the vanishing point.

Great intellects are skeptical.

—FRIEDRICH NIETZSCHE

The view that we can't know what isn't certain is often espoused by *philosophical skeptics.* According to these thinkers, most of us are deluded about the actual extent of our knowledge. In defense of their position, philosophical skeptics often cite examples like the lottery case, which seem to suggest that nothing less than conclusive proof can give us knowledge. But for each such example, there are many that suggest otherwise. That the Earth is inhabited, that cows produce milk, that water freezes at 32 degrees Fahrenheit, and so on are all propositions we would ordinarily claim to know, yet none of them is absolutely certain. In light of these counterexamples, can philosophical skeptics legitimately claim to *know* that knowledge requires certainty? No, for, unless they are certain that knowledge requires certainty, they can't know that it does. (Philosophical skeptics, remember, claim that we can only know what is certain.) And they can't be certain that knowledge requires certainty because the counterexamples just cited provide good reason for doubting that it does.

So if knowledge doesn't require certainty, how much evidence does it require? It doesn't require enough to put the claim beyond *any* possibility of doubt but, rather, enough to put it beyond any *reasonable* doubt. There comes a point beyond which doubt, although possible, is no longer reasonable. It's possible, for example, that our minds are being controlled by aliens from outer space, but to reject the evidence of our senses on that basis would not be reasonable. The mere possibility of error is not a genuine reason to doubt. To have knowledge, then, we must have adequate evidence, and our evidence is adequate when it puts the proposition in question beyond a reasonable doubt.

A proposition is beyond a reasonable doubt when it provides the best explanation of something. In Chapter 6, we spell out the notion of best explanation in some detail. For now, it's important to realize that a claim doesn't have to possess any particular degree of probability in order to be beyond a reasonable doubt. All that is required is that it explain the evidence and account for it better than any of its competitors.

Even though we can't be absolutely sure that we're not living in the Matrix, we're justified in believing that we're not because the matrix hypothesis does not provide the best explanation of our sense experience. The hypothesis that our sensations are caused by a computer that directly stimulates our brains is not as simple as the hypothesis that they are caused by physical objects; it raises more questions than it answers; and it makes no testable predictions. The acceptability of a hypothesis is determined by the amount of understanding it produces, and the amount of understanding produced by a hypothesis is determined by how well it systematizes and unifies our knowledge. Since the physical object hypothesis systematizes and unifies our knowledge better than the matrix hypothesis, we're justified in believing that we're not living in the Matrix.

Ignorance is not bliss—it's oblivion.

—Phillip Wylie

We are justified in convicting someone of a crime if we have established his or her guilt beyond a reasonable doubt. Similarly, we are justified in believing a proposition if we have established its truth beyond a reasonable doubt. But being justified in believing a proposition no more guarantees its truth than being justified in convicting someone guarantees his or her guilt. It is always possible that we have overlooked something that undermines our justification. Since we are not omniscient, we can never be sure that we have considered all the relevant evidence. Nevertheless, if we are justified in believing a proposition, we are justified in *claiming* that it is true; indeed, we are justified in *claiming* that we know it. Such a claim could be mistaken, but it would not be improper, for our justification gives us the right to make such a claim.

If our belief in a proposition is not justified—if we have good reason to doubt it—then we have no right to claim that we know it.

In all affairs it's a healthy thing now and then to hang a question mark on the things you have long taken for granted.
—BERTRAND RUSSELL

We have reasonable grounds for doubt when we have credible evidence to the contrary. Suppose, for example, that we are looking at a surface that appears to be pink and are told either that there is no pink surface in the room or that there is a red light shining on the surface. In such a case, as epistemologist Ernest Sosa explains:

> Anyone who still believes in a pink surface before him after accepting either testimony would lack justification—this because we consider rational coherence the best overall guide. Even if the testimony is in each case false, given only adequate reason to accept it, one still loses one's justification to believe in the pink surface.[9]

In other words, if we have good reason for believing a proposition to be false, we are not justified in believing it to be true, even if all of our sensory evidence indicates that it is. When two propositions conflict with one another, we know that at least one of them must be false. Until we determine which one it is, we cannot claim to know either. Thus:

There is good reason to doubt a proposition if it conflicts with other propositions we have good reason to believe.

The conflict of credible propositions provides reasonable grounds for doubt. And where there are reasonable grounds for doubt, there cannot be knowledge.

Doubt grows with knowledge.
—GOETHE

The search for knowledge, then, involves eliminating inconsistencies among our beliefs. When the conflict is between different reports of current observations, as in the case of the surface that appears to be pink, it's easy enough to find out which one is mistaken: Look more closely. When the conflict involves propositions that can't be directly verified, finding the mistaken belief can be more difficult.

Sometimes we observe or are informed about things that seem to conflict with our background information—that vast system of well-supported beliefs we use to guide our thought and action, much of which falls under the heading "common sense." When this conflict happens, we have to decide whether the new piece of information is credible enough to make us give up some of our old beliefs. When we cannot directly verify a questionable claim, one way to assess its credibility is to determine how much is at stake in accepting it. When all other things are equal:

The more background information a proposition conflicts with, the more reason there is to doubt it.

The structure of our belief system can be compared to that of a tree. Just as certain branches support other branches, so certain beliefs support other beliefs. And just as bigger branches support more branches than little ones, so fundamental beliefs support more beliefs than ancillary ones. Accepting some dubious claims is equivalent to cutting off a twig, for it requires giving up only peripheral beliefs. Accepting others, however, is equivalent to cutting off a limb or even part of the trunk, for it requires giving up some of our most central beliefs.

The beginning of wisdom is found in doubting; by doubting we come to the question, and by seeking we may come upon the truth.
—PIERRE ABÉLARD

For example, suppose that after listening to the nightly weather report you come to believe that it will be sunny tomorrow. Suppose further that when you get to work the next morning, a trusted friend informs you that it is going to rain that afternoon. Your friend's report conflicts with what you heard on the news last night, but given the variability of the weather and the possibility that your friend might have heard a more recent weather report, the claim is not altogether implausible. You may even decide to change your belief about the day's weather on its basis. Such a change would have little effect on your overall belief system, for not much hangs on your beliefs about the weather.

Now suppose that somebody claimed to be able to walk through walls without using doors. On the credibility scale, such a claim would be close to zero because it conflicts with so much of what we believe about the physical world. Unlike the case of the weather report, you would be right in dismissing such a claim out of hand, for if it were true, large portions of your belief system would be false.

But suppose your claimant offers to provide you with supporting evidence. Suppose he proposes to demonstrate his ability by walking through as many different walls in as many different buildings as you choose. If he could perform this feat regularly and repeatedly, you would have little choice but to start pruning your belief system. But if he could perform the feat only under special circumstances controlled by him, there would be less reason to alter your beliefs, for, in that case, you couldn't be sure that the feat wasn't just a conjuring trick.

When it is not in our power to determine what is true, we ought to follow what is most probable.
—RENÉ DESCARTES

Most of the dubious claims we encounter fall somewhere between the extremes of the weather report and wall-walker cases. They are not so outrageous that we can simply dismiss them, but the evidence in their favor is not compelling enough to justify their acceptance. What should be our attitude toward such propositions? We should believe as the evidence warrants. In other words:

When there is good reason to doubt a proposition, we should proportion our belief to the evidence.

The Ethics of Belief

"Everybody's entitled to their own opinion" goes the platitude, meaning that everybody has the right to believe whatever they want. But is that really true? Are there no limits on what is permissible to believe? Or, as in the case of actions, are some beliefs immoral? Surprisingly, perhaps, many people have argued that just as we have a moral duty not to perform certain sorts of actions, so we have a moral duty not to have certain sorts of beliefs. No one has expressed this point of view more forcefully than the distinguished mathematician W. K. Clifford: "It is wrong always, everywhere, and for anyone to believe anything on insufficient evidence."[10] Others of similar stature have echoed this sentiment. Biologist Thomas Henry Huxley, for example, declared, "It is wrong for a man to say that he is certain of the objective truth of any proposition unless he can produce evidence which logically justifies that certainty."[11] And Brand Blanshard has proclaimed that "where great human goods and ills are involved, the distortion of belief from any sort of avoidable cause is immoral, and the more immoral the greater the stakes."[12] These men think it wrong for belief to outstrip the evidence because our actions are guided by our beliefs, and if our beliefs are mistaken, our actions may be misguided. As Blanshard indicates, the more important the decision, the greater our duty to align our beliefs with the evidence, and the greater the crime if we don't.

Where not much hangs on the belief, it might be thought that what one believes has little importance. But Clifford claims that even in trivial matters we have a duty to proportion our belief to the evidence:

> Every time we let ourselves believe for unworthy reasons, we weaken our powers of self-control, of doubting, of judicially and fairly weighing evidence. We all suffer severely enough from the maintenance and support of false beliefs and the fatally wrong actions which they lead to. . . . But a greater and wider evil arises when the credulous character is maintained and supported, when a habit of believing for unworthy reasons is fostered and made permanent."[13]

According to Clifford, responsible believing is a skill that can be maintained only through constant practice. And since responsible believing is a prerequisite for responsible acting, we have a duty to foster that skill.

The more evidence we have for a proposition, the more credence we should give it.

The probability of a proposition may range from close to 0 (e.g., "Humans can walk through walls") to 1 (e.g., "Either it's raining or it isn't"). Similarly, our belief in a proposition may range from total incredulity to complete acceptance. Ideally, our belief in a proposition should correspond to its probability. If there's a good chance that the proposition is true, we should believe it strongly. If not, we shouldn't. This match with probability is needed because, if the strength of our convictions doesn't match the strength of our evidence, we dramatically increase our chances of error. As any good gambler will tell you, the more you miscalculate the odds, the more you stand to lose. Unfortunately, many of us are not good gamblers, especially when it comes to estimating the chances of a proposition's truth. As a result, we end up believing all sorts of outlandish things for no good reason.

EXPERT OPINION

Nothing is so firmly believed as what we least know.

—MICHEL DE MONTAIGNE

Bertrand Russell was acutely aware of the difficulty many of us have in getting our beliefs to correspond to the evidence. To remedy this situation, he suggested that we adopt the following principle: "It is undesirable to believe a proposition when there is no ground whatever for supposing it true."[14] Russell felt that "if such an opinion became common, it would completely transform our social life and our political system" because it would not only require rejecting many of our most cherished beliefs but also "tend to diminish the incomes of clairvoyants, bookmakers, bishops, and others who live on the irrational hopes of those who have done nothing to deserve good fortune here or hereafter."[15] More to the point, adopting such a proposal would help alleviate a good deal of unnecessary suffering.

To adopt his proposal, Russell claimed, we need only accept the following propositions:

> (1) that when the experts are agreed, the opposite opinion cannot be held to be certain; (2) that when they are not agreed, no opinion can be regarded as certain by a non-expert; and (3) that when they all hold that no sufficient grounds for a positive opinion exist, the ordinary man would do well to suspend his judgment.[16]

If our beliefs were guided by these principles, he insisted, the world would be completely transformed:

> These propositions may seem mild, yet, if accepted, they would absolutely revolutionize human life.
>
> The opinions for which people are willing to fight and persecute all belong to one of the three classes which this skepticism condemns. When there are rational grounds for an opinion, people are content to set them forth and wait for them to operate. In such cases, people do not hold their opinions with passion; they hold them calmly, and set forth their reasons quietly. The opinions that are held with passion are always those for which no good ground exists; indeed the passion is the measure of the holder's lack of rational conviction.[17]

Unfortunately, Russell seems to be right. There often appears to be an inverse correlation between degree of conviction and evidence—the less evidence there is for a proposition, the more fervently it is believed. Such a situation, as Russell realized, is not conducive to harmonious human relations.

Men will cease to commit atrocities only when they cease to believe absurdities.
—VOLTAIRE

To avoid holding unjustified beliefs, then, it's important to develop a healthy *commonsense skepticism.* Unlike philosophical skepticism, commonsense skepticism does not consider everything that lacks certainty suspect. Rather, it considers everything that lacks adequate evidence suspect. Commonsense skeptics won't believe something unless they have a good reason for believing it, and their belief will be proportionate to the evidence.

Russell argues that one way to foster such commonsense skepticism is to give experts their due. We should not defer to the experts because they are always right—they aren't. But they are more likely to be right than we are. One reason they are usually right is that they are usually privy to more information than we are. Another reason is that they are usually better judges of that information than we are. They know, for example, what kinds of observations are accurate, what kinds of tests are valid, and what kinds of studies are reliable. Since they are more knowledgeable than we are, their judgments are usually more trustworthy than ours. Consequently:

There is good reason to doubt a proposition if it conflicts with expert opinion.

But the opinion of experts is superior to our own *only* in their fields of expertise. Outside their specialties, what experts say carries no more weight than what anyone else says. Unfortunately, people have a tendency to treat the opinions of experts as authoritative even when they're speaking out of their depth.

The trouble with people is not that they don't know, but that they know so much that ain't so.
—HENRY WHEELER SHAW

For example, Cleve Backster was one of the FBI's foremost lie detector experts. One day while sitting in his office, he decided to see what would happen if he put a lie detector on his philodendron. After the machine was attached, he decided to see what would happen if he burned one of its leaves. To his surprise, just as he formulated this idea, the lie detector jumped off the scale. Backster concluded that his philodendron was responding to his thoughts! After conducting a number of other experiments, he published his results in an article titled "Evidence of a Primary Perception in Plant Life."[18] Backster's experiments and others like them were chronicled in a 1975 book by Peter Tompkins and Christopher Bird called *The Secret Life of Plants,* which became an international best-seller. As a result of the claims made in this book, people all over the world began playing music and talking to their plants. When scientists tried to replicate Backster's results, however, they failed.[19] It turned out that his experiments had not been conducted with adequate controls. Backster may have been an expert in the use of the lie detector, but that did not make him an expert in scientific method or plant physiology. What this example shows is that:

Just because someone is an expert in one field doesn't mean that he or she is an expert in another.

Just as disturbing as our tendency to treat experts in one area as experts in others is our tendency to treat nonexperts as experts, especially when they're famous. You may have heard the television commercial for a medicine that began, "I'm not a doctor, but I play one on TV, and I recommend . . ." Playing a doctor on television hardly qualifies someone as a medical expert. Consequently, any medical advice this actor offers should be taken with a grain of salt.

To cite a nonexpert as an expert is to make a *fallacious appeal to authority.* It's fallacious because it doesn't provide the type of evidence it purports to. Instead, it attempts to deceive us about the quality of the evidence presented. To avoid being taken in by this kind of subterfuge, we need to know what makes someone an expert.

An expert is someone who knows some of the worst mistakes that can be made in his subject, and how to avoid them.

—Werner Heisenberg

Contrary to what the Wizard of Oz says, being an expert requires more than having a certain piece of paper. Where the paper comes from is also important. The opinions of people with degrees from institutions that advertise on the inside of matchbook covers are not as credible as those of people with degrees from Ivy League institutions. But even having a degree from a reputable institution does not necessarily qualify you as an expert, especially if you have never practiced in the field in which you offer expert opinion. The designation *expert* is something you earn by showing that your judgments are reliable. To be considered an expert, you must have demonstrated an ability to correctly interpret data and arrive at conclusions that are justified by the evidence. In other words, you must have shown yourself capable of distinguishing truth from falsehood in a particular field. If you have a good education but make faulty judgments, you can't be considered an expert. A good indication of the quality of someone's judgment is to be found in the recognition he or she has received from his or her peers. The views of those who have achieved positions of authority or won prestigious awards are to be trusted more than those who have not, for such distinctions are usually a mark of intellectual virtue.

Expert testimony, like any testimony, is credible only to the extent that it is unbiased. If there is reason to believe that an expert is motivated by something other than the search for truth, there is good reason to doubt his or her testimony. If, for example, the expert has something to gain or lose by espousing one position rather than another, that expert's testimony cannot be trusted. Where there is a conflict of interest, there are reasonable grounds for doubt. When considering the opinions of others, then, we must always look for the presence of bias.

When you know a thing, hold that you know it; when you know not a thing, allow that you know it not; this is knowledge.
—CONFUCIUS

According to Russell, any proposition that flies in the face of expert opinion cannot be certain. More important, because credible opinion to the contrary provides reasonable grounds for doubt, any proposition that flies in the face of expert opinion cannot be known (unless, of course, we can show beyond a reasonable doubt that the experts are mistaken). These considerations have important implications for our beliefs about weird things. Such beliefs often conflict with expert opinion. When they do, we cannot claim to know them. We can believe them, but, without adequate evidence showing that the experts are mistaken, we cannot know them. If we do claim to know them, it is *we* who are weird.

COHERENCE AND JUSTIFICATION

Ordinarily, if a proposition fails to cohere with the rest of our beliefs, we are not justified in believing it. So coherence is a necessary condition for justification. But is it also sufficient? If a proposition coheres with the rest of our beliefs, are we justified in believing it? Remarkably enough, the answer to this question is no. Just because a proposition coheres with our beliefs, it is not necessarily likely to be true.

To see this point, consider the case of David Koresh, the former leader of the Branch Davidians, who died when the cult's headquarters near Waco, Texas, burned down in 1993. Koresh believed that he was Jesus Christ. He maintained that this belief was based on a coherent interpretation of the Scriptures. Suppose it was. And suppose that everything else that he believed cohered with that belief. Does that mean that he was justified in believing that he was God? Of course not. Just because someone consistently believes something doesn't mean that it's likely to be true.

But suppose that it wasn't only Koresh who believed he was God; suppose (as is likely) that all his followers did, too. Does that justify his belief that he is God? Does the number of people who believe a proposition increase its likelihood? Again, the answer is no. When it comes to knowledge, there is no safety in numbers. Even if a large number of people consistently believe something, its credibility may be negligible.

If cohering with a certain group's beliefs justified a proposition, then both a proposition and its negation could be equally justified because both could be consistently believed by different groups. Do we want to say that Koresh's position is or could be just as justified as the denial of his position (as long as *that denial* is part of a coherent belief system)? If we do, we must give up the notion that justification is a reliable indication of truth, because whatever justification a proposition had, its denial could have as well. The price for taking coherence to be a sufficient condition for justification, then, is rather high.

Coherence alone is not enough for justification because a coherent set of propositions may not be grounded in reality. A fairy tale may be coherent, but that doesn't justify our believing it. Since justification is supposed to be a reliable guide to the truth, and since truth is grounded in reality, there must be more to justification than mere coherence.

SOURCES OF KNOWLEDGE

All our knowledge has its origins in our perceptions.

—LEONARDO DA VINCI

Perception has traditionally been considered our most reliable guide to the truth. That perception is considered a source of knowledge should not surprise us, for most of our information about the world comes to us through our senses. If our senses weren't reliable, we could not have survived as long as we have. But even though senses are reliable, they're not infallible. The existence of illusions and hallucinations demonstrates that our senses can't always be trusted.

Illusions and hallucinations occur only under certain circumstances, however. Only when we, our tools, or our environment are in a state that impedes the accurate flow of information do our senses lead us astray. For example, if we are injured, anxious, or drugged; if our glasses are cracked, our hearing aid broken, or our measuring devices malfunctioning; or if it is dark, noisy, or foggy, then our observations may be mistaken. But if we have good reason to believe that no such impediments to accurate perception are present, then we have good reason to believe what we perceive.

Just as perception is considered a source of knowledge about the external world, introspection is considered a source of knowledge about the internal world, that is, about our mental states. Some people have considered this source of knowledge to be infallible. We may be mistaken about many things, they argue, but we cannot be mistaken about the contents of our own minds. We may be mistaken, for example, about whether we see a tree, but we cannot be mistaken about whether we *seem* to see a tree. But we must be careful here. While we may infallibly *know what* our experience is like, we may not infallibly *know that* it is of a certain sort. In other words, we may miscategorize or misdescribe what we experience. Infatuation, for example, may be mistaken for love, jealousy for envy, rage for anger.

So the beliefs we form through introspection about our current experience are not infallible.

Similarly, the beliefs we form through introspection about our dispositional mental states are not infallible. There are certain mental states (like believing, wanting, hoping, fearing, and so on) that we may be in even though we are not currently feeling or doing anything in particular. Such states are called *dispositional* because to be in them is to have a tendency to feel or do certain things under certain conditions. For example, if you are afraid of snakes, you will normally have a tendency to feel fear and run away when you see one. Unfortunately, we can deceive ourselves about our dispositional mental states. We may believe, for example, that we are in love when we really aren't. Or we may believe that we don't have a certain desire when we really do. Since introspection is not error free, it is not an infallible source of knowledge about our mental states.

Though introspection is fallible, it can still be trusted. Our beliefs about our mental states are about as certain as they come. We rarely misdescribe our current mental states, and when we do, the fault often lies not with our faculty of introspection but with our carelessness or inattentiveness.[20] While mistakes regarding our dispositional mental states are more common, they, too, can often be traced to our being in an abnormal state. Normally, then, beliefs arrived at through introspection are justified. As long as we have no reason to doubt what our introspection tells us, we are justified in believing it.

Everyone complains of his memory, and no one complains of his judgment.

—Duc François de La Rochefoucauld

Although much of what we know originates in introspection and perception, we have to rely on our memory to preserve and retrieve that information. So memory is also a source of knowledge, not in the sense of generating it, but in the sense of transmitting it. Memory, like perception and introspection, is not infallible. We may forget certain details of events we've experienced, or we may embellish them with imaginative flourishes. We may even seem to remember events that never happened. Psychologist Jean Piaget had a vivid memory of his nurse fighting off a kidnapper on the Champs-Elysées when he was only two. Years later, his nurse confessed in a letter to his parents that she made up the whole story about that event. Even though our memory is fallible, it's not totally unreliable. If we seem to clearly remember something, then, as long as we have no good reason to doubt it, we are justified in believing it.

Reason has also been considered a source of knowledge, for it too can reveal how things are. Consider the proposition "Whatever has a shape has a size." We know that it's true, but we don't have to perform any experiments or gather any data to see that it is. Through the use of reason alone we can see that these concepts necessarily go together. Reason is the ability we have to discern the logical relationships between concepts and propositions. Reason shows us, for example, that if A is bigger than B, and B is bigger than C, then A is bigger than C.

Some people think that reason, like introspection, is an infallible guide to the truth. History has taught us otherwise, however. Many propositions once thought to be self-evident are now known to be false. That every event has a cause, that every property determines a class, that every true mathematical theorem has a proof were all thought, at one time, to be self-evident. We now know that they're not. Even the clear light of reason does not shine only on the truth.

But most of the time, reason is not wrong. What seems to be self-evident usually is. Self-evident propositions are ones whose denial is unthinkable, like "Whatever has a shape has a size." To understand a self-evident proposition is to believe that it's true. If someone denies a self-evident proposition, the burden of proof is on them to provide a counterexample. If they can't, their denial is groundless. So in the absence of any evidence to the contrary, we are justified in believing what reason reveals.

Reason in man is rather like God in the world.

—Saint Thomas Aquinas

The traditional sources of knowledge—perception, introspection, memory, and reason—are not infallible guides to the truth, for our interpretation of them can be negatively affected by all sorts of conditions, many beyond our control. But if we have no reason to believe that such conditions are present, then we have no reason to doubt what these sources of knowledge tell us. The principle that emerges from these considerations is this:

If we have no reason to doubt what's disclosed to us through perception, introspection, memory, or reason, then we're justified in believing it.

In other words, the traditional sources of knowledge are innocent until proven guilty. Only if we have good reason for believing that they are not functioning properly should we doubt them.

THE APPEAL TO FAITH

Faith, as it is ordinarily understood, is "belief that does not rest on logical proof or material evidence."[21] To believe something on faith is to believe it in spite of, or even because of, the fact that we have insufficient evidence for it. No one has expressed this cavalier attitude

I respect faith, but doubt is what gets you an education.

—Wilson Mizner

Mind Viruses

Biologist Richard Dawkins, author of *The Selfish Gene* and *The Blind Watchmaker,* argues that certain thoughts can function in the mind like computer viruses in a computer, subverting its normal functioning. The thought that faith is a source of knowledge, he argues, is one such:

> Like computer viruses, successful mind viruses will tend to be hard for their victims to detect. If you are the victim of one, the chances are that you won't know it, and may even vigorously deny it. Accepting that a virus might be difficult to detect in your own mind, what telltale signs might you look out for? I shall answer by imagining how a medical textbook might describe the typical symptoms of a sufferer (arbitrarily assumed to be male).
>
> 1. The patient typically finds himself impelled by some deep, inner conviction that something is true, or right, or virtuous: a conviction that doesn't seem to owe anything to evidence or reason, but which, nevertheless, he feels as totally compelling and convincing. We doctors refer to such a belief as "faith." . . .
> 2. Patients typically make a positive virtue of faith's being strong and unshakable, in spite of not being based upon evidence. Indeed, they may feel that the less evidence there is, the more virtuous the belief. . . .
> 3. A related symptom, which a faith-sufferer may also present, is the conviction that "mystery," *per se,* is a good thing. It is not a virtue to solve mysteries. Rather we should enjoy them, even revel in their insolubility. . . .
> 4. The sufferer may find himself behaving intolerantly toward vectors of rival faiths, in extreme cases even killing them or advocating their deaths. He may be similarly violent in his disposition toward apostates (people who once held the faith but have renounced it); or toward heretics (people who espouse a different—often, perhaps significantly, only very slightly different—version of the faith). He may also feel hostile toward other modes of thought that are potentially inimical to his faith, such as the method of scientific reason that may function rather like a piece of anti-viral software.[22]

Source: Richard Dawkins, *Viruses of the Mind* (1993), pp. 34–41.

toward evidence better than Tertullian: "It is to be believed," he said, "because it is absurd."[23] Saint Thomas Aquinas considered faith to be superior to opinion because it is free from doubt, but inferior to knowledge because it lacks rational justification. In the case of faith, the gap between belief and evidence is filled by an act of will—we choose to believe something even though that belief isn't warranted by the evidence. Can such a belief be a source of knowledge? No, for we cannot make something true by believing it to be true. The fact that we believe something doesn't justify our believing it. Faith, in the sense we are considering, is unquestioning, unjustified belief, and unjustified belief cannot constitute knowledge.

The problem with the appeal to faith is that it is unenlightening; it may tell us something about the person making the appeal, but it tells us nothing about the proposition in question. Suppose someone presses you about why you believe something and you say, "My belief is based on faith." Does this answer help us evaluate the truth of your belief? No. To say that you believe something on faith is not to offer any justification for it; in fact, you are admitting that you have no justification. Since believing something on faith doesn't help us determine the plausibility of a proposition, faith can't be a source of knowledge.

THE APPEAL TO INTUITION

The only real valuable thing is intuition.
—ALBERT EINSTEIN

Intuition is sometimes claimed to be a source of knowledge. "How did you know that they would get married?" we might ask. "I knew by intuition," might be the reply. But what sort of thing is this intuition? Is it a sixth sense? Are those who claim to know by intuition claiming to have extrasensory perception? Perhaps they are, but to take such a claim seriously, we would need evidence showing that there is such a thing as ESP and that it is a reliable guide to the truth. Without such evidence, intuition in this sense can't be considered a source of knowledge.

But the claim to know by intuition need not be construed as a claim to possess ESP. It can instead be construed as a claim to possess what might be called HSP—*hypersensory perception*. Some people, like the fictional Sherlock Holmes, are much more perceptive than others. They notice things that others don't and consequently make inferences that others may think are unwarranted but really aren't—they are simply based on data that most people aren't aware of. To know by intuition that a couple will get married, for example, you need not have read their minds. You need only to have noticed them exhibiting some of those subtle behaviors that indicate true love.

One of the most remarkable examples of HSP comes from the animal kingdom. In 1904, a retired Berlin schoolteacher, Wilhelm von Osten, claimed that his horse—who came to be known as "Clever Hans"—possessed an intelligence equivalent to humans. He seemed to be able to correctly answer arithmetic problems, tell time, and correctly recognize photographs of people he had met, among other things. Clever Hans would answer the questions put to him by tapping his hoof. He had learned the alphabet, and when he was asked a word problem, he would spell out the answer in German by tapping once for "A," twice for "B," and so on. A panel of thirteen of the best scientists in Germany rigorously tested Clever Hans to determine whether his master was somehow communicating the answers to him. Since he performed almost as well without his master as with him, they concluded in their report that Clever Hans was a genuine phenomenon worthy of the most serious scientific consideration.

One of those assisting in this investigation, however, remained skeptical. Oskar Pfungst couldn't believe that a horse possessed such extraordinary intellectual powers. What made him skeptical was the fact that Clever Hans would not get the right answer when the answer was unknown to any of those present or when he was unable to see those who did know the right answer. Pfungst concluded that the horse needed some sort of visual aid. The remarkable thing was, the aid did not have to be given intentionally.[24]

It turns out that Hans would get the right answer by attending to very subtle changes in people's posture—some of those changes were by less than one-fifth of a millimeter. Those who knew the answer, for example, would unconsciously tense their muscles until Hans produced it. Hans perceived this tension and used it as a cue. Pfungst learned to consciously make the same body movements that were unconsciously made by Hans's examiners and was thus able to elicit from Hans all of his various reactions without asking him any questions or giving him any commands.[25] Pfungst's experiment showed beyond a reasonable doubt that Clever Hans's cleverness lay not in his intellectual prowess but in his perceptual acuity.

Intuition comes very close to clairvoyance; it appears to be the extrasensory perception of reality.
—ALEXIS CARREL

Our ability to perceive subtle behavioral cues is no less remarkable than Clever Hans's. Psychologist Robert Rosenthal has studied this ability in depth. In an attempt to determine the extent to which psychological experimenters can nonverbally influence their subjects, he devised the following experiment. Student subjects were asked to look at photographs of ten people and rate them in terms of their success or failure. The scale ranged from +10 (extreme success) to −10 (extreme failure). The photographs used had been independently determined to elicit a success rating of close to 0 from most people. The experimenters were told that their task was to replicate the results achieved in previous experiments. They were paid one dollar an hour for conducting the experiment, but were promised two dollars an hour if they achieved the desired results. One group of experimenters was told that the people in the photographs had received an average rating of +5 in previous experiments, while the other group was told that they had received an average rating of −5. The experimenters were not allowed to talk to their subjects; they could read the experimental instructions to them but could say nothing else. Without telling their subjects how to evaluate the people in the photographs, the experimenters who expected high scores nevertheless received higher scores than any of those who expected low ones.[26] This result has been repeated in other, similar experiments.[27] How did the subjects know what ratings the experimenters wanted? By attending to subtle behavioral cues. Call it intuition if you will, but it is really nothing more than acute sensory perception.

Researchers investigating ESP must be particularly wary of these sorts of experimenter effects. Any experiment that does not eliminate them cannot provide evidence for ESP, for the results obtained could be due to experimenter signaling. Early telepathy experiments did not take these effects into account, and consequently their results are unconvincing. Simon Newcomb, first president of the American Society for Psychical Research and a distinguished astronomer, describes one of these early experiments: "When the agent drew cards from a pack one by one, and at each drawing the percipient named a card at random, it was found that the proportion of correct guesses was much greater than it should have been as the result of chance, which would, of course, be 1 out of 52."[28] If the percipient could see the agent, however, the success of the experiment could be due to hypersensory perception rather than extrasensory perception. These experimental results thus do not provide evidence for ESP. An experiment can provide evidence for extraordinary abilities only if its results can't be accounted for in terms of ordinary abilities.

Intuition is reason in a hurry.

—Holbrook Jackson

THE APPEAL TO MYSTICAL EXPERIENCE

Beyond the senses, beyond the intellect, beyond these mundane means we use to acquire knowledge lies a more direct path to truth: mystical experience. So say many people who claim that mystical experience bypasses our normal modes of cognition and yields a "deeper" insight into the nature of reality. According to the physicist Fritjof Capra, author of the best-selling *The Tao of Physics*, "What the Eastern mystics are concerned with is a direct experience of reality which transcends not only intellectual thinking but also sensory perception."[29] Attaining such an experience, however, often requires years of preparation and involves practices that are both mentally and physically taxing. Because such practices are known to induce altered states of consciousness, many people dismiss mystical experience as nothing more than delusion or hallucination. As Bertrand Russell put it: "From a scientific point of view we can make no distinction between the man who eats little and sees heaven and the man who drinks much and sees snakes. Each is an abnormal physical condition, and therefore has abnormal perception."[30]

If the doors of perception were cleansed, everything would appear to man as it is—infinite.

—William Blake

But Capra argues that the mystics' claim to knowledge can't be so easily dismissed because their vision of reality agrees with that of modern physics. "The principal theories and models of modern physics," he says, "lead to a view of the world which is internally consistent and in perfect harmony with the views of Eastern Mysticism."[31] Mystics, like scientists, are seekers after truth. But whereas scientists use their senses to explore nature's mysteries, mystics use only their intuition. What is remarkable, contends Capra, is that the reality revealed by these two types of experience appears to be the same. Psychologist Lawrence LeShan agrees:

> The physicist and the mystic follow different paths: they have different technical goals in view; they use different tools and methods; their attitudes are not the same. However, in the world-picture they are led to by these different roads they perceive the same basic structure, the same reality.[32]

Mysticism is just tomorrow's science dreamed today.
—Marshall McLuhan

According to Capra and LeShan, although the mystic and the scientist have traveled different paths, they have arrived at the same destination. Consequently, they claim, mystical experience must be considered a privileged source of knowledge.[33]

But is there really such a royal road to the truth? Has modern physics vindicated the visions of the mystics? To find out, we'll have to take a closer look at what the mystics tell us about the nature of reality.

Mystical experiences are ecstatic, awesome, extraordinary experiences in which you seem to enter into a mysterious union with the source and ground of being. During this encounter, it seems as if the deepest secrets of the universe are revealed to you. What you formerly took to be real seems nothing more than an illusion. You become convinced that now, as never before, you understand the true nature of reality. The Christian mystic, Saint John of the Cross, described the experience this way:

> The end I have in view is the divine Embracing, the union of the soul with the divine Substance. In this loving, obscure knowledge God unites Himself with the soul eminently and divinely. . . . This knowledge consists in a certain contact of the soul with the Divinity, and it is God Himself Who is then felt and tasted, though not manifestly and distinctly, as it will be in glory. But this touch of knowledge and of sweetness is so deep and so profound that it penetrates into the inmost substance of the soul. This knowledge savors in some measure of the divine Essence and of everlasting life.[34]

For some, the union appears to be almost a sexual one. Saint Theresa, another Christian mystic, writes:

> I saw an angel close by me, on my left side, in bodily form. . . . I saw in his hand a long spear of gold, and at the iron's point there seemed to be a little fire. He appeared to me to be thrusting it at times into my heart, and to pierce my very entrails; when he drew it out, he seemed to draw them out also and to leave me all on fire with a great love of God. The pain was so great that it made me

moan; and yet so surpassing was the sweetness of this excessive pain that I could not wish to be rid of it. The soul is satisfied now with nothing less than God.[35]

The God of which Saint John and Saint Theresa speak is the God of the Bible: a personal being with thoughts, feelings, and desires. For them, mystical experiences are the result of entering into a peculiarly intimate relationship with Him. But in their view, even though you unite with God, you don't become God. You may be deeply moved—even transformed—by the experience, but you're not annihilated by it. Through it all, you retain your personal identity.

Not all mystics describe their experience this way, however. Hindus of the Advaita Vedanta school, for example, do not believe that mystical union is a relationship between two persons, for, in their view, the world does not contain two persons. According to them, there is only one thing in the universe—Brahman—and mystical experience reveals that we are identical to it. As the founder of this school, Shankara (AD 686–718), relates: "Through his transcendental vision he [the mystic] has realized that there is no difference between man and Brahman, or between Brahman and the universe—for he sees that Brahman is all."[36] In the mystical state, according to Shankara, all individuality, all distinctions, all boundaries disappear. Reality is experienced as a seamless, indivisible whole. No line can be drawn between the self and the nonself, for the self is all. You are God.

Not I, but the whole world says it: Everything is one.
—HERACLITUS

Shankara holds that Brahman, the one and only true reality, is unchanging and eternal. The Buddha (563–483 BCE), another Eastern mystic and teacher, maintains that reality is constantly changing and ephemeral. As he remarked to one of his followers, "The world is in continuous flux and is impermanent."[37] The Buddha, then, denies the existence of Shankara's Brahman. As theologian John Hick notes, "This notion of an immutable *atman* [soul], without beginning or end, which each of us ultimately is, is explicitly rejected by the Buddha's anatta [no soul] doctrine."[38]

Capra can't claim that modern physics vindicates the worldview of Eastern mystics in general because the Eastern mystics don't share a common worldview. Hindus and Buddhists have radically different conceptions of the nature of reality. In fact, mystical worldviews seem to be at least as various as mystical traditions themselves. Mystics, even Eastern ones, do not speak with a single voice. Consequently, it can't coherently be maintained that modern physics confirms their view of things.

Even the more limited claim that modern physics vindicates the worldview of one particular group of mystics is problematic, for if

The Miracle of Marsh Chapel

Timothy Leary was not the only person experimenting with hallucinogens at Harvard in the early 1960s. Walter Pahnke, a graduate student in theology, was also exploring inner space by means of drugs. His interest, however, was the relationship between drug-induced hallucinations and mystical experience. Here's an account of his experiment.

> Walter Pahnke was interested in the literature and experience of religious ecstasy. He trained housewives, presumably for their lack of bias, to identify passages in literature that qualified as transcendental or ecstatic accounts. Then he fed a group of divinity students controlled doses of psilocybin on Good Friday, 1962. The theology students soon after described their experiences while under the influence, and the housewives rated those confessions, mixed in among other narratives of religious ecstasy as well as other nonecstatic accounts, without knowing where they came from. The results were remarkable. The brigade of housewife readers identified a large proportion of the students' narratives as bona fide mystical encounters, and Pahnke concluded that drugs could simulate the transcendent ecstasy that lay at the source of so much religious tradition. Pahnke's work became known as the Good Friday Experiment and the reports by students as the Miracle of Marsh Chapel, named after the site on Harvard's campus where Pahnke collected his results. The age of scientific study of hallucinogens and their role in religious ecstasy had begun. But Pahnke's research raised a storm of criticism. If experience of God could be induced by a chemical, then what did that say about all the regalia and ritual of institutional religion?[39]

one group of mystics is right, the others must be wrong. How, then, would we account for the fact that Christian mystics were mistaken? Is the answer that their experiences weren't really mystical? But how would we distinguish real mystical experiences from false ones? Is the answer that the Christians didn't interpret their experiences correctly? But how would we distinguish correct interpretations from incorrect ones? Once we admit that only certain mystical experiences are revelatory, we have abandoned the claim that all mystical experience yields knowledge.

ASTROLOGY REVISITED

I shall always consider the best guesser the best prophet.

—CICERO

Now that we have a better idea of what's involved in making claims about knowledge, what are we to make of astrology? Is it reasonable to believe that the position of the stars and planets at the time and place of your birth controls your destiny? Let's examine the evidence.

Astrology, as noted at the beginning of this chapter, was invented by the Babylonians as a means of foretelling the future. Their belief was (and the belief of present-day astrologers is) that all people's physical and emotional makeup is caused not by their heredity and environment but by the particular arrangement of stars and planets at their birth. Given what the Babylonians knew about the universe at that time, such a view was not unreasonable. Anyone can see that the position of heavenly bodies is correlated with the seasons. The belief that heavenly bodies cause the seasons is therefore quite a natural one. And if heavenly bodies control the Earth's destiny, maybe they control ours as well. Although such a view makes sense from a Babylonian perspective, the question is whether it makes sense from ours.

Science must begin with myth and with the criticism of myth.

—KARL POPPER

There is no evidence that the Babylonian astrologers established the alleged correlations between personal characteristics and star positions by conducting statistical surveys. They do not appear to have sent out questionnaires asking people to describe themselves and to give the time and place of their birth. Rather, it appears that they assumed that people born under the influence of a particular planet or constellation would acquire the characteristics of the person, god, or animal for which the planet or constellation was named.[40] Thus people born under the sign of Aries, for example, are said to be ramlike—courageous, impetuous, and energetic—while those born under the sign of Taurus are said to be oxlike—patient, persistent, and obstinate.[41]

Saint Augustine, one of the patriarchs of the Roman Catholic Church, realized long ago that if the stars really determined our fate, then astral twins (people who are born at the same time and place) should lead the same sort of lives. When he learned of a pair of astral twins—a slave and an aristocrat—who were as different as night and day, he gave up his belief in astrology and became an outspoken critic of it. The twins, for him, were conclusive proof that our destiny is not written in the stars.

In our century, many attempts have been made to statistically verify the predictions of astrology, but none has succeeded. Psychologists Zusne and Jones describe some of these studies:

> In 1937, Farnsworth failed to find any correspondence between artistic talent and either the ascendant sign or the sun in the sign of Libra for the birth dates of 2000 famous painters and musicians. Bok and Mayall (1941) found no predominance of any one sign of the zodiac among scientists listed in a directory of scientists, the *American Men of Science.* Barth and Bennett (1973) did a statistical study on whether more men who had chosen a military career had been born under the influence of the planet Mars than men who had chosen non-military careers. They found no such relationship. Very large numbers of birth dates were used by McGervey (1977), who tabulated the number of

scientists and politicians (a total of 16,634 scientists and 6,475 politicians) born on each day of the year, and found no astrological sign favoring either one of the callings. . . . In another recent study, Bastedo (1978) tested statistically whether persons with such characteristics as leadership ability, liberalism/conservatism, intelligence, and 30 other variables, many of them attributed to astral influence, would cluster on certain birth dates—that is, according to the astrological sign that governs the appropriate characteristics. The results for a 1000-person, cross sectional, stratified cluster sample taken from the San Francisco Bay area were entirely negative.[42]

More recent research confirms these findings. R. B. Culver and P. A. Ianna surveyed hundreds of people to determine if there is any truth to the astrologists' claim that there is a correlation between sun sign (the zone of the zodiac that the sun was in when you were born) and physical features. They studied such attributes as neck size, skin complexion, body build, height, and weight. Contrary to what the astrologers would have us believe, no set of physical features occurred more in one sign than another.[43]

David Voas, professor of population studies at the University of Manchester, recently conducted the largest study ever of the "love sign" hypothesis, namely, that people born under certain astrological signs are more compatible than those born under others. Using the 2001 census data for England and Wales (which contains records of over twenty million people), he was able to determine whether those born under certain signs are more likely to get married or stay married than those born under others. He found that "astrological sign has no impact on the probability of marrying—and staying married to—someone of any other sign."[44] It looks like that old pickup line—"What's your sign?"—isn't going to help you predict whether you're going to get lucky.

You can make a better living in the world as a soothsayer than as a truthsayer.

—GEORGE LICHTENBERG

Professional astrologers might find these studies unconvincing, because they focus on the sun sign rather than the astrological chart. To get an accurate prediction, they might argue, the positions of the planets at the time of birth must also be taken into account. When this casting is done, however, the results are still negative. For his doctoral dissertation at North Texas State University, Jonus Noblitt tried to determine if the angular relations among planets could predict an individual's personality traits. He gave 155 volunteers the 16PF personality questionnaire, which assesses personality characteristics, and compared the results with their horoscopes. None of the predictions of astrology were borne out by the data.[45]

In a study published in *Nature,* physicist Shawn Carlson gave thirty prominent American and European astrologers the natal charts of 116 subjects.[46] For each subject, the astrologers were given three personality profiles: one from the subject and two others chosen at random. The personality profiles were based on the California Personality Inventory (CPI), a standard test for measuring personality traits. The astrologers' task was to match the subject's natal chart with his or her personality profile. Although the astrologers predicted that they would be able to select the correct CPI profile over 50 percent of the time, they chose the correct profile only 34 percent of the time, which is how well anyone should do if they were just guessing. So, once again, the astrologers demonstrated no unusual knowledge.

Geoffrey Dean and Arthur Mather, after reviewing more than 700 astrology books and 300 scientific works on astrology, concluded:

> Astrology today is based on concepts of unknown origin but effectively deified as "tradition." Their application involves numerous systems, most of them disagreeing on fundamental issues, and all of them supported by anecdotal evidence of the most unreliable kind. In effect, astrology presents a dazzling and technically sound superstructure supported by unproven beliefs; it starts with fantasy and then proceeds entirely logically. Speculation is rife, as are a profusion of new factors (each more dramatically "valid" than the last) to be conveniently considered where they reinforce the case and ignored otherwise.[47]

There are simply no reliable data establishing any of astrology's claims.

Not only is there no trustworthy evidence supporting astrology, but the very notion that stars and planets determine our physical and psychological makeup conflicts with a good deal of what we know about human physiology and psychology. Research has shown that our physical characteristics are determined by the information encoded in our genes. All the tissues in our body are manufactured according to this information, and all our genes are present in the fertilized egg from which we developed. So our basic physical constitution is determined by our genes at the moment of conception—not by the heavens at the moment of birth, as astrologers would have us believe.

It is the difficulty of explaining how stars and planets could possibly influence our personalities and careers that makes the claims of astrology so hard to swallow. To the best of our knowledge, the universe contains only four forces: gravity, electromagnetism, the strong nuclear force, and the weak nuclear force. Everything that happens in the world results from the action of one or more of these forces. The range of the strong and weak nuclear forces, however, is very limited—they can only affect things in and around atoms. So if stars and planets affect us, it cannot be by their means.

That leaves gravity and electromagnetism. Their range is potentially unlimited. But the strength of these forces diminishes the farther they get from their source. The gravitational and electromagnetic forces reaching us from the stars and planets are extremely weak. The book you are now reading, for example, exerts a gravitational force about a billion times greater at the point you're holding it than does Mars when it is closest to Earth. Similarly, the electromagnetic radiation from the radio and television transmitters all around us is hundreds of millions of times greater than that from the planets.[48] Thus there is no known way that stars or planets could significantly affect us. That's not to say that they don't; it's just to say that no one has given us a plausible theory of how they do.

In 1975, 186 scientists published a letter alerting the public to the fact that there is no evidence for the claims of astrology. They proclaimed:

> We, the undersigned—astronomers, astrophysicists, and scientists in other fields—wish to caution the public against the unquestioning acceptance of the predictions and advice given privately and publicly by astrologers. Those who wish to believe in astrology should realize that there is no scientific foundation for its tenets. . . . It is simply a mistake to imagine that the forces exerted by stars and planets at the moment of birth can in any way shape our futures. Neither is it true that the positions of distant heavenly bodies make certain days or periods more favorable to particular kinds of action, or that the sign under which one was born determines one's compatibility or incompatibility with other people.[49]

Unfortunately, the letter seems to have had little effect. A 2005 Gallup poll found that 25 percent of Americans believe that astrology works. Even more ominous, during the 1980s, then president Ronald Reagan was making decisions regarding affairs of state on the basis of astrological predictions.[50]

Why, with so little evidence to support it, do people continue to believe in astrology? For one thing, most people are probably unaware of the many studies that have found no substantiation for astrology. These studies have not received much media coverage, and newspapers running astrology columns don't usually preface them with caveats such as "for entertainment purposes only." For another, astrologers like to give the impression that it all makes perfectly good scientific sense. Linda Goodman, for example, writes, "Science recognizes the Moon's power to move great bodies of water. Since man himself consists of seventy percent water, why should he be immune to such forceful planetary pulls?"[51] He isn't. But, as we have seen, the effect must be negligible given the miniscule level of the force, and there is no reason to believe that extraterrestrial gravity significantly affects our physical or psychological development.

Why, then, does belief in astrology persist? Some, like the scientists objecting to its widespread acceptance, claim that its appeal derives from the diminished sense of personal responsibility it provides:

> In these uncertain times many long for the comfort of having guidance in making decisions. They would like to believe in a destiny predetermined by astral forces beyond their control. However, we must all face the world, and we must realize that our futures lie in ourselves, and not in the stars.[52]

Others believe that its appeal derives from an increased sense of unity it provides. Historian Theodore Roszak writes, "The modern fascination with astrology—even in its crudest forms—stems from a growing nostalgia for that older, more unified sense of nature in which the sun, moon and stars were experienced as a vast network of living consciousness."[53] There is probably an element of truth in both these assessments.

Many people probably find astrology appealing because it seems to describe them accurately. It seems to do so because the descriptions offered are so general that they apply to practically everybody (see the discussion of the Forer effect in Chapter 5). One of the most dramatic examples of the Forer effect comes from Michel Gauquelin. Gauquelin placed an advertisement in a French newspaper offering a personalized horoscope to anyone who would send him their name, address, birthday, and birthplace. About 150 people responded to the ad, and Gauquelin sent them a ten-page horoscope, a questionnaire, and a return envelope. The horoscope read, in part, as follows:

> As he is a Virgo-Jovian, instinctive warmth of power is allied with the resources of the intellect, lucidity, wit. . . . He may appear as someone who submits himself to social norms, fond of property, and endowed with a moral sense which is comforting—that of a worthy, right-thinking, middle-class citizen. . . . The subject tends to belong wholeheartedly to the Venusian side. His emotional life is in the forefront—his affection towards others, his family ties, his home, his intimate circle . . . sentiments . . . which usually find their expression in total devotion to others, redeeming love, or altruistic sacrifices . . . a tendency to be more pleasant in one's own home, to love one's house, to enjoy having a charming home.[54]

Ninety-four percent of those who returned the questionnaire said that the horoscope described them accurately, and 90 percent said that their friends and relatives agreed with that assessment. The horoscope, however, was that of notorious mass murderer, Dr. Marcel Petiot, who lured unsuspecting Nazi escapees into his home with promises of aid only to rob them, murder them, and dissolve their bodies in quicklime (calcium oxide). He was accused of twenty-seven murders but boasted of sixty-three. Funny that so many fine upstanding citizens of France would claim the horoscope of a mass murderer as their own.

How, then, should we think about astrology? The first thing to note is that no one can legitimately claim to know that astrology is true. Such a claim conflicts with expert opinion and, as we have seen, claims that conflict with expert opinion cannot be known (unless it can be shown beyond a reasonable doubt that the experts are mistaken). Astrology also conflicts with a lot of our background beliefs. Accepting astrology would mean rejecting large tracts of physics, astronomy, biology, and psychology. When faced with such conflicts, the thing to do is to proportion our belief to the evidence. In the case of astrology, however, there is no evidence to proportion it to, for none of its claims has been verified. So the degree of belief it warrants is negligible.

Although perception, introspection, reason, and memory are sources of knowledge, they can also be sources of error. The mind is not just a blank slate that passively records the information it receives. Instead, it is an active information processor that manipulates that information in an attempt to make sense of it. If that information is inaccurate, incomplete, or inconsistent, the conclusions we draw from it can be mistaken. In the next chapter, we will examine the myriad ways in which our senses can fool us.

SUMMARY

Factual knowledge concerns the truth of propositions and is therefore referred to as propositional knowledge. We possess this kind of knowledge when we have a true belief supported by good reasons. Reasons confer probability on propositions. The better the reasons, the more likely it is that the proposition they support is true. Some think that to know a proposition, we must have reasons that establish it beyond a shadow of a doubt. But knowledge requires only that we have reasons good enough to put the proposition beyond a reasonable doubt. A proposition is beyond a reasonable doubt when it provides the best explanation of something.

If we have good reasons to doubt a proposition, then we cannot be said to know it. We have good reasons to doubt it if it conflicts with other propositions we have good reason to believe. We also have good reasons to doubt it if it conflicts with our background information—our massive system of well-supported beliefs, many of which we would regard as common sense. The more background information a proposition conflicts with, the more reason there is to doubt it. Likewise, since the opinions of experts are generally reliable, we have good reason to doubt a proposition if it conflicts with such opinions. But we must be careful: Just because someone is an expert in one field doesn't mean that he or she is an expert in another.

The traditional sources of knowledge are perception, introspection, memory, and reason. They are not infallible guides to the truth, for our use of them can be distorted by many factors. But if we have no reason to doubt what's disclosed to us through these, then we're justified in believing it. Faith—unjustified belief—is often considered to be another source of knowledge. But unjustified belief cannot constitute knowledge. Intuition conceived as a kind of sixth sense like ESP cannot be regarded as a source of knowledge without evidence showing that it is in fact a reliable guide to truth. Intuition as a type of heightened sensory perception, however, has been shown to be actual. Some people consider mystical experiences reliable guides to deep truths. They may be correct, but we cannot simply assume that they are—we must corroborate the experiences by applying our usual tests of knowledge.

In light of all this, we can ask whether we have good reasons for believing in astrology. The answer is no: The claim that astrology is true is not supported by any good evidence, and it conflicts with expert opinion and with a tremendous amount of our background information.

STUDY QUESTIONS

1. What besides true belief do you need in order to have knowledge?
2. When are you justified in believing a proposition to be true?
3. When do you have good reason for doubting that a proposition is true?
4. What are the sources of knowledge?
5. Is faith a source of knowledge?
6. Are we justified in believing the claims of astrology?

EVALUATE THESE CLAIMS. ARE THEY REASONABLE? WHY OR WHY NOT?

1. Dr. Thomson says that crystals have no healing power. He's just saying that so you won't go to crystal healers.
2. As a practicing physicist, I can assure you that adding fluoride to our water will cause serious mental problems.
3. Madam X said they would find the body in the ditch and they did. Doesn't that prove that some psychic detectives are real?
4. Some say that love is possible only between people with the same color aura. My aura is orange and my girlfriend's aura is green. Orange and green are not compatible. I guess we should break up.
5. Morey Gomez, the famous psychic, announced that the stock market would go up by 20 percent in the next six months. So now is the time to invest.

DISCUSSION QUESTIONS

1. Suppose you are a scientifically minded person and find yourself in a culture that believes in astrology. What could you do to show others the error of their ways?

2. Tarot cards are another ancient form of divination. A recent series of television commercials claims, "Tarot cards never lie." Is this true? Are you justified in believing it? Why or why not? Discuss how one might go about assessing this claim.

FIELD PROBLEM

Assignment: Do research on the internet to determine which of the following statements conflicts with expert opinion:

- Current scientific evidence shows that *intercessory* prayer can improve people's medical conditions.
- The images of ghosts (disembodied spirits) have been captured on film.
- Some of the world's ancient feats of architecture (e.g., the Great Pyramid, Mayan temples, etc.) could have been accomplished only with the help of intelligent visitors from outer space.
- Roswell, New Mexico, is the site of an actual crash of an alien spacecraft.

CRITICAL READING AND WRITING

I. Read the passage below and answer the following questions:
   1. What is the claim being made in this passage?
   2. Are any reasons offered to support the claim?
   3. Does the claim conflict with expert opinion? Who are the experts in this case?
   4. Does the idea that extraterrestrials are visiting Earth conflict with our background knowledge? If so, how?
   5. What kind of evidence would convince you that extraterrestrials are visiting Earth?

II. Write a 200-word critique of this passage, focusing on how well its claim is supported by good reasons, whether the claim conflicts with our background knowledge or other statements we have good reason to believe, and why you think accepting the claim would be reasonable (or unreasonable).

Passage 3

The evidence that extraterrestrials are visiting Earth and currently operating in our skies on a regular uninterrupted basis is extensive beyond a shadow of a doubt both in scope and detail. In its totality it comprises a body of evidence so profound that it has numbed the human experience of all government and religious leaders around the world into an absolute de facto policy of denial. This would also include most if not all members of the mainstream scientific community who fear the social stigma associated with the subject. (From a UFO/alien visitation website.)

NOTES

1. Proverbs 4:7–9; Francis Bacon, "De Haeiresibus," *Meditationes Sacrae.*
2. Richard Lewinsohn, *Science, Prophecy, and Prediction* (New York: Harper Brothers, 1961), p. 53.
3. Ibid., p. 54.
4. Ibid.
5. Ibid., p. 59.
6. Plato, *The Meno of Plato* (Clarendon Press, 1887).
7. We sometimes say things that seem to suggest that knowledge doesn't require belief. For example, after winning a prize we might remark, "I know that I won, but I still don't believe it." What we mean, though, is not that we doubt that we've won the prize but that we haven't gotten used to the fact that we did. Intellectually we've accepted the situation, but emotionally we haven't.
8. Plato, "Meno," 98a, p. 381.
9. Ernest Sosa, *Knowledge in Perspective: Selected Essays in Epistemology* (Cambridge University Press, 1991).
10. W. K. Clifford, "The Ethics of Belief," in *Philosophy and Contemporary Issues,* ed. J. Burr and M. Goldinger (New York: Macmillan, 1984), p. 142.
11. Thomas Henry Huxley, *Science and Christian Tradition* (London: Macmillan, 1894), p. 310.
12. Brand Blanshard, *Reason and Belief* (New Haven: Yale University Press, 1975), p. 410.
13. William Kingdon Clifford, *Ethics of Belief,* p. 142.
14. Bertrand Russell, *Let the People Think* (Watts & Company, 1996), p. 281.
15. Ibid.
16. Ibid., p. 2.
17. Ibid.
18. Cleve Backster, "Evidence of a Primary Perception in Plant Life," *International Journal of Parapsychology* 10 (1968): 329–48.
19. K. A. Horowitz, D. C. Lewis, and E. L. Gasteiger, "Plant 'Primary Perception': Electrophysical Unresponsiveness to Brine Shrimp Killing," *Science* 189 (1975): 478–80.
20. Sosa, "Knowledge and Intellectual Virtue," p. 230ff.
21. *The American Heritage Dictionary of the English Language* (Boston: Houghton Mifflin, 1970), p. 471.
22. Richard Dawkins, "Viruses of the Mind," *Free Inquiry* 13, no. 3 (Summer 1993): 37–39.
23. Tertullian, "On the Flesh of Christ," *Apology.*
24. Oskar Pfungst, *Clever Hans: The Horse of Mr. von Osten,* ed. Robert Rosenthal (New York: Rinehart and Winston, 1965), p. 261.
25. Ibid., pp. 262–63.
26. Robert Rosenthal, *Experimenter Effects in Behavioral Research* (New York: Irvington, 1976), pp. 143–46.

27. Ibid., pp. 146–49.
28. Paul Kurtz, *A Skeptic's Handbook of Parapsychology* (Buffalo: Prometheus Books, 1985), p. 151.
29. Fritjof Capra, *The Tao of Physics* (Shambhala, 1975).
30. Bertrand Russell, *Mysticism,* quoted in Walter Kaufmann, *Critique of Philosophy and Religion* (Garden City, NY: Doubleday, 1961), p. 315.
31. Capra, *Tao of Physics,* p. 294.
32. Lawrence LeShan, *The Medium, The Mystic, and The Physicist: Toward a General Theory of the Paranormal* (Turnstone Books, 1974).
33. A number of writers have made similar claims. See, for example, Michael Talbot, *Mysticism and the New Physics* (New York: Bantam Books, 1981); Amaury de Riencourt, *The Eye of Shiva* (New York: William Morrow, 1981); and Gary Zukav, *The Dancing Wu Li Masters* (New York: William Morrow, 1979).
34. Paul Kurtz, *The Transcendental Temptation: A Critique of Religion and the Paranormal,* 12th ed. (Buffalo: Prometheus Books, 1991).
35. Evelyn Underhill, *Mysticism: A Study in the Nature and Development of Man's Spiritual Consciousness* (Penguin Group, 1974).
36. *Sankaracharya, Shankara's Crest-Jewel of Discrimination = Viveka-Chudamani* (Vedanta Press, 1978).
37. Cited in Walpola Rahula, *What the Buddha Taught* (New York: Grove Press, 1974), pp. 25 26.
38. John Hick, *Death and Eternal Life* (San Francisco: Harper and Row, 1976), p. 339.
39. "A Short History of Consciousness," *Omni,* October 1993, p. 64.
40. George O. Abell, "Astrology," in *Science and the Paranormal* (New York: Scribner's, 1981), pp. 83–84.
41. Ellic Howe, "Astrology," in *Man, Myth, and Magic,* ed. Richard Cavendish (New York: Marshall Cavendish, 1970), p. 155.
42. Leonard Zusne, *Anomalistic Psychology: A Study of Extraordinary Phenomena of Behavior and Experience* (Erlbaum Associates, 1982), p. 219.
43. R. B. Culver and P. A. Ianna, *The Gemini Syndrome: A Scientific Evaluation of Astrology* (Buffalo: Prometheus Books, 1984).
44. David Voas, "Ten Million Marriages: An Astrological Detective Story," *Skeptical Inquirer* 32, no. 2 (March/April 2008), p. 55.
45. Cited in I. W. Kelly, "Astrology, Cosmobiology, and Humanistic Astrology," in *Philosophy of Science and the Occult,* ed. Patrick Grim (Albany: State University of New York Press, 1982), p. 52.
46. Shawn Carlson, "A Double-Blind Test of Astrology," *Nature* 318 (1985).
47. Geoffrey Dean and Arthur Mather, *Recent Advances in Natal Astrology: A Critical Review 1976–1990* (Rockport, MA: Para Research, 1977), p. 1.
48. Abell, "Astrology," p. 87.
49. Bart Jan Bok, *Objections to Astrology* (Prometheus Books, 1975), p. 9.

50. Donald T. Regan, *For the Record: From Wall Street to Washington* (San Diego: Harcourt Brace Jovanovich, 1988).
51. Linda Goodman, *Linda Goodman's Sun Signs* (Pan Books, 1972), p. 477.
52. Bart Jan Bok, *Objections to Astrology* (Prometheus Books, 1975).
53. Theodore Roszak, *Why Astrology Endures* (San Francisco: Robert Briggs Associates, 1980), p. 3.
54. Michel Gauquelin, *Astrology and Science* (London: Peter Davies, 1969), p. 149.

FIVE
Looking for Truth in Personal Experience

If you believe everything, you are not a believer in anything at all.
—IDRIES SHAH

"I SAW IT WITH MY own eyes."

"I *know* what I heard and felt."

"I could no longer doubt my own senses—what seemed utterly impossible was . . . *real.*"

Such words have come from many of us who've experienced, up close and personal, the extraordinary, the bizarre, the *weird.* They're often spoken with conviction, with an air of certainty. After all, we trust our own sensory experiences and the interpretations we put on them. We trust them because relying on our senses works, at least for most purposes. Doing so proves accurate enough, often enough, for us to make our way in the world. So, in the aftermath of an extraordinary personal experience, it's no wonder when someone asks, "Can we reasonably deny the evidence of our own senses?"—and concludes, "No!"

SEEMING AND BEING

In the fields of observation chance favors only the mind that is prepared.
—LOUIS PASTEUR

Everard Feilding, an amateur magician and researcher of psychic phenomena, was such a someone. In the first decade of the twentieth century, he investigated Eusapia Palladino, the world-famous medium (a person said to contact spirits). Feilding was a skeptic concerning such matters and had helped to expose trickery among many who claimed paranormal powers. But he changed his tune after the unforgettable experience of sitting in on several seances with Palladino. Here's what he said about those encounters:

> All my own experiments in physical mediumship had resulted in the discovery of the most childish frauds. Failure had followed upon failure. . . . The first seance with Eusapia, accordingly, provoked chiefly a feeling of surprise; the second, of irritation—irritation at finding oneself confronted with a foolish but apparently insoluble problem. . . . After the sixth, for the first time, I find that my mind, from which the stream of events has hitherto run off like rain from a macintosh, is at last beginning to be capable of absorbing them. For the first time I have the absolute conviction that our observation is not mistaken. I realize, as an appreciable fact in life, that, from an empty cabinet I have seen hands and heads come forth, that from behind the curtain of that empty cabinet I have been seized by living fingers, the existence and position of the very nails of which could be felt. I have seen this extraordinary woman sitting visible outside the curtain, held hand and foot by my colleagues, immobile except for the occasional straining of a limb, while some entity within the curtain has over and over again pressed my hand in a position clearly beyond her reach. I refuse to entertain the possibility of a doubt that we were the victims of hallucination.[1]

Such compelling stories of personal experience leading to belief in the paranormal are numerous in past and present. Maybe you even have one of your own. In several surveys, people who believe in the paranormal have cited personal experience as the most important reason for their belief. In one study, believers were asked their main reasons for their belief in ESP. Personal experience got more votes than media reports, experiences of friends or relatives, and laboratory evidence. Even many of the skeptics in this study put a high premium on personal experience. They said that they disbelieved because they hadn't yet experienced ESP.[2] So Feilding's emphasis on personal experience seems typical.

But there's a problem here. Despite Feilding's experience being direct and firsthand, despite his impressive experience, despite his certainty in concluding that the paranormal phenomena in question were real, there are good reasons to believe that his conclusion was in fact *wrong.* (We'll return to his case later in this chapter.) These reasons do not involve questioning Feilding's integrity, intelligence, or sanity. Neither do they involve the unjustified assertion that paranormal events are impossible. More important, what we've said about Feilding's conclusion could be said about many similar conclusions based on other equally impressive extraordinary experiences.

The fact is, though our experiences (and our judgments about those experiences) are reliable enough for most practical purposes, they often mislead us in the strangest, most unexpected ways—especially when the experiences are exceptional or mysterious. This is because our perceptual capacities, our memories, our states of consciousness, our information-processing abilities have perfectly natural but amazing powers and limits. Apparently, most people are unaware of these powers and limits. But these odd characteristics of our minds are very influential. Because of them, as several psychologists have pointed out, we should *expect* to have many natural experiences that seem for all the world like supernatural or paranormal events. So even if the supernatural or paranormal didn't exist, *weird things would still happen to us.*

The point is not that every strange experience must indicate a natural phenomenon—nor is it that every weird happening must be supernatural. The point is that some ways of thinking about personal experience help increase our chances of getting to the truth of the matter. If our minds have peculiar characteristics that influence our experience and how we judge that experience, we need to know about those characteristics and understand how to think our way through them—all the way through, to conclusions that make sense. This feat involves critical thinking. But it also requires *creative* thinking—a grand leap powered by an open mind past the obvious answer, beyond the will to believe or disbelieve, toward new perspectives, to the best solution among several possibilities. This chapter shows you how to take the first step. The chapters that follow tell you how to finish the job.

That first step is to understand and apply a simple but potent principle:

Just because something seems (feels, appears) real doesn't mean that it is.

We can't know for sure that an event or phenomenon has objective reality—that it's not imagination, not "all in our heads"—just because it appears to us to have objective reality. This is simply a logical fact. We can't infer what is from what seems. To draw such a conclusion is to commit an elementary fallacy of reasoning. It's clearly fallacious to say, "This event or phenomenon seems real; therefore, it *is* real." What's more, the peculiar nature of our minds guarantees that what seems will frequently *not* correspond to what is.

Heaven and hell have been located inside the human brain.

—John Taylor

Now, in our daily routines, we usually do assume that what we see is reality—that seeming is being. And we're generally not disappointed. But we're at much greater risk for being dead wrong with such assumptions when (1) our experience is uncorroborated (no one else has shared our experience), (2) our conclusions are at odds with all known previous experience, or (3) any of the peculiarities of our minds could be at work.

Here's how some of these peculiarities operate and how powerful they can be.

PERCEIVING: WHY YOU CAN'T ALWAYS BELIEVE WHAT YOU SEE

The idea that our normal perceptions have a direct, one-to-one correspondence to external reality—that they are like photographs of the outer world—is wrong. Much research now suggests that perception is *constructive,* that it's in part something that our minds manufacture. Thus what we perceive is determined, not only by what our eyes and ears and other senses detect but also by what we know, what we expect, what we believe, and what our physiological state is. This constructive tendency has survival value—it helps us make sense of and deal successfully with the world. But it also means that seeing is often *not* believing—rather, the reverse is true.

Believing is seeing.

—John Slader

Perceptual Constancies

Consider what psychologists call perceptual constancies—our tendency to have certain perceptual experiences regardless of the relevant input from our senses. Research has demonstrated these constancies again and again; they're stock items in basic psychology texts. Psychologist Terence Hines believes that they're some of the best illustrations of our constructive perception at work, and he cites three examples.[3]

One is color constancy. People often perceive an object as a certain color because they know that the object is supposed to be that color—even if the object is not that color at all. In one early experiment, people were shown cutouts of trees and donkeys, which they perceived as green and gray, as they should be—even though all the cutouts were made from the same green material and lit by a red light to make them appear gray.[4] Such findings help explain how we sometimes can be quite wrong when remembering colors.

Then there's the example of size constancy. If you watch a truck rumble past you and speed into the distance, do you perceive the truck to become smaller? Of course not. You perceive the size of familiar objects as roughly constant no matter how far away they are. The image on your retinas shrinks as an object gets farther away, but you perceive the size of the object as unchanging. The reason is that you *know* that distance has no effect on the actual size of physical objects. With this knowledge your brain gives you perceptions of size constancy, despite shrinking retinal images.

Amazingly enough, our knowledge of size constancy is learned. We're not born with it. And there have been reports of people in the world who haven't learned it. Anthropologist Colin Turnbull told of the Ba Mbuti people who didn't get a chance to learn about size constancy because they lived in thick jungle where the only objects that could be seen were always just a few yards away. When Turnbull took one of these people out on an open plain, they saw several buffalo grazing a few miles away. The Ba Mbuti asked what kind of insects they were! Turnbull told him that they were buffalo twice the size of the ones his people were used to. Turnbull's companion refused to believe him. So they drove to where the buffalo were. As they got closer to the animals, and the buffalo appeared to get larger and larger, the Ba Mbuti became frightened and said that it was witchcraft. Turnbull writes, "Finally, when he realized that they were real buffalo he was no longer afraid, but what puzzled him still was why they had been so small, and whether they *really* had been small and had so suddenly grown larger, or whether it had been some kind of trickery."[5]

The Role of Expectation

Whatever one believes to be true either is true or becomes true in one's mind.

—JOHN C. LILLY

We're usually completely unaware of our many perceptual constancies—just as we're often oblivious to all the other ways that our brains get into the construction business. One of these other ways is based on the power of expectancy: We sometimes perceive exactly what we *expect* to perceive, regardless of what's real.

Research has shown that when people expect to perceive a certain stimulus (for example, see a light or hear a tone), they often do perceive it—even when no stimulus is present. In one experiment, subjects were told to walk along a corridor until they saw a light flash.

Sure enough, some of them stopped, saying they had seen a flash—but the light hadn't flashed at all. In other studies, subjects expected to experience an electric shock, or feel warmth, or smell certain odors, and many did experience what they expected even though none of the appropriate stimuli had been given. All that was really given was the suggestion that a stimulus might occur. The subjects had hallucinated (or perceived, or apparently perceived, objects or events that have no objective existence). So if we're normal, expectancy or suggestion can cause us to perceive what simply isn't there. Studies show that this perception is especially true when the stimulus is vague or ambiguous or when clear observation is difficult.

We've all had such hallucinations. Psychologist Andrew Neher cites the common experience of looking at a clock and "seeing" the second hand move—then realizing that the clock isn't running.[6] Have you ever seen someone standing in the shadows on a dark night as you walk home alone and then discovered that the person was a shrub? Have you ever been in the shower and heard the phone ring, only to realize that the ringing was all in your mind?

Looking for Clarity in Vagueness

Things are not always what they seem.

—PHAEDRUS

Another kind of perceptual construction happens every time we're confronted with a vague, formless stimulus but nevertheless perceive something very distinct in it. Take the moon, for instance. In the United States, we see the figure of a man in it. But East Indians see a rabbit, Samoans a woman weaving, and Chinese a monkey pounding rice. We often look at clouds, wallpaper, smoke, fire, fuzzy photos, murky paintings, water stains on walls and see elephants, castles, faces, demons, nude figures—you name it. This trick is technically a type of illusion, or misperception, called *pareidolia*. We simply see a vague stimulus as something it's not. We etch meaning into the meaningless. Psychologists point out that once we see a particular image in the clouds or smoke, we often find it difficult to see anything else, even if we want to. This tendency takes on more importance when we consider some of the conclusions people have reached when they failed to take it into account.

Consider: On the surface of the planet Mars, there's a monument of a human face, one mile wide—and this amazing artifact is clearly revealed in a NASA photograph. This startling claim has been made by several people in books, magazines, and on television. They have suggested that the face is the work of an alien civilization.

The NASA photo is real enough (see next page). It was taken by the Viking spacecraft in 1976, along with many others. But it's an ambiguous mixture of light and shadow, suggestive of a face but subject

The famous face on Mars, photographed by the Viking 1 orbiter in 1976, is one mile across and has a nose and mouth formed by shadows.

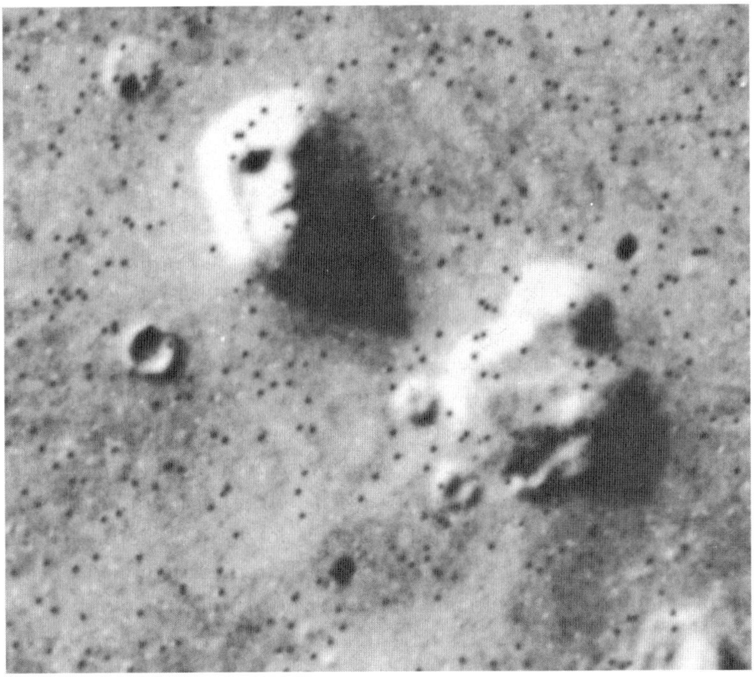

Source: NASA

to various interpretations. Planetary scientists have emphasized that the photo shows a natural formation. Indeed, Mars experts who've seen the photo don't consider it to show anything unusual at all. A key space scientist who was involved in the Viking mission said, "The object does not even look very much like a face, but the correlating sense of the human brain fills in the missing details to make one think of a face."[7]

Now it is possible that an alien civilization sculpted a massive human face on Mars. But given our tendency to overlay our own patterns onto vague stimuli, it's a mistake to look at something as ambiguous as the Mars photo and conclude that it is, in fact, a sculpted human face. To do so is to ignore at least one other very good possibility: our own constructive perception.

Overlooking or rejecting this possibility plays a part in countless bizarre cases of pareidolia—like Maria Rubio, the New Mexico housewife who in 1977 noticed the odd shape of skillet burns on one of her tortillas. She thought that the tortilla looked like the face of Jesus Christ with a crown of thorns—and took it as a sign of Christ's Second Coming. Pilgrims by the thousands came to see the tortilla, encased in glass. Or what about the woman who said in 2004 that her ten-year-old grilled cheese sandwich—with a bite taken out of it—bore the very image of the Virgin Mary? The sandwich sold on eBay for $28,000.

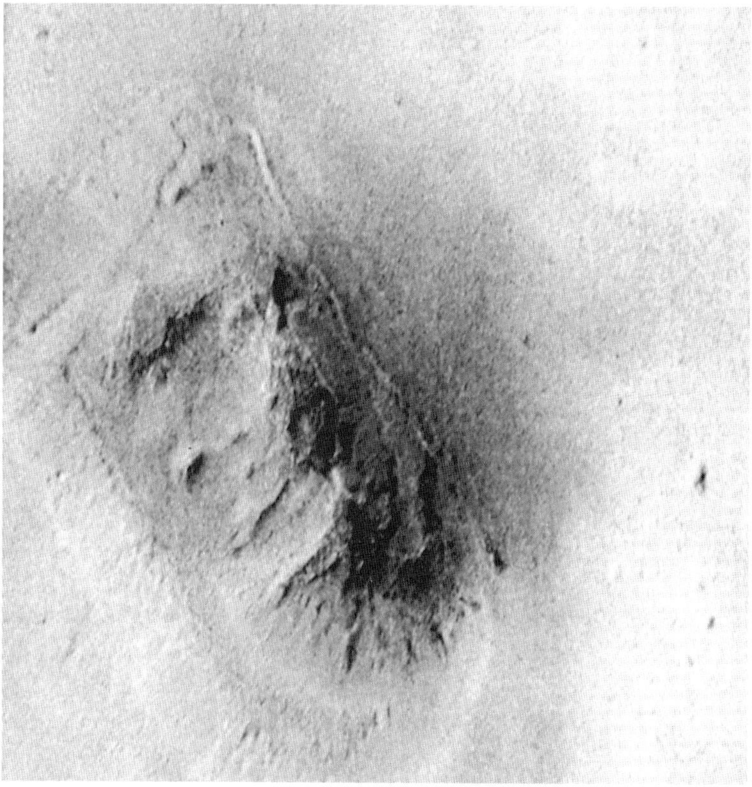

Source: NASA

This photo shows the famous face on Mars photographed by the Mars Global Surveyor in 1998. Planetary geologists say that the feature is due to natural processes.

Similarly, in 1991, Georgia choir member Joyce Simpson saw the face of Jesus in a forkful of spaghetti on a Pizza Hut billboard. She was debating whether to quit the choir when she looked up and saw Christ's face. After the sighting was reported in a local paper, dozens of motorists claimed to see Christ in the billboard. Jesus was not the only figure seen, however. Others saw Willie Nelson, Jim Morrison, and John Lennon.[8]

Another example of pareidolia is "backward masking," the belief that certain messages are placed on a recording backward to mask their true meaning. The idea is that the brain will unconsciously decipher the message and be affected by it. In 1989, the parents of suicide victim James Vance sued the heavy metal rock group Judas Priest and CBS Records on the grounds that a series of backward-masked messages (as well as forward subliminal ones) on the album *Stained Class* caused him to commit suicide. They didn't win their case, however, because there was no evidence that Judas Priest had intentionally put any subliminal messages in its album. But even if it had, there is no evidence that backward or subliminal messages can have any effect on people's behavior[9]—something to keep in mind if you ever consider investing in subliminal self-help tapes.

Maria Rubio and her tortilla image of Jesus.

At least one group has intentionally put a backward message on one of its albums. At the end of the song "Goodbye Blue Sky" on Pink Floyd's album *The Wall*, there is some very faint muffled speech. When played backward, someone is clearly saying: "Congratulations, you have just discovered the secret message. Please send your answer to Old Pink, care of the funny farm."[10] Not a particularly satanic message, but a hidden one nonetheless.

Besides learning to see, there is another art to be learned—not to see what is not.
—Maria Mitchell

The Blondlot Case

Perceptual construction, in all its forms, explains some of the strangest episodes in the history of science. It explains why scientists in Nazi Germany thought they could see nonexistent physical differences between the blood particles of Jews and those of the Aryan man.

It explains why over one hundred years ago the Italian astronomer Giovanni Schiaparelli (and later the American astronomer Percival Lowell) claimed to see canals on Mars. (Lowell even published a detailed map of the canals.) Photos taken by Mariner 9 show nothing on Mars that corresponds to what Schiaparelli and Lowell said they saw.[11] And perceptual construction explains the infamous case of Professor René Blondlot.

Blondlot (1849–1930) was a member of the French Academy of Sciences and a highly respected physicist at the University of Nancy in France. In 1903, not long after scientists discovered X-rays and other forms of radiation, Blondlot announced the discovery of yet another type of radiation. He called it N rays, after his university. His research indicated that the presence of N rays could be detected by the human eye and that they were emitted by certain metals (but not wood). They increased the brightness of a spark. When they were directed at objects coated with luminous paint, the objects became brighter. And when N rays were present, they helped the eye see better in dim light. Soon dozens of research studies confirmed Blondlot's discovery. Many scientists reported other amazing properties of N rays.[12]

But all was not well. Scientists outside France weren't able to duplicate Blondlot's results. Many physicists doubted the existence of N rays because all the tests were based on subjective judgments. Instead of using instruments to gather objective data, researchers relied on people's observations to determine the results. For example, people were used to judge whether there was an increase in brightness of an object (a standard test for the presence of N rays). Most scientists knew then, as they know now, that such subjective judgments can be affected by belief or expectancy.

"I can't believe that," said Alice. "Can't you?" the Queen said in a pitying tone. "Try again: draw a long breath and shut your eyes."

—Lewis Carroll

One of those skeptical scientists was American physicist Robert W. Wood. In 1904 he paid a visit to Blondlot's laboratory. There, without Blondlot's knowledge, he tested Blondlot and others to see if N rays were real or just wishful thinking. In one N-ray experiment, Wood was to assist Blondlot by placing a sheet of lead between a source of N rays and a card coated with luminous paint. N rays were supposed to make the paint brighter, except when the lead sheet was placed in their path. (Blondlot had found that lead completely blocked N rays.) Blondlot was to observe the changes in the paint's brightness as the lead sheet was inserted or removed. But without Blondlot's knowledge, Wood tried something that revealed the truth about N rays. Wood repeatedly told Blondlot that the lead sheet was in place when in fact it wasn't or that the sheet had been removed when it was really still there. Blondlot's observations then followed an amazing pattern. If he believed that the lead sheet wasn't in place, and thus not blocking N rays, he reported that the paint was brighter. If he believed that the lead sheet was there, blocking N rays, he reported that the paint was dimmer. His observations depended on his belief and had *nothing to do with whether the lead sheet was actually in place.*

Wood secretly manipulated other experiments in Blondlot's laboratory with similar results. If Blondlot, or some other observer, believed N rays were present, he could see that they were—even in situations where Wood had secretly changed the experiments so that N rays should have been impossible to detect.

In 1904 Wood published his findings in the British scientific journal *Nature.* It became clear that Blondlot and other French scientists had been victims of perceptual construction. They weren't lying about their observations, and they didn't imagine their experience. Their strong belief in N rays simply changed the way they perceived. Being scientists didn't protect them from a kind of perceptual distortion that affects us all.

"Constructing" UFOs

It is easier to attribute UFO sightings to the known irrationalities of terres-trials than to the unknown efforts of extraterrestrials.
—Richard Feynman

This uncomfortable fact—that a phenomenon can be radically misperceived by people who are sane, sober, honest, educated, and intelligent—is seen even more clearly in UFO reports. Case in point: On March 3, 1968, a UFO was sighted by multiple witnesses in several states. In Tennessee, three intelligent, educated people (including the mayor of a large city) saw a light in the night sky moving rapidly toward them. They reported that they saw it pass overhead at about 1,000 feet up; what they saw was a huge, metallic craft moving in silence. They observed orange-colored flames shooting out from behind it, with many square-shaped windows lit from inside the object. In a report to the U.S. Air Force, one of the witnesses said that the craft was shaped "like a fat cigar . . . the size of one of our largest airplane fuselages, or larger."

At about the same time, six people in Indiana spotted the same UFO. Their report to the Air Force said that it was cigar-shaped, moving at treetop level, shooting rocketlike exhaust from its tail, and it had many brightly lit windows. Around the same time, two people in Ohio saw it too. But they said that they saw three luminous objects, not one. One of these witnesses used her binoculars to get a good look at the UFO. She submitted a detailed report to the Air Force that said the objects were shaped like "inverted saucers," flying low and in formation, silently cruising by.[13]

Fortunately, we know exactly what these witnesses (and many others) saw in the sky that night. Records from the North American

Image of Bigfoot from the 1967 Patterson film.

Air Defense Command (NORAD) and other evidence show that at the time of the UFO sighting, the rocket used to launch the Soviet *Zond 4* spacecraft reentered the atmosphere, breaking into luminous fragments as it sped across the sky. It zoomed in the same southwest-to-northeast trajectory noted by the witnesses, crossing several states. The witnesses simply saw the light show produced by the breakup of a rocket.[14]

So where did those interesting details come from—the giant craft, the inverted saucers, the square-shaped windows, the metallic cigar shape? They were constructed. As Hines says,

> These additions and embellishments were purely the creation of the witnesses' minds: not because they were crazy, drunk, or stupid, but because that is the way the human brain works. It can be said that these witnesses did perceive what they said they did. This doesn't mean, however, that what they perceived was the same as what was really there. Note, too, how inaccurate was the estimate of the object's altitude. . . . [Witnesses] estimated about 1,000 feet while, in fact, the reentering rocket was miles high and scores of miles away. This type of gross inaccuracy frequently occurs when one sees a light in the

Tracking Down Bigfoot

North America is said to be inhabited not just by ordinary humans and familiar animals but by a mysterious species seldom seen—an outsized two-legged ape-man called Bigfoot, or Sasquatch. He is thought to be a hairy and smelly primate, standing 7 to 10 feet tall and weighing in at 500 to 1,000 pounds. He is reclusive and skittish, roaming alone or in small family groups in the forests of North America, especially western United States and Canada. He's a famous guy, the subject of movies, books, websites, and news accounts, and he's studied and hunted relentlessly by Bigfoot enthusiasts and investigators.

Bigfoot is unknown to science, yet his followers have amassed an enormous amount of evidence for his existence. There are thousands of eyewitness accounts, stories told by people who claim to have seen a Bigfoot monster firsthand. There are also many oversized footprints (or plaster casts of footprints) thought to belong to the creature. (It was the gigantic footprints that inspired the name Bigfoot.) The evidence also is said to include photographs, film, and sound recordings of Bigfoot vocalizations. Among these, the most impressive is the so-called Patterson film, a short 16-mm film shot in 1967 by Roger Patterson and Bob Gimlin showing what they said was Bigfoot walking through a wilderness area in northern California.

Though a tiny handful of scientists believe that Bigfoot is real and are dedicated to Bigfoot investigations, most scientists (anthropologists, for example) are not impressed by claims for his existence. Part of the reason for skepticism is the quality of the evidence, which is generally thought to be poor.

For example, a large part of the evidence for Bigfoot consists of eyewitness accounts. But as discussed in this chapter, eyewitness accounts are generally unreliable. They are unreliable because of the influence of expectancy and belief, the effects of stress, selective attention, memory construction, poor observational conditions (darkness, faint stimuli, etc.), and other factors. It's well known that in many alleged sightings, people mistake large animals such as elk or bear for Bigfoot. Some Bigfoot researchers say that 70 to 80 percent of sightings are hoaxes or mistakes. To establish the existence of a previously unknown animal, scientists insist on better evidence than eyewitness reports.

Bigfoot footprints seem to be plentiful, but they too are problematic as evidence. Countless Sasquatch footprints have been faked by pranksters who strap on huge feet and tramp around the woods. Bigfoot investigators have sometimes disagreed about the authenticity of footprints, and even some veteran Bigfoot researchers have been fooled by bogus footprints. All these factors raise doubts about footprint evidence.

There are no good-quality photos of Bigfoot. Existing photos are generally indistinct or grainy and offer no reliable evidence for Bigfoot. The Patterson film has been controversial practically from the day it was made. Bigfoot enthusiasts claim that the film could not have been faked. Many critics disagree. And some scientists have argued that because of the dubious quality of the film, it cannot provide evidence either for or against the existence of Sasquatch. All of this shows that as evidence, the film is dubious.

Probably the main reason scientists do not accept the Bigfoot claim is that it conflicts with what we already know. Anthropology, biology, and other sciences give us no reason to expect that a creature like Bigfoot exists in North America. There simply is nothing in our experience that unequivocally shows that such a creature exists. Someday maybe we will discover that Bigfoot does exist after all. But based on what we know now, we must give this possibility a low probability.

> sky with no background, as is the case at night. Under these circumstances, the many cues the brain uses to judge distance are not present, so no accurate basis for judgment exists.[15]

Even pilots, who are presumed to be experts at accurately observing objects in the sky, can be fooled by UFO construction of the perceptual kind. For example, on June 5, 1969, near St. Louis, the pilots of two airliners and an Air National Guard fighter plane had a close encounter with what they said was a whole squadron of UFOs. It was late afternoon when the copilot of one of the airliners first spotted the UFOs. A Federal Aviation Administration traffic controller who happened to be riding in the cockpit as an observer later reported that it seemed that the squadron would collide with the airliner. He said they seemed to come frighteningly close—within several hundred feet of the airliner! They were the color of "burnished aluminum" and shaped like a "hydroplane." Moments later, the crew of the other airliner (8 miles west of the first) radioed the tower reporting that the UFOs had just zoomed past them. Later, the fighter pilot, flying behind the second airliner at 41,000 feet, radioed a near collision with the UFOs. "Damn, they almost got me," he said. At the last moment the UFOs seemed to suddenly change course and climb out of his way, suggesting that they were "under intelligent control."

What was going on up there? UFO investigator Philip Klass has shown that

> The identity of this "squadron of UFO's" not only is now known beyond all doubt, but they were photographed by an alert newspaper photographer in Peoria, Illinois, named Alan Harkrader, Jr. His photo shows a meteor fireball, with a long, luminous tail of electrified air, followed by a smaller flaming fragment, also with a long tail, flying in trail behind. Harkrader told me that he saw another fragment break off but was unable to get a photo of it.[16]

The Harkrader photo and many eyewitness reports from the ground in Illinois and Iowa show that the fireball and its fragments were *not* just a few hundred feet from the planes. The actual distance was at least *125 miles.*

UFO sightings are also complicated by another kind of perceptual construction, called the *autokinetic effect.* This effect refers to how, for most people, a small stationary light in the dark will be perceived as moving. This perception happens even if the person's head remains perfectly still. Psychologists theorize that the cause of this apparent movement is small, involuntary movements of the eyeball. So a star or bright planet can appear to move, creating the illusion of a UFO. Research has shown that the autokinetic effect can be influenced by

Robert Wilson's 1934 photo of Nessie.

©Matt84/E+/Getty Images

the opinion of others. If someone says a light in the dark is moving in a certain way, others will be more likely to report similar observations.[17] Klass says that no single object has been mistaken as a flying saucer more often than the planet Venus, a very bright object in the morning sky, and the autokinetic effect helps explain why.[18]

Perceptual construction in UFO sightings has been documented many times, enough to demonstrate that no one is immune to it—not pilots, not astronomers, not reliable witnesses of all kinds, not pillars of the community. This fact, of course, doesn't explain every UFO sighting. (To explain many more sightings, other facts would need to be—and have been—brought to bear.) But it does help show that personal observations alone aren't proof that UFOs—that is, spacecraft of extraterrestrial origin—are real. In fact, when clear observation is difficult (which is usually the case, as in the examples above), personal experience by itself can never tell us whether or not a UFO is real. What *seems* real may not *be* real.

REMEMBERING: WHY YOU CAN'T ALWAYS TRUST WHAT YOU RECALL

Your memory is like a mental tape recorder—it whirrs day and night, picking up your experience, making a literal record of what happens, and letting you play back the parts you want to review. Does this description sound about right? It's wrong.

The Loch Ness Monster

For centuries, legends and eyewitness reports have claimed that a large, mysterious creature inhabits a deep lake called Loch Ness in the Scottish highlands. The so-called Loch Ness monster is said to be a plesiosaur, a beast left over from the age of dinosaurs. Few people take the early accounts of "Nessie" seriously, but many stand by the alleged sightings and other evidence accumulated since the 1930s.

In 1934 the now-famous photo of Nessie was allegedly taken by Robert Wilson, a physician from London. The photo shows the silhouette of a beast with a long neck and small head, looking very plesiosaur-like, floating on the surface of the water. Eyewitness accounts also suggested that the creature had a long neck and small head.

Starting around 1960, many sonar searches have been conducted in Loch Ness, most notably by researchers from Cambridge and Birmingham Universities and the Academy of Applied Science. Most of these searches found nothing unusual in the Loch. Some showed large underwater moving objects, which researchers have identified as large fish, boat wakes, gas bubbles, lake debris, or something simply unidentified. Most recently, a BBC research team hoping to find the elusive creature used 600 separate sonar beams and satellite navigation technology to scour the entire loch from shore to shore and top to bottom. The team members were hoping to encounter Nessie herself, but they found nothing out of the ordinary.

The most dramatic evidence for the existence of Nessie is some 1972 underwater photographs taken in combination with sonar. The published photos show what looks like a diamond-shaped flipper attached to a large body.

All of this evidence for the existence of the Loch Ness monster, however, is in dispute. The famous Wilson photograph has been reported to be a fake, a staged picture of a model of a sea serpent attached to a toy submarine. In 1993, one of the original hoaxers confessed shortly before his death that the whole charade had been hatched by his stepfather with Wilson as an accomplice. More recently, some have questioned whether this story of a faked photograph was itself faked! Many other Nessie photos are just too indistinct to constitute reliable evidence. Researchers allege that the original flipper photos were too fuzzy to reveal much of anything but that they were doctored before publication to make the image resemble a flipper. As for eyewitness reports, critics have pointed out the unreliability of eyewitness accounts generally and the fact that there are many things in Loch Ness that an honest and sober person can mistake for a lake monster: floating logs, boat wakes, birds, otters, and hoaxed monsters. In addition, scientists have proposed these possibilities: Baltic sturgeon (a giant fish); underwater waves caused by volcanic activity; and rotting, gas-filled logs that rise from the lakebed and violently break the surface before sinking again.

Scientists are generally very skeptical of the notion that Nessie is a plesiosaur that time forgot. They point out, among other things, that for the monster to be a remnant of the dinosaur era, there would have to be not one Nessie, but several—and the lake habitat cannot sustain such large creatures.

Of course, to some, the biggest sticking point is that after hundreds of years of monster-hunting, no one has found a shred of physical evidence. No bones, no skin, no scales.

False Memories

We're all aware that memory is fallible—that we forget where we put our keys, whether we locked the door, what we went to the store to buy, and so forth. But you may not realize that we can seem to remember events that never happened. Known as "false memories," they can be created by suggestion, imagination, and hypnosis, and can seem just as real as true memories. When false memories are traumatic, they can profoundly affect the lives of those who have them.

In 1992, for example, Beth Rutherford sought help from a church counselor who used what is called "recovered memory therapy" to allegedly uncover memories she had repressed. Beth was asked to recall details about her childhood and placed in a trancelike state to supposedly improve her recall. As a result of the therapist's guided questioning, Beth came to believe that she had been repeatedly raped by her father, a member of the clergy, from the time she was 7 to the age of 14, sometimes with the aid of her mother. She even came to believe that her father had impregnated her twice and forced her to abort the fetus herself with a coat hanger. When these allegations were made public, Beth's father was forced to resign his position. A subsequent medical examination, however, revealed that Beth was still a virgin and had never been pregnant. Beth sued the counselor and received a $1 million settlement in 1996.[19]

Beth's case is not unique. Many others who have falsely come to believe that they were abused as children have successfully sued their therapists. But many more are living with the painful consequences of false memories. Elizabeth Loftus, an award-winning psychologist who has done groundbreaking work on the malleability of memory, says that therapist-induced false memories has taken an enormous toll:

> There are still hundreds, perhaps thousands of families who have been devastated by repressed memory accusations. There are elderly parents who have one wish left in life—simply to be reunited with their children. There are talented mental health professionals who have found their profession tarred by the controversy. And there are the genuinely abused patients who have felt their experiences trivialized by the recent sea of unsubstantiated, unrealistic, and bizarre accusations.[20]

A lot of research now indicates that our memories *aren't* literal records or copies. Like our perceptual powers, our memories are constructive or, rather, creative. When we remember an experience, our brains reach for a representation of it; then, piece by piece, they *reconstruct* a memory based on this fragment. This reconstructive process is inherently inexact. It's also vulnerable to all kinds of influences that guarantee that our memories will frequently be inaccurate.

For an example of your memory's reconstructive powers, try this: Remember an instance when you were sitting today. Recall your surroundings, how you were dressed, how you positioned your legs and arms. Chances are, you see the scene from the perspective of someone looking at it, as though you were watching yourself on television. But this memory can't be completely accurate because during the experience you never perceived yourself from this perspective. You now remember certain pieces of the experience, and your brain constructed everything else, television perspective and all.

For well over a half century, research has been showing that the memory of witnesses can be unreliable, and the constructive nature of memory helps explain why. Studies demonstrate that the recall of eyewitnesses is sometimes wrong because they reconstruct events from memory fragments and then draw conclusions from the reconstruction. Those fragments can be a far cry from what actually transpired. Further, if eyewitnesses are under stress at the time of their observations, they may not be able to remember crucial details, or their recall may be distorted. Stress can even distort the memories of expert witnesses, which is one of several reasons why reports of UFOs, seances, and ghosts must be examined carefully: The experiences are stressful. Because memory is constructive and liable to warping, people can sincerely believe that their recall is perfectly accurate—and be perfectly wrong. They may report their memory as honestly as they can, but alas, it's been worked over.

Like perception, memory can be dramatically affected by expectancy and belief. Several studies show this effect, but a classic experiment illustrates the point best. Researchers asked students to describe what they had seen in a picture. It portrayed a white man and a black man talking to each other on the subway. In the white man's hand was an open straight razor. When the students recalled the picture, one-half of them reported that the razor was *in the hand of the black man.* Memory reconstruction was tampered with by expectancy or belief.[21]

Our beliefs are not automatically updated by the best evidence available. They often have an active life of their own and fight tenaciously for their own survival.

—D. F. Marks

The same kind of thing can happen in our successful "predictions." After some event has occurred, we may say, "I knew that would happen; I predicted it." And we may truly believe that we foretold the future. But research suggests that our desire to believe that we accurately predicted the future can sometimes alter our memories of the prediction. We may remember our prediction even though we actually made no such prediction. Apparently, such an incident can occur despite our knowing that our memories can be checked against records of the actual predictions.[25]

Research also shows that our memory of an event can be drastically changed if we later encounter new information about the event—even if the information is brief, subtle, and dead wrong. Here's a classic example: In one experiment, people were asked to watch a film depicting a car accident. Afterward, they were asked to recall what they had seen. Some of the subjects were asked, how fast were the cars going when they smashed into each other? The others were asked the same

Past Life Remembered or Cryptomnesia?

If, under hypnosis, you recall living 200 years ago and can vividly remember doing and seeing things that you've never experienced in your present life, isn't this proof that you lived a "past life"? Isn't this evidence of reincarnation? Some people would think so. There is, however, another possibility, explained by Ted Schultz:

> Beatle George Harrison got sued for rewriting the Chiffons' "He's So Fine" into "My Sweet Lord." He was the innocent victim of the psychological phenomenon of cryptomnesia. So was Helen Keller, the famous blind and deaf woman, when she wrote a story called "The Frost King." After it was published in 1892, she was accused of plagiarizing Margaret Canby's "The Frost Fairies," though Helen had no conscious memory of ever reading it. But, sure enough, inquiries revealed that Canby's story had been read to her (by touch) in 1888. She was devastated.[22]

Cryptomnesia or "hidden memory" occurs when you recall a forgotten memory but don't recognize it as something that happened to you. Such recollections may not only lead you to claim someone else's artistic work as your own, but also to believe that you are the reincarnation of someone who lived before. Virginia Tighe's recollections of Bridey Murphy provide a case in point.

In 1952, Virginia Tighe was placed in a hypnotic trance and began to recall a past life as Bridey Murphy, an Irishwoman who grew up in Cork during the nineteenth century. Virginia seemed to know a great deal about Bridey Murphy's life, claiming that she was born on December 20, 1798, that she grew up in a wooden house called "The Meadows," that, at the age of 17 she married a barrister named Sean Brian MacCarthy who taught at Queens University, that she died in 1864, and that she witnessed her own funeral. Her remarkable story was published as *The Search for Bridey Murphy* and became an international best-seller.[23]

Although some of Virginia's story checked out, such as her description of the northern Irish countryside (to which she had never traveled), much of it turned out to be inaccurate or unverifiable. There was no record of Bridey Murphy's birth or death, of a house named "The Meadows," or of a Sean Brian MacCarthy teaching at Queen's University (because Queen's University did not exist at the time).

Hypothesizing that Virginia's recollections might stem from early childhood experiences, reporters from the *Chicago American* and later Melvin Harris found that Virginia Tighe grew up across the street from a Mrs. Anthony Corkell whose maiden name was Bridie Murphy! Mrs. Corkell regularly regaled Virginia with tales of the old country. In high school, Virginia learned to recite several Irish monologues with a thick Irish brogue, and both her parents turned out to be part Irish. "The more reporters talked to relatives and friends of Virginia," reports Martin Gardner, "the more it became obvious that in her trances she had simply dredged up childhood memories."[24] Not all cases of alleged reincarnation can be chalked up to cryptomnesia, but when investigating such cases, it is one of the first things that must be ruled out.

question with a subtle difference. The word *smashed* was replaced by *hit*. Strangely enough, those who were asked the "smashed" question estimated higher speeds than those asked the "hit" question. Then, a week later, all the subjects were asked to recall whether they had seen broken glass in the film. Compared to the subjects who got the "hit" question, more than twice as many of those who got the "smashed" question said they had seen broken glass. But the film showed *no broken glass at all.*[26] In a similar study, subjects recalled that they had seen a stop sign in another film of a car accident even though no stop sign had appeared in the film. The subjects had simply been asked a question that presupposed a stop sign and thus created the memory of one in their minds.[27]

These studies put in doubt any long-term memory that's subjected to leading questions or is evoked after exposure to a lot of new, seemingly pertinent information. Psychologist James Alcock cites the example of reports of near-death experiences collected by Raymond Moody in his books *Life after Life* (1975) and *Reflections on Life after Life* (1977). These books contain stories of people who had been close to death (for example, clinically dead but later resuscitated) and later reported that while in that state they felt the sensation of floating above their body, traveling through a dark tunnel, seeing dead loved ones, or having other extraordinary experiences. Researchers generally agree that people do experience such things; whether their experiences show that they literally leave their bodies and enter another world is another question. Moody's cases were based on the memories of people who came to him with their stories, sometimes years after the experience, frequently after they had heard Moody lecture or read newspaper stories about his work. Alcock explains:

> Since there was such great similarity in the reports, Moody argued that these reports must reflect reality. (There are physiological reasons for expecting such similarities. . . .) Considering how memory can be shaped after the event, it is not unlikely that one's memory of near-death experience will conform to the pattern described in the lecture or reading one has just experienced. Moreover, Moody's questions to his subjects certainly would not have been without influence.[28]

But our memories are more than just constructive—they're also selective. We selectively remember certain things and ignore others, setting up a memory bias that can give the impression that something mysterious, even paranormal, is going on. Our selective memories may even lead us to believe that we have ESP. As Hines says:

> A classic example is to be thinking of someone and, minutes later, having them call. Is this sort of instance amazing proof of direct

> mind-to-mind communication? No—it's just a coincidence. It seems amazing because we normally don't think about the millions of telephone calls made each day and we don't remember the thousands of times we have thought of someone when they *haven't* called.[29]

Selective memory is also at work in many cases of seemingly prophetic dreams. Research has shown that we all dream during sleep. Most dreams occur during the four or five periods of REM—rapid eye movement—sleep that we experience every night. These dreams do not form one continuous narrative, however. Instead, they consist of a number of different dream themes. In fact, if we're normal, we experience around 250 dream "themes" a night which Hines characterizes as "snippets of more or less (often less) coherent 'story.'" Each REM period can contain upward of 50 dream themes. We won't remember most of them. But, as Hines points out, we're likely to remember the ones that "come true":

> If a dream doesn't "come true" there is very little chance that it will be remembered. We have all had the experience of awakening and not remembering any dreams. Then, sometime later during the day, something happens to us, or we see or hear something, that retrieves from our long-term memory a dream we had had, but which, until we were exposed to what is called a *retrieval cue,* we were unable to recall voluntarily. Of course, if we had not been exposed to the retrieval cue, we would never have been aware that the dream had occurred. Thus, the nature of memory for dreams introduces a strong bias that makes dreams appear to be much more reliably prophetic than they are—we selectively remember those dreams that "come true."[30]

When asked questions like "How can you explain that I dreamed that my brother broke his leg, and I found out the next day that he broke his leg at summer camp?" the late Dr. Silas White, professor of physiological psychology at Muhlenberg College, used to respond: "How can you explain that I've dreamed dozens of times that I was walking around downtown Allentown, and I panicked when I realized I wasn't wearing any clothing, but it has never happened to me?" The fact that something appears to us in a dream is no reason to believe that it is likely to happen.

CONCEIVING: WHY YOU SOMETIMES SEE WHAT YOU BELIEVE

Nothing is so easy as to deceive one's self, for what we wish we readily believe.

—DEMOSTHENES

Our success as a species is due in large part to our ability to organize things into categories and to recognize patterns in the behavior of things. By formulating and testing hypotheses, we learn to predict and control our environment. Once we have hit upon a hypothesis that works, however, it can be very difficult to give it up. Francis Bacon was well aware of this bias in our thinking:

> The human understanding when it has once adopted an opinion . . . draws all things else to support and agree with it. And though there be a greater number and weight of instances to be found on the other side, yet these it either neglects and despises, or else by some distinction sets aside, and rejects, in order that by this great and pernicious predetermination, the authority of its former conclusion may remain inviolate.[31]

While this intellectual inertia can keep us from jumping to conclusions, it can also keep us from seeing the truth.

Denying the Evidence

No man was ever so much deceived by another as by himself.
—LORD GREVILLE

Our reluctance to give up seemingly well-confirmed hypotheses was dramatically demonstrated by psychologist John C. Wright.[32] Wright constructed a device consisting of a panel containing sixteen unmarked buttons arranged in a circle. In the middle of the circle was a seventeenth button, identical to the others. Above the circle was a three-digit counter. Subjects were told that they were participating in an experiment in problem solving. Their goal was to get as high a score as possible by pushing the buttons in the circle in the right sequence. To determine whether a button had been pushed in the correct order, the subjects were instructed to push the button in the center after each push of a button in the circle. If it was correct, a buzzer would sound and the counter would be increased by one. What the subjects didn't know is that there was no correct sequence.

A complete run consisted of 325 consecutive button pushes divided into thirteen blocks of 25. During the first ten blocks (250 button pushes), the buzzer randomly indicated that the subject had pushed the correct button a certain percentage of the time. During the eleventh and twelfth block, the buzzer did not sound once. During the thirteenth block, the buzzer sounded every time. As a result, the subjects came to believe that whatever hypothesis they were working on at the time was correct.

When they were told that there was no correct sequence, many couldn't believe it. Their belief in the truth of their hypotheses was so strong that some of them didn't believe that there was no correct sequence until the experimenters opened the device and showed them the wiring! Max Planck was well aware of how tenaciously we can cling to a hypothesis when we have invested a lot of time and effort in it. He once remarked, "A new scientific truth does not triumph by convincing its opponents and making them see the light, but rather because its opponents eventually die, and a new generation grows up that is familiar with it."[33]

The refusal to accept contrary evidence is found not only among scientists, however. Religious groups predicting the end of the world also have a remarkable ability to ignore disconfirming evidence. Perhaps the most famous of these groups is the Millerites. In 1818, after devising a mathematical interpretation of a certain passage in the Book of Daniel, William Miller concluded that Christ would return to Earth and the world would come to an end sometime between March 21, 1843, and March 21, 1844. As news of his prediction spread, he gained a small group of followers. In 1839, Joshua V. Hines entered the fold and spread the word by publishing the newspaper *Signs of the Times* in Boston. *The Midnight Cry,* published in New York City, and the *Philadelphia Alarm* also contributed to the movement's popularity.

A rumor arose in the Millerite camp that April 23, 1843, was the exact date of the coming of Christ. Even after that day passed without incident, the faith of Miller's followers was not shaken. Attention became focused on January 1, 1844. When that day came and went, the Millerites eagerly awaited March 21, 1844, the final date indicated in Miller's original prophecy. Christ's nonarrival was a blow to the faithful, but, remarkably enough, the movement did not break up.

One of Miller's disciples did some recalculations and came up with a new date of October 22, 1844. Although Miller was originally skeptical of this date, he too came to accept it. Faith in this date became greater than that in any of the others. This fourth failure finally led to the end of the movement. But its offspring live on to this day. Some of the disillusioned Millerites went on to found the Adventist movement. Others formed the Jehovah's Witnesses. Although these groups refrain from giving exact dates, they both believe that the end is near.

Reluctance to change one's views in the face of contrary evidence can be found in all walks of life, from doctors who refuse to change their diagnoses to scientists who refuse to give up their theories. In one study of student psychotherapists, it was found that once the students had arrived at a diagnosis, they could look through an entire folder of contrary evidence without changing their minds. Instead they interpreted the evidence to fit their diagnoses.[34]

The moment we want to believe something, we suddenly see all the arguments for it, and become blind to the arguments against it.
—George Bernard Shaw

Subjective Validation

Our ability to fit data to theory accounts for the apparent success of many methods of divination such as palmistry, tarot cards, and astrology. Consider the following personality profile:

> Some of your aspirations tend to be pretty unrealistic. At times you are extroverted, affable, sociable, while at other times you are introverted, wary and reserved. You have found it unwise to be too frank in revealing

Failed End of the World Prophecies

The Millerites, of course, were not the first to establish an exact date for the end of the world. Many different people have proposed many different dates, but so far, none of them has been correct. Here's a sampling of failed end times prophecies.

- **Jan. 1, 1000.** Claimant: Pope Sylvester II.
- **1033.** Claimant: Various Christians. Some believed this to be the 1,000th anniversary of the death and resurrection of Jesus, and his Second Coming was anticipated.
- **1284.** Claimant: Pope Innocent III. Pope Innocent III predicted that the world would end 666 years after the rise of Islam.
- **1346–1351.** Claimant: Various Europeans. The black plague spreading across Europe was interpreted by many as a sign of the end times.
- **1600.** Claimant: Martin Luther. Iconic figure of the Protestant reformation predicted the end of the world would occur no later than 1600.
- **1658.** Claimant: Christopher Columbus. Columbus claimed that the world was created in 5343 BCE, and would last 7,000 years. Assuming no year zero, that means the end would come in 1658.
- **1967.** Claimant: Rev. Jim Jones. The founder of the Peoples Temple stated he had visions that a nuclear holocaust was to take place in 1967.
- **1969.** Claimant: Charles Manson. Manson predicted that an apocalyptic race war would occur in 1969 and ordered the Tate-Labianca murders in an attempt to bring it about.
- **July 1999.** Claimant: Nostradamus. A prediction attributed to Nostradamus stating the "King of Terror" would come from the sky in "1999 and seven months" led to fears of the end.
- **Jan. 1, 2000.** Claimant: Various. A Y2K computer bug was predicted that would cause computer crashes, major catastrophes, and the end of the world as we know it.
- **April 29, 2007.** Claimant: Pat Robertson. In his 1990 book, *The New Millennium,* Robertson suggests this date as the day of Earth's destruction.
- **Oct. 21, 2011.** Claimant: Harold Camping. Camping predicted the rapture and devastating earthquakes would occur on May 21, 2011, with God taking approximately 3 percent of the world's population into heaven, and that the end of the world would occur five months later on October 21. When his previous (fifth) prediction failed to come about, Camping revised it and said that on May 21, a "spiritual judgment" took place, and that both the physical rapture and the end of the world would occur October 21, 2011.
- **Dec. 21, 2012.** Claimant: Various. The end of the Mayan calendar gives many different scenarios including a galactic alignment, a geomagnetic reversal of the poles, a collision with an unknown planet called Nibiru, an alien invasion, Earth being destroyed by a giant supernova, the moon exploding . . . and the list goes on.[35]

> yourself to others. You pride yourself on being an independent thinker and do not accept others' opinions without satisfactory proof. You prefer a certain amount of change and variety, and become dissatisfied when hemmed in by restrictions and limitations. At times you have serious doubts as to whether you have made the right decision or done the right thing. Disciplined and controlled on the outside, you tend to be worrisome and insecure on the inside.
>
> Your sexual adjustment has presented some problems for you. While you have some personality weaknesses, you are generally able to compensate for them. You have a great deal of unused capacity which you have not turned to your advantage. You have a tendency to be critical of yourself. You have a strong need for other people to like you and for them to admire you.[36]

Now answer this question honestly: How well does this profile match your personality? Most people, if told that the profile is created specifically for them, think that it describes them fairly well—maybe even perfectly. Even though the profile could apply to almost anyone, *people believe that it describes them specifically and accurately.* This phenomenon of believing that a general personality description is unique to oneself, which has been thoroughly confirmed by research, is known as the *Forer effect* (named after the man who first studied it). For the Forer effect to work, people have to be told that the catch-all description really pinpoints them specifically. If people suspect what's really going on, they're less likely to fall for the phenomenon.

But why *do* we fall for it? Psychologists David Marks and Richard Kammann explain it this way:

> From our point of view, Forer's result is a special case of subjective validation in which we find ways to match ourselves up with the description given. Our personalities are not fixed and constant as we usually imagine. Everybody is shy in one situation, bold in another, clever at one task, bumbling at another, generous one day, selfish the next, independent in one group of people but conforming in another group. Thus, we can usually find aspects of ourselves that will match up with a vague statement, although the specific examples of self will be different from one person to the next.[37]

Astrology, biorhythms, graphology (determining personality characteristics from handwriting), fortune-telling, palmistry (palm reading), tarot card reading, psychic readings—all these activities generally involve the Forer effect. So if the Forer effect is likely to be at work in any of these systems in any instance, we can't conclude that the system has any special power to see into our character. Our sincere feeling that the readings are true does not—and cannot—validate the system.

One-time palm reader and psychologist Ray Hyman learned this the hard way. Hyman had learned palm reading to help put himself through college. He became quite good at it and was convinced that there was something to it. A friend of his, however, was skeptical. He bet Hyman that Hyman could tell his clients the exact opposite of what the palm said and they would still believe him. Hyman took the bet and, to his surprise, found that his friend was right. Some of his clients even thought that his "incorrect" readings were more profound than his "correct" ones.

Our ability to make sense of things is one of our most important abilities. But we are so good at it that we sometimes fool ourselves into thinking something's there when it's not. Only by subjecting our views to critical scrutiny can we avoid such self-delusion.

Probably no prophet has a bigger reputation than Michel Nostradamus (1503–1566), who composed a thousand verses that some people believe foretold many historical events. He's been credited with predicting both World Wars, the atomic bomb, the rise and fall of Hitler, and more. Now, clearly, if a prophet consistently offers unequivocal, precise predictions of events that can't reasonably be expected, we must take serious notice of that seer. How about Nostradamus?

In fact, his predictions are neither unequivocal nor precise, and this fact has allowed subjective validation to convince some people that his prophecies have come true. Nostradamus himself said that he deliberately made his verses puzzling and cloudy. As a result, they are open to multiple interpretations. For example:

Century I, verse XXII

That which shall live shall leave no direction,
Its destruction and death will come by stratagem,
Autun, Chalons, Langres, and from both sides,
The war and ice shall do great harm.[38]

Century I, verse XXVII

Underneath the cord, Guien struck from the sky,
Near where is hid a great treasure,
Which has been many years a gathering,
Being found, he shall die, the eye put out by a spring.[39]

What do you think these verses from Nostradamus mean? Andrew Neher asks that people compare their own interpretations of the verses with those of Henry Roberts, one of several authors of books on Nostradamus's prophecies. According to Roberts, verse XXII is "a forecast of the use of supersonic weapons, traveling in the near absolute zero temperature above the stratosphere." And Roberts

©Chris Hellier/Corbis Historical/Getty Images

Michel de Nostradame (1503–1566), from the frontispiece of one of his early publications.

says verse XXVII means "paratroopers alight near the Nazi's plunder hoard and, captured, they are executed."[40] Did you come to a different conclusion? Do you see how easy it is to come up with alternative interpretations that seem to fit?[41]

Neher also suggests a telling comparison between the interpretations offered by two Nostradamus experts commenting on the same verses. On one verse Roberts and Erika Cheetham, also a Nostradamus author, had this to say:

> Roberts: "A remarkably prophetic description of the role of Emperor Haile Selassie, in World War II."[42]

> Cheetham: "Lines 1–2 . . . refer . . . to Henry IV. The man who troubles him from the East is the Duke of Parma. . . . Lines 3–4 most probably refer to the siege of Malta in 1565."[43]

And on another verse:

> Roberts: "The taking over of Czechoslovakia by Hitler, the resignation of President Benes, the dissensions over the matter between France and England and the dire warning of the consequences of this betrayal, are all remarkably outlined in this prophecy."[44]

> Cheetham: "The first three lines here may apply to the assassinations of the two Kennedy brothers."[45]

As Neher points out, "In comparing the conflicting interpretations of the quatrains, it is apparent that Roberts and Cheetham are projecting into them meanings that exist in their own minds, which leads them to think that Nostradamus had great precognitive ability."[46]

These examples are subjective validation at work. And once an interpretation is overlaid on a vague prophecy, it may be difficult to see any other possibility.

Despite the obscure references and conflicting interpretations, Nostradamus's writings are still considered by many to be prophetic. So much so that he was credited with predicting the 9/11 attack on the World Trade Center. Immediately following the attack, email boxes across the country began receiving letters containing the following prophecy:

> In the city of God there will be a great thunder,
> Two brothers torn apart by Chaos, while the fortress endures, the great leader will succumb,
> The third big war will begin when the big city is burning
>
> —NOSTRADAMUS 1654

Anyone familiar with Nostradamus would suspect that something is amiss because Nostradamus died in 1566. Ironically, it turns out that the foregoing prophecy was written several years earlier by Neil Marshall, a Canadian college student who wanted to demonstrate "just how easy it is to dupe the gullible."[47] Quite an impressive demonstration indeed.

Of course, prediction is much easier after the fact. What Nostradamus interpreters actually do is a form of retrodiction; they take a quatrain and try to fit it to an event that's already occurred. There's only one quatrain that contains an unambiguous reference to a specific date, quatrain X:72:

> In the year 1999 and seven months
> From the sky will come the great King of Terror
> He will bring back to life the great king of the Mongols
> Before and after war reigns happily
>
> —NOSTRADAMUS

Some thought that this prophesied the end of the world; others thought it foretold a world revolution. Both camps were mistaken because no such cataclysm occurred in July 1999. Nostradamus's one specific prediction turns out to be false. When a theory's predictions are not borne out by the facts, it should be rejected. So it should be with the theory that Nostradamus is a great prophet.

Confirmation Bias

Not only do we have a tendency to ignore and misinterpret evidence that conflicts with our own views; we also have a tendency to look for and recognize only evidence that confirms them. A number of psychological studies have established this *confirmation bias.*

A wise man knows his own ignorance. A fool knows everything.

—CHARLES SIMMONS

Crop Circles

Crop circles are swirled patterns of bent-over plants, such as wheat, corn, or soybeans, that mysteriously appear in large fields. First noticed in southern England, crop circles have started to appear all over the world. They range from simple, circular shapes to elaborate pictograms. Originally, some people thought that the circles were produced by extraterrestrials or some other paranormal phenomenon. Others thought that they were produced by "plasma vortex phenomena" that consisted of a spinning mass of air containing electrically charged matter. Still others thought that they were produced by clever human beings.

In 1991, two pubmates in their sixties—Doug Bower and Dave Chorley—claimed to have produced many of the English crop circles by attaching a rope to both ends of a long narrow plank, holding it between themselves and the plants, and stepping on the plank to bend over the plants. To substantiate their claim, they produced a circle for a tabloid newspaper, which was later claimed to be of extraterrestrial origin by one of the believers in the extraterrestrial hypothesis. Since then, other crop circles thought impossible to be hoaxes have turned out to be human-made. Apparently there is no reliable way to distinguish crop circles of terrestrial origin from those of extraterrestrial origin. Nevertheless, people continue to believe that crop circles are messages from outer space.

Consider the following simplified representation of four cards, each of which has a letter on one side and a number on the other:[48]

A D 4 7

Subjects were told that their task was to determine the most effective means for deciding whether the following hypothesis were true: If a card has a vowel on one side, it has an even number on the other. Specifically, the subjects were instructed to indicate which cards needed to be turned over to establish the truth of the hypothesis.

Which cards would you turn over? Most subjects thought that only the A and the 4 cards needed to be turned over. But they were mistaken. The 7 card also needed to be turned over, because it too could have a bearing on the truth of the hypothesis.

Turning the A card over was a good choice, because if there were an even number on the other side, it would support the hypothesis. And if there were an odd number, it would refute it. Turning the 4 card over could also lend support to the hypothesis if there were a vowel on the other side. If there were a consonant on the other side, however, it would not refute the hypothesis, because the hypothesis says that if there is a vowel on one side, there is an even number on the other side. It does not say that if there is an even number on one side, there is necessarily a vowel on the other side.

People were right to ignore the D card, because whatever is on the other side is irrelevant to the truth of the hypothesis. The 7 card

Superstitious Pigeons

The tendency to notice and look for confirming instances is not unique to human beings. The same tendency can be found in other creatures as well. As a result, they, too, can appear to be superstitious.

In an experiment with pigeons, psychologist B. F. Skinner fed the pigeons at random intervals.[49] During the time between feedings, the pigeons would engage in various behaviors: pecking on the ground, turning their heads from side to side, flapping their wings, and so on. If food appeared while a pigeon was performing one of these behaviors, the pigeon associated the behavior with the food and thus produced the behavior more frequently. Because the behavior was produced more frequently, however, it was rewarded more frequently. As a result, the pigeon seemed to acquire a superstitious belief, namely, the belief that the behavior caused the feeding. The same sort of process lies behind some of our superstitious beliefs. If a good thing happens to us while we are wearing a particular item of clothing, say, we may come to associate that item with the happy event. As a result, we may wear it more often. And if good things happen to us only on a statistically random basis, we may come to believe that the item brings good luck.

was crucial, however, because, like the A card, it could refute the hypothesis. If there were a vowel on the other side of the 7 card, the hypothesis would be false.

This experiment demonstrates that we tend to look for confirming rather than disconfirming evidence, even though the latter can often be far more revealing. Disconfirming evidence can be decisive when confirming evidence is not.

Consider the hypothesis: All swans are white. Each white swan we see tends to confirm that hypothesis. But even if we've seen a million white swans, we can't be absolutely sure that all swans are white because there could be black swans in places we haven't looked. In fact, it was widely believed that all swans were white until black swans were discovered in Australia. Thus:

When evaluating a claim, look for disconfirming as well as confirming evidence.

Our tendency to confirm rather than disconfirm our beliefs is reflected in many areas of our lives. Members of political parties tend to read literature supporting their positions. Owners of automobiles tend to pay attention to advertisements touting their make of car. And all of us tend to hang out with people who share our views about ourselves.

Facts do not cease to exist because they are ignored.

—ALDOUS HUXLEY

One way to cut down on confirmation bias is to keep a number of different hypotheses in mind when evaluating a claim. In one experiment, subjects were shown a sequence of numbers—2, 4, 6—and were informed that it follows a certain rule. Their task was to identify this rule by proposing other triplets of numbers. If a proposed triplet fit the rule—or if it did not—the subjects were informed. They were not supposed to state the rule until they were sure of it.[50]

Most subjects picked sets of even numbers like 8, 10, 12 or 102, 104, 106. When told that these too followed the rule, subjects often announced that they knew the rule: Any three consecutive even numbers. But that rule was incorrect. This fact led some people to try out other triplets such as 7, 9, 11 or 93, 95, 97. When told that these triplets fit the rule, some claimed that the rule was any three numbers ascending by two. But that rule, too, was incorrect. What was the correct rule? Any three numbers in ascending order.

Why was this rule so difficult to spot? Because of confirmation bias: Subjects tried only to confirm their hypotheses; they did not try to disconfirm them.

If subjects were asked to keep two hypotheses in mind—such as, any three numbers in ascending order and any three numbers not in ascending order—they did much better. They picked a wider range of triplets, each of which confirmed or disconfirmed one of the rules. Thus, keeping a number of different hypotheses in mind can help you avoid confirmation bias.

The Availability Error

Mankind, in the gross, is a gaping monster that loves to be deceived and has seldom been disappointed.
—Harry Mackenzie

Confirmation bias can be exacerbated by the *availability error*. The availability error occurs when people base their judgments on evidence that's vivid or memorable instead of reliable or trustworthy. Those who buy something on the basis of a friend's recommendation, for example, even though they are aware of reviews that do not give their choice high marks, are guilty of the availability error. College students who choose courses on the basis of personal recommendations even when those recommendations contradict statistically accurate student surveys are also guilty of the availability error. Although anecdotal evidence is often psychologically compelling, it is rarely logically conclusive.

Those who base their judgments on psychologically available information often commit the fallacy of hasty generalization. To make a hasty generalization is to make a judgment about a group of things on the basis of evidence concerning only a few members of that group. It is fallacious, for example, to argue like this: "I know one of those insurance salespeople. You can't trust any of them." Statisticians refer to this error as the failure to consider sample size. Accurate judgments about a group can be made on the basis of a sample only if the sample is sufficiently large and every member of the group has an equal chance to be part of the sample.

The availability error also leads us to misjudge the probability of various things. For example, you may think that amusement parks are dangerous places. After all, they are full of rides that hurl people around at high speeds, and sometimes those rides break. But statistics show that riding the rides at an amusement park is less dangerous than riding a bicycle on main roads.[51] We tend to think that amusement parks are dangerous places because amusement park disasters are psychologically available—they are dramatic, emotionally charged, and easy to visualize. Because they stick in our minds, we misjudge their frequency.

When confirming evidence is more psychologically compelling than disconfirming evidence, we are likely to exhibit confirmation bias. In cases of divination, prophecy, or fortune-telling, for example, confirming instances tend to stand out. Disconfirming instances are easily overlooked. An experiment concerning prophetic dreams illustrates this phenomenon.[52]

Subjects were asked to read a "diary" of a student who had an interest in prophetic dreams. It purportedly contained a record of the student's dreams as well as the significant events in her life. Half the dreams were followed by events that fulfilled them and half were not.

When subjects were asked to remember as many of the dreams as possible, they remembered many more of the dreams that were fulfilled than those that were not. Events that confirmed the dreams were more memorable (and thus more available) than those that did not. Consequently, prophetic dreams were thought to be more frequent than they actually were. To avoid the availability error, then, it's important to realize that the available data are not always the only relevant data.

When evaluating a claim, look at all the relevant evidence, not just the psychologically available evidence.

To be ignorant of one's ignorance is the malady of ignorance.

—Amos Bronson Alcott

Confirming evidence is not always more available than disconfirming evidence. For example, losing a bet, which constitutes a disconfirming instance, can be a very memorable experience.[53] Gambling losses are emotionally significant and thus psychologically available. Because we usually don't have as much invested in other sorts of prediction, other failures are not as memorable.

Our predilection for available evidence helps account for the persistence of many superstitious beliefs. As Francis Bacon realized, "All superstition is much the same whether it be that of astrology, dreams, omens, retributive judgment or the like . . . [in that] the deluded believers observe events which are fulfilled, but neglect or pass over their failure, though it be much more common."[54] A superstition is a

Psychic Detectives

Psychic detectives are people thought to have paranormal powers in solving crimes—to find missing persons or the bodies of crime victims or to identify criminals. Their supposed successes in helping law enforcement officials solve cases have been widely publicized in the media, most notably on television shows like Court TV's *Psychic Detectives*, *Larry King Live*, and the drama series *Medium*. In *Psychic Detectives*, dramatized re-creations portray psychics as eerily on the mark in fingering murderers and discovering the whereabouts of missing people. Some police departments use psychic sleuths in investigations, and occasionally a law enforcement detective will say that a psychic provided useful information. Some who have seen a psychic detective in action say they were converted from skeptics to believers by the psychic's performance. And psychics themselves tout their track record in cracking famous cases.

Should we conclude, then, that psychic detectives are for real? If we did, our judgment would be premature. The central problem is that evidence in favor of psychic detection is weak, and there are many ways to be fooled into thinking it strong. Only carefully controlled scientific tests could confirm the psychics' claims, and there has been no such confirmation. (Tabloid TV re-creations and observations under uncontrolled conditions don't count.) No scientific evidence demonstrates that any crime has been solved or any missing person found through psychic means. In fact, despite decades of scientific experiments examining ESP and other psychic phenomena, no good evidence shows that any of them exist. (See the discussion of parapsychology in Chapter 6.)

On the other hand, there are countless ways people can be misled about the reality of psychic detection. To name just a few:

- Psychic detectives and the media often overstate the psychics' crime-solving exploits. For example, several years ago psychic detective Carla Baron claimed that she had solved fifty cases and that she had worked with the Brown family in the O. J. Simpson case. But investigators reported that both these claims were false. The lead character in the TV series *Medium* is based on the experiences of the famous clairvoyant Allison Dubois. The *Medium* website has stated that she was a consultant on cases for the Glendale (Arizona) police department and the Texas Rangers. But both organizations deny ever using Dubois. Media reports described the case of a psychic named Nancy Meyer who worked with police to locate the body of an elderly man who had been missing. She was said to have drawn maps and homed in precisely on the location of the body. (Meyer's story was later presented on *Psychic Detectives*.) But the police officers involved said later that the psychic's information was

belief that an action or situation can have an effect on something even though there is no logical relation between the two. When we believe that there is a cause-and-effect relation between things, we tend to notice and look for only those events that confirm the relation.

Take, for example, the lunar effect. It is widely believed that the moon has an effect on our behavior. It supposedly can drive people crazy. (Hence the label *lunatic*.) But research has failed to bear this out. In a review of thirty-seven studies dealing with the moon's effect on unimpressive—too vague and general to be of much use. She told them, for example, that the corpse would be found near a body of water (which could have referred to several different objects, including ponds, lakes, or streams) and railroad tracks (which were everywhere).

- The media rarely report psychics' failures, and psychics are frequently wrong. In famous murder or kidnapping cases, police often receive hundreds or thousands of tips from psychics, yet the cases are never solved (or solved by someone connected with the crimes). Sometimes the police waste hours or days following up erroneous information from a psychic. Such dead ends generally don't make the news.
- Psychics (and sometimes their clients and the police) employ *retrofitting*, a technique used after the case is solved to match earlier vague tips with the facts. For example, suppose the psychic says that in a vision she sees the victim's corpse and the number 18, a bridge, and a body of water. After the body is located, it would be easy for people (including the police) to force a match to these pronouncements—to see the number 18 in a street address near the crime scene, on a billboard near the victim's home, on a highway sign somewhere in the area, even in the fact that it is 1.8 miles from the body to some landmark. Or to see a bridge within a mile or two of the body, or on a nearby store sign, or in the name of a road. Or to see either a lake, stream, or pond in every direction. Retrofitting is often reinforced by people's tendency to interpret the psychic's incorrect statements as correct. If the prediction is that the missing person will be found dead but is later discovered alive, the investigators or family members may assert that the person was actually dead in some other sense, perhaps psychologically or spiritually. The will to believe can be strong.
- Psychics often use their *normal* faculties—their natural intelligence, talents, and senses—to gather information. They may consult newspaper accounts, websites, maps, and witnesses for clues. They may use all the skills and resources of any good police investigator—careful observations, hunches, inferences, and interviews with everyone involved in the case. They may even rely on cold reading, the old "mind reader" trick of surreptitiously extracting information from people by asking them questions or making statements and observing their facial expressions and other bodily clues to the truth.

Perhaps psychic detectives really do have paranormal powers, but neither the available evidence nor *Medium* nor Court TV's *Psychic Detectives* provide us with good reasons for believing it.

behavior, psychologists I. W. Kelly, James Rotton, and Roger Culver concluded, "There is no causal relationship between lunar phenomena and human behavior."[55] Why is the belief in the lunar effect so prevalent? Kelly and colleagues suggest that it is due to slanted media reporting, an ignorance of the laws of physics, and the sorts of cognitive errors we have been discussing. Bizarre behavior during a full moon is much more memorable—and thus much more available—than normal behavior. So we are apt to misjudge its frequency.

And because we tend to look only for confirming instances, we do not become aware of the evidence that would correct this judgment.

The availability error not only leads us to ignore relevant evidence; it also leads us to ignore relevant hypotheses. For any set of data, it is, in principle, possible to construct any number of different hypotheses to account for the data. In practice, however, it is often difficult to come up with many different hypotheses. As a result, we often end up choosing among only those hypotheses that come to mind—that are available.

In the case of unusual phenomena, the only explanations that come to mind are often supernatural or paranormal ones. Many people take the inability to come up with a natural or normal explanation for something as proof that it is supernatural or paranormal. "How else can you explain it?" they often ask.

This sort of reasoning is fallacious. It's an example of the appeal to ignorance. Just because you can't show that the supernatural or paranormal explanation is false doesn't mean that it is true. Unfortunately, although this reasoning is logically fallacious, it is psychologically compelling.

The extent to which the availability of alternate hypotheses can affect our judgments of probability was demonstrated in the following experiment.[56] Subjects were presented with a list of possible causes of a car's failure to start. Their task was to estimate the probability of each of the possible causes listed. Included on every list was a catchall hypothesis labeled "all other problems [explanations]." Researchers discovered that the probability the subjects assigned to a hypothesis was determined by whether it was on the list—that is, by whether it was available. If more possibilities were added, subjects lowered the probability of the existing possibilities instead of changing the probability of the catchall hypothesis (which they should have done if they were acting rationally).

Although the unavailability of natural or normal explanations does not increase the probability of supernatural or paranormal ones, many people think that it does. To avoid this error, it's important to remember that just because you can't find a natural explanation for a phenomenon doesn't mean that the phenomenon is supernatural. Our inability to explain something may simply be due to our ignorance of the relevant laws or conditions.

Although supernatural or paranormal claims can be undercut by providing a natural or normal explanation of the phenomenon in question, there are other ways to cast doubt on such claims. A hypothesis is acceptable only if it fits the data. If the data are not what you would expect if the hypothesis were true, there is reason to believe that the hypothesis is false.

Take the case of the infamous Israeli psychic, Uri Geller. Geller claims to have psychokinetic ability: the ability to directly manipulate objects with his mind. But the data, psychologist Nicholas Humphrey says, do not fit this hypothesis:

> If Geller has been able to bend a spoon merely by mind-power, without his exerting any sort of normal mechanical force, then it would immediately be proper to ask: Why has this power of Geller's worked only when applied to metal objects of a certain shape and size? Why indeed only to objects anyone with a strong hand could have bent if they had the opportunity (spoons or keys, say, but not pencils or pokers or round coins)? Why has he not been able to do it unless he has been permitted, however briefly, to pick the object up and have sole control of it? Why has he needed to touch the object with his fingers, rather than with his feet or with his nose? Etcetera, etcetera. If Geller really does have the power of *mind over matter,* rather than muscle over metal, none of this would fit.[57]

Humphrey calls this sort of skeptical argument the argument from "unwarranted design" or "unnecessary restrictions," because the phenomena observed are more limited or restricted than one would expect if the hypothesis were true. To be acceptable, a hypothesis must fit the data: This means not only that the hypothesis must explain the data but also that the data explained must be consistent with what the hypothesis predicts. If the hypothesis makes predictions that are not borne out by the data, there is reason to doubt the hypothesis.

The Representativeness Heuristic

Our attempt to comprehend the world is guided by certain rules of thumb known as *heuristics.* These heuristics speed up the decision-making process and allow us to deal with a massive amount of information in a short amount of time. But what we gain in speed we sometimes lose in accuracy. When the information we have to work with is inaccurate, incomplete, or irrelevant, the conclusions we draw from it can be mistaken.

He that is not aware of his ignorance will only be misled by his knowledge.

—RICHARD WHATELY

One of the heuristics that governs both categorization and pattern recognition is this one: Like goes with like. Known as the representativeness heuristic, this rule encapsulates the principles that members of a category should resemble a prototype and that effects should resemble their causes. While these principles often lead to correct judgments, they can also lead us astray. A baseball game and a chess game are both games, but their dissimilarities may be greater than their similarities. A tiny microbe can produce a big epidemic. So if we blindly follow the representative heuristic, we can run into trouble.

To see how the representativeness heuristic can affect our thinking, consider the following problem:[58]

> Linda is 31 years old, single, outspoken, and very bright. She majored in philosophy. As a student, she was deeply concerned with issues of discrimination and social justice and also participated in antinuclear demonstrations.
>
> Now, based on the above description, rank the following statements about Linda, from most to least likely:
>
> a. Linda is an insurance salesperson.
> b. Linda is a bank teller.
> c. Linda is a bank teller and is active in the feminist movement.

Most people rank *c* as most likely, because it seems to provide a better representation of Linda than either *a* or *b*. But *c* cannot possibly be the most likely statement because there have to be more bank tellers than there are bank tellers who are active in the feminist movement. The set of bank tellers who are active in the feminist movement is a subset of the set of bank tellers, so it cannot have more members than the set of bank tellers. This fallacy is known as the *conjunction fallacy* because the probability of two events occurring together can never be greater than the probability of one of them occurring alone. By taking an unrepresentative description (being a bank teller) and adding a more representative one (being a feminist), the description of Linda was made more representative but less likely.

Man's mind is so formed that it is far more susceptible to falsehood than to truth.

—DESIDERIUS ERASMUS

The influence of the representativeness heuristic is most apparent in the realm of medicine. In China, ground-up bats used to be prescribed for people with vision problems, because it was mistakenly assumed that bats had good vision. In Europe, the lungs of foxes used to be prescribed for asthmatics, because it was mistakenly believed that foxes had great stamina. In America, some alternative medical practitioners prescribed raw brains for mental disorders. In all these cases, the underlying assumption is that by consuming something you will acquire some of its properties. You are what you eat.

The notion that like causes like is the basic principle behind what anthropologist Sir James Frazer calls "homeopathic (or imitative) magic." By imitating or simulating a desired result, people the world over have thought that they can get their wish. For example, the Cora Indians of Mexico attempted to increase their flocks by placing wax or clay models of the animals they wanted in caves on the side of mountains. Barren Eskimo women placed small dolls under their pillows in hopes of becoming pregnant. And by drawing a figure in sand, ashes, or clay and poking it with a sharp stick, North American Indians thought that they could inflict a corresponding wound on the intended victim.[59]

Taboos found in many cultures are also based on the principle that like causes like. To prevent bad luck or ill fortune, people refrained from engaging in certain behaviors. For example, Eskimo children were forbidden to play cat's cradle because it was feared that, as adults, their fingers would become entangled in their harpoon lines. Pregnant Ainos women were advised not to spin yarn or twist rope at least two months before delivery lest the umbilical cord of their unborn baby become twisted around the baby's neck. Galearese fishermen didn't cut their lines after they caught a fish for fear that their next catch would break the line and get away.[60]

Superstition, which is widespread among the nations, has taken advantage of human weakness to cast its spell over the mind of almost every man.

—CICERO

These practices may seem silly to us now, but many modern practices are based on the same principle that like causes like. For example, the notion that like causes like also lies behind two prominent pseudosciences: astrology and graphology. Astrology, as we have seen, claims that persons born under certain signs will have certain mental and physical characteristics. This claim was not established through empirical investigation because there is no significant correlation between a person's sign and his or her features. How was it established then? Apparently by means of the representativeness heuristic. It is natural to assume, for example, that those born under the sign of Taurus (the bull) should be strong-willed. Similarly, it is natural to assume that those born under the sign of Virgo (the Virgin) should be shy and retiring. The naturalness of these assumptions may help explain the continuing popularity of astrology.

Graphology also makes use of the representativeness heuristic. Graphologists claim to be able to identify personality traits by examining people's handwriting. Again, the connections between handwriting characteristics and personality have not been established empirically. Instead, they, too, seem to be based on the representativeness heuristic. For example, one graphologist claimed that the small, neat handwriting of Gandhi showed that he was a man of peace while the jagged, hard-edged handwriting of Napoleon showed that he was a man of war.[61] When put to the test, however, graphologists do no better than chance at predicting occupational success.[62]

Even trained scientists can have their thinking clouded by the representativeness heuristic. When Barry Marshall, an internal medicine resident in Australia, claimed in 1983 that ulcers were caused by a simple bacteria, Martin Blaser, director of the Division of Infectious Medicine at Vanderbilt University, responded by calling Marshall's claim "the most preposterous thing I'd ever heard."[63] The received view at the time was that ulcers were caused by stress. This view seems to have been based on the representativeness heuristic. People thought that ulcers were caused by stress because having an ulcer feels like being under

Man prefers to believe what he prefers to be true.

—FRANCIS BACON

stress. We now know that assumption isn't true. The only way to avoid being misled by the representativeness heuristic is to be sure that any claim of cause and effect is based on more than just similarity.

Anthropomorphic Bias

Not only do we have a tendency to assume that like causes like, we have a tendency to assume that things are like us—even nonhuman things. As Scottish philosopher David Hume recognized long ago:

> There is an universal tendency among mankind to conceive all beings like themselves, and to transfer to every object, those qualities with which they are familiarly acquainted, and of which they are intimately conscious. We find human faces in the moon, armies in the clouds; and by a natural propensity, if not corrected by experience and reflection, ascribe malice and good-will to everything that hurts or pleases us. Hence . . . trees, mountains and streams are personified, and the inanimate parts of nature acquire sentiment and passion.[64]

Hume here is describing not only the phenomena of pareidolia—projecting human physical features onto nonhuman objects—but also the phenomena of anthropomorphism—attributing human thoughts, feelings, and desires to nonhuman objects.

We all anthropomorphize from time to time. How often have you talked to (or yelled at) your computer, your car, or your cell phone as if it had a mind of its own? Herodotus recounts the story of King Xerxes who, after having been prevented by a storm from crossing the Hellespont (a strait connecting the Aegean Sea and the Sea of Marmara), commanded that the waters of the Hellespont be given 300 lashes and cursed as punishment. Anthopologist Stewart Guthrie has documented cases of people anthropomorphizing everything from airplanes to umbrellas.[65]

One of the most compelling demonstrations of our tendency to anthropomorphize comes from an experiment conducted by psychologists Fritz Heider and Simmel in 1944.[66] They showed subjects a film of geometric shapes—circles, squares, and triangles—moving around on a screen. When asked what the film depicted, the subjects claimed that the figures represented various types of people—bullies, victims, and heroes—whose actions were guided by specific desires and goals. They didn't just see geometric figures moving around, they saw intentional, purposeful action. Other investigators have observed the same phenomena using moving dots and swarms or tiny squares.

These experiments indicate that humans are primed to detect agency—conscious, purposeful action—on the basis of remarkably little evidence. Because this tendency is universal, and because it is possessed even by young children, psychologists believe that it's innate—that it's hardwired into our genes. From an evolutionary perspective, this makes perfectly good sense. The biggest threat to the survival of early humans may well have been other humans. Those with the ability to detect the presence of their enemies would be more likely to live long enough to reproduce (and thus pass on their agent detection genes). The ability to sense other agents, then, became widespread throughout the human population.

The more sensitive our agency-detecting ability, the more likely it is that we will survive. The price we pay for an overly sensitive agent detector is a lot of false positives. We may jump to the conclusion that an agent is present when there isn't. This is a small price to pay, however, because it's better to be safe than sorry. It's better to falsely detect an agent who isn't there than not to detect one that is there. Failure to detect an agent could result in your death.

Many psychologists, however, claim that there is another price we pay for our overly sensitive agency detection system: a belief in supernatural beings. Justin Barrett, for example, asserts: "Part of the reason people believe in gods, ghosts, and goblins also comes from the way in which our minds, particularly our agency detection device (ADD) functions. Our ADD suffers from some hyperactivity, making it prone to find agents around us, including supernatural ones, given fairly modest evidence of their presence."[67] Psychologists Scott Atran and Ara Norezayan agree. They write: "Supernatural agents are readily conjured up because natural selection has trip-wired cognitive schema for agency detection in the face of uncertainty."[68] When we hear a suspicious noise or see a mysterious figure, we don't always assume it's another human being. Sometimes we assume it's something supernatural like a ghost or an evil spirit, especially if we're in a place where such things are supposed to exist.

When we think we're dealing with a human agent, it's easy enough to confirm (or disconfirm) our assumption: just look for physical clues. But in those cases where we think we're dealing with something supernatural, confirmation or disconfirmation may be next to impossible because such beings aren't physical. That may be one reason that the belief in supernatural beings has such staying power—their existence can't be disproven. So the next time you think you're in the presence of something supernatural, realize that it may just be your agency-detection system playing a trick on you.

Is God Just a Face in the Clouds?

The first person to suggest that our belief in the supernatural is a by-product of our tendency to anthropomorphize was anthropologist Stewart Guthrie. In his book *Faces in the Clouds: A New Theory of Religion*, he argues that our tendency to infer the presence of an agent when presented with only fragmentary evidence led us to postulate the existence of supernatural beings. He writes: "the progenitors of religions are our perceptual uncertainty and our need to see any people who are present. Religions are a family in that all are born from the search for human form and behavior."[69] But, one might wonder, why infer the presence of a supernatural agent, that is, one without physical form? All the humans we're acquainted with have a physical body; why assume that there are humanlike creatures without one? The answer comes from recent research in developmental psychology. It turns out that children naturally assume that the mind is separate from the body. They recognize that the brain is important for some mental activities, but not for all. This affinity for dualism (the view that the mind and the body are two different things) is dramatically displayed in an experiment conducted by J. M. Bering and D. F. Bjorkland.[70] They told children of different ages a story about a mouse that was eaten by an alligator. When asked what happened to the mouse, the children admitted that it could no longer eat or perform any biological functions. But they insisted that it could still feel hunger, have desires, and hold beliefs. Psychologist Paul Bloom concludes: "the notion that consciousness is separable from the body is not learned at all; it comes for free."[71]

This innate dualism has an evolutionary explanation. It is in our biological best interest not only to detect the presence of other humans, but also to anticipate their next move. To do that, however, we need to know what they're thinking, and that requires a theory of mind—what psychologists and philosophers call a "folk psychology." This theory tells us how beliefs and desires work together to create actions. We use folk psychology to explain the behavior of humans while we use our understanding of natural laws like gravity and motion to explain the behavior of everything else. As a result, "we perceive the world of objects as essentially separate from the world of minds, making it possible for us to envision soulless bodies and bodiless souls."[72] We have two separate systems for understanding the world, and that encourages us to postulate supernatural beings.

The foregoing account of religious belief raises the question: "If religion is generalized and systematized anthropomorphism, can it be said simply to be a mistake?"[73] For Guthrie, the answer is "yes" because he believes that such anthropomorphizing is not backed by sufficient evidence. For Barrett, however, the answer is "no" because he believes that God would want us to believe in him. As he puts it: "Why wouldn't God, then, design us in such a way as to find belief in divinity quite natural?"[74] Who's right? What do you think?

Against All Odds

Consider: A woman finds herself thinking about an old friend she hasn't thought about for ages or seen in twenty years. Then she picks up the newspaper and is stunned to see her friend's obituary. Or a man reads his daily horoscope, which predicts that he'll meet someone who'll change his life. The next day he's introduced to the woman he eventually marries. Or a woman dreams in great detail that the house next door catches fire and burns to the ground. She wakes up in a cold sweat and writes down the dream. Three days later her neighbor's house is struck by lightning and is damaged by fire. Are these stories simply cases of coincidence? Could the eerie conjunction of events have happened by chance?

Many would say absolutely not—the odds against mere coincidence are too great, astronomical. But research shows that people—even trained scientists—are prone to misjudge probabilities. When we declare that an event couldn't have occurred by chance, we're frequently way off in our estimates of the odds. Test yourself: Let's say you're at a party, and there are twenty-three people present including yourself. What are the chances that two of those twenty-three people have the same birthday? Is it (a) 1 chance in 365, or 1/365; (b) 1/1,000; (c) 1/2; (d) 1/40; or (e) 1/2,020? Contrary to most people's intuitive sense of the probabilities, the answer is (c) 1 chance in 2, or fifty-fifty.[75] Here's another one: You toss an unbiased coin five times in a row. The chances of it landing heads on the first toss is, of course, 1 in 2. Let's say it does land heads on the first toss—and, amazingly enough, on each of the other four tosses. That's five heads in a row. What are the chances of it landing heads on the sixth toss? The answer is fifty-fifty, the same as on the first toss. The probability of heads (or tails) on any toss is always fifty-fifty. What happened in previous tosses has no effect on the next toss; coins have no memory. The idea that previous events can affect the probabilities in a current random event is called the *gambler's fallacy.* And most people act as though this idea were valid.

One problem is that most of us don't realize that because of ordinary statistical laws, *incredible coincidences are common and must occur.* An event that seems highly improbable can actually be highly probable—even virtually certain—given enough opportunities for it to occur. Drawing a royal flush in poker, getting heads five times in a row, winning the lottery—all these events may seem incredibly unlikely in any instance. But they're virtually certain to happen *sometime* to *someone.* With enough chances for something to happen, it will happen.

Consider prophetic dreams, mentioned earlier. If a normal person experiences about 250 dream themes per night and over 250 million people live in the United States, there must be billions of dream themes dreamed every night and trillions in a year. With so many dreams and so many life events that can be matched up to the dreams, it would be astounding if some dreams didn't seem prophetic. The really astonishing thing may not be that there are prophetic dreams but that there are so few of them.

What Are the Odds? You Wouldn't Believe It

When we try to judge the probabilities involved in events, we're often wrong. Sometimes we're *really* wrong because the true probabilities are completely counter to our intuitive "feel" for the odds. Mathematician John Allen Paulos offers this surprising example of a counterintuitive probability:

> First, take a deep breath. Assume Shakespeare's account is accurate and Julius Caesar gasped "You too, Brutus" before breathing his last. What are the chances you just inhaled a molecule which Caesar exhaled in his dying breath? The surprising answer is that, with probability better than 99 percent, you did just inhale such a molecule.
>
> For those who don't believe me: I'm assuming that after more than two thousand years the exhaled molecules are uniformly spread about the world and the vast majority are still free in the atmosphere. Given these reasonably valid assumptions, the problem of determining the relevant probability is straightforward. If there are N molecules of air in the world and Caesar exhaled A of them, then the probability that any given molecule you inhale is from Caesar is A/N. The probability that any given molecule you inhale is not from Caesar is thus $1 - A/N$. By the multiplication principle, if you inhale three molecules, the probability that none of these three is from Caesar is $[1 - A/N]^3$. Similarly, if you inhale B molecules, the probability that none of them is from Caesar is approximately $[1 - A/N]^B$. Hence, the probability of the complementary event, of your inhaling at least one of his exhaled molecules, is $1 - [1 - A/N]^B$. A, B (each about 1/30th of a liter, or 2.2×10^{22}), and N (about 10^{44} molecules) are such that this probability is more than .99. It's intriguing that we're all, at least in this minimal sense, eventually part of one another.[76]

It is likely that unlikely things should happen.

—ARISTOTLE

Suppose you're reading a novel. Just as you get to the part that mentions the peculiar beauty of the monarch butterfly, you look up and see one on your window. Suppose you're sitting in an airport, musing over the last name of an old classmate. Just then the person sitting next to you says that very name aloud in a conversation with someone else. These are indeed uncanny pairings of events, strange couplings that provoke wonder—or the idea that psychic forces are at work. But just how likely are such pairings? The answer is *very*. A demonstration of this fact by psychologists David Marks and Richard Kammann goes something like this: Let's say that in an ordinary day a person can recall 100 distinct events. The total number of pairings of these events for a single person in a single day is thus 4,950 ($99 + 98 + 97 \ldots + 3 + 2 + 1$).[77] Over a period of ten years (or about 3,650 days), 1,000 people are thus expected to generate over 18 billion pairs (that is, $4{,}950 \times 3{,}650 \times 1{,}000 = 18{,}067{,}500{,}000$). Out of so many pairs of events, it's *likely* that some of those 1,000 people will experience some weird, incredible pairings.[78] Thus, the seemingly impossible becomes commonplace.

Rationalizing *Homo Sapiens*

People not only jump to conclusions; they frequently rationalize or defend whatever conclusion they jump to. Psychologist Barry Singer summarizes research findings that show just how good our rationalizing skills are:

> Numerous psychological experiments on problem solving and concept formation have shown that when people are given the task of selecting the right answer by being told whether particular guesses are right or wrong, they will tend to do the following:
>
> 1. They will immediately form a hypothesis and look only for examples to confirm it. They will not seek evidence to disprove their hypothesis, although this strategy would be just as effective, but will in fact try to ignore any evidence against it.
> 2. If the answer is secretly changed in the middle of the guessing process, they will be very slow to change the hypothesis that was once correct but has suddenly become wrong.
> 3. If one hypothesis fits the data fairly well, they will stick with it and not look for other hypotheses that might fit the data better.
> 4. If the information provided is too complex, people will cope by adopting overly simple hypotheses or strategies for solution, and by ignoring any evidence against them.
> 5. If there is no solution, if the problem is a trick and people are told "right" and "wrong" about their choices at random, people will nevertheless form all sorts of hypotheses about causal relationships they believe are inherent in the data, will believe their hypotheses through thick and thin, and will eventually convince themselves that their theories are absolutely correct. Causality will invariably be perceived even when it is not present.
>
> It is not surprising that rats, pigeons, and small children are often better at solving these sorts of problems than are human adults. Pigeons and small children don't care so much whether they are always right, and they do not have such a developed capacity for convincing themselves they are right, no matter what the evidence is.[80]

How easy it would be to gather some eerie pairings into a book and offer them as proof that something psychic or cosmic had transpired.

How likely is it that someone will recall a person he knew (or knew of) in the past thirty years and, within exactly five minutes, learn of that person's death? More likely than you might think. In fact, it's possible to calculate the approximate probability of this strange occurrence. One such calculation assumes that a person would recognize the names of 3,000 people from the past thirty years and that the person would learn of the death of each of those 3,000 people in the thirty years. With these assumptions and some statistical math, it can be determined that the chance of the strange occurrence happening is 0.00003. This is, as you would expect, a low probability. But in a population of 100,000 people, even this low probability means that about ten of these experiences should occur every day.[79]

> *The mathematical probabilities of rare events, in particular, often run counter to intuition, but it is the mathematics, not our intuition, that is correct.*
>
> —Barry Singer

Now none of this discussion shows that truly prophetic dreams or psychic connections among events can't happen. But it does demonstrate that our personal experience of improbabilities doesn't prove that they're miraculous or paranormal. Our personal experience alone simply can't reveal to us the true probability of a single impressive event, despite the strong feelings that an odd conjunction of events may cause in us. When events that people view as too much of a coincidence happen, we may be awestruck, mystified, or frightened. We may get a sense of strangeness that invites us to believe that something unusual is happening. But these feelings aren't evidence that something significant is occurring, any more than the feeling of dizziness means that the world is swaying from side to side.

ANECDOTAL EVIDENCE: WHY TESTIMONIALS CAN'T BE TRUSTED

Now that you know some of the mind's peculiarities that affect personal experience, we can say more clearly how much personal experience can tell you about what's real and what isn't:

It's reasonable to accept personal experience as reliable evidence only if there's no reason to doubt its reliability.

When there's reason to suspect that any of the limitations discussed above are influencing our thoughts—like when we experience something that seems to be impossible—then we should withhold judgment until we gather more evidence.

Our beliefs may predispose us to misinterpret the facts, when ideally the facts should serve as the evidence upon which we base beliefs.

—Alan M. MacRobert and Ted Schultz

When there's reason to think that any of these limitations or conditions may be present, our personal experience can't prove that something is true. In fact, when we're in situations where our subjective limitations could be operating, the experiences that are affected by those limitations not only can't give us proof that something is real or true; they can't even provide us with low-grade evidence. The reason is that at those moments, we can't tell where our experience begins and our limitations end. Is that an alien spacecraft in the night sky or Venus, embellished for us by our own high level of expectancy? Is that strange conjunction of events a case of cosmic synchronicity or just our inability to appreciate the true probabilities? If subjective limitations might be distorting our experience, our personal evidence is tainted and can't tell us much at all. That is why anecdotal evidence—evidence based on personal testimony—carries so little weight in scientific investigations. When we can't establish beyond a reasonable doubt that a person was not influenced by these limitations, we aren't justified in believing that what they report is real.

By now you probably have guessed why Everard Feilding's personal experience in Palladino's seances wasn't a good enough reason for him to conclude that he had witnessed genuine paranormal phenomena. As an eyewitness, in a darkened room, in unusual circumstances, feeling the stress of the situation, he was open to possible distortions of perception and judgment. The testimony of any eyewitness—or several eyewitnesses—in similar circumstances would be suspect. (In Palladino's case, there are additional grounds for doubting that she had extraordinary powers. She cheated. Like countless other mediums of her day, she used trickery to deceive her sitters. Some say she used trickery only occasionally; others say, all the time. In any case, she was caught red-handed several times. In one instance, she was caught skillfully using her foot to reach behind her into the spirit cabinet from which objects often appeared.)

We need not look to the annals of the paranormal, however, to see why anecdotal evidence is so unreliable. We can find good examples of the problem close at hand in countless personal experiments with unconventional, or alternative, treatments—acupuncture, homeopathy, magnetic therapy, therapeutic touch, herbs, vitamins, and the like. A large proportion of the claims made for unconventional therapies are based solely on personal experience, and testimonials by those who believe they've been cured are common and often highly persuasive. "I had multiple sclerosis," the typical story goes, "and the doctors could do nothing for me. So I tried megadoses of vitamin E, and all my symptoms soon disappeared. Vitamin E really works." But appearances are often deceiving. There are good reasons why personal experience generally cannot tell you if a treatment really works. There are, in fact, good grounds to be guided by this principle:

Personal experience alone generally cannot establish the effectiveness of a treatment beyond a reasonable doubt.

Distance Healing Treatments: Experience positive healing energy in the comfort of your own home by distance. Treatments $35.00 per session. Call for appt.

—CLASSIFIED AD

There are three reasons why this principle is true: Many illnesses simply improve on their own; people sometimes improve even when given a treatment known to be ineffective; and other factors may cause the improvement in a person's condition.

The Variable Nature of Illness

Human physiology is immensely complicated. Drawing conclusions about what causes what inside the body is not as easy as figuring

Firewalking to Well-Being

For a fee, you can have an amazing personal experience and learn to do an extraordinary feat—you can walk barefoot across a red-hot bed of burning charcoal and not get burned! Yes, seminars are teaching the art of firewalking. They're promoting the idea that the practice requires esoteric skills and that mastering them can increase self-confidence, cure impotence and chronic depression, heal failing eyesight, help people stop smoking, or enhance powers of communication and persuasion. Anthony Robbins has been a major advocate of firewalking, leading many seminars and asserting that successful firewalking requires psychic or mental energy that protects the walker from burns. Science and health writer Kurt Butler, however, disputes Robbins's claims, pointing out—as several experts have—that firewalking is actually a matter of simple physics, not psychics:

> In response to [Robbins's] skullduggery, some friends and I held a firewalk and invited the public to join us for free. We received front-page newspaper coverage as well as coverage on local television news. In that event and others since, our coals have been at least as hot as Robbins's and our fire at least as long. We have been thanked for our demonstrations by grateful relatives for helping to dissuade loved ones from continuing to waste money on firewalking seminars and experiences. One mother said her daughter had already spent $35,000 following her firewalking guru to seminars and firewalks around the country. . . .
>
> In our events we have no seminar, positive thinking, or praying to invoke special powers or awaken dormant parts of our brain. In fact, following two minutes of safety instructions, our participants chant "hot coals" as they stride across the glowing bed. In over one hundred individual crossings, only one person was ever burned badly enough to raise a blister. Other groups of skeptics, most notably members of the Southern California Skeptics, have done similar demonstrations of firewalking. (Nevertheless, we all strongly urge against anyone trying to do it without advice and preferably direct supervision from an experienced person. Several safety and legal precautions are absolutely essential.)
>
> Firewalking is a physical feat, not a mental one. It is possible because charcoal, especially when coated with ashes, does not transfer heat rapidly to other objects. Its heat-transmission characteristics are similar to those of air. You can stick your hand into a very hot oven without burning yourself, but if you touch metal in the oven, you can be badly burned. The metal is no hotter than the air, but it transfers its heat much more quickly. . . .
>
> Glowing hot charcoals, of course, are not the same as hot air. The firewalkers walk (usually rapidly) on the charcoals—they don't stand around. If they did so they would be burned. Each foot is in contact with the heat for only about a second before being lifted. Moreover, the entire walk generally lasts less than seven seconds. Any longer exposure and the risk of burns is much greater.
>
> Walking on hot coals without sustaining injury is not a miraculous feat.[81]

out what causes a car engine to misfire or a billiard ball to drop into the side pocket. One of the complexities that frequently confounds efforts to discover whether a treatment works is the self-limiting nature of illness. The fact is, most human ailments improve on their own—whether a treatment is administered or not. Diseases often simply disappear without any help from anybody. Plus, the symptoms of illnesses, even serious or terminal ones, can vary dramatically from day to day, with periods of both decline and improvement. Some chronic diseases like rheumatoid arthritis and multiple sclerosis (MS) can have spontaneous remissions, with symptoms vanishing for long periods of time—MS symptoms can disappear for years.

Even the course of cancer is variable. One cancer patient may live a few months; another patient with the same kind of cancer may live years. It's possible to calculate average survival times for certain cancers, but it's often extremely difficult to predict what will happen to a particular patient who gets a certain treatment or no treatment. This variability is one reason why doctors who predict how long a specific patient has to live are often wrong. When a patient does outlive a doctor's prediction, people sometimes credit whatever unconventional therapy the patient was taking at the time. Spontaneous remissions of cancer, even particularly lethal types, have also been documented. They're rare, and their frequency varies according to tumor type. But because they do happen, they undermine attempts to legitimately claim that a single instance of a cure was due to any particular treatment.

Often a treatment is administered when the patient's condition is deteriorating. Due to the natural variation in illness, such bad times are frequently followed by inevitable high points of improvement, so the treatment may get credit that it doesn't deserve.

The Placebo Effect

A peculiar fact about people is that sometimes even if they're given a treatment that's inactive or bogus, they'll respond with an improvement in the way they feel. This response, called the *placebo effect,* is not all in the mind—it can involve both psychological and physiological changes. What exactly is behind this effect isn't clear, but many experts say it depends on suggestibility, operant conditioning (previous experience with healing acts), expectation, and other factors.

The power of suggestion to alter body function is well established by research with hypnosis. Blisters have been induced and warts made to disappear through suggestion.

—William T. Jarvis

In many illnesses about one-third or more of patients will get better when given a placebo. (Placebos can also cause negative side effects, just as drugs can.) People taking placebos have experienced relief of headaches, hay fever, tension, arthritis, nausea, colds, high blood pressure, premenstrual tension, mood changes, cancer, and other conditions. Many times the relief is only temporary. Placebo effects can be induced by sugar pills, worthless injections and devices, a practitioner's reassuring manner, and incantations—even by the act of walking into the doctor's office.[82]

Some people are more likely than others to get relief from placebos; in most cases, people don't respond to placebos at all. But it's difficult to tell who will respond and who won't. Having trust in the practitioner or believing in a therapy raises the chances that a placebo effect will happen. Even those who don't believe in a treatment, however, may have a placebo response.

The placebo effect can be especially impressive in the relief of pain. Psychologists Leonard Zusne and Warren H. Jones explain:

> It is well-known that expectations have a profound effect on the degree of distress that an individual will experience when in pain. Objectively measured, the anticipation of pain can be quite literally worse than the pain itself. . . . The placebo, a physiologically inert substance, can be as effective as a drug if there is expectation that it will work. The placebo effect has an obvious bearing on the relief of pain in faith healing. Clinical studies show that severe post-operative pain can be reduced in some individuals by giving them a placebo instead of a pain-killing drug, such as morphine. Some 35% of the cases studied experienced relief. On the other hand, only 75% of patients report relief from morphine.[83]

Miracle of the Roses—Blooms from Shrine Are Curing Cancer, Arthritis and Even AIDS!
—TABLOID

The risk of being misled by the placebo effect is why scientists include a placebo group in medical studies. The changes shown in the treatment group are compared to any changes in the placebo group. To be considered effective, the treatment under study must do better than sugar pills or sham therapies. Placebos may have a place in the modern practice of medicine. But they can also make worthless remedies look potent.

Overlooked Causes

You've had an upset stomach for two days. A friend rubs a crystal amulet across your belly, and in a few hours your stomach settles. Did the crystal heal you?

Maybe. But there are other possible causes of your relief, besides the placebo effect and natural fluctuations in your illness. Was there a change in your diet in the last day that finally eased your digestion? Was your cure caused by exercise, lack of exercise, change in bowel habits, altered daily routine, or standing on your head in yoga class? Was it the medication you took—or stopped taking? Was it the tremendous relief you got when you heard that your car was not going to be repossessed? Unfortunately, in personal experience it's extremely difficult to rule out such possible causes for any given improvement (or deterioration) in your condition. People, however, frequently ignore other possibilities and adopt the explanation that suits them. This habit is a reliable formula for reaching false conclusions.

The formula, nevertheless, is widespread. It's sometimes used, for example, by people who've undergone cancer treatment. They may have received both conventional and unconventional treatment, but they choose to credit only the unconventional.[84]

"Life would certainly be simpler if medical treatments could be tested as easily as puddings," says psychologist Ray Hyman.

> But healing is far more complicated than cooking. If a woman says she sleeps better after being advised to change her position, should we accept this as evidence that a pendulum can determine "polarity"? If two patients improve after undergoing intense emotional experiences with Miss F [who practices "regression therapy," believing that most illnesses and emotional problems result from problems in previous lives], does this argue for the reality of "previous existences"? If scar tissue or abnormal cervical cells disappear after a patient consults a psychic healer, does this prove that psychic forces did the job?[85]

It's this whirl of possible causes that scientists try to control in properly conducted research. By controlling these confounding factors, scientists hope to narrow the possibilities to the true cause or causes of a condition. This task requires a systematic, objective approach—something that personal experience, by definition, isn't.

It's not surprising, then, that numerous claims of the effectiveness of treatments, though affirmed by many testimonials, have been shown to be false by controlled scientific testing. Some examples: Vitamin C prevents the common cold; Laetrile (the trade name for a synthetic relative of the chemical amygdalin, found in apricot pits and other plants) fights cancer; the Feingold diet can prevent or treat attention-deficit/hyperactivity disorder in children.[86]

Enjoy a longer and healthier life with Bible Healing Plants
—TABLOID

SCIENTIFIC EVIDENCE: WHY CONTROLLED STUDIES CAN BE TRUSTED

Science is a systematic attempt to get around the limitations of personal experience. It is a set of procedures designed to keep us from fooling ourselves. By performing controlled experiments, scientists seek to ensure that what they observe is not affected by these limitations, or at least is affected as little as possible. Thus, scientific work is largely the business of not taking any one person's word for it. Scientists know that the biasing, distorting powers of their unaided experience work overtime, and prestige and authority and good intentions are no protection. So they

Immunizations and Autism

Over a dozen years ago, a scientific paper published in the medical journal *Lancet* suggested that there may be a link between autism and the children's vaccine against measles, mumps, and rubella (MMR). The study was not proof of cause and effect; it merely hinted at a possibility. Nevertheless a worldwide furor over the alleged connection began, with many parents refusing to have their children vaccinated and many others blaming the vaccine for their children's autism. The number of vaccinations in Western countries plummeted, and an increase in cases of measles followed. (Measles can be serious; every year tens of thousands of people, mostly children in developing countries, die of measles.) Eventually *Lancet* retracted the study; an independent analysis of the research showed that it was fraudulent; and a later study found no evidence of an MMR-autism connection. More recently, the National Academy of Medicine (formerly the Institute of Medicine) conducted a thorough review of all available evidence and concluded that no causal relationship exists between the MMR vaccine and autism.

The most obvious lesson here is about the perils of leaping from tenuous, preliminary research to firm conclusions. But an equally important moral to this story concerns the dangers of the post hoc fallacy. Some parents came to believe that MMR caused autism in their children because autism symptoms appeared *after their children were vaccinated*. This coincidence can occur because children are usually vaccinated around the age that signs of autism would appear. Post hoc reasoning led to an outcry against the MMR vaccine (and perhaps vaccines generally), an unknown number of unvaccinated children at risk for measles, and a dramatic surge in measles cases throughout the Western world.

try to remove the element of unsystematic personal experience from the scientific process. Science requires the use of objective measurements, not subjective judgments, wherever possible. Findings must be corroborated by other scientists and must be public evidence open to public scrutiny, not private data subject to personal confirmation. Facts must rest not on the say-so of some authority, but on objective evidence. When scientists err (as did Professor Blondlot), it's often because the limitations of the subjective creep in. When science progresses, it's in large measure because these limitations are overcome.

Controlled studies, then, are generally much better guides to the truth than anecdotal evidence is. This is so even when the anecdotal evidence is of very high quality, as it often is when it's in the form of medical case reports.

Case reports are accounts of a doctor's observations of individual patients (also called case series, case histories, and descriptive studies). They can be extremely valuable to other doctors and to medical scientists. "They are . . . invaluable documentaries that, once filed, may lead to exciting discoveries," says epidemiologist Stephen H. Gehlbach. Gehlbach goes on to note:

> Accounts of an unusual episode of poisoning or an atypical rash developing after administration of a new medication are examples of descriptive studies at their simplest. These reports alert clinicians about possible drug side effects, unusual complications of illnesses, or surprising presentations of disease.[87]

But, as Gehlbach points out, such accounts "do not provide detailed explanations for the cause of disease or offer the kind of evidence we need to evaluate the efficacy of a new treatment."[88]

Perhaps you've already guessed some of the reasons for this limitation of case reports. The variable nature of disease, the placebo effect, and overlooked causes can confound the doctor's attempt to draw firm conclusions about treatment efficacy, just as these factors confound attempts to pinpoint causes of symptom relief in our own personal experience. Though doctors monitor patients and keep records, case studies are compiled without the strict controls found in scientific studies, so confounding factors usually can't be ruled out. The doctor administered a treatment; the patient got better. But would the patient have gotten better anyway? Was it a placebo effect? Was some other factor involved? While the patient was being treated by the doctor, did the patient change his diet, his daily routine, his sleep patterns, his physical activities, his stress level? Was he taking some other treatment (maybe a self-treatment) while under the doctor's care? Case reports usually can't help us answer all these questions.

Case reports are also vulnerable to several serious biases that controlled research is better able to deal with. One is called *social desirability bias.* It refers to patients' tendency to strongly wish to respond to treatment in what they perceive as a correct way. People will sometimes report improvement in their condition after treatment simply because they think that's the proper response or because they want to please the doctor.

> *Doctors Reveal Amazing Healing Powers of Water*
> —TABLOID

Another bias can come from doctors themselves. Called *investigator bias,* it refers to the well-documented fact that investigators or clinicians sometimes see an effect in a patient because they want or expect to see it.

> One's investment in the results or anticipation of how subjects are likely to respond can easily become a self-fulfilling prophecy. This is not to impugn the integrity of investigators. Objectivity is difficult to master. It is difficult for surgeons not to find benefits from their favorite operative procedures to alleviate hemorrhoids or for social workers looking for evidence of child abuse and neglect not to uncover child maltreatment in a group known to be at high risk.[89]

Scientists use several techniques in medical research to try to minimize the effects of such biases. In case studies, bias is harder to control, and it often has sway.

We therefore reach an inevitable conclusion about the doctor's evidence:

Case studies alone generally cannot establish the effectiveness of a treatment beyond a reasonable doubt.

There's gold in them thar' hills! And the rush is on. Pandering publishers, manufacturers, drugstores, "health food" stores, pharmaceutical firms, and bookstores all profit from the misinformation and mythology.

—KURT BUTLER

This principle and the preceding one (about personal experience) are especially handy tools in thinking about proposed treatments because often the only evidence such treatments offer in their favor is case studies or personal experience.

Our senses can fool us and our minds can play tricks on us. Unfortunately, we are often unaware of our perceptual and cognitive errors because they come so naturally. They're often an unintended byproduct of the inference rules (heuristics) that served us so well in the struggle for survival. To avoid these errors, we need a method that will help us spot them. Science provides that method. In the next chapter, we will examine the scientific method in an attempt to understand how it can improve our search for knowledge.

SUMMARY

An important principle to use when evaluating weird phenomena is that just because something seems real doesn't mean that it is. Part of the reason for this caution is the constructive nature of our perceptions. We often perceive exactly what we expect to perceive, regardless of what's real, and we sometimes experience the misperception of seeing distinct forms in vague and formless stimuli. These constructive processes are notoriously active in UFO sightings, where under poor viewing conditions average people mentally transform lights in a dark sky into alien spacecraft.

Our memories are also constructive and easily influenced by all sorts of factors: stress, expectation, belief, and the introduction of new information. Added to all this is the selectivity of memory—we selectively remember certain things and ignore others, setting up a recall bias. No wonder the recall of eyewitnesses is often so unreliable.

How we conceive the data we encounter is also problematic. We often refuse to accept contrary evidence, a reluctance that can be found in just about everyone, including scientists and trained investigators. We have a tendency to believe that a very general personality description applies uniquely to ourselves, a phenomenon known as the Forer effect. The Forer effect is at work in the readings of astrology, biorhythms, fortune-telling, tarot cards, palmistry (palm reading), and psychic performances. We are often prey to confirmation bias, the tendency to look for and recognize only evidence that confirms our own views. We fall for the availability error and base our judgments on evidence that's vivid or memorable instead of reliable or trustworthy. We are sometimes led astray by the representative heuristic, the rule of thumb that like goes with like. And we are generally poor judges of probabilities and randomness, which leads us to erroneously believe that an event could not possibly be a mere coincidence.

All this points to the fact that anecdotal evidence is not a reliable guide to the truth. Our principle should be that it's reasonable to accept personal experience as reliable evidence only if there's no reason to doubt its reliability. The problems with this kind of evidence are illustrated well in people's personal attempts to judge the effectiveness of treatments and health regimens. The reality is that personal experience alone generally cannot establish the effectiveness of a treatment beyond a reasonable doubt—but controlled scientific studies can.

STUDY QUESTIONS

1. How might the constructive nature of your perceptions play a role in what you experience while you're walking at night through a graveyard said to be visited by spirits of the dead?
2. What are some of the factors that could influence the accuracy of your memory of an event that happened three years ago?
3. Let's say that an incredible coincidence occurs in your life, and your friend argues that the odds against the occurrence are so astronomical that the only explanation must be a paranormal one. What is wrong with this argument?
4. How is it possible for the prophecies of Nostradamus to appear to be highly accurate and yet not be?
5. What is the principle that explains how much trust we should put in personal experience as reliable evidence?
6. What is confirmation bias? How does it affect our thinking?
7. What is the availability error? How does it affect our thinking?
8. How do confirmation bias and the availability error lead to superstitious beliefs?
9. What is the argument from unnecessary restrictions? How can it be used to undercut supernatural or paranormal claims?
10. What is the representativeness heuristic? How does it affect our thinking?
11. Why can't personal experience alone establish the effectiveness of a treatment?
12. What is the placebo effect?

EVALUATE THESE CLAIMS. ARE THEY REASONABLE? WHY OR WHY NOT?

1. Last night in bed, I had the experience of being transported to a spaceship where I was placed on an examining table and probed with various instruments. You can't tell me that UFOs aren't real.

2. Sometimes Chinese fortune cookies can be extremely accurate. In January I opened one that said I would soon be starting a long and difficult journey, and, sure enough, in May I got into medical school.
3. I had my aura read three times and each time I learned something new. Auras must be real.
4. Magnet therapy works. I applied an ordinary magnet to my painful elbow for fifteen minutes, and the next day I was pain free.
5. Compared to automobile travel, air travel is very dangerous. Last year there were three big airliner crashes overseas. All passengers and crew perished.
6. Gun violence in schools is caused mainly by the lack of religious instruction in grades 1 through 12.

DISCUSSION QUESTIONS

1. The only way to tell whether something is real is to see if it works for you. Is this a legitimate principle?
2. In 1977, Maria Rubio of Lake Arthur, New Mexico, was cooking tortillas in her kitchen. One of them had a burn mark that resembled a human face. She concluded that it was an image of Jesus Christ, and, after the word got out, 600 to 1,000 people a day visited the shrine to the tortilla that she set up in her home. The Bible does not contain any detailed descriptions of Jesus's physical appearance. Is Mrs. Rubio justified in believing that the face she sees in the tortilla is the face of Jesus? Why or why not?
3. In a random survey, if people were asked whether one is more likely to die from asthma or a tornado, what do you think the majority would say? Why?
4. Jane wants to buy a new car and is deciding between a Mazda and a Toyota. The most important factor in her decision is reliability. Consumer surveys indicate that the Toyota is more reliable. But her Uncle Joe owns a Toyota, and it has given him nothing but trouble. So she buys the Mazda. Is Jane's conclusion reasonable? Why or why not?

FIELD PROBLEM

Some people may believe certain statements so strongly that no evidence could possibly compel them to change their minds. Are you like that? Are any of your friends?

Assignment: Examine the following statements. Pick one that you strongly believe (or make up one of your own) and ask yourself: What evidence would persuade me to change my mind about the statement? If confronted with that evidence, would I really change my mind? Would I try to find an excuse to deny or ignore the evidence? Next, try this same test on a friend.

- Heaven—a transcendent or celestial place—does exist.
- Bill Clinton was a much better president than Ronald Reagan.

- Ronald Reagan was a much better president than Bill Clinton.
- Alien spacecraft have visited Earth.
- An all-powerful, all-knowing, all-good God exists.
- I have experienced an actual instance of ESP.
- Some people can predict the future.

CRITICAL READING AND WRITING

I. Read the passage below and answer the following questions:
   1. The speaker in the passage says that she saw the Loch Ness monster. What is her evidence to support this claim?
   2. Is her claim justified? Why or why not?
   3. Are there any reasons for doubting the evidence of her personal experience? If so, what are they?
   4. Do you find her argument convincing? Why or why not?
   5. What kind of evidence when added to her observations would make her argument stronger?

II. Write a 200-word paper critiquing the argument in the passage, stating whether you think it is strong or weak and why you think that.

Passage 4

Well, the day that I saw the [Loch Ness] monster, it was the end of September 1990, and I was driving back from Inverness. I came up the hill where we came in sight of the bay, glanced out across it, and saw this large lump, is the best way to describe it. The nearest I can tell you is it looked like a boat that had turned upside down. Pretty much like that one out there, actually, same sort of size. If you took that boat and put it in the entrance to the bay, which is where I saw the monster, that's the size of it. About 30 feet in length, and nearly 10 feet in height from the water to the top of the back. It was a bright, sunny day, the water was bright blue, and it really showed up against it. It was a mixture of browns, greens, sludgy sort of colors. I looked at it on and off for a few seconds, because I was driving. Must have seen it three or four times, and the last time I looked, it was gone! (Val Moffat, eyewitness quoted in NOVA Online, "The Beast of Loch Ness," accessed December 2, 2003.)

NOTES

1. E. Feilding, W. W. Baggally, and H. Carrington, *Proceedings of the SPR* 23 (1909): 461–62, reprinted in E. Feilding, *Sittings with Eusapia Palladino and Other Studies* (New Hyde Park, NY: University Books, 1963).
2. James Alcock, *Parapsychology: Science or Magic?* (Oxford: Pergamon Press, 1981), pp. 35–37, 64.

3. The following discussion is drawn from Terence Hines, *Pseudoscience and the Paranormal* (Buffalo: Prometheus Books, 1988), pp. 168–70.
4. K. Duncker, "The Influence of Past Experience upon Perceptual Properties," *American Journal of Psychology* 52 (1939): 255–65.
5. C. M. Turnbull, "Some Observations Regarding the Experiences and Behavior of the Ba Mbuti Pygmies," *American Journal of Psychology* 74 (1961): 304–08.
6. Andrew Neher, *The Psychology of Transcendence* (Englewood Cliffs, NJ: Prentice-Hall, 1980), p. 64.
7. Kendrick Frazier, ed. *The Skeptical Inquirer* (Summer 1988): 340–43.
8. L. Guevara-Castro and L. Viele, "Dozens Say They Have Seen Christ on a Pizza Chain Billboard," *Atlanta Journal Constitution,* May 21, 1991, p. D1.
9. John R. Vokey, "Subliminal Messages," in *Psychological Sketches,* 6th ed., ed. John R. Vokey and Scott W. Allen (Lethbridge, Alberta: Psyence Ink, 2002), pp. 223–46.
10. Ibid., p. 249.
11. Carl Sagan and P. Fox, "The Canals of Mars: An Assessment after Mariner 9," *Icarus* 25 (1975): 602–12.
12. The following account draws on I. Klotz, "The N-Ray Affair," *Scientific American* 242, no. 5 (1980): 168–75.
13. Philip J. Klass, *UFOs Explained* (New York: Random House, 1974), pp. 9–14.
14. Philip J. Klass, "UFOs," in *Science and the Paranormal* (New York: Scribner's, 1981), pp. 313–15.
15. Terence Hines, *Pseudoscience and the Paranormal: A Critical Examination of the Evidence* (Prometheus Books, 1988), p. 175.
16. Philip J. Klass, *UFOs–identified*, 1968, p. 129
17. Leonard Zusne and Warren Jones, *Anomalistic Psychology: A Study of Magical Thinking,* 2nd ed. (New York: Psychology Press, 2014), p. 336.
18. Klass, *UFOs Explained,* p. 77.
19. Beth Rutherford, "A Retractor Speaks," accessed September 16, 2018, http://www.stopbadtherapy.com/retracts/beth.shtml.
20. Elizabeth F. Loftus, "The Prince of Bad Memories," *Skeptical Inquirer* 21 (March/April 1998): 24.
21. G. W. Allport and L. J. Postman, "The Basic Psychology of Rumor," *Transactions of the New York Academy of Science,* 2d ser., 8 (1945): 61–81.
22. Ted Schultz, "Voices from Beyond: The Age-Old Mystery of Channeling," in *The Fringes of Reason: A Whole Earth Catalog* (New York: Harmony Books, 1989), p. 60.
23. Martin Gardner, *Fads and Fallacies in the Name of Science* (New York: Dover, 1957), pp. 315–20.
24. Ibid.
25. B. Fischhoff and R. Beyth, "'I Knew It Would Happen': Remembered Probabilities of Once-Future Things," *Organizational Behavior and Human Performance* 120 (1972): 159–72.

26. E. F. Loftus and J. C. Palmer, "Reconstruction of Automobile Destruction: An Example of the Interaction between Language and Memory," *Journal of Verbal Learning and Verbal Behavior* 13, no. 5 (1974): 585–89.
27. E. Loftus, D. Miller, and H. Burns, "Semantic Integration of Verbal Information into a Visual Memory," *Journal of Experimental Psychology: Human Learning and Memory* 4 (1978): 19–31.
28. James Alcock, *Parapsychology-Science or Magic?: A Psychological Perspective* (Pergamon Press, 1981), p. 76.
29. Terence Hines, *Pseudoscience and the Paranormal* (Prometheus Books, 2003), p. 81.
30. Ibid.
31. Francis Bacon, *Novum Organum: Or, True Suggestions for the Interpretation of Nature*, 1884.
32. John C. Wright, "Consistency and Complexity of Response Sequences as a Function of Schedules of Noncontingent Reward," *Journal of Experimental Psychology* 63 (1962): 601–09.
33. Max Planck, *Transactions of the North American Wildlife and Natural Resources Conference* (Wildlife Management Institute, 1966), p. 383.
34. L. J. Chapman and J. P. Chapman, "The Genesis of Popular but Erroneous Psychodiagnostic Observations," *Journal of Abnormal Psychology* 72 (1967): 193–204.
35. "Failed Doomsday and Apocalyptic Predictions," *Relatively Interesting,* May 8, 2012, http://www.relativelyinteresting.com/failed-doomsday-and-apocalyptic-predictions/.
36. C. R. Snyder and R. J. Shenkel, "The P. T. Barnum Effect," *Psychology Today,* 1977.
37. David Marks, *The Psychology of the Psychic* (Prometheus Books, 1980), p. 181.
38. Neher, *Psychology of Transcendence*, p. 157.
39. Ibid., p. 18.
40. Robert Henry, *The Psychology of Transcendence* (Prentice-Hall, 1980), p. 158.
41. In these verses there is another problem, as noted by James Randi, an expert on the Nostradamus legend: Their translation is wildly inaccurate.
42. Roberts, p. 12, as cited in Neher, *Psychology of Transcendence,* p. 188.
43. Erika Cheetham, *The Prophecies of Nostradamus* (Perigee, 1974).
44. Roberts, p. 17, as cited in ibid.
45. Cheetham, p. 33, as cited in ibid.
46. Neher, *Psychology of Transcendence,* p. 159.
47. Derek Brown, "Nostradamus Foresaw the Calamity, and Other Stupid Urban Myths," accessed September 18, 2001, https://www.theguardian.com/world/2001/sep/18/september11.usa23.
48. P. N. Johnson-Laird and P. C. Wason, eds., *Thinking: Readings in Cognitive Science* (Cambridge: Cambridge University Press, 1977), pp. 143–57.

49. B. F. Skinner, "'Superstition' in the Pigeon," *Journal of Experimental Psychology* 38 (1948): 168–72.
50. P. C. Wason, "On the Failure to Eliminate Hypotheses in a Conceptual Task," *Quarterly Journal of Experimental Psychology* 12 (1960): 129–40.
51. Stuart Sutherland, *Irrationality* (New Brunswick, NJ: Rutgers University Press, 1992), p. 23.
52. S. F. Madey and T. Gilovich, "Effect of Temporal Focus on the Recall of Expectancy-Consistent and Expectancy-Inconsistent Information," *Journal of Personality and Social Psychology* 65 (1993): 458–68.
53. T. Gilovich, "Biased Evaluation and Persistence in Gambling," *Journal of Personality and Social Psychology* 44 (1983): 1110–26.
54. Thomas Gilovich, *How We Know What Isn't So* (New York: Free Press, 1991), p. 178.
55. I. W. Kelly, James Rotton, and Roger Culver, "The Moon Was Full and Nothing Happened," in *The Hundredth Monkey,* ed. Kendrick Frazier (Buffalo: Prometheus Books, 1991), p. 231.
56. B. Fischoff, P. Slovic, and S. Lichtenstein, "Fault Trees: Sensitivity of Estimated Failure Probabilities to Problem Representation," *Journal of Experimental Psychology: Human Perception and Performance* 4 (1978): 330–44.
57. Nicholas Humphrey, *Leaps of Faith* (New York: Basic Books, 1996), p. 87.
58. A. Tversky and D. Kahneman, "Extensional versus Intuitive Reasoning: The Conjunction Fallacy in Probability Judgment," *Psychological Review* 90 (1983): 293–315.
59. Sir James Frazer, *The Illustrated Golden Bough* (New York: Doubleday, 1978), pp. 36–37.
60. Ibid., pp. 39–40.
61. Robert Basil, "Graphology and Personality: Let the Buyer Beware," in Frazier, *The Hundredth Monkey,* p. 207.
62. G. Ben-Shakhar, M. Bar-Hillel, Y. Blui, E. Ben-Abba, and A. Flug, "Can Graphology Predict Occupational Success?" *Journal of Applied Psychology* 71 (1989): 645–53.
63. T. Monmaney, "Marshall's Hunch," *New Yorker* 69 (1993): 64–72.
64. David Hume, *The Natural History of Religion*, ed. by H. E. Root (Palo Alto, CA: Stanford University Press, 1957), p. 29.
65. Stewart Guthrie, *Faces in the Clouds: A New Theory of Religion* (New York: Oxford University Press, 1993).
66. F. Heider and M. Simmel, "An Experimental Study of Apparent Behavior," *American Journal of Psychology* 57 (1944): 243–59.
67. Justin L. Barrett, *Why Would Anyone Believe in God?* (Walnut Creek, CA: AltaMira Press, 2004), p. 31.
68. Scott Atran, *In Gods We Trust: The Evolutionary Landscape of Religion* (Oxford University Press, 2004).
69. Guthrie, *Faces in the Clouds*, p. 197.
70. J. M. Bering and D. F. Bjorkland, "The Natural Emergence of Afterlife Reasoning as a Developmental Regularity," *Developmental Psychology* 40 (2004): 217–33.

71. Paul Bloom, "Religion Is Natural," *Developmental Science* 10 (2007): 149.
72. Paul Bloom, "Is God an Accident?" *The Atlantic Monthly* 296 (2005): 107.
73. Guthrie, *Faces in the Clouds*, p. 200.
74. Justin Barrett, quoted in Robin Marantz-Henig, "Darwin's God," *The New York Times Magazine*, March 4, 2007, p. 20.
75. John Allen Paulos, *Innumeracy* (New York: Hill and Wang, 1988), p. 27.
76. Ibid., p. 24.
77. You can understand better why this formula works by considering a smaller number of events, say five (A, B, C, D, E). Event A can be paired with B, C, D, and E, producing four possible pairs. Event B can be paired with C, D, and E (not A, to avoid repeating a pair), producing three pairs. Event C can be paired with D and E (not A and B, to avoid repeats), and so on. So the total possible pairs (without duplicates) of five events is given by the formula $4 + 3 + 2 + 1$, or 10.
78. Marks, *The Psychology of the Psychic*, p. 166.
79. L. W. Alvarez, letter to the editors, *Science*, June 18, 1965, p. 1541.
80. Barry Singer, "To Believe or Not to Believe," in *Science and the Paranormal*, ed. George Abell and Barry Singer (New York: Scribner's, 1981), p. 18.
81. Kurt Butler, *A Consumer's Guide to "Alternative Medicine"* (Buffalo: Prometheus Books, 1992), pp. 182–84.
82. Howard Brody, *Placebos and the Philosophy of Medicine* (Chicago: University of Chicago Press, 1980), pp. 8–24. See also Harold J. Cornacchia and Stephen Barrett, *Consumer Health: A Guide to Intelligent Decisions* (St. Louis: Mosby–Year Book, 1993), pp. 58–59.
83. Zusne and Jones, *Anomalistic Psychology*, p. 60.
84. American Cancer Society, *Dubious Cancer Treatment* (Baltimore: Port City Press, 1991), pp. 24, 75–76.
85. Stephen Barrett and William T. Jarvis, *The Health Robbers: A Close Look at Quackery in America* (Prometheus Books, 1993), p. 58.
86. See Charles W. Marshall, "Can Megadoses of Vitamin C Help against Colds?" *Nutrition Forum*, September/October 1992, pp. 33–36; Office of Technology Assessment, Congress of the United States, *Unconventional Cancer Treatments* (Washington, DC: U.S. Government Printing Office, 1990), pp. 102–07; and E. H. Wender and M. A. Lipton, "The National Advisory Committee on Hyperkinesis and Food Additives—Final Report to The Nutrition Foundation" (Washington, DC: The Nutrition Foundation, 1980).
87. Stephen H. Gehlbach, *Interpreting the Medical Literature: Practical Epidemiology for Clinicians* (New York: Macmillan, 1988), p. 14.
88. Ibid. The exceptions to this rule are rare, occurring only when cause-and-effect relationships are clear-cut and dramatic. One example is the effect of insulin on diabetic hyperglycemia; another is the effect of penicillin on pneumococcal pneumonia. These effects were accepted by scientists without demands for rigorously controlled studies.
89. Ibid., p. 90.

SIX

Science and Its Pretenders

> *Scientists are peeping Toms at the keyhole of eternity.*
>
> —ARTHUR KOESTLER

THE SCIENTIFIC METHOD is the most powerful tool we have for acquiring knowledge. By its means we've discovered the structure of the atom and the composition of the stars, the causes of disease and cures for infection, the blueprint for life and the mechanisms of growth. Use of the scientific method is not confined to scientists, however. Whenever we try to solve a problem by systematically evaluating the plausibility of various solutions, we are proceeding scientifically. To improve our problem-solving ability, then, it's useful to know what's involved in conducting a scientific investigation.

Scientists use the scientific method to acquire knowledge about the nature of reality. Many people don't think of science as a search for the truth, however. Instead, they think of it as a means for creating commodities. When they think of science, they think of such things as televisions, DVDs, and microwave ovens.

Although scientific knowledge is used in the manufacture of these items, the production of such goods is not the goal of science. Science seeks to understand the general principles that govern the universe–not to produce gadgets.

Gadget production is the province of technology, which applies scientific knowledge to practical problems. The line between science and technology is often difficult to draw, because the same persons may engage in both pursuits. Scientists, in conducting their investigations, may fabricate special apparatus, while technologists, in designing their mechanisms, may perform systematic experiments that lead to scientific discoveries. In general, however, we may say that science produces knowledge while technology produces goods. Scientists are primarily interested in knowing how something works while technologists are primarily interested in making something that works. The best indication for scientists that they know how something works is that they can successfully predict what it will do. Thus science seeks to understand the world by identifying general principles that are both explanatory and predictive.[1]

The dangers that face the world can, every one of them, be traced back to science. The salvations that may save the world will, every one of them, be traced back to science.

—ISAAC ASIMOV

SCIENCE AND DOGMA

It's tempting to say that what distinguishes science from all other modes of inquiry is that science takes nothing for granted. But this statement is not strictly true, for there is at least one proposition that must be accepted before any scientific investigation can take place–that the world is *publicly understandable.* This proposition means at least three things: (1) The world has a determinate structure; (2) we can know that structure; and (3) this knowledge is available to everyone. Let's examine each of these claims in turn.

It is not what the man of science believes that distinguishes him, but how and why he believes it.

—BERTRAND RUSSELL

If the world had no determinate structure–if it were formless and nondescript–it couldn't be understood scientifically because it couldn't be explained or predicted. Only where there is an identifiable pattern can there be explanation or prediction. If the world lacked a discernible pattern, it would be beyond our ken.

But a determinate structure is not enough for scientific understanding; we also need a means of apprehending it. As we've seen, humans possess at least four faculties that put us in touch with the world: perception, introspection, memory, and reason. There may be others, but at present, these are the only ones that have proven themselves to be reliable. They're not 100 percent reliable, but the beauty of the scientific method is that it can determine when they're not.

Science commits suicide when it adopts a creed.

—THOMAS HENRY HUXLEY

The scientific method is self-correcting, and as a result it is our most reliable guide to the truth.[2]

What makes scientific understanding public is that the information upon which it is based is, in principle, available to everyone. All people willing to make the appropriate observations can see for themselves whether any particular claim is true. No one has to take anybody's word for anything. Everything is out in the open, and it is open season on everything. To be accepted as true, a scientific claim must be able to withstand the closest scrutiny, for only if it does can we be reasonably sure that it's not mistaken.

SCIENCE AND SCIENTISM

Science is the great antidote to the poison of enthusiasm and superstition.
—ADAM SMITH

Some critics of science say that far from being an impartial search for the truth, science is an imperialistic ideology that champions a particular worldview, namely, a mechanistic, materialistic, and atomistic one. This ideology is often referred to as *scientism.* Scientism, they claim, is committed to the view that the world is a great machine, composed of minuscule particles of matter that interact with each other like tiny billiard balls. Such a world is inimical to human flourishing because it treats us like machines. Stripping us of our dignity and humanity, it denies the importance of our thoughts, feelings, and desires. The devastating effects of this approach to reality, they claim, can be witnessed by anyone who turns on the nightly news.[3]

What we need, these critics suggest, is a different worldview, one that is more organic, holistic, and process oriented. The world should be viewed not as a giant machine composed of isolated entities, but as a giant organism composed of interdependent processes. Only by adopting this sort of worldview can we regain the social, psychological, and ecological balance necessary for continued survival on this planet.[4]

While it may be true that, at any one time, a particular worldview is dominant in the scientific community, it would be a mistake to identify science with any particular worldview. Science is a method of discerning the truth, not a particular body of truths. It is a way of solving problems, not a particular solution to them. Just as you cannot identify science with its applications, so you cannot identify it with its results. The worldviews held by scientists have changed radically over the years: The worldview of quantum mechanics is far from the mechanistic worldview of the seventeenth century.

Those critics who believe that we should adopt a more organic and holistic worldview do so on the grounds that it offers a more accurate description of reality than does a mechanistic and atomistic one. That may well be true, but the only way to find out is to determine whether there is any evidence to that effect, and the best way to make such a determination is to use the scientific method. The scientific method provides the best means of assessing competing theories.

SCIENTIFIC METHODOLOGY

The scientific method is often said to consist of the following four steps:

1. Observe
2. Induce general hypotheses or possible explanations for what we have observed
3. Deduce specific things that must also be true if our hypothesis is true
4. Test the hypothesis by checking out the deduced implications[5]

Science is nothing but developed perception, interpreted intent, common sense rounded out and minutely articulated.
—GEORGE SANTAYANA

But this conception of the scientific method provides a misleading picture of scientific inquiry. Scientific investigation can occur only after a hypothesis has been formulated, and induction is not the only way of formulating a hypothesis.

A moment's reflection reveals that data collection in the absence of a hypothesis has little or no scientific value. Suppose, for example, that one day you decide to become a scientist, and having read a standard account of the scientific method, you set out to collect some data. Where should you begin? Should you start by cataloging all the items in your room, measuring them, weighing them, noting their color and composition, and so on? Should you then take these items apart and catalog their parts in a similar manner? Should you note the relationship of these objects to one another, to the fixtures in the room, to objects outside? Clearly, there's enough data in your room to keep you busy for the rest of your life.

How odd it is that anyone should not see that all observation must be for or against some view if it is to be of any service!
—CHARLES DARWIN

From a scientific point of view, collecting these data wouldn't be very useful because it wouldn't help us evaluate any scientific hypotheses. The goal of scientific inquiry is to identify principles that are both explanatory and predictive. Without a hypothesis to guide our investigations, there is no guarantee that the information gathered would help us accomplish that goal.

Philosopher Karl Popper graphically demonstrated the importance of hypotheses for observation:

> Twenty-five years ago I tried to bring home the same point to a group of physics students in Vienna by beginning a lecture with the following instructions: "Take pencil and paper; carefully observe, and write down what you have observed!" They asked, of course, what I wanted them to observe. Clearly the instruction, "Observe!" is absurd.

(It is not even idiomatic, unless the object of the transitive verb can be taken as understood.) Observation is always selective. It needs a chosen object, a definite task, an interest, a point of view, a problem.[6]

Scientific inquiry begins with a problem—why did something occur? How are two or more things related? What is something made of? An observation, of course, is needed to recognize that a problem exists, but any such observation will have been guided by an earlier hypothesis.[7] Hypotheses are needed for scientific observation because they tell us what to look for—they help us distinguish relevant from irrelevant information.

Scientific hypotheses indicate what will happen if certain conditions are realized. By producing these conditions in the laboratory or observing them in the field, we can assess the credibility of the hypotheses proposed. If the predicted results occur, we have reason to believe that the hypothesis in question is true. If not, we have reason to believe that it's false.

In scientific work, those who refuse to go beyond fact rarely get as far as fact.
—THOMAS H. HUXLEY

Although hypotheses are designed to account for data, they rarely can be derived from data. Contrary to what the traditional account of the scientific method would have us believe, inductive thinking is rarely used to generate hypotheses. It can be used to formulate certain elementary hypotheses such as this one: Every fish ever caught in this lake has been a bass; therefore, every fish that ever will be caught in this lake will be a bass. But it can't be used to generate the more sophisticated hypotheses scientists commonly use because scientific hypotheses often postulate entities that aren't mentioned in the data. The atomic theory of matter, for example, postulates the existence of atoms. All of the data upon which the atomic theory rests, however, can be described without mentioning atoms. Since scientific hypotheses often introduce concepts not found in their data, there can be no mechanical procedure for constructing them.[8]

Hypotheses are created, not discovered, and the process of their creation is just as open-ended as the process of artistic creation. There is no formula for generating hypotheses. That's not to say that the process of theory construction is irrational, but it *is* to say that the process is not mechanical. In searching for the best explanation, scientists are guided by certain criteria, such as testability, fruitfulness, scope, simplicity, and conservatism. Fulfilling any one of these criteria, however, is neither a necessary nor a sufficient condition for being a good hypothesis. Science therefore is just as much a product of the imagination as it is of reason.

Science is our century's art.
—HORACE FREELAND JUDSON

Even the most beautifully crafted hypotheses, however, can turn out to be false. That's why scientists insist on checking all hypotheses against reality. Let's examine how this check might be done in a particular kind of scientific work—medical research.

In medical research, clinical studies offer the strongest and clearest support for any claim that a treatment is effective because they can establish cause and effect beyond a reasonable doubt. Clinical trials allow scientists to control extraneous variables and test one factor at a time. Properly conducted clinical trials have become the gold standard of medical evidence, having proven themselves again and again.

In clinical trials designed to test treatment efficacy, an experimental group of subjects receives the treatment in question. A control group that's as similar to the experimental group as possible doesn't get the treatment. (Use of a control group makes the study a *controlled trial.*) Scientists then compare pertinent differences between the two groups to verify whether the treatment has any effect. The control group is essential. Without it, there's generally no way to tell whether the treatment really worked. With no control group, it's usually not possible to know whether the subjects' condition would have changed even without treatment, or that some factor besides the treatment (like the subjects' lifestyle) was responsible for any positive results, or that the placebo effect was at work, or that some change in the subjects' behavior after getting the treatment was what made the difference. By comparing results in the experimental group to those in the control group, researchers can determine whether the experimental treatment was more effective than would be expected because of these other factors alone.

> *The most important quality of the scientific method is its capacity to eliminate bias. That's what randomisation, blinding, proper sampling and so on is all about. That's where almost all non-scientific medicine breaks down.*
>
> —PATRICK BRAMWELL-WESLEY

To minimize confounding factors, subjects in the control group often receive a placebo. (Such a study is then referred to as a *placebo-controlled trial.*) Placebos are given as if they're effective therapy because, as mentioned in the previous chapter, many people experience signs of improvement even when they're given a worthless treatment (the placebo effect). Scientists compare the results in the experimental group with that in the placebo-control group. If the experimental treatment is truly effective—and not merely a placebo itself—it should perform much better than the placebo.

Frequently, especially in drug testing, the control group gets not a placebo but an already proven treatment. The purpose of the study is to determine if the new treatment works better than the established, or standard, one.

Another extremely important element in clinical trials is *blinding*—a practice used to ensure that subjects (and, if possible, researchers) don't know which subjects are getting the experimental treatment or the placebo. This practice is followed to avoid having knowledge of the experiment taint the results. If subjects know

Benjamin Franklin and the Origin of Blind Testing

Benjamin Franklin's most famous scientific accomplishment is the discovery of electricity. But perhaps his most important is the invention of the blind controlled experiment, which remains the gold standard against which all other experimental protocols are compared.

In 1784, King Louis XVI of France commissioned a group of scientists, headed by Franklin, to investigate the claims of Franz Anton Mesmer, the father of hypnotism. Mesmer claimed to be able to heal various physical and mental ailments by manipulating an invisible magnetic fluid, known as *animal magnetism,* which flows through the bodies of all animals, much as traditional Indian doctors claim to heal their patients by manipulating the life force they call "prana" and traditional Chinese doctors, "qi." Mesmer believed that various illnesses were caused by the obstruction of the flow of animal magnetism through the body. By infusing additional animal magnetism into his patients, the obstruction could be overcome and the natural flow restored.

When working one-on-one with his patients, Mesmer would "mesmerize" them by sitting directly across from them, knee to knee, holding their thumbs in his hands and staring deeply into their eyes. He would then direct animal magnetism into their bodies, in the same way therapeutic touch practitioners do today, by moving his hands in the air over the affected region. In this way, Mesmer could induce in his patients feelings of heat or pain that sometimes led to a "crisis" in which the patient would go into a convulsive fit signaling that the treatment had worked and the blockage had been dislodged.

To determine whether this fluid really existed or was just a figment of Mesmer's (and his patients') imaginations, Franklin's commission identified subjects who seemed particularly sensitive to animal magnetism. They then blindfolded them and had a magnetic healer direct the fluid to specific parts of their bodies. When blindfolded, however, the subjects could not correctly identify which part of the body it was directed upon.[9] In another series of experiments, the subjects were blindfolded and made to believe that a healer was in the room when none in fact was. Nevertheless, they felt the

Finding the occasional straw of truth awash in a great ocean of confusion and bamboozle requires intelligence, vigilance, dedication and courage.

—Carl Sagan

which therapy is the placebo and which the true treatment, some of them may feel better when they get the treatment whether it's truly effective or not. Or if they know they've received a placebo, they may change their health habits to compensate. Or they may even try to obtain the true therapy on their own. Similar problems can affect the scientists conducting the study. If researchers know who received which treatment, they may unconsciously bias the test data. Well-designed clinical trials are *double-blind,* which means that neither the subjects nor the scientists know who's getting which treatment.

Conducting medical research is exacting work, and many things can go wrong—and often do. Several scientific reviews of medical studies have concluded that a large proportion of published studies are seriously flawed. (In the words of one review: "The mere fact that research reports are published, even in the most prestigious journals, is no guarantee of their quality."[10] An expert on the medical literature effects of being magnetized. The commission concluded, therefore, that the effect was the result of the imagination, not of the actions of an invisible fluid.

In their most convincing experiment, the commission had Mesmer's protégé, Charles Deslon, magnetize a tree. According to Mesmer's theory, a sensitive enough person would be able to detect its elevated magnetism. So as not to prejudice the experiment, the commission had Deslon identify a suitably sensitive subject (in this case, a 12-year-old boy). The commissioners then blindfolded him and led him to the wooded area that contained the magnetized tree. He was placed in front of four different nonmagnetized trees one at a time, and at the last one he had a crisis where "he lost consciousness, his limbs stiffened & he was carried to a nearby lawn where M. Deslon gave him first aid & revived him." The commission concluded: "The result of this experiment is totally contrary to magnetism. . . . Had the young man not felt anything, even under the magnetized tree, it could have been said that he was not sensitive enough, at least on that day: but the young man fell into a crisis under a non-magnetized tree; consequently it is an effect which has no physical cause, & which can have no cause other than the imagination."[11] The commission's report was widely circulated, and Mesmer was forced to leave Paris in 1785. He died in relative obscurity in 1815.

In these first "blind" controlled experiments, the subjects were literally blind because they had a blindfold over their eyes. Nowadays, any experiment in which the subject doesn't know whether he or she has come into contact with the object under investigation is referred to as a blind experiment.

Although the commission's experiments were blind, they were not double blind, because the commissioners themselves knew whether the subjects were in the presence of a source of magnetic fluid. Since experimenters can give subjects unconscious clues as to whether the object in question is present, a double-blind experiment, where even the experimenters are in the dark about the object's presence, are an even more reliable form of testing.

cautions, "the odds are good that the authors [of published clinical research] have arrived at invalid conclusions."[12]) Confounding variables and bias may creep in and skew results. The sample studied may be too small or not representative. The statistical analysis of data may be faulty. In rare cases, the data may even turn out to be faked or massaged. There may be many other detected or undetected inadequacies, and often these problems are serious enough to cripple a study and cast substantial doubt on its conclusions.

To minimize this potential for error, inadequacy, or fraud, medical scientists seek replication—they repeat the experiment to see if they get the same result. Several studies yielding essentially the same results can render a hypothesis more probable than would a lone study. "Two studies seldom have identical sources of error or bias," says epidemiologist Thomas Vogt. "With three or four studies, the chance is even less that the same flaws are shared."[13] Replication means that evidence for or against a certain treatment generally accumulates slowly. Despite the impression often left by the media, medical breakthroughs arising out of a single study are extremely rare.

Science is intelligence in action with no holds barred.
—P. W. BRIDGMAN

It should be clear from this sketch of medical research why the scientific method is such an effective means of acquiring knowledge. Knowledge, you will recall, requires the absence of reasonable doubt. By formulating their hypotheses precisely and controlling their observations carefully, scientists attempt to eliminate as many sources of doubt as possible. They can't remove them all, but often they can remove enough of them to give us knowledge.

Not all sciences can perform controlled experiments, because not all natural phenomena can be controlled. Much as we might like to, there's little we can do about earthquakes, volcanoes, and sinkholes, let alone comets, meteors, and asteroids. So geological and astronomical hypotheses can't usually be tested in the laboratory. They can be tested in the field, however. By looking for the conditions specified in their hypotheses, geologists and astronomers can determine whether the events predicted actually occur.

Since many legitimate sciences don't perform controlled experiments, the scientific method can't be identified with the experimental method. In fact, the scientific method can't be identified with *any* particular procedure because there are many different ways to assess the credibility of a hypothesis. In general, *any procedure that serves systematically to eliminate reasonable grounds for doubt can be considered scientific.*

You don't have to be a scientist to use the scientific method. In fact, many of us use it every day; as biologist Thomas H. Huxley realized, "Science is simply common sense at its best—that is, rigidly accurate in observation, and merciless to fallacy in logic."[14] When getting the right answer is important, we do everything we can to ensure that both our evidence and our explanations are as complete and accurate as possible. In so doing, we are using the scientific method.

CONFIRMING AND REFUTING HYPOTHESES

Science is organized common sense where many a beautiful theory was killed by an ugly fact.
—THOMAS H. HUXLEY

The results of scientific inquiry are never final and conclusive but are always provisional and open. No scientific hypothesis can be conclusively confirmed because the possibility of someday finding evidence to the contrary can't be ruled out. Scientific hypotheses always go beyond the information given. They not only explain what has been discovered; they also predict what will be discovered. Since there's no guarantee that these predictions will come true, we can never be absolutely sure that a scientific hypothesis is true.

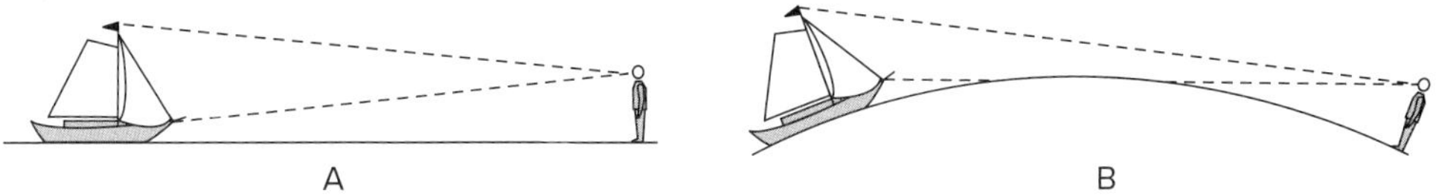

In a world where light travels in straight lines, Figure A shows what we should see if the Earth is flat, while Figure B shows what we should see if the Earth is round.

Just as we can never conclusively confirm a scientific hypothesis, we can never conclusively refute one either. There is a widespread belief that negative results prove a hypothesis false. This belief would be true if predictions followed from individual hypotheses alone, but they don't. Predictions can be derived from a hypothesis only in conjunction with a background theory. This background theory provides information about the objects under study as well as the apparatus used to study them. If a prediction turns out to be false, we can always save the hypothesis by modifying the background theory. As philosopher Philip Kitcher notes:

> Individual scientific claims do not, and cannot, confront the evidence one by one. Rather . . . "hypotheses are tested in bundles." . . . We can only test relatively large bundles of claims. What this means is that when our experiments go awry we are not logically compelled to select any particular claim as the culprit. We can always save a cherished hypothesis from refutation by rejecting (however implausibly) one of the other members of the bundle.[15]

To see this point, let's examine Christopher Columbus's claim that the Earth is round.

Both Christopher Columbus and Nicholas Copernicus rejected the flat Earth hypothesis on the grounds that its predictions were contrary to experience. They argued that if the Earth were flat, all parts of a ship should disappear from view at the same rate as it sails out to sea. But that's not what is observed. To someone onshore, the lower part of a ship disappears before the upper part. As a result, they concluded that the Earth must not be flat. Furthermore, they argued, if the Earth were round, the lower part of a ship would disappear before the upper part. Because this is what is observed, the latter hypothesis is the more credible one.

But if the Earth were flat, all parts of a ship would fade from view at the same rate only if light traveled in straight lines. If it traveled in curved lines, concave upward, the lower part of a ship could well disappear from view before the upper part. As a ship sailed farther out to sea, the light from the lower part would curve into the ocean before the light from the upper part did, thus making the lower part invisible before the upper part.[16] So we can maintain the view that the Earth is flat as long as we're willing to change our view of the

The Duhem Hypothesis

Pierre Duhem, a French philosopher of science, was perhaps the first to realize that hypotheses cannot be tested in isolation. Harvard philosopher Willard Van Orman Quine puts Duhem's insight this way: "Hypotheses meet the tribunal of experience as a corporate body." Here's how Duhem put it:

> People generally think that each one of the hypotheses employed in Physics can be taken in isolation, checked by experiment, then when many varied tests have established its validity, given a definitive place in the system of Physics. In reality, this is not the case. Physics is not a machine which lets itself be taken apart; we cannot try each piece in isolation, and in order to adjust it, wait until its solidity has been carefully checked; physical science is a system that must be taken as a whole; it is an organism in which one part cannot be made to function without the parts that are most remote from it being called into play, some more so than others, but all to some degree. If something goes wrong, if some discomfort is felt in the functioning of the organism, the physicist will have to ferret out through its effect on the entire system which organ needs to be remedied or modified without the possibility of isolating this organ and examining it apart. The watchmaker to whom you give a watch that has stopped separates all the wheelworks and examines them one by one until he finds the part that is defective or broken; the doctor to whom a patient appears cannot dissect him in order to establish his diagnosis; he has to guess the seat and cause of the ailment solely by inspecting disorders affecting the whole body. Now, the physicist concerned with remedying a limping theory resembles the doctor and not the watchmaker.[17]

nature of light. In general, any hypothesis can be maintained in the face of seemingly adverse evidence if we're willing to make enough alterations in our background beliefs. Consequently, no hypothesis can be conclusively refuted.

In a world where light travels in curved lines, Figure C shows what we should see if a ship is close by, and Figure D shows what we should see if the ship is farther away.

It is not true, however, that every hypothesis is as good as every other. Although no amount of evidence logically compels us to reject a hypothesis, maintaining a hypothesis in the face of adverse evidence can be manifestly unreasonable. So even if we cannot conclusively say that a hypothesis is false, we can often conclusively say that it's unreasonable.

The flat Earth hypothesis, for example, is manifestly unreasonable—and yet it has defenders to this day. Although the voyages of Columbus and other seafaring explorers nearly killed the theory in

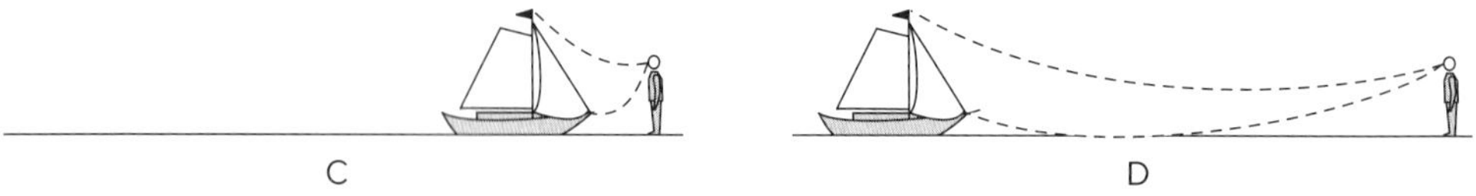

the fifteenth century, it was resurrected in England in 1849 by an itinerant lecturer who called himself Parallax (his real name was Samuel Birley Rowbotham). The world, he argued, is a flat disk with the North Pole at its center and a 150-foot wall of ice—the South Pole—encircling its perimeter. According to Parallax, those who sail around the world simply travel in a big circle. What makes the lower part of a ship disappear before the upper part is atmospheric refraction and what he called the *zetetic law of perspective.*[18]

Exactly what the zetetic law of perspective is, is unclear. But its use by Rowbotham is instructive, for it illustrates a popular method for shielding hypotheses from adverse evidence: constructing *ad hoc hypotheses.* A hypothesis threatened by recalcitrant data can often be saved by postulating entities or properties that account for the data. Such a move is legitimate if there's an independent means of verifying their existence. If there is no such means, the hypothesis is ad hoc.

In days of old, When Knights were bold, And science not invented, The Earth was flat, And that was that, With no man discontented.

—ENGLISH VERSE

Ad hoc literally means "for this case only." It's not simply that a hypothesis is designed to account for a particular phenomenon that makes it ad hoc (if that were the case, *all* hypotheses would be ad hoc). What makes a hypothesis ad hoc is that it can't be verified independently of the phenomenon it's supposed to explain.

For example, by 1844, it was known that the planet Uranus didn't follow the orbit predicted by Newton's theories of gravity and planetary motion. The observed orbit differed from the predicted orbit by two minutes of arc, a discrepancy much greater than that of any other known planet. In 1845, the astronomer Urbain Jean Joseph Leverrier hypothesized that the gravitational force of an unknown planet affected Uranus's motion. Using Newton's theories of gravity and motion, he calculated the planet's position. On the basis of those calculations, he requested that astronomer Johann Gottfried Galle in Berlin search a particular region of the sky for it. In less than an hour after Galle began his search, he noticed something that was not on his charts. When he checked again the next night, it had moved a considerable distance. He had discovered the planet that we now call Neptune!

If the aberrant orbit of Uranus had not been accounted for, Newton's theory would have been in jeopardy. So Leverrier's postulation of another planet can be seen as an attempt to save Newton's theory from negative evidence. But his hypothesis was not ad hoc, for it could be independently verified. If he had claimed, however, that some unknown and undetectable (occult) force was responsible for Uranus's erratic behavior, that would have been an ad hoc hypothesis. For, by definition, there would be no way to confirm the existence of such a force.

The Flat Earthers Are Back!

We've known for some 2,500 years that the Earth is spherical because that fact provides the best explanation of a wide range of data—not least of which is the observation that hulls of ships disappear before their masts as they sail out to sea. In the fourth century BCE, Aristotle noted that different constellations of stars are seen in different places on Earth, that as one travels south, the southern constellations rise higher in the sky, and that the shadow of the Earth on the moon during a lunar eclipse is round[19]—none of which would happen if the Earth were flat but all of which make sense if the Earth is spherical. In the third century BCE, Eratosthenes learned that during the summer solstice, the sun was directly overhead at noon in Syrene, Egypt, but still cast a shadow in Alexandria. Assuming that the sun's rays are coming in at the same angle in both cities, Eratosthenes realized that the Earth must be spherical. He went on to accurately calculate the circumference of the Earth using nothing more than a stick, the angle of the shadow cast by the stick in Alexandria, and the distance from Syrene to Alexandria. In the sixteenth century, Ferdinand Magellan became the first to sail around the Earth, thus providing direct evidence of the Earth's sphericity. In the twentieth century, of course, not only have we traveled to the moon and taken pictures of the Earth, but we have put thousands of satellites in orbit around the Earth.

And yet, there are still people who believe the Earth is flat, including hip-hop star B.o.B., basketball star Kyrie Irving, and rocketeer Mike Hughes. So determined was Mike Hughes to see for himself that the Earth is round that he built a steam-powered rocket to launch himself into the sky. On March 24, 2018, the rocket took off, reached an altitude of 1,875 feet, and parachuted back to Earth. Unfortunately, Hughes didn't get high enough to observe the curvature of the Earth. But that has not deterred him. He plans on building a "rockoon"—a rocket launched from a balloon—to reach the requisite altitude.[20]

B.o.B., Irving, and Hughes are not alone in believing the Earth is flat. A survey conducted by YouGov in April 2018 found that about 2 percent of Americans believe the Earth is flat.[21] Of that 2 percent, 52 percent said they did so for religious reasons. This is not surprising because belief in a flat Earth has long

When a scientific theory starts relying on ad hoc hypotheses to be saved from adverse data, it becomes unreasonable to maintain belief in that theory. The phlogiston theory of heat provides a case in point.

The scientific study of heat began in earnest shortly after Galileo's invention of the thermometer (or *thermoscope,* as he called it) in 1593. Over the years it was discovered that different substances absorb heat at different rates, that different substances change state (solid, liquid, gas) at different temperatures, and that different substances expand at different rates when heated. To explain these phenomena, German chemist Georg Ernst Stahl proposed in the late seventeenth century been associated with a literal reading of the Bible. Although the Bible never explicitly says that the Earth is flat, some verses are taken to imply that it is, like Daniel 4:10–11: "I saw, and behold a tree in the midst of the earth, and the height thereof was great. The tree grew, and was strong, and the height thereof reached unto heaven, and the sight thereof to the end of all the earth." Only if the Earth were flat could you see a tree from every point on it. Others claim that the Bible tells us that the Earth is a sphere, citing verses like Isaiah 40:22: "It is he that sitteth upon the circle of the earth, and the inhabitants thereof are as grasshoppers; that stretcheth out the heavens as a curtain, and spreadeth them out as a tent to dwell in."[22] Many of the early church founders such as Saints Basil, Ambrose, and Augustine took the Earth to be spherical. By the eighth century, the acceptance of a spherical Earth was so widespread that "no cosmographer worthy of note has called into question the sphericity of the Earth."[23]

Our worldview is an interdependent and interlocking web of beliefs. Change one, and you usually have to change others or the whole structure collapses. Accepting the belief that the Earth is flat requires rejecting many other beliefs we hold, like the belief that stars are extremely distant objects. In order to account for the shifting position of southern constellations as we travel south, flat earthers claim that stars "are small and a few thousand miles above the sea level of the earth."[24] For them, the view that stars are many times bigger than the Earth and light-years away from us is part of an elaborate hoax. People who study the heavens—astronomers, astrophysicists, cosmologists, and the like—supposedly know the truth, but they are keeping it from us. Why? According to Charles Johnson, the late president of the Flat Earth Society: to replace religion with science.[25] Scientists have been espousing the spherical Earth theory for millennia. It stretches the bounds of credulity to think that so many people could have been involved in so massive a coverup and no one leaked it to the press. It's hard enough for one person to keep a secret, let alone thousands for centuries. There simply is no evidence for such a conspiracy. Since the flat Earth theory makes no sense without one, it shouldn't be hard to tell who the deluded party is here.

that all combustible substances and metals contain an invisible substance that came to be known as *phlogiston.*

Phlogiston was considered to be an elastic fluid composed of particles that repel one another. (This explained why things expand when heated.) These particles were thought to be attracted to particles of other substances with different strengths. (This explained why some things heat faster than others.) When particles of phlogiston come into contact with particles of another substance, they supposedly combine to form a new state of matter. (This explained why ice turns into water when heated.) Phlogiston also seemed to explain such mysteries as why a substance turns to ash when burned (it loses phlogiston); why a metallic oxide turns back into a metal when heated with charcoal (it gains phlogiston); and why pounding on a substance can make it expand (it releases stored phlogiston). Because the phlogiston theory seemed to explain so much, it became the dominant theory of combustion in the eighteenth century.

It always had its detractors, however, for phlogiston was a very mysterious substance. Not only was it colorless and odorless; it was weightless as well. Even though phlogiston was supposed to flow into substances that were heated, careful experiments had found that increases in temperature did not produce increases in weight. Phlogiston was also thought to flow out of substances that were burned. What ultimately led to the theory's demise, however, was the discovery that some substances actually gain weight when burned. French chemist Antoine Lavoisier found that when tin was burned, for example, the resulting metallic oxide weighed more than the original tin. If phlogiston were lost during burning, he argued, this weight gain wouldn't be possible.

Defenders of the phlogiston theory tried to account for this phenomenon by hypothesizing that the phlogiston in tin possessed negative weight, so that when it was lost, the tin gained weight. But this hypothesis was soon seen for what it really was—a desperate attempt to save the theory from the facts. Unlike Leverrier's postulation of the existence of the planet that was named Neptune, there was no way to independently confirm or refute the negative weight hypothesis. It was ad hoc in the truest sense of the term.

The moral of this story is that for a hypothesis to increase our knowledge, there must be some way to test it, for if there isn't, we have no way of telling whether or not the hypothesis is true.

CRITERIA OF ADEQUACY

The aim of science is not to open the door to everlasting wisdom, but to set a limit on everlasting error.
—Bertolt Brecht

To explain something is to offer a hypothesis that helps us understand it. For example, we can explain why a penny left outside turns green by offering the hypothesis that the penny is made out of copper and that when copper oxidizes, it turns green. But for any set of facts, it's possible to devise any number of hypotheses to account for them. Suppose that someone wanted to know what makes fluorescent lights work. One hypothesis is that inside each tube is a little gremlin who creates light (sparks) by striking his pickax against the side of the tube. In addition to the one gremlin hypothesis, there is the two-gremlin hypothesis, the three-gremlin hypothesis, and so on. Because there is always more than one hypothesis to account for any set of facts and because no set of facts can conclusively confirm or refute any hypothesis, we must appeal to something besides the facts in order to decide which explanation is the best. What we appeal to are *criteria of adequacy.* As we saw in Chapter 3, these criteria are used in any inference to the best explanation to determine how well a hypothesis accomplishes the goal of increasing our understanding.

Hypotheses produce understanding by systematizing and unifying our knowledge. They bring order and harmony to facts that may have seemed disjointed and unrelated. The extent to which a hypothesis systematizes and unifies our knowledge is determined by how well it meets the criteria of adequacy. In its search for understanding, science tries to identify those hypotheses that best meet these criteria. As anthropologist Marvin Harris puts it: "The aim of scientific research is to formulate explanatory theories which are (1) predictive (or retrodictive), (2) testable (or falsifiable), (3) parsimonious [simple], (4) of broad scope, and (5) integratable or cumulative within a coherent and expanding corpus of theories."[26] The better a hypothesis meets these criteria, the more understanding it produces. Let's take a closer look at how these criteria work.

Testability

The practical effect of a belief is the real test of its soundness.

—James A. Froude

Since science seeks understanding, it's interested only in those hypotheses that can be tested—if a hypothesis can't be tested, there is no way to determine whether it's true or false. Hypotheses, however, can't be tested in isolation, for as we've seen, hypotheses have observable consequences only in the context of a background theory. So to be testable, a hypothesis, in conjunction with a background theory, must predict something more than what is predicted by the background theory alone.[27] If a hypothesis doesn't go beyond the background theory, it doesn't expand our knowledge and hence is scientifically uninteresting.

Take the gremlin hypothesis, for example. To qualify as scientific, there must be some test we can perform—other than turning on the lights—to detect the presence of gremlins. Whether there is such a test will depend on what the hypothesis tells us about the gremlins. If it tells us that they are visible to the naked eye, it can be tested by simply breaking open a fluorescent light and looking for them. If it tells us that they are invisible but sensitive to heat and capable of emitting sounds, it can be tested by putting a fluorescent light in boiling water and listening for tiny screams. But if it tells us that they are incorporeal or so shy that any attempt to detect them makes them disappear, it can't be tested and hence is not scientific.

Falsification and Psychoanalysis

Many writers have concurred with one of Popper's assertions, which is that psychoanalysis is not a legitimate scientific theory because it can't be falsified. No observation or experimental test can show the theory to be false because psychoanalysts can always invent a just-so story to account for any possible behavior. Popper explains his dissatisfaction with psychoanalysis as follows:

> The Freudian analysts emphasized that their theories were constantly verified by their "clinical observations." As for Adler, I was much impressed by a personal experience. Once, in 1919, I reported to him a case which to me did not seem particularly Adlerian, but which he found no difficulty in analyzing in terms of his theory of inferiority feelings, although he had not even seen the child. . . . But this means very little, I reflected, since every conceivable case could be interpreted in the light of Adler's theory, or equally of Freud's. I may illustrate this by two very different examples of human behavior: that of a man who pushes a child into the water with the intention of drowning it; and that of a man who sacrifices his life in an attempt to save the child. Each of these two cases can be explained with equal ease in Freudian and in Adlerian terms. According to Freud the first man suffered from repression (say, of some component of his Oedipus complex), while the second man had achieved sublimation. According to Adler the first man suffered from feelings of inferiority (producing perhaps the need to prove to himself that he dared to commit some crime), and so did the second man (whose need was to prove to himself that he dared to rescue the child). I could not think of any human behavior which could not be interpreted in terms of either theory. It was precisely this fact—that they always fitted, that they were always confirmed—which in the eyes of their admirers constituted the strongest argument in favor of these theories. It began to dawn on me that this apparent strength was in fact their weakness.[28]

Source: Karl Raimund Popper, *Conjectures and Refutations: The Growth of Scientific Knowledge* (Psychology Press, 2002), p. 61.

Scientific hypotheses can be distinguished from nonscientific ones, then, by the following principle:

A hypothesis is scientific only if it is testable, that is, only if it predicts something more than what is predicted by the background theory alone.

The gremlin hypothesis predicts that if we turn on a fluorescent light, it will emit light. But this action doesn't mean that the gremlin hypothesis is testable, because the fact that fluorescent lights emit light is what the gremlin hypothesis was introduced to explain. That fact is part of its background theory. To be testable, a hypothesis must make a prediction that goes beyond its background theory. A prediction tells us that if certain conditions are realized, then certain results will be observed. If a prediction can be derived from a hypothesis and its background theory that cannot be derived from its background theory alone, then the hypothesis is testable.

Karl Popper realized long ago that untestable hypotheses cannot legitimately be called scientific. What distinguishes genuine scientific hypotheses from pseudoscientific ones, he claims, is that the former are *falsifiable*. A hypothesis is falsifiable if it is, in principle, possible to discover some evidence that would refute it. For example, the hypothesis that there's life in other galaxies is falsifiable because even if we never travel beyond the Milky Way, in principle it's possible to do so. The hypothesis that either it's raining or it's not raining is not falsifiable, however, because no possible evidence could count against it. It's consistent with all possible weather conditions and thus tells us nothing about the weather. In order for a hypothesis to be informative, it has to rule out something. If it doesn't, it carries no information about the world.

Although Popper's insight is a good one, it has two shortcomings: First, the term is unfortunate, for no hypothesis is, strictly speaking, falsifiable because it's always possible to maintain a hypothesis in the face of unfavorable evidence by making suitable alterations in the background, as we've seen in the case of the flat Earth theory and the zetetic law of perspective.[29]

The second weakness in Popper's theory is that it doesn't explain why we hold on to some hypotheses in the face of adverse evidence. When new hypotheses are first proposed, there is often a good deal of evidence against them. As philosopher of science Imre Lakatos notes, "When Newton published his *Principia*, it was common knowledge that it could not properly explain even the motion of the moon; in fact, lunar motion refuted Newton. . . . All hypotheses, in this sense, are born refuted and die refuted."[30] Nonetheless, we give credence to some and not others. Popper's theory is hard-pressed to explain why this is so. Recognizing that other criteria play a role in evaluating hypotheses makes sense of this situation.

In making theories, always keep a window open so that you can throw one out if necessary.

—BELA SCHICK

Fruitfulness

One thing that makes some hypotheses attractive even in the face of adverse evidence is that they successfully predict new phenomena and thus open up new lines of research. Such hypotheses possess the virtue of *fruitfulness*. For example, Einstein's theory of relativity predicts that light rays traveling near massive objects will appear to be bent because the space around them is curved. At the time Einstein proposed his

Truth in science can be defined as the working hypothesis best suited to open the way to the next better one.

—KONRAD LORENZ

The effect of light bending near the sun.

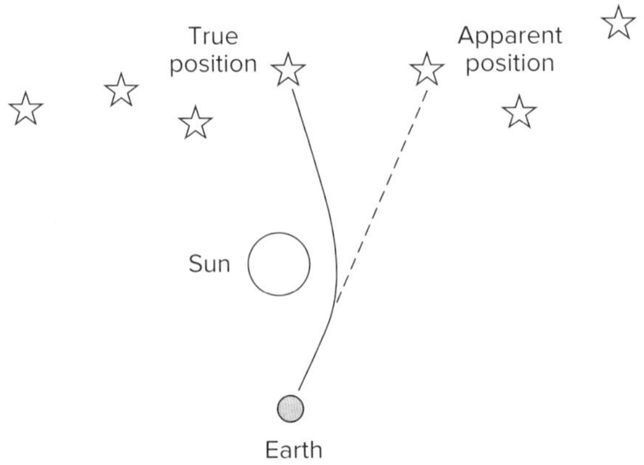

theory, common wisdom was that since light has no mass, light rays travel in Euclidean straight lines. To test Einstein's theory, physicist Sir Arthur Eddington mounted an expedition to Africa in 1919 to observe a total eclipse of the sun. If light rays are bent by massive objects, he reasoned, then the position of stars whose light passes near the sun should appear to be shifted from their true position. The shift should be detectable by comparing a photograph taken during the eclipse with one taken at night of the same portion of the sky. When Eddington compared the two photographs, he found that stars near the sun during the eclipse did appear to have moved more than those farther away and that the amount of their apparent movement was what Einstein's theory predicted. (Einstein's theory predicted a deflection of 1.75 seconds of arc. Eddington observed a deflection of 1.64 seconds of arc, well within the possible error of measurement.)[31] Thus Einstein's theory had successfully predicted a phenomenon that no one had previously thought existed. In so doing, it expanded the frontiers of our knowledge.

Since hypotheses make predictions only in the context of a larger body of background information, Lakatos prefers to talk of *research programs* rather than hypotheses. According to Lakatos, what distinguishes good (progressive) research programs from bad (degenerating) ones is their fruitfulness.

> All the research programs I admire have one characteristic in common. They all predict novel facts, facts which had been either undreamt of, or have indeed been contradicted by previous or rival programs. . . . What really count are dramatic, unexpected, stunning predictions; a few of them are enough to tilt the balance; where theory lags behind the facts, we are dealing with miserable degenerating research programs.[32]

The classic case of a degenerating research program, he tells us, is Marxism:

> Has, for instance, Marxism ever predicted a stunning novel fact successfully? Never! It has some famous unsuccessful predictions. It predicted the absolute impoverishment of the working class. It predicted that the first socialist revolutions would take place in the industrially most developed society. It predicted that socialist societies would be free of revolutions. It predicted that there will be no conflict of interests between socialist countries. Thus the early predictions of Marxism were bold and stunning but they failed. Marxists explained all their failures: they explained the rising living standards of the working class by devising a theory of imperialism; they even explained why the first socialist revolution occurred in industrially backward Russia. They "explained" Berlin 1953, Budapest 1956, Prague 1968. They "explained" the Russian-Chinese conflict. But their auxiliary hypotheses were all cooked up after the event to protect Marxian theory from the facts. The Newtonian program led to novel facts; the Marxian lagged behind the facts and has been running fast to catch up with them.[33]

Marxism is a degenerating research program not only because it failed to predict any novel facts but also because it is riddled with ad hoc hypotheses. The lesson is clear:

Other things being equal, the best hypothesis is the one that is the most fruitful, that is, makes the most successful novel predictions.

If two hypotheses do equally well with regard to all the other criteria of adequacy, the one with greater fruitfulness is better.

Having greater fruitfulness by itself does not necessarily make a hypothesis superior to its rivals, however, because it might not do as well as they do with respect to other criteria of adequacy. Velikovsky's theory of Venus's genesis demonstrates this point.

In 1950 Immanuel Velikovsky published *Worlds in Collision,* in which he argued that many of the ancient myths depicting worldwide catastrophes can be explained on the assumption that around 1500 BCE. Jupiter expelled a glowing ball of hot gases toward the Earth. This great ball of fire, which looked to observers on Earth like a gigantic comet, was later to become the planet Venus. As the Earth passed through its tail, Velikovsky claims, showers of meteorites fell to the Earth, exploding balls of naphtha filled the sky, and oil rained from the heavens. The gravitational pull of the comet became so great that it caused the Earth to tilt on its axis and slow its rate of rotation. Cities were laid waste by earthquakes, rivers reversed their course, and a gigantic hurricane

He who proves things by experience increases his knowledge; he who believes blindly increases his errors.
—CHINESE PROVERB

ravaged the planet. Before Venus finally settled into its current orbit, it pulled Mars off course and sent that planet hurtling toward the Earth, thus igniting a whole new wave of catastrophes.[34]

Because Velikovsky thought that Venus had been recently expelled from Jupiter, he predicted that it would still be hot. This prediction flew in the face of current scientific thinking, which held that Venus was cold and lifeless. The Pioneer space probe revealed, however, that Velikovsky was right: Venus is hot. At the time it was offered, then, Velikovsky's theory could claim fruitfulness among its virtues because it predicted a novel fact. Many of its other claims, however, appear to be physically impossible. Carl Sagan, for example, has calculated that the energy necessary to eject a mass the size of Venus from Jupiter is 10^{41} ergs, "which is equivalent to all the energy radiated by the Sun to space in an entire year, and one hundred million times more powerful than the largest solar flare ever observed."[35] Velikovsky does not say how Jupiter was able to generate such energy. Nor does he explain how the Earth was able to resume its normal rate of rotation after it slowed down. Other claims conflict with well-established laws in biology, chemistry, and astrophysics.[36] These laws may be mistaken, but unless Velikovsky can identify the correct laws and show that they explain astronomical events better than the currently accepted laws do, there is no reason to believe that those currently accepted laws are mistaken.

Scope

The glory of science is that it is freeing the soul, breaking the mental manacles, getting the brain out of bondage, giving courage to thought, filling the world with mercy, justice, and joy.

—ROBERT G. INGERSOLL

The *scope* of a hypothesis—or the amount of diverse phenomena explained and predicted by it—is also an important measure of its adequacy: the more a hypothesis explains and predicts, the more it unifies and systematizes our knowledge and the less likely it is to be false. For example, one reason that Einstein's theory of relativity came to be preferred over Newton's theories of gravity and motion is that it had greater scope. It could explain and predict everything that Newton's theories could, as well as some things that they couldn't. For instance, Einstein's theory could explain a variation in Mercury's orbit, among other phenomena.

It had been known since the middle of the nineteenth century that the planet Mercury's *perihelion* (the point at which it is closest to the sun) does not remain constant—that point rotates slowly, or *precesses,* around the sun at the rate of about 574 seconds of arc per century. Using Newton's laws of motion and gravity, it was possible to account for about 531 seconds of arc of this motion. Leverrier tried to account for the missing 43 seconds of arc in the same way he had accounted for the discrepancies in the orbit of Uranus—by postulating the existence of another planet between Mercury and the sun. He named this planet

Vulcan (*Star Trek* fans take note), but repeated observations failed to find it. Einstein's theory of relativity, however, can account for the precession of Mercury's perihelion without postulating the existence of another planet. According to relativity theory, space is curved around massive objects. Since Mercury is so close to the sun, the space it travels through is more warped (again, *Star Trek* fans take note) than is the space that the rest of the planets travel through. Using relativity theory, it is possible to calculate the extent to which space is thus bent. It turns out to be just enough to account for the missing 43 seconds of arc in the precession of Mercury's perihelion.[37]

The fact that Einstein's theory had greater scope than Newton's was a powerful argument in its favor. As the physicist P. Langevin proclaimed at the Paris Academy of Sciences:

> This theory is the *only one* that permits one actually to represent all the known experimental facts and that possesses moreover the remarkable power of prediction confirmed in so astonishing a manner by the deviation of light rays and the displacement of spectral lines in the gravitational field of the sun.[38]

For Langevin, Einstein's theory is superior to Newton's because it has greater explanatory and predictive power. The principle he's relying on is this one:

Other things being equal, the best hypothesis is the one that has the greatest scope, that is, that explains and predicts the most diverse phenomena.

Simplicity

Seek simplicity and distrust it.

—Alfred North Whitehead

Interestingly enough, even though considerations of fruitfulness and scope loomed large in the minds of many of those scientists who accepted Einstein's theory, *simplicity* was what Einstein saw as its main virtue. He wrote, "I do not by any means find the chief significance of the general theory of relativity in the fact that it has predicted a few minute observable facts, but rather in the simplicity of its foundation and in its logical consistency."[39] For Einstein, simplicity is a theoretical virtue *par excellence.*

Simplicity is notoriously difficult to define.[40] For our purposes, we may say that the simpler of two hypotheses is the one that makes the fewest assumptions.[41] Simplicity is valued for the same reason that scope is—the simpler a theory is, the more it unifies and systematizes our knowledge and the less likely it is to be false because there are fewer ways for it to go wrong.

Parallax: As Earth travels around the sun, the stars that appear to be behind the nearest star change.

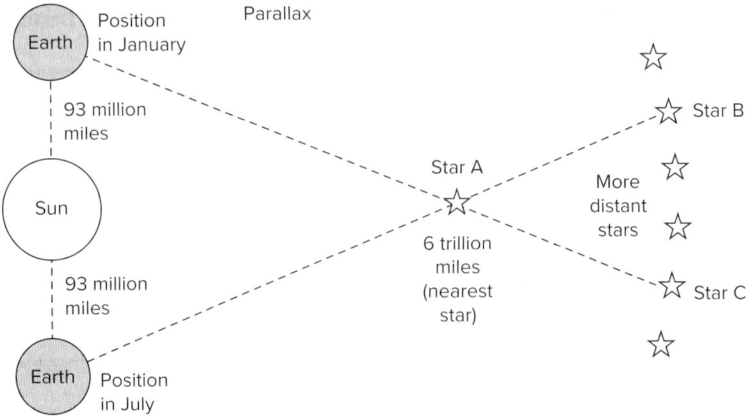

Since the time of Thales (arguably the West's first scientist), simplicity has been an important criterion of theory selection. To take but one example: Copernicus's heliocentric theory, which claims that the Earth revolves around the sun, could explain no more than Ptolemy's geocentric theory, which claims that the sun revolves around the Earth. In terms of scope and fruitfulness, then, Copernicus's theory has no advantage over Ptolemy's. In fact, Copernicus's theory had the disadvantage of being inconsistent with observed data. If Copernicus's theory were true, opponents charged, then stars nearer to Earth should seem to change their position relative to more distant stars as the Earth moved around the sun. But no such apparent change in position (known as *parallax*) was observed. This predictive failure did not move Copernicus and his followers to abandon the theory, however, for they believed that stars were too far away to exhibit parallax. It turns out that they were right: The nearest star is 6 trillion miles away. It wasn't until 1838, almost 300 years after Copernicus's death,

The Ptolemaic system of planetary motion.

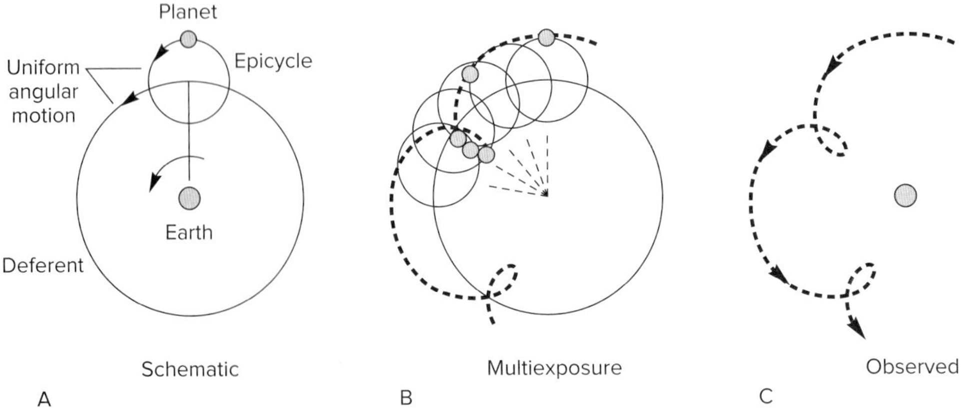

that stellar parallax was finally observed. (The parallax was observed when more powerful telescopes were available to observe stars more precisely.) Copernicus's theory, however, had long since become the accepted explanation of the structure of the solar system.

Scientists accepted Copernicus's theory in the face of such seemingly adverse evidence because it was simpler than Ptolemy's. One of the most difficult features of planetary motion to account for is the fact that certain planets, at certain times, seem to reverse their direction of travel. Ptolemy accounted for this retrograde motion by assuming that planets orbit their orbits, so to speak. He assumed that they travel in a circle (known as an *epicycle*) around a point that is itself traveling in a circle around the Earth (known as a *deferent*).

Copernicus showed that many of these epicycles were unnecessary hypotheses adduced to maintain the view that planets travel in circles around the Earth. Because Copernicus's theory could explain planetary motion without using as many epicycles, it was simpler than Ptolemy's. The criterion at work here is this:

Other things being equal, the best hypothesis is the simplest one, that is, the one that makes the fewest assumptions.

As we've seen, hypotheses often explain phenomena by assuming that certain entities exist. The simplicity criterion tells us that, other things being equal, the fewer such assumptions a theory makes, the better it is. When searching for an explanation, then, it's wise to cleave to the principle known as *Occam's Razor* (in honor of the medieval philosopher, William of Occam, who formulated it): Do not multiply entities beyond necessity. In other words, assume no more than is required to explain the phenomenon in question. If there's no reason to assume that something exists, it's irrational to do so.

One of the most famous applications of this principle was made by the French mathematician and astronomer Pierre Laplace. After Laplace presented the first edition of his theory of the universe to Napoleon, Napoleon is said to have asked, "Where does God fit into your theory?" Laplace matter-of-factly replied, "I have no need of that hypothesis."[42]

Conservatism

The least questioned assumptions are often the most questionable.
—Paul Broca

Since consistency is a necessary condition of knowledge, we should be wary of accepting a hypothesis that conflicts with our background information. As we've seen, not only does accepting such a hypothesis undermine our claim to know; it also requires rejecting the beliefs it conflicts with. If those beliefs are well established, the chances of the new hypothesis being true are not good. In general, then, the more *conservative* a hypothesis is (that is, the fewer well-established beliefs it conflicts with), the more plausible it is.[43] The criterion of conservatism can be stated as follows:

Other things being equal, the best hypothesis is the one that is the most conservative, that is, the one that fits best with established beliefs.

Things aren't always equal, however. It may be perfectly reasonable to accept a hypothesis that is not conservative provided that it possesses other criteria of adequacy. Unfortunately, there's no foolproof method for determining when conservatism should take a backseat to other criteria.

Indeed, there is no fixed formula for applying *any* of the criteria of adequacy. We can't quantify how well a hypothesis does with respect to any of them, nor can we definitively rank the criteria in order of importance. At times we may rate conservatism more highly than scope, especially if the hypothesis in question is lacking in fruitfulness. At other times we may rate simplicity higher than conservatism, especially if the hypothesis has at least as much scope as our existing hypothesis. Choosing between theories is not the purely logical process it is often made out to be. Like judicial decision-making, it relies on factors of human judgment that resist formalization.

The process of theory selection, however, is not subjective. There are many distinctions we can't quantify that nevertheless are perfectly objective. We can't say, for example, exactly when day turns into night or when a person with a full head of hair turns bald. Nevertheless, the distinctions between night and day or baldness and hirsuteness are as objective as they come. There are certainly borderline cases that reasonable people can disagree about, but there are also clear-cut cases where disagreement would be irrational. It would simply be wrong to believe that a person with a full head of (living) hair is bald. If you persisted in such a belief, you would be irrational. Similarly, it would simply be wrong to believe that the phlogiston theory is a good scientific theory. In general, if someone believes a theory that clearly fails to meet the criteria of adequacy, that person is irrational.

CREATIONISM, EVOLUTION, AND CRITERIA OF ADEQUACY

Criteria of adequacy are what we appeal to when trying to decide which hypothesis best explains a phenomenon. The best hypothesis is the one that explains the phenomenon and meets the criteria of adequacy better than any of its competitors. To make a rational choice among hypotheses, then, it's important to know what these criteria are and how to apply them. Philosopher and historian Thomas Kuhn agrees. "It is vitally important," he tells us, "that scientists be taught to value these characteristics and that they be provided with examples that illustrate them in practice."[44]

In recent years, a number of people (as well as a number of state legislatures) have claimed that the theory of creationism is just as good as the theory of evolution and thus should be given equal time in the classroom. Our discussion of the criteria of adequacy has given us the means to evaluate this claim. If creationism is just as good a theory as evolution, then it should fulfill the criteria of adequacy just as well as evolution does. Let's see if that is the case.

The theory of evolution, although not invented by Darwin, received its most impressive formulation at his hand. In 1859, he published *The Origin of Species,* in which he argued that the theory of evolution by natural selection provided the best explanation of a number of different phenomena:

> It can hardly be supposed that a false theory would explain, in so satisfactory a manner as does the theory of natural selection, the several large classes of facts above specified. It has recently been objected that this is an unsafe method of arguing; but it is a method used in judging of the common events of life, and has often been used by the greatest natural philosophers.[45]

If God indeed exists, then one of his greatest gifts to us was our reason. To deny evolution is not to be truly religious or truly moral. . . . There is nothing in modern evolutionary theory which stands in the way of a deep sense of religion or of a morally worthwhile life.

—Michael Ruse

Darwin found that organisms living in isolated habitats (such as islands) have forms related to but distinct from organisms living in neighboring habitats, that there are anatomical resemblances between closely related species, that the embryos of distantly related species resemble one another more than the adults of those species, and that fossils show a distinct progression from the simplest forms to the most complex.[46] The best explanation of these facts, Darwin argued, was that organisms adapt to their environment through a process of natural selection. The hypothesis that all creatures were created by God in one fell swoop, he argued, offers no explanation for these facts.

Darwin realized that many more creatures are born than live long enough to reproduce, that these creatures possess different physical characteristics, and that the characteristics they possess are often inherited from their parents. He reasoned that when an inherited characteristic (like an opposable thumb) increased an organism's chances of living long enough to reproduce, that characteristic would be passed to the next generation. As this process continued, the characteristic would become more prevalent in succeeding generations.

This process Darwin called *natural selection,* which was the driving force behind evolution. Darwin was not aware of the mechanism by which these characteristics were transmitted. The discovery of that mechanism—the science of genetics—has further bolstered Darwin's theory, for it has been found that the number of chromosomes and their internal organization is similar among closely related species.[47]

Scientific Creationism

The only way we can determine the true age of the earth is for God to tell us what it is.
—Henry Morris

Creation science, or scientific creationism, holds that the universe, energy, and life were created from nothing relatively recently (around 6,000 to 10,000 years ago), whereas modern science claims that the universe was created about 14 billion years ago and the Earth, about 4.5 billion years ago; that, contrary to what evolution claims, living things could not have developed from a single organism through mutation and natural selection; that there is very little variation among members of the same species; that humans did not develop from the apes; and that the Earth's geology can be explained by the occurrence of various catastrophes, including a worldwide flood.[48] This account of the creation of the universe and its inhabitants is derived primarily from the Bible's Book of Genesis.[49]

Those who espouse this view believe the theory of evolution to be a pernicious doctrine with disastrous social consequences. Henry Morris, president emeritus of the Institute for Creation Research, and Martin Clark, for example, assert:

> Evolution is thus not only anti-Biblical and anti-Christian, but it is utterly unscientific and impossible as well. But it has served effectively as the pseudo-scientific basis of atheism, agnosticism, socialism, fascism, and numerous other false and dangerous philosophies over the past century.[50]

Teaching creationism, they believe, will help counter these consequences by putting God back in the classroom. Promoting religion in the public schools, however, is a violation of the establishment clause of the First Amendment, which reads, "Congress shall make no law respecting an establishment of religion." Consequently, the courts have consistently found laws requiring the teaching of creationism to be unconstitutional. Supreme Court Justice William Brennan explains:

> Because the primary purpose of the Creationism Act is to advance a particular religious belief, the act endorses religion in violation of the First Amendment. . . . The act violates the establishment clause of the First Amendment because it seeks to employ the symbolic and financial support of government to achieve a religious purpose.[51]

Creationism and Morality

On the wall of the lobby of the Museum of Creation and Earth History run by the Institute for Creation Research hang two posters: one titled "Creationist Tree" and the other, "Evolutionary Tree." The "Creationist Tree," on the one hand, depicts a lush, verdant tree around whose branches float phrases like "True Christology," "True Gospel," "True Faith," "True Morality," "True Americanism," "True Government," "True Family Life," "True Education," "True History," and "True Science." The "Evolutionary Tree," on the other hand, depicts a withered, barren tree around whose branches float phrases like "Communism," "Nazism," "Atheism," "Amoralism," "Materialism," "Pornography," "Slavery," "Abortion," "Euthanasia," "Homosexuality," "Child Abuse," and "Bestiality." The message here is obvious: evolution is the root of all evil. Georgia judge Braswell Dean agrees. As he so alliteratively put it, "This monkey mythology of Darwin is the cause of permissiveness, promiscuity, pills, prophylactics, perversions, pregnancies, abortions, pornotherapy, pollution, poisoning, and the proliferation of crimes of all types."[52] This view lies at the heart of the creation/evolution controversy. It's not so much about the nature of science as it is about the nature of morality.

Creationists believe that evolution undercuts the authority of the Bible by contradicting a literal reading of Genesis. What's more, they believe that if any part of the Bible is untrue, we cannot trust any of it. Without the Bible, however, we have no way of distinguishing right from wrong. So by undercutting the authority of the Bible, evolution undermines the basis of morality.

The theory of morality that lies behind this view is known as the Divine Command Theory. According to this view, what makes an action right is that God wills it to be done. Remarkably enough, even though this view may be widespread, very few professional ethicists or theologians subscribe to it because they believe that it not only endorses the mistaken view that might makes right, but also takes away the only reason we have for worshipping God. Leibniz, the discoverer of modern calculus and one of the most God-fearing men in the Western intellectual tradition, explains:

> In saying, therefore, that things are not good according to any standard of goodness, but simply by the will of God, it seems to me that one destroys without realizing it, all the love of God and all his glory; for why praise him for what he has done, if he would be equally praiseworthy in doing the contrary? Where will be his justice and his wisdom if he has only a certain despotic power, if arbitrary will takes the place of his reasonableness, and if in according with the definition of tyrants, justice consists in that which is pleasing to the most powerful. Besides it seems that every act of willing supposes some reason for the willing and this reason, of course, must precede the act.[54]

Leibniz's point is that if actions are neither right nor wrong prior to God's willing them, then God cannot choose one set over another because one is morally better than another. Thus if God does choose one over another, his choice must be arbitrary. But a being whose actions are arbitrary is not a being worthy of worship.

According to Leibniz, God's choosing an action to be done is not what makes it right. Instead God chooses an action to be done because it is right. Its rightness is independent of His will and thus can guide His choices. Morality doesn't depend on God any more than mathematics does. God can't make the number 3 an even number because by its very nature, 3 is odd. Similarly God can't make justice or mercy bad things because by their very nature, they are good. So even if evolution did undercut the authority of the Bible—which most denominations say it doesn't—it wouldn't thereby undermine the basis of morality.

Our concern, however, is not with the constitutionality of the teaching of creationism, but with its adequacy as a scientific theory. We want to know whether creationism really is as good a theory as evolution.

Ironically, even though creationists have taken to calling their theory scientific in an attempt to garner public support, they openly admit that it's nothing of the sort. They don't see this as a problem, however—because they don't believe that evolution is a scientific theory either. Duane Gish, senior vice president of the Institute for Creation Research, explains, "There were no human witnesses to the origin of the Universe, the origin of life or the origin of a single living thing. These were unique, unrepeatable events of the past that cannot be observed in nature or recapitulated in the laboratory. Thus, neither creation nor evolution qualifies as a scientific theory, and each is equally religious."[53] Gish here is appealing to the principle of testability discussed earlier in this chapter. His claim is that since neither creationism nor evolution is testable, neither can be considered a scientific theory.

But is it true that neither is testable? A hypothesis is testable if it predicts something more than what is predicted by the background theory alone. Evolution clearly meets this criterion, for it correctly predicts that animals inhabiting islands will be more closely related to those living on the nearest mainland than to those living on more distant lands, that different types of fossils will be found in different layers of rock, and that series of fossils exhibiting gradual change over time will be discovered. Evolution makes numerous other predictions that help explain facts discovered by immunology, biochemistry, and molecular biology.[55] So evolution is testable. If these predictions had turned out to be false, evolution might well have been abandoned.

If superior creatures from space ever visit Earth, the first question they will ask in order to assess the level of our civilization, is: "Have they discovered evolution yet?"
—RICHARD DAWKINS

Creationism is also testable because it makes a number of claims that can be checked by observation. It claims, for example, that the universe is 6,000 to 10,000 years old, that all species were created at the same time, and that the geographical features of the Earth can be explained as the result of tidal waves created by the great flood of Noah. All these claims can be tested. All these claims conflict with well-established scientific findings.[56] So not only is creationism testable; it has been tested—and failed the tests.

Gish writes as if the lack of human witnesses makes the two theories untestable and therefore religious. But if that lack rendered a theory religious, a lot of what passes for science would have to be reclassified as religion, for many phenomena studied by scientists

Is Evolution Just a Theory?

The most recent battle in the war between creation and evolution was fought in Dover, Pennsylvania. The school board there voted to have the following statement read in biology classes:

> Because Darwin's Theory is a theory, it continues to be tested as new evidence is discovered. The theory is not a fact. Gaps in the theory exist for which there is no evidence. A theory is defined as a well-tested explanation that unifies a broad range of observations. Intelligent Design is an explanation of the origin of life that differs from Darwin's view.

Eleven parents of the Dover Area School District sued the school board on the grounds that this statement promoted a particular religious belief under the guise of science education. Judge Jones found in favor of the parents.

What's interesting about this statement is not just its attempt to sneak religion into the science classroom, but its misunderstanding of the nature of facts and theories. Its definition of a theory is essentially correct. Its claim that evolution is not a fact because it continues to be tested, however, is mistaken. What distinguishes a theory from a fact is not whether it's still being tested or even how certain we are of it, but whether it provides the best explanation of some phenomena.

A fact is a true statement. A theory is a statement about the way the world is. If the world is the way the theory says it is—if the theory is true—then the theory is a fact. For example, if the Copernican theory of the solar system is true—if planets revolve around the sun—then the Copernican theory is a fact. If Einstein's theory of relativity is true—if $E = mc^2$—then Einstein's theory is a fact. Similarly, if the theory of evolution is true, then it's a fact.

So the question arises: when are we justified in believing something to be true? We have already seen the answer: when it provides the best explanation of some phenomena. Biologists consider evolution to be a fact because, in the words of Theodosius Dobzhansky, "Nothing in biology makes sense except in the light of evolution."[57] Evolution is a fact because it's the best theory of how biological change occurs over time.

What often goes unnoticed in these discussions is that every fact is a theory. Take the fact that you're reading a book right now, for example. You're justified in believing that to be a fact because it provides the best explanation of your sense experience. But it's not the only theory that explains your sense experience. After all, you could be dreaming, you could be hallucinating, you could be a brain in a vat, you could be plugged into the matrix, you could be receiving telepathic messages from extraterrestrials, and so on. All of those theories explain your sense experience. You shouldn't accept any of them, however, because none of them is as good an explanation as the ordinary one.

The intelligent design theory is on a par with the theory that extraterrestrials are putting thoughts in your head. It's a possible explanation of the evidence, but not a very good one because, like the extraterrestrial theory, it doesn't identify the designer nor does it tell us how the designer did it. Consequently, it doesn't meet the criteria of adequacy as well as the evolutionary theory does. In a court of law, no one would take seriously an explanation of a crime that didn't identify the criminal or how he committed the crime. Similarly, in a science classroom, no one should take seriously an explanation that doesn't identify the cause or how the cause brings about its effect. Evolution does both and does it better than any competing theory. So we're justified in believing it to be true.

can't be witnessed by humans. Nobody, for example, ever has seen or ever will see the interior of the sun. But that fact doesn't mean that any theory about what goes on inside the sun is theological. Theories about the internal structure of stars can be tested by observing their behavior. Similarly, theories about the creation of the universe or living things can be tested by observing the behavior of objects in the universe or creatures on the Earth.

Religion, which should most distinguish us from the beasts, and ought most particularly to elevate us, as rational creatures, above brutes, is that wherein men often appear most irrational, and more senseless than beasts themselves.
—John Locke

One piece of evidence that Darwin cited in favor of the theory of evolution is that there is a progression among fossils from the simplest, in the oldest strata, to the most complex, in the most recent layers. Creationists claim that this evidence is no evidence at all because—they say—the age of rock strata is determined by the complexity of the fossils it contains. In other words, creationists claim that evolutionists argue in a circle—they date rock strata by the fossils they contain and then date fossils by the rock strata in which they're found.[58]

Creationists don't deny that the simplest fossils are often found at the lowest point in fossil beds. They account for this fact by assuming that after the great flood of Noah, the simplest forms of life (marine life) would be the first to be deposited on the seafloor. All creatures—dinosaurs as well as humans—came into existence at the same time. They were all washed away in a great flood, and the fossils that remain are found in their present order not because of their relative age but because of their relative buoyancy.

Creationists who make this argument must then explain how the creatures alive today survived the flood. Most follow the Bible and claim that they were saved by Noah and his ark. The ark, of course, presents a problem. To save all living creatures, according to one calculation, the ark had to carry at least 25,000 species of birds, 15,000 species of mammals, 6,000 species of reptiles, 2,500 species of amphibians, and more than 1 million species of insects.[59] Moreover, since creationists believe that men and dinosaurs walked the Earth at the same time, the ark must have contained two of each species of dinosaur; that is, it included two Supersauruses (which were 100 feet long and weighed up to 55 tons each) and two Apatosauruses (up to 70 feet long and 20 tons)—not to mention two hungry 7-ton Tyrannosauruses. How Noah, his wife, and three sons, and their wives could possibly have built an ark big enough to hold all these creatures—let alone feed and water them and clean out their stalls—is something that creationists are curiously silent about.

The fact is that no geological or anthropological evidence indicates that a worldwide flood occurred during the past 10,000 years.[60]

Furthermore, the claim that the evolutionist's argument from the fossil record is circular is simply mistaken, for there are many ways to date fossils independent of the rock strata they're found in.

The age of the universe can also be calculated independently of both fossils and rock strata. By determining how far apart the galaxies are and how rapidly they are moving away from each other, it's possible to determine when the outward expansion of the universe began. Present estimates put the age of the universe at something like 15 to 20 billion years, a far cry from the 6,000 years claimed by creationists.

This disagreement about the age of the universe and living things points out one of the major failings of creationism: It does not cohere with well-established beliefs. In other words, it fails to meet the criterion of conservatism. As Isaac Asimov has pointed out, creationism cannot be adopted "without discarding all of modern biology, biochemistry, geology, astronomy—in short, without discarding all of science."[61] That's a pretty high price to pay for adopting a theory. If the creationists can't make up for this lack of conservatism by demonstrating that their theory has greater fruitfulness, scope, or simplicity than evolution, it can't be considered as good a theory as evolution.

Creationism is not a fruitful theory because it hasn't predicted any novel facts. It has made some novel claims—such as that the universe is from 6,000 to 10,000 years old, that all creatures were created at the same time, that there was a worldwide flood, and so on—but none of them has been borne out by the evidence. Evolution, on the other hand, has predicted that the chromosomes and proteins of related species should be similar, that mutations should occur, that organisms should adapt to changing environments, and so on, all of which have been verified. In terms of fruitfulness, then, evolution is superior to creationism.

Evolution is also superior to creationism in terms of simplicity. Simplicity, remember, is a measure of the number of assumptions a theory makes. Evolution assumes a lot less than creationism. For one thing, it doesn't assume the existence of God. For another, it doesn't assume the existence of unknown forces. That creationism makes both of these assumptions was made clear by Gish:

Nothing in biology makes sense except in the light of evolution.

—THEODOSIUS DOBZHANSKY

> We do not know how the Creator created, what processes He used, *for He used processes which are not now operating anywhere in the natural universe.* This is why we refer to creation as Special Creation. We cannot discover by scientific investigation anything about the creative processes used by the Creator.[62]

Creationism, then, assumes the existence of a supernatural being with supernatural powers. Since evolution makes neither of these assumptions, it is the simpler theory.

The major advantage of evolution over creationism, however, is its scope, or explanatory power. Evolution has served to systematize and unify discoveries from a number of different fields. "In fact," claims Isaac Asimov, "the strongest of all indications as to the fact of evolution and the truth of the theory of natural selection is that all the independent findings of scientists in every branch of science, when they have anything to do with biological evolution at all, *always* strengthen the case and *never* weaken it."[63] Evolution fits well with what we know about the universe. It explains the facts uncovered by not only Darwin, but many others as well. Creationism, on the other hand, does not fit well with what we know about the universe and can't even explain Darwin's data. Furthermore, it raises more questions than it answers. How did the creator create? What caused the worldwide flood? How did creatures survive it? Why does the world seem so much older than it is? A theory that raises more questions than it answers doesn't increase our understanding; it decreases our understanding.

It stands to the everlasting credit of science that by acting on the human mind it has overcome man's insecurity before himself and before nature.
—Albert Einstein

Moreover, appealing to the incomprehensible can never increase our comprehension. To see this, suppose that you're an engineer charged with explaining why a bridge collapsed, and suppose someone came to you claiming to know why it did. Not wanting to leave any possibility unexplored, you ask him what he knows. He tells you that the bridge was brought down by a gremlin with a ray gun. Not wanting to seem rude, you ask him if he can tell you anything about the gremlin. He replies that no one has ever seen the gremlin and that if you go looking for him, he will hide where no one can find him. You then ask him why the gremlin destroyed the bridge. He replies that his motives are inscrutable, and nobody knows why he does what he does. Finally, you ask him if he can tell you anything about the ray gun he used. He replies that the ray gun uses a force different from any known to exist in nature. At that point it would probably be best to show him to the door. He has failed to answer the three questions that any explanation that appeals to the actions of an agent must answer: who did it, why he did it, and how he did it. But the creationist and intelligent design explanations fail to answer these questions. They don't tell us who the creator is, why the creator created, or how the creator created. As a result, their explanations are as vacuous as the gremlin explanation—they don't increase our understanding and leave us with more questions than when we started. The real problem with creationism and intelligent design, then, is not that they are pseudosciences, but that they are pseudoexplanations.

Did Adam and Eve Have Navels?

If the universe is only 10,000 years old, why does it seem so much older? Why, for example, do we find fossils that seem to be millions of years old? One possible response is to say that God put them there to test our faith. This view is not favored by modern-day creationists, however, for it puts God in a bad light. As one creationist remarks: "This would be the creation, not of an appearance of age, but of an appearance of evil, and would be contrary to Gods [*sic*] nature."[64] The creationists do not want to make God out to be a deceiver.

Nineteenth-century British naturalist Philip Gosse, however, argued that if God created the world, he had to create it with vestiges of a past, so why not assume that God created it with vestiges of a great past? Martin Gardner elucidates Gosse's argument:

Gosse admitted geology had established beyond any doubt that the earth had a long geological history in which plants and animals flourished before the time of Adam. He was also convinced that the earth was created about 4,000 B.C.E., in six days, exactly as described in *Genesis*. How did he reconcile these apparently contradictory opinions? Very simply. Just as Adam was created with a navel, the relic of a birth which never occurred, so the entire earth was created with all the fossil relics of a past which had no existence except in the mind of God!

Just as God couldn't create a tree without growth rings, Gosse argued that God couldn't make a man without a naval. What do you think?[65]

If creationism met the criteria of adequacy as well as evolution does, it would be as good a theory as evolution—but it doesn't. With respect to each criterion of adequacy—testability, conservatism, fruitfulness, simplicity, and scope—creationism actually does much worse than evolution. Consequently, the creationists' claim that creationism is as good a theory as evolution is totally unfounded. As Plato realized over 2,500 years ago, to say that "God did it" is not to offer an explanation, but to offer an excuse for not having an explanation (*Cratylus* 426a).

Creationists often object that various organs or limbs couldn't have evolved gradually because a half-formed organ or limb has no survival value. "What good is half a wing?" they ask. The answer is that half a wing is better than none. Richard Dawkins explains:

> What use is half a wing? How did wings get their start? Many animals leap from bough to bough, and sometimes fall to the ground. Especially in a small animal, the whole body surface catches the air and assists the leap, or breaks the fall, by acting as a crude aerofoil. Any tendency to increase the ratio of surface area to weight would help, for example, flaps of skin growing out in the angles of joints. From here, there is a

> continuous series of gradations to gliding wings, and hence to flapping wings. Obviously there are distances that could not have been jumped by the earliest animals with proto-wings. Equally obviously, for any degree of smallness or crudeness of ancestral air-catching surfaces, there must be some distance, however short, which can be jumped with the flap and which cannot be jumped without the flap.[66]

What's more, creatures all along the continuum are alive today. "Contrary to the creationist literature," Dawkins asserts, "not only are animals with 'half a wing' common, so are animals with a quarter of a wing, three quarters of a wing, and so on."[67] So intermediate stages in the development of organs and limbs are not only possible, they are actual.

Intelligent Design

One cannot look at this Universe with all living productions and man without believing that all has been intelligently designed.
—CHARLES DARWIN

Recently, a similar objection has been made at the molecular level. Michael Behe, a Lehigh University biochemist, claims that a light-sensitive cell, for example, couldn't have arisen through evolution because it is "irreducibly complex." Unlike the scientific creationists, however, he doesn't deny that the universe is billions of years old. Nor does he deny that evolution has occurred. He only denies that every biological system arose through natural selection.

Behe defines "irreducibly complex" this way:

> By irreducibly complex I mean a single system composed of several well-matched, interacting parts that contribute to the basic function, wherein the removal of any one of the parts causes the system to effectively cease functioning. An irreducibly complex system cannot be produced directly, (that is, by continuously improving the initial function, which continues to work by the same mechanism) by slight, successive modifications of a precursor system, because any precursor to an irreducibly complex system that is missing a part is by definition nonfunctional.[68]

The operative phrase here is "cannot be produced directly." Behe is claiming that it's physically impossible for certain biological systems to have been produced naturally. To refute this claim, then, all one has to show is that these systems can be produced without violating any natural laws.

Behe's favorite example of an irreducibly complex mechanism is a mouse trap. A mouse trap consists of five parts: (1) a wooden platform, (2) a metal hammer, (3) a spring, (4) a catch, and (5) a metal bar that holds the hammer down when the trap is set. What makes this mechanism irreducibly complex is that if any one of the parts were removed, it would no longer work. Behe claims that many biological systems, such as cilium, vision, and blood clotting, are also irreducibly

God the Extraterrestrial

When Michael Behe gives lectures on intelligent design theory, he often opens the floor to questions. During one of those question-and-answer sessions, he was asked, "Could the designer be an alien from outer space?" to which he answered, "Yes." The intelligent design theory itself tells us nothing about the nature of the designer. So it's entirely possible for the designer to be an extraterrestrial.

Remarkably enough, this is the basic premise upon which the religion known as "Raelianism" is founded. Raelianism is the brainchild of the French journalist Claude Vorilhon. He was moved to create this religion after he was contacted by an extraterrestrial while walking along the rim of the extinct Puy de Lassolas volcano in central France. The extraterrestrial told him that all life on Earth was created by aliens from outer space using advanced genetic engineering technology. According to the Raelian website, the messages dictated to Rael explain how life on Earth is not the result of random evolution, nor the work of a supernatural "God." It is a deliberate creation, using DNA, by a scientifically advanced people who made human beings literally "in their image"—what one can call "scientific creationism."[69]

The Raelians became internationally infamous after their subsidiary, Clonaid, claimed on December 26, 2002, to have cloned a human being. Immediately after their announcement, they agreed to have independent investigators verify their claim. They later reneged on that agreement, however, citing the need to preserve the privacy of the family involved. As of 2004, they claimed to have successfully cloned 13 human beings.[70] Ultimately, they hope to use cloning to achieve eternal life. They are currently trying to figure out how to transfer the memory and personality of someone into their clone.

complex because each of these systems would cease to function if any of their parts were removed.

Irreducibly complex biochemical systems pose a problem for evolutionary theory because it seems that they could not have arisen through natural selection. A trait such as vision can improve an organism's ability to survive only if it works. And it works only if all the parts of the visual system are present. So, Behe concludes, vision couldn't have arisen through slight modifications of a previous system. It must have been created all at once by some intelligent designer.

Behe tells us nothing about the intelligent designer nor the means used to implement the design. The designer could be a supernatural being, or it could be an alien from outer space. It could be benevolent, or it could be malevolent. It could even be more than one being. Perhaps irreducibly complex biochemical systems were designed by a committee. In any event, it should be clear that even if Behe's argument were sound, it does not provide evidence for the existence of God.

The logic turns out to be no more convincing than this: 'I [insert own name] am personally unable to think of any way in which [insert biological phenomenon] could have been built up step by step. Therefore it is irreducibly complex.

—Richard Dawkins

Most biologists do not believe that Behe's argument is sound, however, because they reject the notion that the parts of an irreducibly complex system could not have evolved independently of that system. As Nobel Prize–winning biologist H. J. Muller noted in 1939, a genetic sequence that is, at first, inessential to a system may later become essential to it. Biologist H. Allen Orr describes the processes as follows: "Some part (A) initially does some job (and not very well, perhaps). Another part (B) later gets added because it helps A. This new part isn't essential, it merely improves things. But later on A (or something else) may change in such a way that B now becomes indispensable."[71] For example, air bladders—primitive lungs—made it possible for certain fish to acquire new sources of food. But the air bladders were not necessary to the survival of the fish. As the fish acquired additional features, such as legs and arms, lungs became essential. So, contrary to what Behe would have us believe, the parts of an irreducibly complex system need not have come into existence all at once.

In fact, we know that some parts of the systems Behe describes are found in other systems. Thrombin, for example, is essential for blood clotting but also aids in cell division and is related to the digestive enzyme trypsin.[72] Because the same protein can play different roles in different systems, the fact that it is part of an irreducibly complex system doesn't indicate that it couldn't have arisen through natural selection.

Darwin himself recognized that many systems are composed of parts that originally evolved for other purposes. He writes:

> When this or that part has been spoken of as adapted for some special purpose, it must not be supposed that it was originally always formed for this sole purpose. The regular course of events seems to be, that a part which originally served for one purpose, becomes adapted by slow changes for widely different purposes.[73]

The process by which a structure that originally served one function comes to serve another was dubbed "exaptation" by Stephen J. Gould and Elizabeth Vrba and appears to be quite common. Darwin recognized this as well: "Thus throughout nature almost every part of each living being has probably served, in a slightly modified condition, for diverse purposes, and has acted in the living machinery of many ancient and distinct specific forms."[74] Because the same structure can perform different functions in different contexts, we do not need to suppose that all parts of an irreducibly complex structure came into being at the same time. Thus it is physically possible for irreducibly complex structures to arise naturally.

Biologists do not know how all parts of every irreducibly complex biochemical system came into being, and they may never know because there is no fossil record indicating how these systems evolved over time. Nevertheless, biologists do know that it is not, in principle, impossible for irreducibly complex systems to arise through natural selection. So there is no need to invoke an intelligent designer.

Creationists often attack evolution by citing a specific fact that they believe evolution can't account for. But notice how hypocritical this strategy is. On the one hand, they claim that evolution is untestable (and therefore unscientific), while on the other, they claim that it fails certain tests. They can't have it both ways. If evolution is untestable, no data can count against it. If data count against it, it can't be untestable.

We have seen species split, and we continue to see species diverging every day.
—Christie Wilcox

What's more, two facts often cited by creationists are simply false, namely, that there are no transitional fossils and that evolution has never been observed. Creationists maintain that if one species evolved into another, there should be fossil remains of intermediate or transitional organisms. But, they claim, the fossil record contains gaps where the intermediate organisms should be. So, they conclude, evolution did not occur. Given the nature of the fossilization process, however, gaps are to be expected. Very few of the organisms that come into being ever get fossilized. Nevertheless, biologists have discovered thousands of transitional fossils. The transitions from primitive fish to bony fish, from fish to amphibian, from amphibian to reptile, from reptile to bird, from reptile to mammal, from land animal to early whale, and from early ape to human are particularly well documented.[75] In addition, there is a detailed record of the diversification of mammals into rodents, bats, rabbits, carnivores, horses, elephants, manatee, deer, cows, and many others. As Harvard biologist Stephen J. Gould reports, "paleontologists have discovered several superb examples of intermediary forms and sequences, more than enough to convince any fair-minded skeptic about the reality of life's physical genealogy."[76]

Creationists also erroneously claim that no one has ever observed evolution. Biological evolution, in its broadest sense, is simply change in the genetic makeup of a group of organisms over time. This sort of change has been observed many times over. Insects that have developed a resistance to pesticides and bacteria that have developed a resistance to antibiotics are just two examples of biological evolution familiar to us all. These instances of biological evolution do not impress creationists because they are examples of what they call "microevolution"—genetic changes within a particular species. What creationists say has never been observed is "macroevolution"—genetic changes from one species to another. But in fact, this change, too, has been observed. Eight new species of fruit flies have been observed in the laboratory as well as six new species of other insects. A new species of mouse arose on the Faeroe Islands in the past 250 years, and scientists have recently recorded a new species of marine worm. The origin of more than a dozen new species of plants has been observed in the past fifty years.[77] So it is simply inaccurate to claim that either microevolution or macroevolution has never been observed.

Creationists also assume that any data that count against evolution count in favor of creationism.[78] But to argue in this way is to commit the fallacy of false dilemma; it presents two alternatives as mutually exclusive when, in fact, they aren't. Gish sets up the dilemma this way: "Either the Universe arose through naturalistic, mechanistic evolutionary processes, or it was created supernaturally."[79] This argument is a false dilemma for a number of reasons. In the first place, there is no need to assume that the universe was created even if evolution is not supported. The universe, as many non-Western peoples believe, may be eternal, that is, without beginning or end. People who believe that the universe was created by God usually believe that God is eternal. If God can be eternal, why not the universe?[80] Second, evolution is not the only natural account of creation, and Genesis is not the only supernatural account. Theories of creation are as varied as the cultures that conceived them. Some believe that the universe developed naturally from the void (the Vikings) while others believe that it's the supernatural work of the devil (the Gnostics). Thus, even if the creationists could totally discredit evolution, they would not thereby prove their own position, for there are many other alternatives.

What's more, if, as the creationists believe, every theory of creation is just as good as every other (because they're all just theories), then if one is taught in the classroom, they all should be taught. Just how ludicrous this would be was brought home to the Kansas State Board of Education in 2005 when Bobby Henderson sent the board an open letter arguing that the theory that the universe was created by the Flying Spaghetti Monster was just as good as the intelligent design theory and thus should be taught alongside it.[81] The letter went viral, was reprinted in *The New York Times, The Washington Post*, and *the Chicago Sun-Times*, and spawned a new religion—Pastafarianism—that is legally recognized in the Netherlands and New Zealand.[82] But, of course, every theory of creation is not as good as every other. The intelligent design theory and the Flying Spaghetti Monster theory are not as good as evolutionary theory because they don't meet the criteria of adequacy as well. Only by demonstrating that creationism meets the criteria of adequacy at least as well as evolutionary theory can creationists hope to show that their theory deserves equal time in the classroom.

Given the manifest inadequacy of the theory of creationism, why does it persist? The answer is not hard to find. Many people believe that evolution is incompatible with religion, for it not only

Are Humans Intelligently Designed?

Bertrand Russell once remarked, "If I were granted omnipotence, and millions of years to experiment in, I should not think man much to boast of as the final result of all my efforts."[83]

Biologists S. Jay Olshansky, Bruce A. Carnes, and Robert N. Butler agree with Russell that our design leaves much to be desired:

> Bulging disks, fragile bones, fractured hips, torn ligaments, varicose veins, cataracts, hearing loss, hernias and hemorrhoids; the list of bodily malfunctions that plague us as we age is long and all too familiar.[84]

As their illustration indicates, the human body could have been designed to last much longer and be much less prone to pain. Does this cast doubt on the intelligent design theory?

©Patricia I. Wynne

contradicts the biblical story of creation, but it suggests that our lives are purposeless and devoid of meaning. This view is not shared by many mainline churches, however. For example, the Roman Catholic Church, United Methodist Church, Evangelical Lutheran Church of America, African Methodist Episcopal Church, Presbyterian Church, Episcopal Church, Greek Orthodox Archdiocese of America, and the United Church of Christ all disavow scientific creationism of the sort espoused by the Institute for Creation Research and instead endorse evolution as a more plausible account of the origin of species.[85]

What's more, there is reason to believe that evolution is the only view that makes a meaningful relationship with God—and thus a meaningful life—possible. Biologist Kenneth R. Miller explains:

> It is often said that a Darwinian universe is one whose randomness cannot be reconciled with meaning. I disagree. A world truly without meaning would be one in which a deity pulled the string of every human puppet, indeed of every material particle. In such a world, physical and biological events would be carefully controlled, evil and suffering could be minimized, and the outcome of historical processes strictly regulated. All things would move toward the Creator's clear, distinct, established goals. Such control and predictability, however, comes at the price of independence. Always in control, such a Creator would deny his creatures any real opportunity to know and worship him—authentic love requires freedom, not manipulation. Such freedom is best supplied by the open contingency of evolution.[86]

A life in which all our actions were determined by God would not be a meaningful one. If what we did were not up to us, we would be little better than robots. Our actions are our own only if they are free. And truly free actions, says Miller, are only possible in a world that is not manipulated by an outside force. So evolution, far from diminishing our relationship with God, actually strengthens it.

PARAPSYCHOLOGY

Welcome to Telepathics Anonymous. Don't bother introducing yourself.
—Benson Bruno

Creationists do not use the scientific method to test their hypotheses, but parapsychologists do. For this reason, among others, the Parapsychological Association was granted affiliate status with the American Association for the Advancement of Science in 1969.

Parapsychology is the study of extrasensory perception (ESP) and psychokinesis. Extrasensory perception, as the name suggests, is perception that is not mediated by an organism's recognized sensory organs. There are three main types of ESP: telepathy, or perception of another's thoughts without the use of the senses; clairvoyance, perception of distant objects without the use of the senses; and precognition, perception of future events without the use of the senses. Psychokinesis is the ability to affect physical objects without the use of the body, that is, by simply thinking about them. These phenomena are often grouped together under the heading *psi phenomena.*

One of the reasons that psi phenomena are so fascinating is that their existence seems to call into question many of our most basic

The Army and ESP

In 1984, the National Research Council was asked by the Army Research Institute to investigate the possibility of using paranormal phenomena to enhance human performance. The Army was particularly interested in its potential military applications.

> In their view, ESP, if real and controllable, could be used for intelligence gathering and, because it includes "precognition," ESP could also be used to anticipate the actions of an enemy. It is believed that PK (psychokinesis), if realizable, might be used to jam enemy computers, prematurely trigger nuclear weapons, and incapacitate weapons and vehicles. More specific applications envisioned involve behavior modification; inducing sickness, disorientation, or even death in a distant enemy; communicating with submarines; planting thoughts in individuals without their knowledge; hypnotizing individuals at a distance; psychotronic weapons of various kinds; psychic shields to protect sensitive information or military installations; and the like. One suggested application is a conception of the "First Earth Battalion," made up of "warrior monks," who will have mastered almost all the techniques under consideration by the committee, including the use of ESP, leaving their bodies at will, levitating, psychic healing, and walking through walls.[87]

Many paranormal phenomena were studied, including remote viewing, psychokinesis, telepathy, and plant perception. The committee drew the following conclusions:

> Overall, the experimental designs are of insufficient quality to arbitrate between claims made for and against the existence of the phenomena. While the best research is of higher quality than many critics assume, the bulk of the work does not meet the standards necessary to contribute to the knowledge base of science. Definitive conclusions must depend on evidence derived from stronger research designs.[88]

beliefs about the nature of knowledge and reality. All forms of ESP, for example, seem to undermine the theory of knowledge underlying modern science, namely, that sense experience is the only source of knowledge of the external world. Telepathy (mind reading) seems to undermine the theory of reality underlying modern science, namely, that all that exists is matter in motion or mass/energy. And precognition seems to undermine the belief that an effect cannot precede its cause. If it turns out that such phenomena are real, we may have to radically restructure our worldview.

Many of us have had experiences that seem to fall into one of these categories. We may have thought of a friend moments before she phoned us, or sensed that a loved one was in danger only to find out that he actually was, or dreamt about winning a jackpot and then won it. Such experiences appear to be common. One study of over 1,400 American adults found that 67 percent had "experienced

ESP."[89] But as we've seen, we can't always take our experiences at face value. What seems to be inexplicable often turns out to have a rather mundane explanation. Before we accept the reality of psi phenomena, then, we should be sure that the phenomena in question can't be explained in terms of well-understood processes.

Some people think that the world would be a much more interesting place if psi were a reality. On a personal level, for example, telepathy could improve our communication skills, precognition could help us prepare for the future, and psychokinesis could help us achieve our goals. On the national and international level, the consequences could be even more remarkable. Imagine being able to read your enemies' minds, examine their secret documents without breaking into their headquarters, and disarm their weapons by thought alone. J. B. Rhine, one of the first to study psi in the laboratory, had this to say about the prospect of harnessing psi energy:

> The consequences for world affairs would be literally colossal. War plans and crafty designs of any kind, anywhere in the world, could be watched and revealed. With such revelation it seems unlikely that war could ever occur again. There would be no advantage of surprise. Every secret weapon and scheming strategy would be subject to exposure. The nations could relax their suspicious fear of each other's secret machinations.
>
> Crime on any scale could hardly exist with its cloak of invisibility thus removed. Graft, exploitation, and suppression could not continue if the dark plots of wicked men were to be laid bare.[90]

Strange thoughts beget strange deeds.
—PERCY BYSSHE SHELLEY

But would a fully developed psi capability really be such a boon? What if there were people who could read your thoughts, see what you're doing every minute of the day, and control your body with their minds? Wouldn't that make possible a form of social control more horrific than that portrayed in either George Orwell's *1984* or Aldous Huxley's *Brave New World?* Martin Gardner thinks so. He sees psi powers as "tools with a far wider scope for repression and terror than the mere tapping of a phone, opening of a letter, or electronic eavesdropping."[91]

The military potential of psi has not escaped the watchful eye of the Pentagon. Columnist Jack Anderson reported in 1981 that the Pentagon's top secret "psychic task force" had spent over $6 million in 1980 alone trying to develop psi weapons. Our military leaders knew that the Soviets had been conducting serious psychic research since the 1930s and that Stalin had hoped to develop psychic weapons to counter America's nuclear threat. Apparently the Pentagon's top brass was anxious to close what they perceived as an ESP gap.

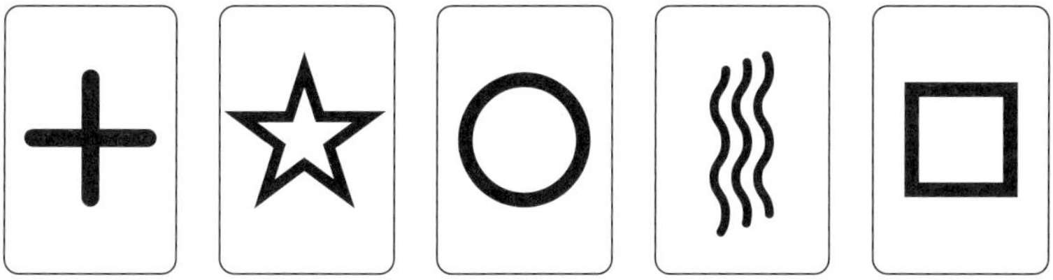

Symbols in a deck of Zener cards.

In the 1970s, books such as Sheila Ostrander and Lynn Schroeder's *Psychic Discoveries behind the Iron Curtain* created the impression that the Soviets were well on the way to harnessing psychic energy. There were stories of Russian women who could separate the white of an egg from its yolk after it had been dropped into an aquarium (an impressive feat because it couldn't have been done with hidden magnets or strings) and psychokinetically stop the heartbeat of frogs. If such energies could be focused and amplified, no American would be safe.

But it wasn't the military implications that got J. B. Rhine interested in psi phenomena. It was the philosophical implications. Like the creationists, Rhine believed that a widespread acceptance of materialism would have disastrous social consequences.

> The most far-reaching and revolting consequence lies in what would happen to volitional or mental freedom. Under a mechanistic determinism the cherished voluntarism of the individual would be nothing but idle fancy. Without the exercise of some freedom from physical law, the concepts of character responsibility, moral judgment, and democracy would not survive critical analysis. The concept of a spiritual order, either in the individual or beyond him, would have no logical place whatever. In fact, little of the entire value system under which human society has developed would survive the establishment of a thoroughgoing philosophy of physicalism.[92]

If psi were real, he thought, the materialist worldview would have to be abandoned and one more in tune with traditional values could take its place.

J. B. Rhine began his research into psi phenomena in 1930 at Duke University. Using a deck of cards designed by his colleague Carl Zener, Rhine tried to determine whether it was possible for a subject to correctly identify the symbols on the cards without coming into sensory contact with them. There are twenty-five cards in a Zener deck: five cards each of five different symbols—a cross, a star, a circle, wavy lines, and a square. One run consists of an attempt to identify the symbol on each card in the deck. By pure chance, in any one run, a respondent should be able to correctly identify the symbols on five of the cards.

Here's something to think about: How come you never see a headline like "Psychic Wins Lottery"?

—Jay Leno

In Rhine's earliest and most successful experiments, the subject and the experimenter sat at opposite ends of a table in the middle of which was a thin partition that prevented the subject from seeing the cards. To test for telepathy, the experimenter would look at the cards one by one, and the subject would try to identify the symbol the experimenter was looking at. To test for clairvoyance, the experimenter, without looking at the symbols on the cards, would pick them up one by one, and the subject would try to identify the symbol that was on the card the experimenter held. Alternatively, the deck would be shuffled and placed face down on the table and the subject would try to identify the symbol on each card starting from the top and reading down through the deck. To test for precognition, the subject would write down ahead of time the order the cards would be in after having been shuffled. (A successful outcome of this test, however, does not necessarily prove the existence of precognition, for the subject could have used psychokinesis to influence the shuffle.)

In 1934 Rhine published his results in a book titled *Extrasensory Perception.* (Rhine coined the term.) Out of nearly 100,000 attempts, Rhine's subjects averaged 7.1 correct identifications per run. Since only five correct identifications per run would be expected by chance, the odds against Rhine's results being due to chance are well over a googol to one. (A googol is a one followed by a hundred zeros.) On the basis of his research, Rhine concluded that there must be some form of nonphysical energy at work:

> Might not the same logic that has produced the concepts of the various energies involved in physical theory profitably be followed to the point of suggesting that psi energy be hypothesized? . . . It is no great jump from the broad concept of energy as it now prevails in physical theory over to the notion of a special state of energy that is not interceptible by any of the sense organs. . . . It may be tentatively proposed, then, that back of the phenomena of psi must exist an energy that interoperates with and interconverts to those other energetic states already familiar to physics.[93]

But is Rhine's conclusion really the best explanation of the evidence? To determine whether it is, we'll have to explore some alternative hypotheses and see whether any of them meet the criteria of adequacy better than Rhine's.

The criteria of simplicity and conservatism tell us that, when we are attempting to explain something,

We should accept an extraordinary hypothesis only if no ordinary one will do.

Rhine's early research, however, does not require an extraordinary hypothesis. It can be fully explained in terms of quite ordinary forms of information transfer. Psychologists Leonard Zusne and Warren Jones explain:

> Chance was clearly not producing Rhine's results. It was opportunities to establish the identity of the cards by sensory means. These were so numerous and so readily available that much of Rhine's work during the 1930s may be safely ignored. Testing often occurred in a face-to-face situation, with minimal screening between the agent and the percipient or none at all. When an agent sits across the table from the percipient, the latter can see the backs of the cards. At one time, the ESP cards had been printed with such a heavy pressure that the symbols became embossed in the card material and could be read from the back. In 1938, it was discovered that the symbols could also be seen through the cards, which, of course, allows room for fingertip reading of the backs of the cards and, if they are marked, of their sides.[94]

Given all the opportunities for sensory leakage, there is no reason to believe that anything extrasensory was going on. The best explanation of Rhine's results, then, is that the subject, either consciously or unconsciously, sensed the identity of the cards by ordinary means. The reason this explanation is the best is that it's the simplest and most conservative one that accounts for the data.

There is something else to notice about Rhine's hypothesis. He tells us that there is some sort of nonphysical energy involved, but he doesn't tell us enough about this energy to allow for any independent confirmation of it. As a result, his hypothesis is ad hoc. It's no better than the hypothesis that gremlins cause fluorescent lights to light up. In fact, it's no better than the hypothesis that gremlins (rather than energy) cause ESP by carrying messages back and forth between the experimenter and the percipient. Until we learn enough about Rhine's energy to make an independent determination of its existence, there is no good reason to believe that it exists.

If Rhine's energy really existed, others should be able to detect it in the same sorts of situations that Rhine did. But very few of the scientists who have repeated Rhine's experiments have gotten his results. Psychologist J. Crumbaugh's experiences are typical:

> At the time [1938] of performing the experiments involved I fully expected that they would yield easily all the final answers. I did not imagine that after 28 years I would still be in as much doubt as when I had begun. I repeated a number of the then current Duke techniques, but the results of 3,024 runs of the ESP cards—as much

The Million-Dollar Paranormal Challenge

If psychic abilities are real, they should be observable under controlled conditions, that is, under conditions that rule out any possibility of fraud, deception, or trickery. Such conditions are hard to find outside of the laboratory, however, and it's often difficult to get alleged psychics into the laboratory. To entice them into demonstrating their abilities in a more convincing way, many organizations have offered a monetary prize. One of the first to do so was the magazine *Scientific American*, which in 1922 offered two $2,500 prizes: one for anyone who could produce a spirit photograph under controlled conditions, and another for anyone who could produce a visible psychic manifestation or apparition. Harry Houdini, the foremost magician of the time, was on the investigating committee, and he was able to show that the effects produced by the claimants were the result of mundane trickery rather than supernatural powers. So the prizes were not awarded.

More recently, the magician, educator, and winner of the MacArthur Genius award, James Randi, offered $1 million to anyone who could exhibit a paranormal, occult, or supernatural power under proper observing conditions. The offer stood from 1996 to 2015, but no one succeeded in winning it. Randi challenged some of the most famous psychics in the world to vie for the prize including Uri Geller, James Van Praagh, Sylvia Browne, and John Edward, but none took him up on it. Sylvia Browne, a renowned medium who claimed to be able to communicate with the dead, agreed on the air during a *Larry King Live* show in 2001 to take the challenge. But she passed away in 2013 without ever submitting herself to a test.

Although Randi is no longer offering a reward for proof of psychic ability, many other organizations are. The Indian Rationalist Organization, the Australian Skeptics, and the Independent Investigation Group, to name but a few, offer significant monetary awards for anyone who can demonstrate paranormal powers under proper observing conditions. To date, no one has won any of these prizes, but even if someone did, that, in itself, would not prove the reality of the individual's powers. Science requires replication to ensure that observed results are not a fluke or the result of some other cause. But if someone could repeatedly demonstrate paranormal abilities under controlled conditions, we would have good reason to believe that they are real.

> work as Rhine reported in his first book—were all negative. In 1940 I utilized further methods with high school students, again with negative results.[95]

Psychologist John Beloff was also unable to find any positive evidence for psi:

> I recently completed a seven-year programme of parapsychological research with the help of one full time research assistant. No one would have been more delighted to obtain positive results than we, but for all the success we achieved, ESP might just as well not have existed. . . . I have not found on comparing notes with other parapsychologists . . . that my experience is in any way out of the ordinary.[96]

Because there are so many ways that an experiment can go wrong, we can't be sure that an effect is real (rather than an artifact of the experimental setup) unless it can be repeated by others. But in the field of parapsychology, there are no repeatable experiments. Even the same researchers, using the same subjects, can't achieve similar results every time. Consequently, there is good reason to doubt that psi is real.

The greatest wonder of all is the regularity of nature.

—GEORGE DANA BOARDMAN

That's not to say that psi is unreal, however. No amount of evidence (or lack of it) could prove that, because it's impossible to prove a universal negative. What the lack of repeatable experiments shows is that no one is justified in believing that psi exists because the evidence available doesn't establish that claim beyond a reasonable doubt.

Perhaps parapsychologists haven't been able to devise a repeatable experiment because they haven't identified the relevant variables yet. Scientists, whenever possible, perform controlled experiments to ensure that the relevant variables remain the same each time an experiment is performed. If they didn't, the experiment would be worthless. So one explanation of the parapsychologists' lack of repeatable experiments is that the factors necessary for proper psi functioning have not been identified.

Parapsychologists have their own explanations for the inability of others to replicate their experiments, however. One of the most common is the *sheep–goat effect,* studied extensively by Gertrude Schmeidler.[97] According to this hypothesis, the results of psi experiments are influenced by the attitudes of the experimenter. If the experimenter doubts the existence of psi (a goat), the experiment won't succeed; if the experimenter believes in the existence of psi (a sheep), the experiment will succeed. But what of experimenters like J. Crumbaugh and John Beloff who claim that they began their research as sheep? Don't they show that the sheep–goat effect is mistaken? Not according to this argument, which holds that while such experimenters may have consciously believed in psi, they must have unconsciously doubted it. D. Scott Rogo, for example, claims that Susan Blackmore's failure to find any evidence for the existence of psi in her sixteen years of research is due to her unconscious bias against it.[98]

The ad hoc character of this hypothesis should be obvious. There's no way to test it because no possible data could count against it. Every apparent counterexample can be explained away by appeal to the unconscious. Moreover, accepting it would make the whole field of parapsychology untestable. No unsuccessful experiments could count against the existence of psi because they could simply be the result of experimenter bias. This sort of reasoning convinces many researchers that parapsychology is a pseudoscience.

But parapsychologists need not reason this way, and many don't. According to Ray Hyman, over 3,000 parapsychological experiments have been performed, many by competent investigators.[99] Some experiments do appear to be successful. But none are consistently repeatable, and many of the most impressive experiments have turned out to be fraudulent.

For example, in London between 1941 and 1943, parapsychologist Samuel Soal tested a subject named Basil Shackleton by using cards that had brightly painted pictures of animals on them instead of the usual Zener symbols. Soal's theory was that subjects might do better if they had more interesting material to work with. Although Shackleton scored only at chance levels with the target cards, his guesses correlated remarkably well with the card immediately following the target card. It was estimated that the odds of that happening by chance were greater than 10^{35} to 1.

Many considered Soal's research to be the best evidence available for psi. Whately Carrington, for example, said:

> If I had to choose one single investigation on which to pin my whole faith in the reality of paranormal phenomena, or with which to convince a hardened skeptic (if this be not a contradiction in terms), I should unhesitatingly choose this series of experiments, which is the most cast-iron piece of work I know, as well as having yielded the most remarkable results.[100]

We now know, however, that Soal fudged his data. An assistant in many of the Shackleton experiments, Gretl Albert, told one of Soal's colleagues that she had seen him altering the records. Later computer analysis of the records has shown that Soal either altered them or didn't get his random numbers in the way he said he did.[101]

Another prominent case of experimenter fraud involves Walter J. Levy Jr., the man Rhine picked to succeed him as head of his parapsychology laboratory. Levy was caught unplugging an automatic scoring machine in an attempt to have it record an abnormally high number of hits.

Certainly not all parapsychologists (nor all parapsychological subjects) are frauds. But because parapsychology has had more than its fair share of them, we should not accept the results of a psi experiment unless we can establish beyond a reasonable doubt that they're not due to fraud. One way to guard against fraud is to enlist the aid of a professional magician. Project Alpha, described in the following box, underscores the importance of this precaution.

The evidence currently available does not establish the existence of psi beyond a reasonable doubt because the experiments on which it is based are not repeatable. The inability of other researchers to replicate the results of a psi experiment suggests that something other than psi may be responsible for the outcome. Perhaps the original experimenters fell prey to one of the perceptual or conceptual errors examined in Chapter 5. Perhaps they failed to employ adequate controls to prevent other factors from producing the result. And perhaps they are guilty of fraud. Replication is necessary to ensure that we're not fooling ourselves or being fooled by others. Without it, there's no way to know what caused the reported effect.

It has been claimed, however, that even though no particular experiment is repeatable, all the successful experiments taken together establish the existence of psi beyond a reasonable doubt. John Beloff, for example, has written:

> It is not my contention that any of the aforegoing experiments were perfect . . . or beyond criticism. . . . Moreover, unless a much higher level of repeatability becomes possible, the skeptical option, that the results can be attributed to carelessness or to conscious or unconscious cheating on the part of one or more of the experimenters, remains open and valid. Nevertheless, it is my personal opinion that these . . . investigations represent an overwhelming case for accepting the reality of psi phenomena.[102]

Everyone's entitled to his or her opinion, of course, but the important question from our point of view is whether Beloff's opinion is justified. Can individually unconvincing studies be collectively convincing? No. What a study lacks in quality cannot be made up in quantity. The evidence generated by questionable studies remains questionable, no matter how many of them there are.

There is a great deal of anecdotal evidence for psi phenomena. Many individuals have had experiences that they believe are inexplicable in terms of known physical laws. But as we saw in Chapter 5, many strange experiences can be accounted for in terms of well-known perceptual processes, such as pareidolia, cryptomnesia, selective attention, subjective validation, the Forer effect, the autokinetic effect, and so on. Because, outside of the laboratory, we can't establish beyond a reasonable doubt that these factors are *not* at work, we can't accept anecdotal evidence at face value.

One further body of evidence must be included in any examination of psi—that obtained by gambling casinos. As Terence Hines observes, "One can consider every spin of the roulette wheel, every throw of the dice, every draw of the card in gambling casinos the

Project Alpha

An experiment provides evidence for ESP only if the results cannot be accounted for in terms of ordinary sensory perception (OSP). Unfortunately, scientists are not particularly adept at determining when a result could be due to OSP because they are not trained in the art of deception. Professional magicians, however, are. As a result, parapsychologists would do well to make use of their expertise. Project Alpha, conceived by James (the Amazing) Randi, provides a dramatic demonstration of the need for magicians in the psi lab.

> In Project Alpha, two young magicians, Steve Shaw and Michael Edwards, with Randi's advice, went to the McDonnell Laboratory for Psychical Research at Washington University in St. Louis, Missouri. The McDonnell Laboratory was probably the best-funded psychical laboratory in the world; it had been created with a $50,000 grant from James McDonnell, chairman of the board of the McDonnell-Douglas Aircraft Corporation.
>
> Shaw and Edwards easily convinced the research staff at the McDonnell Laboratory that they had genuine psychic powers. They were tested by the laboratory for a period of three years. They rarely failed to achieve "psychic" feats. Metal was bent "paranormally," minds were read, the contents of sealed envelopes were mysteriously divined, fuses sealed in protective containers burned out, and mysterious pictures appeared "psychically" on film inside cameras. . . . Randi reports in detail on the simple ways in which these deceptions were carried out.
>
> Before Shaw and Edwards began to be tested at the McDonnell Laboratory, Randi wrote to the director, Dr. Peter Phillips, a physics professor at Washington University. Randi outlined the type of controls that the lab should use to guard against sleight of hand and other such trickery. He also offered to come to the lab, at his own expense and without public acknowledgment, to assist in the preparation of "trick-proof" experiments. Randi's offer was rejected and his advice ignored. The controls that were placed on Shaw and Edwards were totally inadequate to prevent their use of trickery. Even when videotapes of their feats showed fairly clearly, to anyone watching them carefully, how the trick had been done, the enthusiastic laboratory staff failed to catch on.[103]

world over as a single trial in a worldwide ongoing study in parapsychology."[104] If psi were a reality, casino winnings should vary from what's predicted by the laws of chance. But they don't. The billions of trials conducted each year by casinos all over the world provide no evidence for the existence of psi. It has been claimed that the reason for this lack of evidence is that psi cannot be used for personal gain. Such ad hoc hypotheses, however, should not keep us from giving this evidence its due.

There are non–ad hoc hypotheses that can explain the casino data, however. One is that it is just too noisy in casinos for psi to operate. Recent experiments using sensory deprivation techniques seem to lend credibility to this hypothesis.

Recognizing that if psi exists, it must be an extremely weak force, parapsychologist Charles Honorton has tried to detect its presence by reducing normal sensory input to a minimum. Subjects in his experiments are put in a *ganzfeld* designed to block out sensory information. The ganzfeld is produced by having the subjects close their eyes and placing headphones over their ears. A bright red light is shone on their faces and white noise played through the headphones. After being in this condition for about fifteen minutes, the subjects begin to hallucinate. What they see is similar to the hypnogogic images sometimes seen right before falling asleep. Once the subjects have reached this state, the senders—usually relatives or friends—try to transmit to the subjects the contents of a minute-long video. The clip is chosen randomly by a computer out of forty sets of four clips each. Thus, even the experimenter has no way of knowing what clip is being played at any particular time. Once the senders have viewed the clip, the subjects are asked to describe the images they are seeing. Honorton's hypothesis is that if psi exists, the images seen by the subjects should match the images transmitted by the senders more often than would be expected by pure chance. At the end of each session, the subjects are shown all four clips in the set and asked to identify which one most closely resembles the images they were seeing.

By chance alone, the subjects should be able to identify the correct clip 25 percent of the time. Honorton's 240 subjects did so 34 percent of the time. The odds against this high rate happening by chance are more than a million to one. Others tried to replicate his results. Some succeeded; some didn't. Some reported effect sizes much greater than Honorton's. By 1985, over forty ganzfeld studies had been reported in the literature. Ray Hyman, professor of psychology at the University of Washington, performed a meta-analysis of these studies in an attempt to determine whether the results were really due to some sort of psi functioning.[105] A meta-analysis is a statistical procedure that combines the results of similar studies after first grading them in terms of quality. This allows researchers to determine whether significant results are correlated with poor quality. If they are, there's reason to believe something other than psi is responsible for the results. Hyman found that experimental flaws such as sensory leakage and inadequate randomization were indeed correlated with successful outcomes. So he concluded that the original ganzfeld experiments were not convincing evidence for the existence of psi.[106]

In response to Hyman's critique, Honorton performed his own meta-analysis of the studies using a different set of criteria to grade them. Contrary to Hyman, he found the studies to be quite significant, with odds against their being due to chance of over a billion to one.[107] His conclusion differed from Hyman's in part because his criteria identified more flaws in unsuccessful experiments and fewer in successful ones.

To improve the quality of ganzfeld research and to lessen the likelihood of such divergent conclusions, Honorton and Hyman wrote a joint paper in which they outlined the criteria that any credible ganzfeld experiment should meet.[108] Using these criteria, Honorton designed a new type of ganzfeld experiment known as the *autoganzfeld,* because it partially automated the collection of data. In 1990, he published the results of over 355 autoganzfeld sessions with over 241 volunteers. The success rate was far above what would be expected by chance alone. In 1994, Cornell University psychologist Daryl Bem published a joint article with Honorton in one of psychology's most prestigious research journals, *Psychological Bulletin.* Their meta-analysis of a series of ganzfeld experiments also indicated a success rate much greater than chance. They concluded that "the replication rates and effect sizes achieved by one particular experimental method, the ganzfeld procedure, are now sufficient to warrant bringing this body of data to the wider psychological community."[109]

A more recent meta-analysis of 30 additional studies conducted by Richard Wiseman of the University of Hertfordshire and Julie Milton of the University of Edinburgh, however, found no evidence of success above chance.[110] In addition, a more detailed analysis by Ray Hyman of the studies reported in Bem and Honorton's article found a number of statistical anomalies. Specifically, he found that all of the hits were achieved in the second or later appearance of the targets. This suggests that something other than psi may have been responsible for the hits. To rule that out, Hyman suggests that each video clip be run through the machine the same number of times.[111]

Meta-analysis is a relatively new statistical procedure, and some have suggested that the way it has been used in parapsychology yields inaccurate results. To be accurate, a meta-analysis must include all studies of the type under investigation. Not all such studies are reported in the literature, however. Publishing space is limited, and unsuccessful studies are not as noteworthy as successful ones. So unsuccessful studies often get filed away in a drawer somewhere. To counteract this "file drawer" effect, meta-analyses usually include a calculation of how many unsuccessful studies would have to have been conducted in order for the success

Extrasensory Pornception

Daryl Bem recently shocked the psychological establishment by publishing a study in a peer-reviewed journal which seemed to provide evidence of precognition (knowing something before it happens). Bem claims that his experiments, titled "Feeling the Future," show that the future can affect the past by giving us knowledge of what is to come.[112] In one experiment, the subjects (college students) sat in front of a computer screen that displayed two curtains side by side. They were told that one curtain had an image behind it that was neutral, negative, or erotic. Their task was to identify that curtain by clicking on it. On the face of it, the experiment appears to be a test for clairvoyance (distant viewing) because the subjects are trying to detect the presence of an object they cannot see. But Bem arranged things so that the computer didn't choose which curtain to put the image behind until after the subjects had made their choice. So the experiment was really testing for precognition; if the subjects were able to guess which curtain would have the picture behind it more than 50 percent of the time, they would seem to be feeling the future.

Bem found that when the image was neutral, the subjects were able to identify the correct curtain only 50 percent of the time (which is what you would expect by chance alone). But when the image was erotic, the subjects were able to identify the correct curtain 53 percent of the time, which is statistically significant. The subjects apparently could sense which curtain the erotic picture would be placed behind, thus suggesting that they possessed what Stephen Colbert called "extrasensory pornception."

Has science finally proven the existence of ESP? Most psychologists think not. For one thing, if the past is any guide to the future, Bem's experiment will be found to have significant methodological flaws. Many parapsychologists in the past have reported statistically significant results only to find them evaporate under critical scrutiny. For another, Bem did not follow standard scientific protocols in conducting his experiments. For example, halfway through the image guessing experiment, he altered the number of erotic vs. non-erotic images he was using, and made some of them more pornographic. Changing experimental procedure in the middle of an experiment destroys the control needed for the results to be convincing. Finally, and most importantly, other researchers have failed to replicate Bem's results. Replication is important in science because only if an experiment can be replicated can we be sure that error dishonesty was not at work. Three different researchers in three different laboratories ran Bem's most successful experiments to see if the effect was real.[113] In each case the results they got were no better than chance. The failure to replicate Bem's results suggests that something other than ESP may have been at work.

rate to be at the chance level. In his 1985 meta-analysis of 28 ganzfeld studies, Honorton concluded that there would have to have been 423 unsuccessful, unreported studies to bring the success rate down to the chance level. Since the number of researchers conducting ganzfeld experiments is rather small, Honorton concluded that it would be unreasonable to suppose that there were that many such studies.

Statistician Douglas Stokes, however, has pointed out that unsuccessful studies may well have results that are below the chance level.

The number of studies below the chance level needed to explain away the apparent success of the ganzfeld experiments is far fewer than the number required at the chance level. Stokes has calculated that only 62 unreported studies at below the chance level are needed to nullify Honorton's original results, and that number is not outside the realm of probability.[114]

Failed replication and flawed meta-analyses have not put a stop to parapsychological research. In 2010, Lance Storm, Patrizio Tressoldi, and Lorenzo Di Risio published yet another meta-analysis of 29 ganzfeld studies conducted from 1997 to 2008. Out of 1,498 trials, there were 483 hits, resulting in a 32.2 percent hit rate, far above the 25 percent that would be expected by chance. They conclude: "We maintain that some caution is warranted in the interpretation of these results. Nevertheless, our findings indicate the ganzfeld is one of the most consistent and reliable experimental paradigms in parapsychology."[115]

Ray Hyman agrees that some caution is warranted in interpreting these results but disagrees that ganzfeld is a consistent and reliable methodology because it relies so heavily on meta-analysis that "has serious limitations . . . as a method for confirming hypothesis and for establishing the replicability of experiments."[116] Furthermore, attempts by Broughton and Alexander to replicate the type of experiments reported by Storm et al. have failed.[117]

Jeffrey Rouder, Richard Morey, and Jordan Province also examined the results reported by Storm et al. Using Bayesian statistical methods to evaluate the probability of the existence of psi, they found that effect size was not high enough to justify belief in psi. According to them: "this value is unimpressive in the context of psi because there is no plausible mechanism and because there are almost certainly omitted replications failures."[118] Because we don't know how psi works or the extent of the file drawer effect, these studies don't warrant our believing in psi. David Marks's 1986 characterization of parapsychological research remains as true now as it was then: "Parascience has so far failed to produce a single repeatable finding and, until it does, will continue to be viewed as an incoherent collection of belief systems steeped in fantasy, illusion and error."[119]

The ganzfeld procedure remains the most promising way to demonstrate the existence of psi. Bem and other well-respected psychologists remain convinced that these studies identify an anomaly that has not yet been adequately explained. A well-controlled ganzfeld experiment may well turn out to be replicable. If it does, we may have to begin changing our worldview.

There is reason to believe, however, that such a study will not be forthcoming. Not only have ESP investigators failed to come up with a repeatable experiment in over seventy-five years of research, but psychologists at Harvard University have recently carried out a series of experiments which, they claim, provides the strongest evidence yet that ESP does not exist. Samuel Moulton and Stephen Kosslyn hypothesized that "If psi exists, it occurs in the brain, and hence, assessing the brain directly should be more sensitive than using indirect behavioral methods (as have been used previously)."[120] To detect the effect of psi stimuli on the brain, they used functional magnetic resonance imaging (fMRI), a type of brain scanner that records brain activity by tracking blood flow and oxygen level. The experiment was designed to detect the presence of three types of extrasensory perception: telepathy (perceiving another's thoughts), clairvoyance (perceiving distant objects), and precognition (perceiving the future). For each run of the experiment, the receiver was placed in the brain scanner and shown two photographs in succession. At the same time the sender—who was either the receiver's friend, relative, or identical twin—was shown one of the photos on a computer screen and was asked to send it to the receiver. The receiver was then asked to guess which image was being sent and was shown the images a second time. Having the image sent by the sender tested for telepathy; having the image appear on the computer screen tested for clairvoyance, and having the image appear a second time tested for precognition. Nineteen pairs of individuals were tested and 3,687 responses were recorded. If ESP were real, the brain should have responded differently to the psi image. But it didn't. Nor did any of the receivers identify the correct image more than 50 percent of the time, which is exactly what one would expect by pure chance. So Moulton and Kosslyn conclude: "The results support the null hypothesis that psi does not exist. The brains of our participants—as a group and individually—reacted to psi and non-psi stimuli in a statistically indistinguishable manner."[121] The failure to get a positive result does not conclusively prove the nonexistence of psi because new evidence may always turn up. Nevertheless, they believe that their experiment provides strong support for the claim that psi doesn't exist because it employed variables that have traditionally been associated with psi, such as subjects who were emotionally or genetically related to one another as well as emotionally charged stimuli.

Defenders of psi, of course, can use any number of ad hoc explanations to explain away the results. They can claim, for example, that psi doesn't affect the brain or that the people tested were not psychically gifted. But as we've seen, you can explain away the results of any experiment as long as you're willing to make enough changes to our background beliefs. The important point is that we have no compelling reason to make such changes, except to save belief in psi. There is no independent evidence that either of these possibilities are true. The case for ESP is not yet closed, but it is getting harder to make.

Now that we have a better understanding of how science works and what distinguishes good explanations from bad ones, let's see how this knowledge can help us think about weird things. In the next chapter, we'll examine a number of weird things in an attempt to determine the best explanation of them.

SUMMARY

Contrary to what some critics assert, science cannot be identified with any particular worldview. Science is a method of discerning the truth, not a particular body of truths. The worldviews held by scientists have changed radically over the years—the worldview of quantum mechanics is far from the mechanistic worldview of the seventeenth century.

The first step in scientific methodology is not to begin with observations detached from any guiding hypothesis. Scientific inquiry begins with a problem, and hypotheses are needed for scientific observation because they tell us what to look for, helping us distinguish relevant from irrelevant information. Although hypotheses are designed to account for data, they rarely can be derived from data. Hypotheses are created, not discovered, and the process of their creation is just as open-ended as the process of artistic creation. Hypotheses must be checked against reality, and this checking involves controlled tests and systematic observations—all of which must be as free from subjectivity, bias, and extraneous variables as possible. For example, in medical research, controlled clinical studies are the gold standard for discovering whether a particular treatment works. Properly conducting them requires placebo and experimental groups, blinding of both the subjects and researchers, and replication of the results.

No scientific hypothesis can be conclusively confirmed because we can't rule out the possibility of someday finding evidence to the contrary. Neither can we conclusively refute a scientific hypothesis. Predictions can be derived from a hypothesis only in conjunction with a background theory. If a prediction turns out to be false, we can always save the hypothesis by modifying the background theory. Constructing adjunct hypotheses is a way to shield a hypothesis from adverse evidence. Doing so is legitimate if there's a way to independently verify them. If there is no way, the hypotheses are ad hoc. When a scientific theory begins to rely on ad hoc hypotheses to be saved from adverse data, holding onto the theory becomes unreasonable.

The amount of understanding produced by a theory is determined by how well it meets the criteria of adequacy: testability (whether it can be tested), fruitfulness (whether it successfully predicts new phenomena), scope (the amount of diverse phenomena explained by it), simplicity (how many assumptions it makes), and conservatism (how well it fits with established beliefs).

If we use the criteria of adequacy to judge the relative worth of evolution and creationism, we see that the latter gets low marks. It fails the criterion of conservatism, for it doesn't fit with well-established beliefs. It isn't fruitful because it hasn't predicted any new facts. It isn't as simple as evolution: Creationism assumes the existence of an unknown entity (God) and unknown forces. It has far less scope than evolution does. Evolution explains countless phenomena in many fields of science; creationism raises more questions than it answers.

When the criteria of adequacy are applied to the theory that ESP exists, the theory fares poorly. No scientific evidence has established the existence of ESP beyond a reasonable doubt, and ordinary theories (such as chance) are simpler and more conservative.

STUDY QUESTIONS

1. What is the difference between science and technology?
2. What is the function of the scientific method?
3. Why can we never conclusively confirm or confute a scientific hypothesis?
4. What specific features of a hypothesis do each of the criteria of adequacy—testability, fruitfulness, scope, simplicity, and conservatism—try to measure?
5. Is creationism as good a scientific theory as evolution?
6. Are we justified in believing that there is extrasensory perception?

EVALUATE THESE CLAIMS. ARE THEY REASONABLE? WHY OR WHY NOT?

1. Jane has lived in her house for ten years and has just started to see ghosts. She also just started to read horror novels. Therefore, the ghosts must be a figment of her imagination.
2. In order to prove that levitation is real, you've got to believe in it because unless you think it's true, you won't get convincing evidence.
3. Reincarnation is a fact because every person has actually been through many lifetimes.
4. Professor Smith came up with that theory while on LSD. How can anyone take it seriously?
5. Scientists won't accept a paranormal claim because it conflicts with their preconceived notion that all that exists is matter in motion.
6. Have you ever noticed how there are more incidents of violence or strange behavior during a full moon? There is obviously some physical force connected to the full moon that changes the way people behave.

DISCUSSION QUESTIONS

1. What sort of evidence would we need to justifiably claim that intelligent life from another planet was visiting Earth?
2. A scientist sees that the dial on the thermometer reads 105 degrees Fahrenheit. What background information is involved in the inference that the temperature is 105?
3. Dr. Raymond Bernard claims that UFOs do not come from outer space but from the center of the Earth. He believes that the citizens of Atlantis migrated there after their continent sank. Suppose that we had good evidence that UFOs were produced by an advanced civilization. Is Bernard's claim more reasonable than the claim that UFOs come from outer space? Why or why not?

FIELD PROBLEM

Israeli psychic Uri Geller is best known for his alleged ability to bend spoons with his mind. He has demonstrated his psychic spoon bending countless times, in front of large audiences and small, on television shows, and in private gatherings. Some magicians—notably James Randi—have duplicated Geller's feat and declared that it is nothing more than sleight of hand.

Assignment: Do research on the internet to find out exactly how Randi and others do their Geller-like spoon bending. Then answer this question: What are the implications for the Geller hypothesis (spoon bending by mind powers) of the magicians' duplication?

CRITICAL READING AND WRITING

I. Read the passage below and answer the following questions:
   1. What theory is being offered as an explanation for the existence of crop circles?
   2. According to the writer, what evidence supports the theory?
   3. Is the theory conservative? Is it simple?
   4. Is the theory testable? If so, how can it be tested?
   5. What alternative theory could also explain the existence of crop circles?

II. In a 250-word paper, evaluate the worth of the theory espoused in the passage, comparing it to just one competing theory (that crop circles are made by ordinary humans using ordinary means). Use the criteria of adequacy in your analysis and decide which theory is best.

Passage 5

One of the great mysteries of our time is crop circles. Crop circles are large geometric designs pressed or stamped into fields of grain. They are often circular but can be almost any shape, ranging from simple patterns to complex pictograms or symbols. They can measure a few feet in diameter or several hundred feet. Interest in crop circles began in the 1970s when they started mysteriously appearing overnight in the grain fields of southern England. The crops would be neatly flattened with the stalks pressed together. In the 1980s and 1990s, interest in the phenomenon grew as crop circles proliferated throughout the world.

But what theory best explains the existence of crop circles? The answer is this: *Crop circles are created by small whirlwinds of electrified air, also called wind vortices.* That is, crop circles are made by columns of whirling, charged air similar to dust devils or miniature tornadoes. These vortices form above grain fields then plunge to the ground, discharging the electricity and flattening the grain in swirled patterns. But unlike tornadoes, wind vortices leave the stalks of grain undamaged.

The evidence for this theory is impressive. Natural crop-circle vortices are unknown to science, but similar vortices are reported to have been produced artificially in laboratories. A few people claim to have seen the vortices in open fields. An electrified vortex might produce light during discharge, and sure enough some eyewitnesses have reported seeing "balls of light" and other light phenomena in or near crop circles. Some people also report hearing strange sounds near crop circles, such as humming noises.

NOTES

1. Carl Hempel, "Valuation and Objectivity in Science," in *Physics, Philosophy, and Psychoanalysis: Essays in Honor of Adolf Grünbaum,* ed. R. S. Cohen and L. Laudan (Boston: Reidel, 1983), p. 91ff.
2. Charles Sanders Peirce, *Collected Papers,* vol. 5, ed. Charles Hartshorne, Paul Weiss, and Arthur Burks (Cambridge: Harvard University Press, 1931–1958), pp. 575–83.
3. Bruce Holbrook, *The Stone Monkey* (New York: William Morrow, 1981), pp. 50–52.
4. Fritjof Capra, *The Turning Point* (New York: Bantam Books, 1983).
5. Kenneth L. Feder, *Frauds, Myths, and Mysteries* (Mountain View, CA: Mayfield, 1990), p. 20.
6. Karl R. Popper, *Conjectures and Refutations: The Growth of Scientific Knowledge* (New York: Psychology Press, 2002), p. 61.
7. Ibid., p. 62.
8. Carl Hempel, *Philosophy of Natural Science* (Englewood Cliffs, NJ: Prentice-Hall, 1966), p. 14ff.
9. Benjamin Franklin and Antoine Lavoisier, "Report of the Commissioners Charged by the King to Examine Animal Magnetism," trans. Danielle and Charles Salas, *The Skeptic Encyclopedia of Pseudoscience* (Santa Barbara, CA: ABC-CLIO, 2002), p. 809.
10. P. G. Goldschmidt and T. Colton, "The Quality of Medical Literature: An Analysis of Validation Assessments," in *Medical Users of Statistics,* ed. J. C. Bailar and F. Mosteller (Waltham, MA: New England Journal of Medicine Books, 1986), p. 383.
11. Ibid., p. 812.

12. John M. Yancey, "Ten Rules for Reading Clinical Research Reports," *American Journal of Surgery* 159 (June 1990): 533–39.
13. Thomas M. Vogt, *Making Health Decisions* (Chicago: Nelson-Hall, 1983), p. 84.
14. T. H. Huxley, *The Crayfish: An Introduction to the Study of Zoology* (New York: D. Appleton and Company, 1880), p. 1.
15. Philip Kitcher, "Believing Where We Cannot Prove," *Abusing Science* (Cambridge: MIT Press, 1982), p. 44.
16. Irving Copi, *Introduction to Logic,* 6th ed. (New York: Macmillan, 1982), pp. 488–94.
17. Pierre Duhem, *Aim and Structure of Physical Theory* (Princeton: Princeton University Press, 1953), chap. 6, reprinted in *Readings in the Philosophy of Science,* ed. Herbert Feigl and May Brodbeck (New York: Appleton-Century-Crofts, 1953), pp. 240–41.
18. Robert Schadewald, "Some Like It Flat," in *The Fringes of Reason: A Whole Earth Catalog,* ed. Ted Schultz (New York: Harmony Books, 1989), p. 86.
19. Aristotle, *De caelo*, 297a9-21, 297b31-298a10.
20. Tom McKay, "At Long Last, Flat Earth Rocketeer Finally Manages to Blast Himself into Sky at God Knows What Speed," Gizmodo, March 25, 2018, accessed May 16, 2018, https://gizmodo.com/at-long-last-flat-earth-rocketeer-finally-manages-to-b-1824059035.
21. Rob Waugh, "Here's the Real Reason So Many People Now Believe the Earth Is Flat," *Metro News*, April 9, 2018, accessed May 16, 2018, http://metro.co.uk/2018/04/09/real-reason-many-people-now-believe-earth-flat-7451315/.
22. http://reason.landmarkbiblebaptist.net/BibleScience.html, accessed May 16, 2018.
23. Klaus Anselm Vogel, "Sphaera terrae—das mittelalterliche Bild der Erde und die kosmographische Revolution," PhD dissertation Georg-August-Universität Göttingen, 1995, p. 19.
24. Flat Earth Wiki, "Shifting Constellations," accessed May 16, 2018, https://wiki.tfes.org/Shifting_Constellations.
25. Douglas Martin, "Charles Johnson, 76, Proponent of Flat Earth," *New York Times*, March 25, 2001, accessed May 16, 2018, https://www.nytimes.com/2001/03/25/us/charles-johnson-76-proponent-of-flat-earth.html.
26. Marvin Harris, "Cultural Materialism Is Alive and Well and Won't Go Away Until Something Better Comes Along," in *Assessing Cultural Anthropology,* ed. Robert Borofsky (New York: McGraw-Hill, 1994), p. 64.
27. Hempel, *Philosophy of Natural Science,* p. 31.
28. Popper, *Conjectures and Refutations,* p. 35.
29. Popper is not unaware of this method of saving theories from negative evidence. He calls it a *conventionalist twist* or a *conventionalist strategem.* See Popper, *Conjectures and Refutations,* p. 37.

30. Imre Lakatos, "The Methodology of Scientific Research," *Philosophical Papers* (New York: Cambridge University Press, 1977), vol. 1, pp. 6–7.
31. Nathan Spielberg and Byron D. Anderson, *Seven Ideas That Shook the Universe* (New York: Wiley, 1987), p. 178ff.
32. Lakatos, "The Methodology of Scientific Research," p. 6.
33. Ibid.
34. Immanuel Velikovsky, *Worlds in Collision* (New York: Dell, 1969).
35. Carl Sagan, *Broca's Brain*: Reflections on the Romance of Science (New York: Ballantine, 1979), p. 115.
36. Ibid., p. 113ff.
37. Spielberg and Anderson, *Seven Ideas,* pp. 180–81.
38. Paul Langevin, "Sur la theorie de la relativite et l'experience de M. Sagnac," *Comptes Rendus de l'Académie des Sciences* 173 (1921): 831.
39. Albert Einstein, *Forum Philosophicum* 1, no. 173 (1930): 183.
40. Hempel, *Philosophy of Natural Science,* p. 40ff.
41. There is no formula for counting assumptions, but nevertheless their number can be arrived at through various qualitative considerations. See, for example, Paul Thagard, "The Best Explanation: Criteria for Theory Choice," *Journal of Philosophy* 75, no. 2 (February 1978): 86ff.
42. Fritjof Capra, *The Tao of Physics* (Boston: Shambhala, 1975), p. 46.
43. W. V. Quine and J. S. Ullian, *The Web of Belief* (New York: Random House, 1970), pp. 43–44.
44. Thomas Kuhn, "Reflections on My Critics," in *Criticism and the Growth of Knowledge,* ed. Imre Lakatos and Alan Musgrave (Cambridge: Cambridge University Press, 1970), p. 261.
45. Charles Darwin, *On The Origin of Species*. (Trajectory Inc., 2014).
46. I. Michael Lerner, *Heredity, Evolution, and Society* (San Francisco: W. H. Freeman, 1968), pp. 35–39.
47. Ibid., pp. 39–42.
48. Section 4a of Act 590 of the Acts of Arkansas of 1981, "Balanced Treatment for Creation-Science and Evolution-Science Act."
49. Judge William Overton, *McLean v. Arkansas Board of Education,* cited in Jeffrey G. Murphy, *Evolution, Morality, and the Meaning of Life* (Totowa, NJ: Rowman & Littlefield, 1982), p. 146.
50. Henry Morris and Martin Clark, *The Bible Has the Answer* (New Leaf Publishing Group, 1976), pp. 94-95.
51. Garvin McCain and Erwin Segal, *The Game of Science* (Pacific Grove, CA: Brooks/Cole Publishing Company, 1988), pp. 19–20.
52. Judge Braswell Dean, *Time,* March 16, 1981, p. 82.
53. Isaac Asimov and Duane Gish, "The Genesis War," *Science Digest* 89, no. 6–11 (October 1981), p. 82.
54. Philip P. Wiener, *Leibniz Selections* (New York: Charles Scribner's, 1951), p. 292.
55. Lerner, *Heredity, Evolution, and Society,* p. 39ff.
56. Larry Laudan, "Science at the Bar: Causes for Concern," in Murphy, *Evolution, Morality, and the Meaning of Life,* p. 150.

57. Theodosius Dobzhansky, "Nothing in Biology Makes Sense Except in the Light of Evolution," *The American Biology Teacher* 35 (March 1973): 125–29.
58. Martin Gardner, *The New Age: Notes of a Fringe Watcher* (Buffalo: Prometheus Books, 1991), pp. 93–98.
59. Feder, *Frauds, Myths, and Mysteries,* p. 174.
60. Ibid., pp. 176–79.
61. Asimov and Gish, "The Genesis War."
62. Murphy, *Evolution, Morality, and the Meaning of Life,* p. 138.
63. Asimov and Gish, "The Genesis War," p. 87.
64. Henry M. Morris, ed., *Scientific Creationism* (San Diego: Creation-Life Publishers, 1974), p. 210.
65. Martin Gardner, *Fads and Fallacies in the Name of Science* (New York: Dover Publications, 1957), pp. 125–26.
66. Richard Dawkins, *The Blind Watchmaker: Why the Evidence of Evolution Reveals a Universe Without Design* (New York: W.W. Norton & Company, 1987), p. 89.
67. Ibid.
68. Michael J. Behe, *Darwin's Black Box: The Biochemical Challenge to Evolution* (New York: Free Press, 1996), p. 39.
69. "Human Scientists from Another Planet Created All Life on Earth Using DNA," accessed September 2007, www.rael.org/rael_content/rael_summary.php.
70. www.clonaid.com/news.php?3.2.1., accessed September 2007.
71. H. Allen Orr, "Darwin v. Intelligent Design (Again)," *Boston Review,* December/January 1996–1997, p. 22.
72. Jerry A. Coyne, "God in the Details: The Biochemical Challenge to Evolution," *Nature,* September 19, 1996.
73. Charles Darwin, *The Various Contrivances by Which Orchids Are Fertilised by Insects* (New York: D. Appleton & Co., 1877), p. 282.
74. Ibid., p. 284.
75. Kathleen Hunt, "Transitional Vertebrate Fossils FAQ," http://www.talkorigins.org/faqs/faq-transitional.html.
76. Stephen Jay Gould, "Hooking Leviathan by Its Past," *Natural History* (New York: Harmony Books, May 1994).
77. Joseph Boxhorn, "Observed Instances of Speciation," www.talkorigins.org/faqs/faq-speciation.html.
78. Dawkins, *The Blind Watchmaker,* p. 82.
79. Ibid., p. 90.
80. Even though the Big Bang happened only 15 billion years ago, it could have been the result of a prior "big crunch" (gravitational collapse), or our universe may have "budded off" (grown out of) a previously existing universe.
81. Bobby Henderson, "Open Letter to Kansas School Board," Church of the Flying Spaghetti Monster, 2005, accessed May 16, 2018, http://www.venganza.org/about/open-letter/.

82. Wikipedia, "Flying Spaghetti Monster," accessed May 15, 2018, https://en.wikipedia.org/wiki/Flying_Spaghetti_Monster#cite_note-openletter-10.
83. Bertrand Russell, "Cosmic Purpose," *Religion and Science* (New York: Henry Holt, 1935), p. 233.
84. S. Jay Olshansky, Bruce A. Carnes, and Robert N. Butler, "If Humans Were Built to Last," *Scientific American,* March 2001, pp. 50–55.
85. Joel W. Martin, "Compatibility of Major U.S. Christian Denominations with Evolution," *Evolution: Education and Outreach* 3, no. 3 (2010): 420–31.
86. Kenneth R. Miller, "Finding Darwin's God," *Brown Alumni Magazine,* November/December 1999.
87. Daniel Druckman and John Swets, eds., *Enhancing Human Performance: Issues, Theories, and Techniques* (Washington, DC: National Academy Press, 1988), p. 171.
88. Ibid., p. 206.
89. A. Greeley, "Mysticism Goes Mainstream," *American Health,* January/February 1987, pp. 47–49.
90. J. B. Rhine, *The Reach of the Mind* (New York: William Sloane Associates, 1947), p. 195.
91. Martin Gardner, *The Whys of a Philosophical Scrivener* (New York: St. Martin's Press, 1999), p. 58.
92. Jan Ludwig, *Philosophy and Parapsychology* (Prometheus Books, 1978), p. 126.
93. Rhine, "Science of Nonphysical Nature," The *Journal of Philosophy* 51, no. 25 (December 9, 1954), pp. 801–08.
94. Leonard Zusne and Warren H. Jones, *Anomalistic Psychology: A Study of Extraordinary Phenomena of Behavior and Experience* (Hillsdale, NJ: Erlbaum Associates, 1982), pp. 374–75.
95. James C. Crumbaugh, "A Scientific Critique of Parapsychology," *International Journal of Neuropsychiatry* 5 (1966): 521–29.
96. John Beloff, *Psychological Sciences: A Review of Modern Psychology* (London: Crosby Lockwood Staples, 1973), p. 312.
97. G. R. Schmeidler, "Separating the Sheep from the Goats," *Journal of the American Society for Psychical Research* 39, no. 1 (1945): 47–50.
98. D. Scott Rogo, "Making of Psi Failure," *Fate,* April 1986, pp. 76–80.
99. Ray Hyman, "A Critical Historical Overview of Parapsychology," in *A Skeptic's Handbook of Parapsychology,* ed. Paul Kurtz (Buffalo: Prometheus Books, 1985), pp. 3–96.
100. Paul Kurtz, *A Skeptic's Handbook of Parapsychology* (Prometheus Books, 1985), p. 50.
101. C. Scott and P. Haskell, "'Normal' Explanations of the Soal-Goldney Experiments in Extrasensory Perception," *Nature* 245 (1973): 52–54.
102. John Beloff, "Seven Evidential Experiments," *Zetetic Scholar* 6 (1980): 91–94.
103. Terence Hines, *Pseudoscience and the Paranormal: A Critical Examination of the Evidence* (Buffalo: Prometheus Books, 1988), pp. 93–94.

104. Ibid., p. 85.
105. Ray Hyman, "The Ganzfeld Psi Experiment: A Critical Appraisal," *Journal of Parapsychology* 49 (1985): 3–49.
106. Ibid.
107. Charles Honorton, "Meta-analysis of Psi Ganzfeld Research: A Response to Hyman," *Journal of Parapsychology* 49 (1985): 51–86.
108. Ray Hyman and Charles Honorton, "A Joint Communiqué: The Psi Ganzfeld Controversy," *Journal of Parapsychology* 50 (1986): 351–64.
109. Daryl J. Bem and Charles Honorton, "Does Psi Exist? Replicable Evidence for an Anomalous Process of Information Transfer," *Psychological Bulletin* 115, no. 1 (1994): 4–18.
110. J. Milton and R. Wiseman, "Does Psi Exist? Lack of Replication of an Anomalous Process of Information Transfer," *Psychological Bulletin* 125 (1999): 387–91.
111. Ray Hyman, "The Evidence of Psychic Functioning: Claims vs. Reality," *Skeptical Inquirer* 20 (March/April 1996).
112. Daryl Bem, "Feeling the Future: Experimental Evidence for Anomalous Retroactive Influences on Cognition and Affect," *Journal of Personality and Social Psychology* 100 (2011): 407–25.
113. Stuart J. Ritchie, Richard Wiseman, and Christopher C. French, "Failing the Future: Three Unsuccessful Attempts to Replicate Bem's 'Retroactive Facilitation of Recall' Effect," *PLoS ONE* 7, no. 3 (2012): e33423. doi:10.1371/journal.pone.0033423.
114. Douglas M. Stokes, "The Shrinking File Drawer: On the Validity of Statistical Meta-analyses in Parapsychology," *Skeptical Inquirer* 25 (May/June 2001).
115. L. Storm, P. Tressoldi, and L. Di Risio, "Meta-Analysis of Free-Response Studies, 1992–2008: Assessing the Noise Reduction Model in Parapsychology," *Psychological Bulletin* 136, no. 4 (2010): 479.
116. Ray Hyman, "Meta-analysis That Conceals More Than It Reveals: Comment on Storm et al. (2010)," *Psychological Bulletin* 136 (2010): 486.
117. R. S. Broughton and C. H. Alexander, "Autoganzfeld II: An Attempted Replication of the PRL Ganzfeld Research," *Journal of Parapsychology* 61 (1997): 209–26.
118. J.N. Rouder, R.D. Morey, and J.M. Province, "A Bayes Factor Meta-analysis of Recent Extrasensory Perception Experiments: Comment of Storm, Tressoldi, and Di Risio (2010)," *Psychological Bulletin* 139, no. 1 (2013): 241.
119. David F. Marks, "Investigating the Paranormal," *Nature* 320 (March 13, 1986): 119.
120. Samuel T. Moulton and Stephen M. Kosslyn, "Using Neuroimaging to Resolve the Psi Debate," *Journal of Cognitive Neuroscience* 20, no. 1 (2008): 182–192.
121. Ibid., p. 189.

SEVEN

Case Studies in the Extraordinary

> *The pure and simple truth is rarely pure and never simple.*
>
> —Oscar Wilde

LET'S TAKE STOCK.

In the preceding chapters, we've explored several essential principles that can empower our thinking about weird phenomena. We've seen, among other things, that even in the realms of weirdness, it's not true that anything is possible: Some things are logically impossible; some things are physically impossible; some things are technically impossible. On the other hand, some things that people believe are impossible may be possible after all. But we've also seen that just because something is logically or physically possible doesn't mean that it is, or ever will be, real.

We've examined why personal experience doesn't always provide reliable evidence for believing something. We've seen that, in themselves, strong feelings of subjective certainty regarding a personal experience don't increase the reliability of that experience one bit. Only if we have no good reasons to doubt a personal experience can we accept it as a reliable guide to what's real—and there are often many grounds for doubt. As the basis for a claim—whether about UFOs, ghosts, witches, or the curative power of vitamin C—personal experience is frequently shakier than we realize.

We've investigated what it means to say that we know something. We can know many things—including weird things—if we have good reasons to believe them and no good reasons to doubt them. We have good reasons to doubt a proposition when it conflicts with other propositions we have good reasons to believe, when it conflicts with well-established background information, or when it conflicts with expert opinion regarding the evidence. If we have good reason to doubt a proposition, we can't know it. The best we can do is proportion our belief to the evidence. If we don't know something, a leap of faith can never help us know it. We can't make something true just by believing it to be true. To accept a proposition on faith is to believe it without justification. Likewise, mystical experience doesn't provide us with a privileged way of knowing. Claims of knowledge based on mystical experience must pass the same rational tests as any other kind of experience.

The path of sound credence is through the thick forest of skepticism.

—GEORGE JEAN NATHAN

We've explored why—even though the scientific method can never prove or disprove anything conclusively—science is our most reliable means of establishing an empirical proposition beyond a reasonable doubt. It offers us a model for assessing new hypotheses, or claims, about all manner of extraordinary events and entities—a model that can serve scientists and nonscientists alike. If we want to know whether a hypothesis is true, we'll need to use this model in one form or another. The model requires that we judge a new hypothesis in light of alternative, competing hypotheses and apply to each of these alternatives the best yardsticks we have—the criteria of adequacy—to see which hypothesis measures up. Under pressure from the criteria of adequacy, some hypotheses may collapse from the lack of sturdy evidence or sound reasons to support them. Other hypotheses may not tumble completely but will be shown to be built on weak and rickety foundations. One, though, may emerge as the best hypothesis of them all, strong and tall because it rests on a firm base of good reasons.

In this chapter, we bring all these analytical tools together. We try to show how to apply coherently all our preceding principles to actual weird claims. This chapter, then, is the applications section of this volume, which is, as we've mentioned before, essentially a book of *applied epistemology.*

First, we'll sketch out a procedure that can help you evaluate, step-by-step, any extraordinary claim that you come across. It's a formula for inquiry that reminds you of the principles already discussed, suggests when and how they come into play, and guides you toward your own reasoned conclusions about the truth of a claim. The formula isn't carved in stone—it's simply one way to show how to apply the principles that we all must apply if we're to make sense of any unusual (or not so unusual) claim.

The rest of the chapter demonstrates how we authors have already put this formula to work to assess several popular, extraordinary claims and arrive at supportable conclusions. We try to show by example how to, well, think about weird things. The conclusions we reach are neither unique (many scientists and philosophers have reached similar conclusions) nor infallible. We do think, however, that they're based on the best of reasons—which is all anyone can ask of any conclusion worthy of acceptance. You are, of course, free to reject our conclusions. If you do, we hope that you do so for good reasons—and that by now you understand the difference between good and bad reasons and why the difference is crucial.

THE SEARCH FORMULA

Our formula for inquiry consists of four steps, which we represent by the acronym SEARCH. The letters stand for the key words in the four steps:

Judge a man by his questions rather than his answers.

—VOLTAIRE

1. *S*tate the Claim.
2. Examine the *E*vidence for the Claim.
3. Consider *A*lternative Hypotheses.
4. *R*ate, According to the Criteria of Adequacy, Each *H*ypothesis.

The acronym is arbitrary and artificial, but it may help you remember the formula's vital components. Go through these steps anytime you're faced with an extraordinary claim.

Note that throughout this chapter we use the words *hypothesis* and *claim* interchangeably. We do so because any weird claim, like any claim about events and entities, can be viewed as a hypothesis—as an explanation of a particular phenomenon. Thinking of weird claims as hypotheses is important because effectively evaluating weird claims involves essentially the same hypothesis-assessing procedure used in science.

Step 1: *S*tate the Claim

Before you can carefully examine a claim, you have to understand what it is. It's vital to state the claim in terms that are as *clear* and as *specific* as possible. "Ghosts are real" is not a good candidate for examination because it's vague and nonspecific. A better claim is "The disembodied spirits of dead persons exist and are visible to the human eye." Likewise, "Astrology is true" is not much to go on. It's better to say, "Astrologers can correctly identify someone's personality traits by using sun signs." Even these revised claims aren't as unambiguous and definitive as they should be. (Terms in the claims, for example, could be better defined. What is meant by "spirit"? What does it mean to "correctly identify someone's personality traits"?) But many of the extraordinary claims you run into are of this caliber. The point is that before examining any claim, you must achieve maximum clarity and specificity of what the claim is.

Step 2: Examine the *E*vidence for the Claim

Ask yourself what reasons there are for accepting the claim. That is, what empirical evidence or logical arguments are there in the claim's favor? Answering this question entails taking inventory of both the quantity and quality of the reasons for believing that the claim is true. An honest and thorough appraisal of reasons must include:

1. *Determining the exact nature and limitations of the empirical evidence.* You should assess not only what the evidence is but whether there are any reasonable doubts regarding it. You have to try to find out if it's subject to any of the deficiencies we've discussed in this book—the distortions of human perception, memory, and judgment; the errors and biases of scientific research; the difficulties inherent in ambiguous data. Sometimes even a preliminary survey of the facts may force you to admit that there really isn't anything mysterious that needs explaining. Or perhaps investigating a little mystery will lead to a bigger mystery. At any rate, attempting an objective assessment of the evidence takes courage. Many true believers have never taken this elementary step.
2. *Discovering if any of these reasons deserve to be disqualified.* As we've seen, people frequently offer considerations in support of a claim that should be discounted. These considerations include wishful thinking, faith, unfounded intuition, and subjective certainty. The problem is that these factors aren't reasons at all. In themselves, they can't provide any support for a claim.
3. *Deciding whether the hypothesis in question actually explains the evidence.* If it doesn't—if important factors are left out of account—the hypothesis is not a good one. In other words, a good hypothesis must be relevant to the evidence it's intended to explain. If it isn't, there's no reason to consider it any further.

Step 3: Consider *A*lternative Hypotheses

It's never enough to consider *only* the hypothesis in question and its reasons for acceptance. If you ever hope to discover the truth, you must also weigh *alternative* hypotheses and their reasons.

Take this hypothesis, for example: Rudolph the Red-Nosed Reindeer—Santa's funny, flying, furry headlight—is real and lives at the North Pole. As evidence for this hypothesis we could submit these facts: Millions of people (mostly children) believe Rudolph to be real; his likeness shows up everywhere during the Christmas holidays; given the multitude of reindeer in the world and their long history, it's likely that at some time a reindeer with flying capabilities would either evolve or be born with the necessary mutations; some people say that they have seen Rudolph with their own eyes. We could go on and on and build a fairly convincing case for the hypothesis—soon you may even come to believe that we were onto something.

The hypothesis sounds great by itself, but when considered alongside an alternative hypothesis—that Rudolph is a creature of the imagination created in a Christmas song—it looks ludicrous. The song hypothesis is supported by evidence that's overwhelming; it doesn't conflict with well-established theory in biology (as the real-Rudolph hypothesis does); and unlike its competitor, it requires no postulations about new entities.

No man really becomes a fool until he stops asking questions.

—CHARLES STEINMETZ

This third step involves creativity and maintaining an open mind. It requires asking whether there are other ways to account for the phenomenon at hand and, if there are, what reasons there are in favor of these alternative hypotheses. This step involves applying step 2 to all competing explanations.

It's also important to remember that when people are confronted with some extraordinary phenomenon they often immediately offer a hypothesis involving the paranormal or supernatural and then can't imagine a natural hypothesis to account for the facts. As a result, they assume that the paranormal or supernatural hypothesis must be right. But this assumption is unwarranted. Just because you can't think of a natural explanation doesn't mean there isn't one. It may be (as has often been the case throughout history) that you're simply unaware of the correct natural explanation. As pointed out in Chapter 2, the most reasonable response to a mystifying fact is to keep looking for a natural explanation.

We all have a built-in bias that urges us to latch onto a favorite hypothesis and ignore or resist all alternatives. We may believe that we needn't look at other explanations since we know that our favorite one is correct. This tendency may make us happy (at least for a while), but it's also a good recipe for delusion. We must work to counteract this bias. Having an open mind means being willing to consider any possibility and changing your view in light of good reasons.

Step 4: *R*ate, According to the Criteria of Adequacy, Each *H*ypothesis

Now it's time to weigh competing hypotheses and see which are found wanting and which are worthy of belief. Simply cataloging the evidence for each hypothesis isn't enough. We need to consider other factors that can put that evidence in perspective and help us weigh hypotheses when there's no evidence at all, which is often the case with weird things. To command our assent, extraordinary claims must provide exemplary explanations. That is, they must explain the phenomena better than any competing explanation. As we saw in Chapter 6, the way to determine which explanation is best is to apply the criteria of adequacy. By applying them to each hypothesis, we can often eliminate some hypotheses right away, give more weight to some than to others, and decide between hypotheses that may at first seem equally strong.

All is mystery; but he is a slave who will not struggle to penetrate the dark veil.
—Benjamin Disraeli

1. *Testability.* Ask: Can the hypothesis be tested? Is there any possible way to determine whether the hypothesis is true or false? Many hypotheses regarding extraordinary phenomena aren't testable. This does not mean they're false. It means they're worthless. They are merely assertions that we'll never be able to know. What if we claim that there is an invisible, undetectable gremlin in your head that sometimes causes you to have headaches. As an explanation for your headaches, this hypothesis is interesting but trivial. Since by definition there's no way to determine if this gremlin really exists, the hypothesis is amazingly uninformative. You can assign no weight to such a claim.

2. *Fruitfulness.* Ask: Does the hypothesis yield observable, surprising predictions that explain new phenomena? Any hypothesis that does so gets extra points. Other things being equal, hypotheses that make accurate, unexpected predictions are more likely to be true than hypotheses that don't. (Of course, if they yield no predictions, this in itself doesn't show that they're false.) Most hypotheses regarding weird things don't make observable predictions.

3. *Scope.* Ask: How many different phenomena can the hypothesis explain? Other things being equal, the more it explains, the less likely it is to be mistaken. In Chapter 5 we discussed the well-confirmed hypothesis that human perception is constructive. As we pointed out, the hypothesis explains a broad range of phenomena, including perceptual size constancy, misperception of stimuli, hallucinations, pareidolia, certain UFO sightings, and more. A hypothesis that

explains only one of these phenomena (for example, the hypothesis that UFO sightings are caused by actual alien spacecraft) would be much less impressive—unless it had other things in its favor like compelling evidence.

5. *Simplicity.* Ask: Is this hypothesis the simplest explanation for the phenomenon? Generally, the simplest hypothesis that explains the phenomenon is the best, the one least likely to be false. *Simplest* means makes the fewest assumptions. In the realm of weird things, simplicity is often a matter of postulating the existence of the fewest entities. Let's say you get into your car one morning, put the key in the ignition, and try to start the engine but find that it won't start. One hypothesis for this phenomenon is that the car battery is dead. Another is that a poltergeist (a mischievous spirit) has somehow caused your car not to start. The battery hypothesis is the simplest (in addition to being testable, able to yield predictions, and capable of explaining several phenomena) because it doesn't require postulating the existence of any mysterious entities. The poltergeist hypothesis, though, does postulate the existence of an entity (as well as assuming that the entity has certain capabilities and tendencies). Thus the criterion of simplicity shows us that the battery hypothesis has the greater chance of being right.

6. *Conservatism.* Ask: Is the hypothesis consistent with our well-founded beliefs? That is, is it consistent with the empirical evidence—with results from trustworthy observations and scientific tests, with natural laws, or with well-established theory? Trying to answer this question takes you beyond merely cataloging evidence for hypotheses to actually assigning weight to hypotheses *in light of all the available evidence.* Other things being equal, the hypothesis most consistent with the entire corpus of our knowledge is the best bet, the one most likely to be true.

It follows that a hypothesis that flies in the face of extremely well-established evidence must be assigned a very low probability. Say, for example, that someone claims that yesterday thousands of cats and dogs rained down from the sky in Texas. This strange happening is logically possible, of course, but it conflicts with an enormous amount of human experience regarding objects that fall from the sky. Maybe one fine day cats and dogs will indeed tumble from the clouds and surprise us all. But based on a massive amount of experience, we must assign a very low probability to such a possibility.

The mind is like the stomach. It is not how much you put into it that counts, but how much it digests.
—Albert Jay Nock

What if someone claims to have built a perpetual motion machine, a device that, to work, must successfully circumvent one of the laws of thermodynamics. (A perpetual motion machine is supposed to function without ever stopping and without needing to draw on an external source of power—it supplies its own energy; this concept violates the law of conservation of mass-energy, which says that mass-energy can't be created or destroyed.) The laws of thermodynamics are supported by a massive amount of empirical evidence gathered throughout centuries. There have also been numerous failed attempts to build a perpetual motion machine. In light of such evidence, we're forced to conclude that it's very unlikely that anyone could avoid the laws of thermodynamics. Unless someone is able to produce good evidence showing that it can be done, we must say that person's claim is highly improbable.

Likewise, if someone puts forth a hypothesis that conflicts with a highly confirmed theory, the hypothesis must be regarded as improbable until good evidence shows that the hypothesis is right and the theory wrong. Paranormal claims then are, by definition, improbable. They conflict with what we know, with mountains of evidence. Only good evidence to the contrary can change this verdict.

HOMEOPATHY

There have been two great revelations in my life: The first was bepop, the second was homeopathy.
—DIZZY GILLESPIE

Homeopathy is based on the idea that extremely tiny doses of substances that cause disease symptoms in a healthy person can alleviate similar symptoms in a sick person. Samuel Hahnemann (1755–1843), a German physician, was the first to apply this notion systematically. He also added what he called the "law of infinitesimals," the proposition that—contrary to the findings of science—the smaller the dose, the more powerful the medicine. So he treated people with drastically diluted substances—so diluted that, in many homeopathic medicines, not even one molecule of the substance remained. Hahnemann admitted this fact but believed that the substances somehow left behind an imperceptible "spirit-like" essence that effected cures. This essence was supposed to revitalize the "vital force" in the body.

Today, the theory and practice of Hahnemann's homeopathy are still intact. There are hundreds of homeopathic practitioners in the United States (and hundreds more in other countries) and hundreds of thousands of people who try homeopathic treatments.

Homeopathic remedies are derived from raw bovine testicles, crushed honeybees, belladonna (deadly nightshade), hemlock, sulfur, arsenic, Spanish fly, rattlesnake venom, poison ivy, dog milk, and many other substances. They are used to relieve the symptoms of a long list of ills, from allergies and colds to kidney disease, heart trouble, and ear infections.

Through a procedure that Hahnemann called a *proving* he "discovered" that particular remedies could alleviate certain symptoms. In a proving, Hahnemann and his students would simply eat various substances, then observe what symptoms they had. He believed that if a patient complained of certain symptoms, she should be given the (diluted) substance that was said to cause those same symptoms in a proving. The substance was supposed to alleviate the symptoms. The provings became the basis of homeopathic treatments for generations to come.

So let's state the claim here and examine the evidence for it:

Hypothesis 1: *Extremely dilute solutions of substances that produce symptoms in a healthy person can cure those same symptoms in a sick person.* This hypothesis is offered as an explanation of why people taking homeopathic remedies seem to get better. They get better because homeopathy works.

It should come as no surprise that homeopathic provings don't really prove anything. As we saw in Chapter 5, personal experience and case reports generally cannot establish the effectiveness of a treatment. Because of the placebo effect, the variable nature of disease, the possibility of unknown causes, experimenter bias, and other factors, the provings cannot even reliably establish that a substance causes a certain symptom effect.

But there is other evidence that proponents of homeopathy often cite. There have been scores of scientific studies on homeopathic treatments for a variety of conditions. To date, all the research seeming to support homeopathy, however, is undermined by serious problems. One of several recent reviews of the literature explains some of the difficulties:

> J. Kleinjen, P. Knipschild, and G. ter Riet examined 107 controlled clinical trials of homeopathy. They concluded that the evidence was not sufficient to support the claims of homeopathy. C. Hill and F. Doyon examined 40 other clinical studies. They also concluded that there was no acceptable evidence that homeopathy is effective.[1]

In 2002, E. Ernst published "A Systematic Review of Systematic Reviews of Homeopathy" in the *British Journal of Clinical Pharmacology*. Here's what he found:

> Eleven independent systematic reviews were located. Collectively they failed to provide strong evidence in favour of homeopathy. In particular, there was no condition which responds convincingly better to homeopathic treatment than to placebo or other control interventions. Similarly, there was no homeopathic remedy that was demonstrated to yield clinical effects that are convincingly different from placebo.[2]

Magnet Therapy

You can't surf far on the Internet without encountering a website promoting magnet therapy to ease or cure a multitude of ills—knee pain, migraine headaches, arthritis, sports injuries, poor circulation, back pain, even cancer. Magnets sold for curative purposes come in the form of bracelets, necklaces, earrings, wrist bands, shoe insoles, knee pads, seat cushions, mattress pads, hair brushes, you name it. Some of these products cost little; some cost thousands of dollars. Most of them use *static* magnets, which—like common refrigerator or bumper-sticker magnets—create small, unchanging magnetic fields. Pulsed *electromagnets,* however, induce both magnetic and electrical fields and are known to affect biological systems. They have been used to help mend bone fractures that heal slowly, and researchers have been examining their potential for treating depression and several forms of pain.

Do common static magnets have healing power? Many who have used magnets claim therapeutic benefits, including some famous athletes who have endorsed specific magnet products. But testimonials—especially regarding health remedies—prove very little. Because of the placebo effect, the variable course of illnesses, and the difficulties of pinpointing cause-and-effect relationships, personal experience is a poor guide to the efficacy of treatments.

Scientific evidence is a better indicator of effectiveness, but research on static magnet therapy is sparse and inconclusive. Several studies have been done, but most of them suffer from problems that undermine their credibility—for example, too few subjects or no placebo control groups. A number of trials have tested whether static magnetic therapy can alleviate pain, but they have produced contradictory results, with some showing a degree of pain relief and some showing none. A major obstacle in conducting magnet studies is that subjects often invalidate the research by figuring out whether they're getting true magnet therapy or no-magnet placebo treatment. (Discovering whether an object is magnetized is fairly easy.)

In addition, some evidence counts against the idea of magnetic healing. Though promoters of magnet therapy claim that it heals by increasing blood circulation, studies show that static magnetic fields don't affect circulation. Some research suggests that even very powerful magnetic fields—more powerful than those in magnet products—have little or no effect on living tissue. The extremely strong magnetic fields produced by MRI machines, for example, don't seem to affect people at all, either for good or ill.

In 2015, the National Health and Medical Research Council of the Australian government conducted a similar systematic review of systematic reviews and came to the same conclusion:

> Evidence on homeopathy was collected by identifying systematic reviews which evaluated the effectiveness of homeopathy in treating health conditions in humans. In total, 57 systematic reviews were identified that contained 176 individual studies. Studies were only considered by NHMRC if they compared a group of people who were given homeopathic treatment with a similar group of people who were not given homeopathic treatment (controlled studies). . . .

> There was no reliable evidence from research in humans that homeopathy was effective for treating the range of health conditions considered: no good-quality, well-designed studies with enough participants for a meaningful result reported either that homeopathy caused greater health improvements than placebo, or caused health improvements equal to those of another treatment. . . .
>
> Based on the assessment of the evidence of effectiveness of homeopathy, NHMRC concludes that there are no health conditions for which there is reliable evidence that homeopathy is effective.[3]

But let's consider an alternative hypothesis.

Hypothesis 2: *People taking homeopathic remedies feel better because of the placebo effect.* That is, homeopathy does not work as advertised, but people think that it does because of the well-known power of placebos. This hypothesis is the one favored by most medical experts. And for good reason. As we have already seen, the placebo effect is a very well-documented phenomenon that occurs frequently when people try new treatments. What's more, the failure of studies to support the homeopathy hypothesis—specifically, research showing that homeopathy works no better than placebo—lends credence to the notion that homeopathy "cures" *are* placebos.

Now let's examine these two hypotheses in light of the criteria of adequacy. They are both testable, so we must turn to the other criteria to help us judge their worth. The homeopathy hypothesis has yielded no observable, surprising predictions, so it has no advantage in fruitfulness. It could be argued, though, that the homeopathy hypothesis has more scope than the placebo hypothesis since it is offered to explain how *all* symptoms are alleviated.

But in terms of simplicity, the homeopathy hypothesis is in trouble. Homeopathy postulates both an undetectable essence and an unknown mysterious force. Other things being equal, the more unproven assumptions a hypothesis rests on, the less likely it is to be true. These assumptions alone are serious problems for the homeopathy hypothesis. The placebo hypothesis, on the other hand, assumes no unknown forces, entities, or processes.

Even worse, homeopathy runs afoul of the criterion of conservatism. It conflicts with a massive amount of scientific evidence in biochemistry and pharmacology. There isn't a single verified instance of any substance having a stronger effect the more diluted it becomes. There isn't a single documented case of an extremely diluted solution (one in which not one molecule of the original substance remains) affecting any biological system. In addition, as we have noted, all available scientific evidence on the question gives little or no support to homeopathy.

These points all show that homeopathy is a much weaker hypothesis than the placebo hypothesis. In fact, in light of these concerns, the probability of homeopathic remedies being effective seems extremely low.

INTERCESSORY PRAYER

Pray, and let God worry.
—MARTIN LUTHER

The practice of praying for others (called intercessory prayer) is commonplace and strongly believed by millions to be effective. Which of course should not be surprising since the efficacy of prayer has been and still is an article of faith for numerous religious groups worldwide. In recent years some people have claimed that science supports what faith has shown to be obvious—that praying for sick people can make them well, or at least make them feel better. Most attribute the healing effects of intercessory prayer to divine intervention; others to unidentified energies or paranormal forces such as telekinesis. In any case, it seems plain to many that intercessory prayer works, that it can cause positive changes in people's health.

Let's examine that claim—Hypothesis 1: *Intercessory prayer can alleviate symptoms or improve measures of health in people suffering from disease or disability.* This hypothesis is meant to explain why some sick people seem to get better after others pray for their recovery or improved health. Prayers are said, the sick get better, and prayer is the best explanation for the improvement.

Those who take this view usually cite as evidence their personal experience or the experience of others. A friend or loved one was seriously ill, people prayed for her healing, and soon she made a seemingly miraculous recovery. Such stories are innumerable. Here is one told by the famous Christian pastor Rick Warren:

> One of the great evidences of God is answered prayer. I have a friend, a Canadian friend, who has an immigration issue. He's an intern at this church, and so I said, "God, I need you to help me with this," as I went out for my evening walk. As I was walking I met a woman. She said, "I'm an immigration attorney; I'd be happy to take this case." Now, if that happened once in my life I'd say, "That is a coincidence." If it happened tens of thousands of times, that is not a coincidence.[4]

As you might expect, such anecdotal reports are subject to the same reliability problems that so often beset most types of personal experience: confirmation bias, the availability error, constructive memory, hasty generalization, and probability misjudgments. As evidence for the efficacy of prayer, then, these stories—as impressive as they may seem—must be given a very low grade.

Other evidence comes from scientific studies on people suffering from depression and anxiety, alcoholism, infertility, AIDS-related illnesses, and other disorders. Much of the research has focused on patients with heart disease. A famous 1988 study by cardiologist Randolph Byrd compared the extent of medical complications in heart patients who were prayed for with heart patients in a control group who were not prayed for. The prayed-for patients seemed to fare better than the others. In 1999, a larger study tested whether heart patients who were the focus of prayers "for a speedy recovery with no complications" would do better than similar patients without such prayers. The researchers said that the prayed-for group ended up with fewer medical problems. In a 2001 study, researchers divided nearly 800 heart patients into prayed-for and not-prayed-for groups and monitored their medical conditions for six months after they left the hospital. They reported that they could find no significant effect of intercessory prayer on the patients' health. Finally, in 2006 a study of 1,800 people who had undergone heart surgery found that intercessory prayer had no effect on their recovery. Oddly enough, people who knew they were being prayed for had more complications than those who weren't sure.

Most prayer studies have been spoiled by serious design flaws, or have been too small to yield meaningful results, or had other serious problems. So to date the research has not established that intercessory prayer can improve anyone's health.

Moreover, many critics (both religious and nonreligious) say this line of research is doomed from the start. A major concern is that intercessory prayer itself is neither well defined nor explained: Is it communication with a deity or a kind of telekinetic (mind over matter) ability? Does it exert the sort of influence that depends on the number of people praying, or the character or faith of those involved, or the disposition or will of a deity? Can prayers be malevolent, causing harm to others? Can researchers safely rule out the influence of prayers from countless people *not* involved in the studies? Presumably, relatives and friends of sick people will often pray for them to get better—whether or not the patients are part of a scientific study. And, of course, many religious people offer up prayers on behalf of ailing strangers. If a deity can intervene in the course of events at any time—either in response to prayers or not—how can a scientist ever be confident in study results? These issues would seem to undermine any attempts to conduct well-controlled trials of intercessory prayer.

A leading alternative explanation is Hypothesis 2: *The seeming effectiveness of intercessory prayer is due to coincidence and the post hoc*

The Experience behind the Ouija Experience

Have you ever used a Ouija board and wondered what its secret was? Were you really getting messages from the spirit world—or just talking to yourself? Psychologists say the latter is a distinct possibility. Here, psychologist Andrew Neher explains why:

> A Ouija board is a smooth-surfaced board printed with numbers, letters, and words such as yes and no. Ouija players rest their hands on a pointer, which glides easily on felt-covered legs, and concentrate on a question they want answered. Studies have shown that thinking about a certain pattern is sufficient to produce small subconscious movements in the hand in the appropriate directions. Exaggerated, this movement directs the pointer to an answer, which seems to have been arrived at mysteriously since the Ouija player ordinarily has no conscious awareness of having moved the pointer and is often genuinely surprised at the answer. From my own informal experience, it seems possible to elicit memories, as well as subliminal impressions, using a Ouija board, which are otherwise lost to consciousness. . . .
>
> Although the Ouija board, or the planchette, seems to be a handy device for tapping subconscious impressions, there do not seem to be any studies to indicate that Ouija is, in any way, paranormal in its operation.[5]

fallacy. That is, people pray for someone to recover from illness; he coincidentally does recover; and because the praying preceded the recovery, they assume that it *caused* the recovery. The assumption is all the easier to make because of the notorious incompetence of humans in judging probabilities. When people say "This can't possibly be a coincidence," they are too often dead wrong.

Judged by the criteria of adequacy, these two hypotheses are miles apart in plausibility. For reasons already mentioned, Hypothesis 1 seems untestable. It is not simple because it assumes an unknown entity (a deity, spirit, or force) and unknown processes. It is not conservative, for it conflicts with what we know about the physiology and psychology of health and disease. And since it seems to be as puzzling as it is explanatory, we must judge its scope to be nil. It is therefore not credible. Hypothesis 2 has none of these drawbacks—it is by far the better explanation.

It is easier to attribute UFO sightings to the known irrationalities of terrestrials than to the unknown efforts of extraterrestrials.
—RICHARD FEYNMAN

UFO ABDUCTIONS

In recent years, books, magazines, movies, and television talk shows have circulated an amazing hypothesis: Alien beings are abducting ordinary people, manipulating them in strange ways (performing experiments on them, having sex with them, or otherwise terrifying them), and then releasing their victims and vanishing. In the best-selling book *Communion,* author Whitley Strieber suggested that he was abducted by aliens with large heads and strange eyes and that they forced him to endure horrific treatment, including having a needle inserted into his head and an instrument put into his anus.[6] Later the book was made into a movie with the same name. The book *Intruders* by Budd Hopkins presents dramatic case histories of people who claim to have endured UFO abductions.[7] Hopkins suggests that aliens have abducted hundreds of people and used them in disturbing genetic experiments, then released them. On the basis of a Roper poll, Hopkins believes that millions of people have been abducted by aliens.

In 1991, the Roper organization polled almost 6,000 people in an attempt to determine the extent of alien abductions. The respondents were asked to indicate how often they had certain sorts of experiences. These experiences included the following: (1) "Waking up paralyzed with a sense of a strange person or presence or something else in the room," (2) "Feeling that you were actually flying through the air although you didn't know why or how,"

This Earth-drawing, or geoglyph, of a monkey was constructed on a plain in the Andes Mountains by a prehistoric people called Nazca. Such large-scale drawings can be produced with simple tools and require no extraterrestrial help.

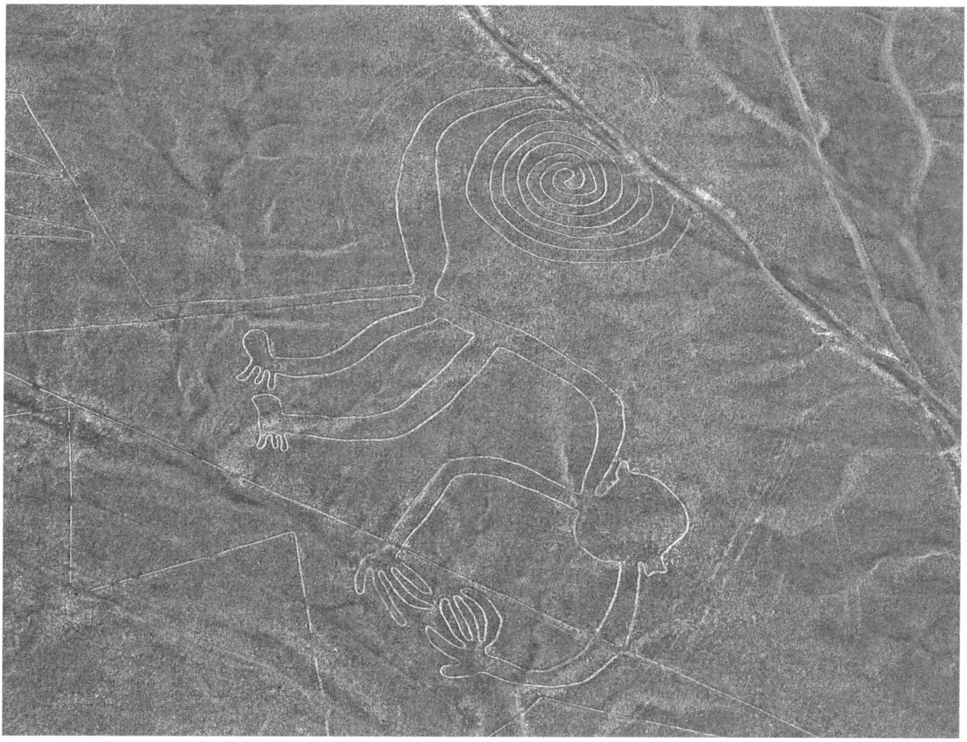

(3) "Experiencing a period of time of an hour or more, in which you were apparently lost, but you could not remember why, or where you had been," (4) "Seeing unusual lights or balls of light in a room without knowing what was causing them, or where they came from," and (5) "Finding puzzling scars on your body and neither you nor anyone else remembering how you received them or where you got them." The designers of the poll, Budd Hopkins and Dave Jacobs, reasoned that if someone answered yes to four or five of these questions, they had been abducted by aliens. About 2 percent of the respondents fell into this category. Since the sample represented 185 million people, they concluded that about 4 million Americans have been abducted by aliens. (The authors of this book have been informed that about 100 percent of fraternity brothers can answer yes to four out of five of these questions. Does that mean they've all been abducted by aliens?)

In many cases, before any abduction story surfaces, the victims first experience a vivid dream or nightmare (sometimes in childhood) involving eerie, otherworldly creatures. Or they experience "missing time," the realization that they don't remember what happened to them during a certain period. Or they see an odd light in the night sky that they identify as a UFO. Later, when the victims are hypnotized to try to learn more about these strange occurrences, an abduction experience is fully revealed. While under hypnosis, the abductees report in stunning detail what they believe they saw or felt during abduction, what the aliens looked like, and, in some cases, what the aliens said. The technique called *regressive hypnosis* has been the favored method for uncovering details of an abduction and for authenticating it. Some people, however, have recounted a UFO-abduction experience or produced details about it without undergoing hypnosis.

Now let's apply the SEARCH formula to the abduction hypothesis and to some of the leading alternatives and see what happens.

He that will not reason is a bigot; he that cannot reason is a fool; and he that dares not reason is a slave.

—William Drummond

Hypothesis 1: *Alien beings have abducted several people, interacted with them in various ways, and then released them.* Proponents of this hypothesis point to several pieces of evidence. First and foremost, there's the striking testimony elicited during hypnosis, which is thought to be a kind of truth serum, a way to retrieve accurate details about a person's experience of past events. There's also testimony that arises without the aid of hypnosis. There's the fact that the alleged abductees' stories seem to be so similar, that many abductees report the experience of missing time, and that a few of them (including Whitley Strieber) have passed lie detector tests. There's also physical evidence, like mysterious scars on abductees' bodies and areas of dead grass on the ground suggesting a UFO landing.

As for hypnosis, it's not the revealer of truth that many believe it to be. Research has shown that even deeply hypnotized people can willfully lie and that a person can fake hypnosis and fool even very experienced hypnotists. More to the point, research also shows that when hypnotized subjects are asked to recall a past event, they will fantasize freely, creating memories of things that never happened. Martin T. Orne, one of the world's leading experts on the use of hypnosis to obtain information about past events, sums up the situation like this:

> The hypnotic suggestion to relive a past event, particularly when accompanied by questions about specific details, puts pressure on the subject to provide information. . . . This situation may jog the subject's memory and produce some increased recall, but it will also cause him to fill in details that are plausible but consist of memories or fantasies from other times. It is extremely difficult to know which aspects of hypnotically aided recall are historically accurate and which aspects have been confabulated [made up and confused with real events]. . . . There is no way, however, by which anyone—even a psychologist or psychiatrist with extensive training in the field of hypnosis—can for any particular piece of information determine whether it is actual memory versus a confabulation unless there is independent verification.[8]

Orne and other experts have also emphasized how extremely suggestible hypnotic subjects are and how easy it is for a hypnotist to unintentionally induce pseudomemories in the subject:

> If a witness is hypnotized and has factual information casually gleaned from newspapers or inadvertent comments made during prior interrogation or in discussion with others who might have knowledge about the facts, many of these bits of knowledge will become incorporated and form the basis of any pseudo-memories that develop. . . . If the hypnotist has beliefs about what actually occurred, it is exceedingly difficult for him to prevent himself from inadvertently guiding the subject's recall so that [the subject] will eventually "remember" what he, the hypnotist, believes actually happened.[9]

Orne describes a simple experiment he has repeatedly conducted that shows the limits of hypnotism. First, he verifies that a subject went to bed at a certain time at night and slept straight through until morning. Then he hypnotizes the subject and asks her to relive that night. Orne asks the subject if she heard two loud noises during the night (noises that didn't, in fact, happen). Typically, the subject says that she was awakened by the noises and then describes how she

The Advanced Aviation Threat Identification Program

In December 2017, the *New York Times* stoked the fires of conspiracy theorists by revealing the existence of a hidden governmental UFO program called the Advanced Aviation Threat Identification Program (AATIP).[10] Created in 2008 by Senator Harry Reid (D-NV) at the urging of his donor Robert Bigelow, it ran until 2012 and cost the taxpayers $22 million. (Bigelow Aerospace received most of the money.) According to Major Audricia Harris, spokesperson for the Department of Defense inside the Pentagon, its mandate "was to assess far-term foreign advanced aerospace threats [to] the United States."[11] Apparently the program looked for aircraft that exhibited unusual abilities or behaviors and tried to identify their country of origin. "What we found many times," says Luis Elizondo, head of the program, "was the fact that the aircraft did not belong to anybody."[12] As evidence for his claim, two videos of unidentified flying objects were included with the online release of the *New York Times* story. Such videos have convinced Elizondo "beyond a reasonable doubt" that we have been visited by aliens from outer space.[13]

The Department of Defense apparently does not share Elizondo's analysis of the situation, however. Although the *New York Times* claims that these videos were released by the Department of Defense, the DoD denies this claim. According to Major Harris, "DoD has not released videos related to this program."[14] So they may have been leaked, or they may have been acquired from some other source, but in any event, they do not appear to have been classified because the classified markings that usually accompany such videos are absent.[15] At any rate, the DoD decided that the objects in such videos were not much of a threat because, as Major Harris tells us, "it was determined that there were other, higher priority issues that merited funding."[16]

Experts who've examined the videos claim they're too short and lack too much supplementary information to make a reasoned judgment concerning them. Others claim that the apparent speed and the quick turns that the UFOs seem to make can be explained by the parallax effect and the rotation of the thermal imaging camera that was tracking them. So there's no reason to think they're otherworldly.[17] But even if a prosaic explanation weren't forthcoming, it would be a mistake to conclude that the aircraft is extraterrestrial in origin. Unidentified does not imply extraterrestrial.

Elizondo hasn't given up his search for extraterrestrials. He has gone to work for former rock star Tom Delonge (of Blink 182 fame) as director of Global Security and Special Programs for the To the Stars Academy. Delonge is convinced that we have been visited by extraterrestrials and that the government knows about it.[18] For Delonge, the truth is out there and right here.

arose from bed to investigate. If Orne asks her to look at the clock, the subject identifies a specific time—at which point the subject was actually asleep and in bed. After hypnosis, the subject remembers the nonevent as though it actually happened. A pseudomemory was thus created by a leading question that may seem perfectly neutral.

A study has even been conducted to see if people who had never seen a UFO nor were well informed about UFOs could, under hypnosis, tell "realistic" stories about being abducted by aliens. The conclusion was that they can. The imaginary abductees easily and eagerly invented many specific details of abductions. The researchers found "no substantive differences" between these descriptions and those given by people who have claimed to be abducted.[19]

Research also suggests that hypnosis not only induces pseudomemories but also increases the likelihood that they'll become firmly established. As psychologist Terence Hines says:

> What hypnosis does do—and this is especially relevant to the UFO cases—is to greatly increase hypnotized subjects' confidence that their hypnotically induced memories are true. This increase in confidence occurs for both correct and incorrect memories. Thus, hypnosis can create false memories, but the individual will be especially convinced that those memories are true. People repeating such false memories will seem credible because they really believe their false memories are true. Their belief, of course, does not indicate whether the memory is actually true or false.[20]

Proponents of the abduction hypothesis, however, point out that a few people have told of being abducted by a UFO before they were hypnotized. This testimony is relevant to the issue—but it's also subject to all the questions of reliability that we must ask of any human testimony. Given what we know about the witnesses and the circumstances of their experience (to be discussed shortly), we must rate this testimonial evidence as weak.

The similarity of abductee stories also gives little support to hypothesis 1. Critics point out that there's little wonder that the stories have so much in common since UFO abduction has become a universally familiar theme, thanks to books, movies, and television. Psychologist Robert A. Baker says:

> Any one of us, if asked to pretend that we had been kidnapped by aliens from outer space or another dimension, would make up a story that would vary little, either in details or in the supposed motives of the abductors, from the stories told by any and all of the kidnap victims reported by [Budd] Hopkins. Our imaginative tales would be remarkably similar in plot, dialogue, description, and characterization to the close encounters of the third kind and conversations with little gray aliens described in *Communion* or *Intruders*. The means of transportation would be saucer-shaped, the aliens would be small, humanoid, two-eyed, and gray or white or green, and the purpose of their visits would be to: 1) save our planet; 2) find a better home for themselves; 3) end nuclear war and the threat we pose to the peaceful life in the rest of the galaxy; 4) bring us knowledge and

> enlightenment; and 5) increase the aliens' knowledge and understanding of other forms of life.[21]

The similarities in many abduction stories can also be created by a hypnotist who has unwittingly cued the same pseudomemories in all his or her subjects. This cuing is most likely to happen when the hypnotist lacks proper training in hypnotism and has strong beliefs about what actually happened to the subject—a state of affairs that may be the norm.

On closer inspection, the phenomenon of missing time seems to provide little support for the abduction hypothesis either. One reason is that the phenomenon is actually a common, ordinary experience—especially when people are anxious or under stress:

> Typically, motorists will report after a long drive that at some point in the journey they woke up to realize they had no awareness of a preceding period of time. With some justification, people will describe this as a "gap in time," a "lost half-hour," or a "piece out of my life."[22]

In addition, many cases of missing time in abduction stories have been investigated and found to have fairly prosaic explanations.[23]

Passing a lie detector test doesn't lend credence to an abduction story either. Polygraph tests are still used in criminal investigations, employment screenings, and elsewhere. Nevertheless, research has established that polygraph testing is an extremely unreliable guide to someone's truthfulness.[24]

The physical evidence is equivocal. Scars or cuts on abductees could have been caused by aliens—or they could have happened accidentally without the subject's knowing how, just as we all occasionally discover scratches or cuts on our bodies without remembering how they got there. They also could have been intentionally self-inflicted. There's no corroborating evidence to show that they are, in fact, alien-inflicted. The story is much the same with dead-grass areas. There's no direct evidence linking them to UFO landings. Some of them, however, have been shown to be the work of a type of fungus that dehydrates the grass (sometimes in a circular pattern called a fairy ring) and makes it appear burnt.

Although hypothesis 1 doesn't violate any laws of logic or science, it still qualifies as extraordinary because it seems technologically impossible. As we saw in Chapter 2, traveling to the stars seems to require much more energy than anyone will ever be able to generate. But beyond that, alien abduction also seems to require a very advanced transporter technology that allows the aliens to beam people out of their beds and into their spacecraft. Scientists

Stephenville Lights

On the night of January 8, 2008, the residents of Stephenville, Texas, witnessed a remarkable aerial display: a series of extremely bright lights created numerous patterns in the night sky. Mike Odom described them this way: "They lined up horizontally, seven of them, changing into an arch. They lined up vertically and I saw two rectangles of bright flame. That's when I knew it was a life-changing experience."[25] Many, like Odom, took the lights to be of extraterrestrial origin. But were they?

When asked whether the lights could have been the result of military aircraft, a public affairs officer at the Naval Air Station Joint Reserve Base at Carswell Field replied, "There were no F-16s from this unit operating." On January 23, however, the Air Force changed its story. In a press release, it stated: "Ten F-16s from the 457th Fighter Squadron were performing training operations in an area which includes the airspace above Erath County."[26] Why the reversal? An internal communications problem, it claimed. To some, however, such reversals smack of a coverup and suggest that a conspiracy is afoot. But isn't human error a simpler explanation?

Retired Air Force pilot James McGaha thinks so.

McGaha says they were flying training maneuvers that involved dropping extraordinarily bright flares. The LUU/2B/B flare is nothing like the standard flares you might think of. These flares have an illumination of about two million candlepower. They are intended to light up a vast area of the ground for nighttime aerial attack. Once released, they are suspended by parachutes (which often hover and even rise due to the heat of the flares) and light up a circle on the ground greater than one kilometer for four minutes. The flare casing and parachute are eventually consumed by the heat. At a distance of 150 miles, a single flare can still be as bright as the planet Venus.[27]

A retired U.S. Army pilot who was flying a helicopter that night corroborated McGaha's analysis, claiming that he saw multiple military aircraft dropping flares in the area of the Brownwood Military Operating Area. Thus there is no need to invoke aliens to explain the Stephenville lights. They are much better explained as the result of military flares and perceptual construction.

at IBM have recently shown such a transporter is physically possible.[28] Unfortunately, it, too, seems to be forever beyond anyone's technological capability because the amount of information needed to reconstruct a human is too great to be transferred in a reasonable amount of time. Physicist Samuel L. Braunstein explains:

> If we forget about recognizing atoms and measuring their velocities and just scale that to a resolution of one-atomic length in each direction that's about 10^{32} bits (a one followed by thirty two zeros). This is so much information that even with the best optical fibers conceivable it would take over one hundred million centuries to transmit all that information! It would be easier to walk! If we packed all that information into CD ROMs it would fit into a cube almost 1000 kilometers on a side![29]

The idea of a transporter capable of beaming humans from one location to another may be good in theory, but it looks like we will never be able to put one into practice.

Hypothesis 2: *People who report being abducted by aliens are suffering from serious mental illness.* In other words, nobody has been abducted; people who make abduction claims are just plain crazy. Actually, it wouldn't be surprising to find that a few of these people were psychotic. But the idea that a large proportion of them are crazy isn't supported by the evidence.

Not every alleged abductee has undergone psychological testing, but a few have. The Fund for UFO Research asked Elizabeth Slater, a professional psychologist, to study nine people who claimed to have been abducted by aliens. During the study, Slater wasn't aware of the subjects' abduction claims. After extensive testing of these nine, she concluded that none of them were psychotic or crazy.[30] Other research has come up with similar findings.

Of course, psychologists and psychiatrists know that a person needn't be insane to exhibit extremely strange behavior or to have very weird experiences. It is also worth noting that Slater commented that the subjects, though sane, couldn't be considered completely normal. She said that they "did not represent an ordinary cross-section of the population," that several of them could be characterized as "odd or eccentric," and that under stressful conditions six of the nine showed a "potential for more or less transient psychotic experiences involving a loss of reality testing along with confused and disordered thinking that can be bizarre."[31]

Men become civilized, not in proportion to their willingness to believe, but in proportion to their readiness to doubt.
—H. L. MENCKEN

Hypothesis 3: *People who report being abducted by aliens are perpetrating a hoax.* A few tales of UFO abduction are suspicious or have been found to be hoaxes. Philip Klass, for example, has shown that the Travis Walton abduction story (eventually made into the movie *Fire in the Sky*) was a probable hoax.[32] But there's no evidence that the majority of abduction tales are put-ons. Most observers agree that those who make abduction claims are apparently sincere.

Hypothesis 4: *Reports of alien abductions are fantasies arising from people with "fantasy-prone personalities," and these fantasies may be further elaborated and strengthened through hypnosis.* Scientists have discovered that some people, though they appear normal and well-adjusted, frequently have very realistic wide-awake hallucinations and fantasies and often have experiences that resemble those induced by hypnosis. The researchers who uncovered this phenomenon describe it this way:

> [This research] has shown that there exists a small group of individuals (possibly 4% of the population) who fantasize a large part of the time,

who typically "see," "hear," "smell," and "touch" and fully experience what they fantasize; and who can be labeled fantasy-prone personalities. Their extensive and deep involvement in fantasy seems to be their basic characteristic and their other major talents—their ability to hallucinate voluntarily, their superb hypnotic performances, their vivid memories of their life experiences, and their talents as psychics or sensitives—seem to derive from or grow out of their profound fantasy life.[33]

When these people are deep in fantasy, they have a decreased awareness of time and place, just as many abductees say they do (the experience of missing time). Also, not only are they easily hypnotized, but they show hypnotic behavior all the time, even when not hypnotized:

> When we give them "hypnotic suggestions" such as suggestions for visual and auditory hallucinations, negative hallucinations, age regression, limb rigidity, anesthesia, and sensory hallucinations, we are asking them to do for us the kind of thing they can do independently of us in their daily lives.[34]

Interestingly enough, some research suggests that people who claim to have been abducted by aliens are in fact fantasy-prone personalities. In one study, a biographical analysis was done on 154 people who said they had been abducted or had several contacts with aliens. It was found that 132 of these subjects seemed normal and healthy but had many fantasy-prone personality characteristics.[35] Baker has suggested that Whitley Strieber, author of *Communion,* fits the fantasy-prone personality mold:

> Anyone familiar with the fantasy-prone personality who reads Strieber's *Communion* will suffer an immediate shock of recognition! Strieber is a classic example of the fantasy-prone type: easily hypnotized, amnesiac, from a very religious background, with vivid memories of his early years and a very active fantasy life—a writer of occult and highly imaginative novels featuring unusually strong sensory experiences, particularly smells and sounds and vivid dreams.[36]

There's also evidence that sleep-related hallucinations happen more frequently to fantasy-prone people. And there's reason to believe that these phenomena play a role in UFO-abduction stories. We know that many UFO abductions allegedly happen after the victim has gone to bed and involve the feeling of being paralyzed or seeming to float outside the body. Such hallucinations seem absolutely real and thus are referred to as waking dreams. They're not an indication of mental illness; they happen to normal, sane, and rational people. Baker explains their telltale signs:

> There are a number of characteristic clues that tell you whether a perception is or is not a hypnogogic or hypnopompic hallucination. First,

> it always occurs before or after falling asleep; second, one is paralyzed or has difficulty in moving, or on the other hand, one may float out of one's body and have an out-of-body experience; third, the hallucination is unusually bizarre, i.e., one sees ghosts, aliens, monsters, etc.; fourth, after the hallucination is over, the hallucinator typically goes back to sleep; and, fifth, the hallucinator is unalterably convinced of the reality of the entire experience.[37]

Finally, it's clear that if a fantasy-prone person experiences a fantasy about being abducted by aliens and then is hypnotized by a hypnotist who asks leading questions and believes in UFO abductions, the fantasy is likely to be confirmed or elaborated, to be very convincing to others, and to be believed as absolutely true by the abductee.

Hypothesis 5: *Reports of alien abductions arise from dreams and are then elaborated or strengthened through hypnosis.* We know that the adventures of many people claiming to be abductees actually began with compelling dreams. First they said that they dreamed that they had had contact with a UFO or were abducted; then—while under hypnosis—they told in detail of an actual alien abduction. Many of the abductees featured in Hopkins's *Intruders,* for example, described such a pattern of events. As Hines says:

> It is thus easy to understand how, for example, a frightening dream about being abducted by a UFO can come to seem real to an individual who is repeatedly hypnotized to recall further details of the experience and is explicitly told by the hypnotist that the experience is real. If the individual already has difficulty telling reality from fantasy, the process of becoming convinced that the dream or fantasy was real will occur more rapidly. It is no rare event for someone to have a dream that, at least briefly, may seem to have really happened. In fact, almost everyone has had dreams that, upon awakening, were so vivid that it was not possible, for a while at least, to decide whether they really happened or not.[38]

Hypothesis 6: *People who report being abducted are suffering from excessive bursts of electrical activity in their temporal lobes.* Neuroscientist Michael Persinger claims that mystical experiences, out-of-body experiences, and even abduction-like experiences are associated with some unusual activity going on inside the brain—specifically, surges of electrical activity in the temporal lobes. Some people have what is called high "temporal lobe lability." Their temporal lobes are "unstable" and frequently surge with electrical activity. Persinger discovered that compared with people who have "normal" lability, those with high temporal lobe lability more often report mystical or psychic experiences and feelings of flying or leaving the body. In experiments, Persinger has actually induced such experiences—including abduction-like experiences—in people by applying magnetic fields across the brain, thereby instigating bursts of electrical activity in the temporal lobes.[39]

Persinger says that people with high lability are likely to have abduction-type experiences occasionally. The surges are likely to occur during sleep, thus inducing a nighttime abduction experience (which is exactly what many people have reported).

Earthquakes, which produce strong magnetic effects, could trigger temporal lobe surges. So Persinger predicted that reports of UFO abductions and sightings would correspond to the dates of seismic activity. When he tested his prediction, he found that he was right; there was a strong correlation between seismic events and the weird experiences.

©Bettmann/Getty Images

Brigadier General Roger M. Ramey and Colonel Thomas Dubose inspecting the debris from the Roswell crash.

The Roswell Incident

On July 8, 1947, the *Roswell Daily Record* ran the headline, "RAAF Captures Flying Saucer on Ranch in Roswell Region." It seems that a local rancher, W. W. Brazel, had discovered some unusual material on his ranch. The July 9 edition of the *Roswell Daily Record* described the material this way: "When the debris was gathered up the tinfoil, paper, tape and sticks made a bundle about three feet long and 7 or 8 inches thick while the rubber made a bundle about 18 or 20 inches thick. In all, he [Brazel] estimated the entire lot would have weighed maybe five pounds."[40] Although one would expect flying saucers to weigh something more than 5 pounds, many people believe this debris to be the wreckage of a crashed flying saucer.

In an attempt to clear up this matter, Congressman Steven H. Stiff (R-NM) requested the General Accounting Office to locate all records relating to the Roswell incident. In support of this effort, the Air Force published the *Report of Air Force Research Regarding the "Roswell Incident."* This report revealed that the material recovered on Brazel's ranch was part of a top-secret program—code named Project MOGUL—that attempted to monitor Soviet nuclear detonations using high-altitude weather balloons and radar reflectors. As the report indicates:

> What was originally reported to have been recovered was a balloon of some sort, usually described as a "weather balloon," although the majority of the wreckage that was ultimately displayed by General Ramey and Major Marcel in the famous photos in Ft. Worth, was that of a radar target normally suspended from balloons. This radar target, discussed in more detail later, was certainly consistent with the description of a July 9 newspaper article which discussed "tinfoil, paper, tape and sticks." Additionally, the description of the "flying disc" was consistent with a document routinely used by most pro-UFO writers to indicate a conspiracy in progress—the telegram from the Dallas FBI office of July 8, 1947. This document quoted in part states: " . . . The disc is hexagonal in shape and was suspended from a balloon by a cable, which balloon was approximately twenty feet in diameter. . . . The object found resembles a high altitude weather balloon with a radar reflector."[41]

Charles B. Moore, one of the three surviving Project MOGUL scientists, agrees with this assessment. Commenting on the markings on the tape that are often taken to be of alien origin he says:

> There were about four of us who were involved in this, and all remember that our targets had sort of a stylized, flowerlike design. I have prepared, in my life, probably more than a hundred of these targets for flight. And every time I have prepared one of the targets, I have always wondered what the purpose of that tape marking was. But . . . a major named John Peterson, laughed . . . and said, "What do you expect when you get your targets made by a toy factory?"[42]

Now let's apply the criteria of adequacy to these alternative hypotheses. All are testable, so we must rely on the other four criteria to help us choose among the possibilities. Using these four criteria, let's first see if we can eliminate some of the hypotheses.

Hypotheses 4 (fantasy-prone personalities), 5 (dream material), and 6 (electrical activity) can probably be given similar weight in terms of fruitfulness, scope, and simplicity (except that 6 has an edge in fruitfulness). Hypotheses 2 (mental illness) and 3 (hoaxes) are clearly inferior to 4, 5, and 6 in conservatism. They conflict with existing evidence; hypotheses 4, 5, and 6, on the other hand, are consistent with a great deal of evidence.

Now the contest is between hypotheses 1 (authentic abductions), 4, 5, and 6. We can now see that hypothesis 1 comes out the loser to the other three on every count. Hypothesis 1 has yielded no novel predictions. Hypotheses 4, 5, and 6 have greater scope, for they offer explanations that can be applied to several phenomena, not just claims of alien abductions. In terms of simplicity, hypothesis 1 must be given less credence than the other hypotheses because it postulates new entities—aliens.

What happened to me was terrifying. It seemed completely real.

—Whitley Strieber

In light of the criterion of conservatism, we see that the evidence in favor of hypothesis 1 is extremely weak; the evidence for the other three alternatives is much stronger. In addition, hypothesis 1 conflicts with a great deal of human experience regarding visitors from outer space; so far, we have no good evidence that anyone has ever detected any aliens. Moreover, the probability of the Earth being visited by aliens from outer space must be considered very low (but not zero) in light of what we know about the size of the universe, the estimated likelihood of extraterrestrial life, and the physical requirements of space travel.

For all these reasons, the abduction hypothesis must be considered improbable. Hypotheses 4, 5, and 6 appear much more likely. If there is a winner among these three, it would have to be hypothesis 6. It excels in fruitfulness, for it has yielded a surprising prediction—the odd correlation between abduction reports and seismic activity. It is still possible, however, that each of our remaining three hypotheses is a correct explanation for a portion of alien abduction claims. Also, these hypotheses may not be the only ones. Our list of alternative hypotheses isn't intended to be exhaustive. Further research could narrow—or widen—the field. In the meantime, our analysis has given us a conclusion supported by good reasons: The abduction hypothesis is untenable, and there are indeed reasonable alternatives.

COMMUNICATING WITH THE DEAD

In the nineteenth century, few were better at mystifying, unsettling, and entertaining people than spiritualist mediums—occult practitioners who claimed to communicate directly with the dead.

In countless darkened parlors, they held seances—gatherings in which they would call forth departed spirits who would speak through the mediums to loved ones present in the room. Sometimes the mediums would levitate, or furniture around them would rise off the floor, or strange rapping sounds would be heard in the room, or objects would fall out of the darkness as though coming from another world.

The heyday of the mediums, however, was not to last. Too many of them were caught cheating. The levitations, rappings, and falling objects were shown to be simple tricks, and the information about the dead that the mediums produced was often shown to be obtained by ordinary means or based on lucky guesses.

Common sense is very uncommon.
—HORACE GREELEY

The old mediums are gone, but the new mediums are here. They are now called psychics, and they are appearing on TV shows, writing books, and promoting their skills. Unlike the mediums of old, the new ones do not produce physical manifestations like rappings and levitations. But they do provide information about people's dead loved ones, information that often seems shockingly accurate and genuinely otherworldly. These modern-day mediums include psychics James Van Praagh, John Edward, and Sylvia Browne. Their promise of direct contact with the minds of the departed has made them famous, beloved, and well compensated. The ethereal contact provides assurances that all is well with the dead on the "other side." For many people, the "contact" experience can be extremely emotional, reassuring, or distressing.

What could explain these amazing performances? There are four main hypotheses.

The medium is the message.
—MARSHALL MCLUHAN

Hypothesis 1: *The psychics are receiving information or messages from the disembodied spirits of people who have died.* That is, the psychics are doing exactly what they say they are doing—communicating with minds beyond the grave. The most important evidence for this claim is the psychics' performance. Typically, they perform before an audience and have conversations with audience members who have lost loved ones. The psychics seem to know facts about dead loved ones that they could know only if they really were in contact with the dead. They are never 100 percent right in the information they produce, but their "hits" (instances of correct information) occur often enough and are impressive enough to convince many observers.

The psychics' ability has rarely been tested in any controlled way. Recently, however, psychologist Gary Schwartz of the University of Arizona has claimed that his research provides evidence that mediums can indeed communicate with the dead. In a series of small studies, he and his colleagues had a few well-known mediums (including

John Edward) give readings to one or two participants (called "sitters"). The mediums gave readings to the sitters about deceased friends and loved ones, and the sitters rated the mediums' statements for accuracy. Schwartz claims that the mediums consistently and accurately provided specific facts and names, and that these readings cannot be explained as cold reading or lucky guesses.

Other scientists, though, have said that these studies are fundamentally flawed in many respects and therefore do not prove anything. They point out, for example, that the accuracy score for the medium depends entirely on the subjective judgments of the sitter. Given vague statements from the medium, a sitter can find many ways to make the statements match up with facts about departed loved ones. In an actual reading from the research, a medium says, "The first thing being shown to me is a male figure that I would say as being above, that would be some type of father image. . . . Showing me the month of May. . . . They're telling me to talk about the Big H-um, the H connection. To me this is an H with an N sound." Psychologist Ray Hyman explains why this sitter could have easily—almost inevitably—judged this information to be right on target:

> The sitter identified this description as applying to her late husband, Henry. His name was Henry, he died in the month of May and was "affectionately referred to as the 'gentle giant.'" The sitter was able to identify other statements by the medium as applying to her deceased spouse.
>
> Note, however, the huge degree of latitude for the sitter to fit such statements to her personal situation. The phrase "some type of father image" can refer to her husband because he was also the father to her children. However, it could also refer to her own father, her grandfather, someone else's father, or any male with children. It could easily refer to someone without children such as a priest or father-like individual—including Santa Claus. It would have been just as good a match if her husband had been born in May, had married in May, had been diagnosed with a life-threatening illness in May, or considered May as his favorite month. The "HN" connection would fit just as well if the sitter's name were Henna or her husband had a dog named Hank.[43]

This kind of judging bias is fatal to studies like this. Unfortunately, this mistake is not the only one. Critics have uncovered other fatal flaws in Schwartz's research as well.

Two facts raise doubts about the performance evidence. First, the actual percentage of hits in a performance is probably much lower than most people think. One investigator who observed several performances by Van Praagh found that the psychic had a hit rate of only 16 to 33 percent (the proportion of accurate statements or questions out of the total). This rate is much lower than the average number of hits on a roulette wheel. The low hit rate, however, may not be apparent on TV shows featuring the psychics because there may be many misses that the television audience does not see in an edited program. Second, the psychics always explain misses with ad hoc hypotheses—explanations that cannot be independently verified. Ad hoc hypotheses do not prove anything and are often just attempts to save a weak explanation.

Hypothesis 2: *The psychics are using telepathy to read the minds of the living to discover facts about the dead.* Perhaps the most important factor in favor of this explanation is that the beyond-the-grave information is always known by a person in the audience. This factor would make sense if telepathy were at work. There is, however, no independent evidence to suggest that the telepathy hypothesis is true.

Don't live on a fault line. It's a zipper.
—THE ENTITY RAMTHA

Hypothesis 3: *The psychics are doing "cold reading."* Cold reading is an ancient art practiced by fortune-tellers and modern-day mentalists (performers who pretend to be able to read minds). It is a clever trick that can appear to be truly paranormal. In this technique, the "psychic" reader gleans information from people (the subjects) simply by asking them questions, making statements, and carefully noting how people react—all the while giving the impression that the information comes from some mysterious source.

There are several ways that a reader may get the relevant information (or appear to have it). Here are a few of them:

1. The reader asks many questions and treats affirmative answers as though they were confirming a statement the reader had made.

> **Reader:** *Who was the person with an illness, or some disease?*
> **Subject:** *That was my mother.*
> **Reader:** *Because I feel that the illness took a heavy toll on her, that she wanted to get well.*

The unity of consciousness is illusory.
—ERNEST R. HILGARD

2. The reader makes statements that could apply to most people. For example, most people have some association with photographs, jewelry, pets, antiques, illness, and other familiar themes.

> **Reader:** *I'm sensing something about a cat or a small dog. I feel this intense image of this animal.*
> **Subject:** *Yes, my brother had a cat.*
>
> **Reader:** *I'm getting a strong impression of a favorite piece of jewelry. I'm feeling that your loved one, before she passed over, had fond feelings about some jewelry.*
> **Subject:** *Oh, my mother had a brooch that she treasured.*

3. The reader infers accurate—and obvious—information from facts mentioned by the subject.

Reader: *What was your (deceased) father's occupation?*
Subject: *He was a farmer.*

Reader: *Yes, he spent many hours in the fields. He had callused hands. He constantly fretted about the weather, and he was always worrying about the prices for his crops.*

Reader: *You say your grandmother suffered from depression before her death?*
Subject: *Yes, a very deep depression.*

Reader: *I'm sensing that she was very sad about the way things had turned out. . . . She even thought about suicide at one point.*
Subject: *Yes, that's right.*

4. The reader makes statements with multiple variables so that a hit is highly probable.

Reader: *I'm sensing that your (deceased) father lived with a great deal of pain, or frustration, perhaps some mental anguish.*
Subject: *Yes, he was in great pain at the end.*

5. The reader invites the subject to fill in the blanks.

Reader: *I'm feeling something about the head or the face.*
Subject: *Yes, my mother had terrible migraines.*

Reader: *I'm getting the impression of medicine, serious medication somewhere. I don't know why.*
Subject: *My father had to have chemotherapy because of cancer.*

Using these cold-reading techniques, along with many others, a reader can easily appear to be reading minds, as a good mentalist does. With practice, almost anyone can be "psychic." More to the point, it is clear that most, or all, of the amazing performances of the professional psychics can be duplicated using cold-reading techniques. Van Praagh, Edward, and other psychics may indeed be mind readers of the dead, but their performances seem to be indistinguishable from those that can be produced by cold reading.

Hypothesis 4: *The psychics are getting information on subjects ahead of time.* Some mediums and mentalists have been known to acquire facts about a subject before a performance. They would research their subjects, looking for some bit of personal information that could make a startling impression—perhaps a loved one's nickname, or an old family story, or an object with sentimental value.

There is no evidence that top psychics consistently use this ploy. But some of them have gone out of their way to acquire information about a subject before a performance—then produced that same information as though it had come from beyond the grave. Some top psychics have been known to interview members of the audience before the performance begins or to question TV producers about subjects who will be present during the psychic's television performance.

[Spiritualists] are lacking not only in criticism but in the most elementary knowledge of psychology. At the bottom they do not want to be taught any better, but merely to go on believing.

—CARL GUSTAV JUNG

Now, which of these hypotheses is best? All the contending hypotheses are testable, but they differ in how they rank according to the other criteria of adequacy. Hypothesis 1, the psychic medium explanation, fares poorly on all counts. It has never yielded any novel predictions, and its scope is limited because it does not explain anything except the mediumistic performances. It assumes entities (departed spirits) and a form of communication that have never been shown to exist, so simple it is not. Finally, it is not conservative, for it conflicts with everything we know about death, the mind, and communication. Its lack of conservatism alone renders it improbable.

Hypotheses 2 (telepathy) is similar to the mediumistic hypothesis in every way. As our analysis in Chapter 6 suggests, the telepathy hypothesis has yielded no novel predictions, assumes unknown entities or forces, and conflicts with available scientific evidence. It could be argued that it has more scope than hypothesis 1, but greater scope cannot save it from improbability.

Hypothesis 4 (advance information) is better than either 1 or 2 in scope, simplicity, and conservatism. But the available evidence does not support the idea that preperformance research is widespread or that most hits are the result of prior knowledge.

Hypothesis 3 (cold reading) is the winner. It is probably equal to the telepathy explanation in scope and simplicity. But it fits the evidence better than any other hypothesis. Investigators have shown that someone using cold reading can duplicate the amazing performances of the psychics—and that top psychics appear to be consistently using cold-reading techniques. We therefore have excellent reasons for believing that Van Praagh, Edward, and other psychics are talented, impressive, and disappointing cold readers.

NEAR-DEATH EXPERIENCES

Benjamin Franklin once remarked in a letter to Jean-Baptist Leroy, "In this world, nothing is certain but death and taxes." A number of researchers, however, believe that Franklin was at best only half right. Taxes may indeed be inevitable, but death—understood as the annihilation of the self—may not even occur. Our physical bodies will no doubt die. But that, they say, doesn't mean that *we* will die, for there is evidence that we can survive the death of our physical bodies. The most impressive evidence for immortality, it is claimed, comes from near-death experiences.

The term near-death experience (NDE) was coined by Dr. Raymond Moody to describe a family of experiences he found common to those who had narrowly escaped death. His initial findings were based on in-depth interviews with some fifty people who had either clinically died (their heart and lungs had stopped functioning) and were later revived or who had faced death as a result of an accident, injury, or illness. What he discovered was that while no two people had exactly the same experience, their experiences shared a number of common elements. In 1975, he published the results of his research in his best-selling *Life after Life.* There he offered the following "ideal" or "complete" account of the near-death experience:

> A man is dying and, as he reaches the point of greatest physical distress, he hears himself pronounced dead by his doctor. He begins to hear an uncomfortable noise, a loud ringing or buzzing, and at the same time feels himself moving very rapidly through a long dark tunnel. After this, he suddenly finds himself outside of his own physical body, but still in the immediate physical environment, and he sees his own body from a distance, as though he is a spectator. He watches the resuscitation attempt from this unusual vantage point and is in a state of emotional upheaval.
>
> After a while, he collects himself and becomes more accustomed to his odd condition. He notices that he still has a "body," but one of a very different nature and with very different powers from the physical body he has left behind. Soon other things begin to happen. Others come to meet and to help him. He glimpses the spirits of relatives and friends who have already died, and a loving, warm spirit of a kind he has never encountered before—a being of light—appears before him. This being asks him a question, nonverbally, to make him evaluate his life and helps him along by showing him a panoramic, instantaneous playback of the major events of his life.[44]

Although none of the people Moody had interviewed for *Life after Life* had experienced all the elements just described, he has since come across a number of people who have had the complete experience.[45]

When it first appeared, Moody's account of the near-death experience was met with a good deal of skepticism. Doctors who had resuscitated hundreds of patients said they had never encountered it. Others claimed that his sample was too small to be significant.[46] Nevertheless it sparked a great deal of interest among both professionals and laypeople. A number of scientists and doctors began their own studies of the phenomena. To disseminate the results of this research, the Association for the Scientific Study of Near-Death Phenomena was founded in 1977.

More extensive and better controlled research has, for the most part, corroborated Moody's findings. The near-death experience as Moody described it is fairly common among those who have survived a close brush with death. In fact, research suggests that if you come close to death or clinically die and are resuscitated, your chances of having such an experience are about fifty-fifty.

Dr. Fred Schoonmaker, chief of cardiovascular services at St. Luke's Hospital in Denver, had been studying near-death experiences for over a decade before Moody published *Life after Life.* He published the results of his research in 1979.[47] Out of the 2,300 cases he examined, most of whom had suffered cardiac arrest, 60 percent reported having near-death experiences of the sort described by Moody. Dr. Michael Sabom, a cardiologist in Atlanta, interviewed seventy-eight people who were known to have nearly died. He found that 42 percent of them had experiences like the one that Moody described.[48] A 1982 Gallup poll found that one in seven Americans had narrowly escaped death and that one in twenty had had a near-death experience.[49] One of the most detailed studies of the near-death experience was conducted by Dr. Kenneth Ring, a psychologist in Connecticut. Using hospital records and newspaper advertisements, he was able to identify 102 people who had been in life-threatening situations. They were asked to provide a general description of their experience and then were questioned about the specific details. Almost 50 percent of the people in his sample had a near-death experience.[50]

Dr. Ring divided the near-death experience into five stages:

1. Peace and a sense of well-being.
2. Separation from the body.
3. Entering the darkness.
4. Seeing the light.
5. Entering the world of light.[51]

The earlier stages were reported more frequently than the latter. Sixty percent of his subjects reached the first stage, 37 percent reached the second, 23 percent reached the third, 16 percent reached the fourth, and 10 percent reached the fifth. What stage (if any) one reached was unaffected by one's age, sex, or religion. In fact, cross-cultural studies have found that the core elements of the experience are the same no matter what the person's background. Psychologists Karlis Osis and Erlendur Haraldsson, for example, examined the

The Biblical View of Souls

Many people believe that the existence of a soul capable of existing independently of the body is a central tenet of Christian teaching. Biblical scholars disagree. The Bible, they tell us, presents a monistic view of the person in which the mind and the body are inseparable from one another. British theologian Adrian Thatcher explains:

> There appears to be a rare unanimity among biblical scholars that the biblical picture of the person is non-dualist, and that the Bible gives little or no support to the idea that a person is essentially a soul, or that the soul is separable from the body. Dualists, of course, may reply that, regardless of what the Bible said about the issue then, dualism offers a convincing framework for Christian teaching now. Even so, they cannot get around the fact that, from a biblical point of view, dualism is very odd. Lynn de Silva summarizes the position thus:
>
>> Biblical scholarship has established quite conclusively that there is no dichotomous concept of man in the Bible, such as is found in Greek and Hindu thought. The biblical view of man is holistic, not dualistic. The notion of the soul as an immortal entity which enters the body at birth and leaves it at death is quite foreign to the biblical view of man. The biblical view is that man is a unity; he is a unity of soul, body, flesh, mind, etc. all together constituting the whole man. None of the constituent elements is capable of separating itself from the total structure and continuing to live after death.[52]
>
> Why are biblical scholars unanimously agreed that the Bible gives us no reason for believing in an immortal soul? Because the words that get translated *soul,* such as "nephesh" and "psuche," mean living, breathing creature, and because the story of the resurrection makes no sense if there are such things as immortal souls. Thatcher explains:
>
>> The resurrection and ascension of Christ seem clearly to exclude dualistic accounts of the human person. The death of Christ was a real and total death, not merely the death of his mortal body. The miracle of the resurrection is precisely that God raises Jesus from the dead, not that he raises Jesus' mortal body and reunites it with his immortal soul. What purpose does the resurrection of Jesus serve, we may ask, if Jesus was not really dead? Was it just to convince the disciples that the bonds of death were forever loosened? Hardly, for if the disciples had believed in immortal souls they would not have required assurance on that point; and if they had needed such assurance, a resurrection miracle would not have provided it; it would merely have created confusion. The ascension of Christ is also rendered superfluous by a dualist account of the person; for the soul of Christ, being alive after his physical death, would presumably have been capable of returning to the Father without its body. What then is the ascension? A highly visual way of saying cheerio? It is, rather, the return of the transformed, transfigured, glorified, yet still embodied, Christ to the Father. No particular historical version of the event is favored by arguing thus. The point is that the theological convictions expressed by the resurrection and ascension narratives make much better sense on the assumption that all men and women are essentially bodily unities, after, as well as before, their bodily deaths.[53] Remarkably, the biblical view of persons seems much closer to that of the neuroscientists than that of the laymen.

Source: Adrian Thatcher, "Christian Theism and the Concept of a Person," *Persons and Personality,* (Oxford: Black-well, 1987).

near-death experiences of Indian swamis and found that they did not differ essentially from those reported in the West.[54]

All of the aforementioned studies were retrospective; that is, they were based on interviews that were conducted up to ten years after the experience occurred. The delay makes it much more difficult to get an accurate assessment of the psychological or physiological factors that may have been involved in the experience. In 2001, however, the Dutch physician Pim van Lommel and three of his colleagues published a prospective study of near-death experiences in the well-respected and peer-reviewed British medical journal, *Lancet*.[55] The study interviewed 344 patients from ten Dutch hospitals immediately after they suffered a heart attack. To gauge the long-term effects of this event, follow-up studies of this group were conducted two and eight years later. Van Lommel and his colleagues found that only 18 percent of their group reported a near-death experience. Whether one had an NDE was unrelated to the length of the heart attack, the period of unconsciousness, the presence of medications, or the fear of death. The depth of the experience, however, was affected by sex (women were more likely to have a deep NDE), place of resuscitation (those resuscitated outside of the hospital were more likely to have a deep NDE), and fear of death (those with a fear of death were more likely to have a deep NDE).

Given that near-death experiences are common and universal, what can we conclude about them? Do they provide evidence for the immortality of the soul? Moody thinks so. He believes that the best explanation of these experiences is that the soul or psyche leaves the body at death and travels to another world.[56] This conclusion is undoubtedly what most people would like to believe, so let's consider this hypothesis first.

Hypothesis 1: *During a near-death experience, the soul or psyche leaves the physical body and travels to another world.* Moody cites two reasons for taking near-death experiences at face value: First, those who have them can often accurately report what was going on around them while they were clinically dead; and second, their personalities are often transformed by the experience.[57] They no longer fear death, and their life becomes infused with a new sense of meaning, purpose, and value.

Let's examine each of these claims in turn.

The discovery that we can perceive the world around us while our brain is no longer functioning would be one of the most momentous in the history of science, for it would completely undermine the fields of psychology and neuroscience. These disciplines have found that the brain is the organ of thought; that we think, perceive, and feel with our brains. If we don't need our brains to perform these functions, then all the psychology and neuroscience textbooks will have to be discarded.

Before we relegate entire fields of study to the trash heap, however, we'd better be sure that the evidence warrants such a dismissal. So let's first examine the evidence in favor of the view that the brain is the seat of the mind. As neurophysiologist Barry Beyerstein indicates, that evidence consists of the following types of data:

> *Phylogenetic:* There is an evolutionary relationship between brain complexity and species' cognitive attributes.
> *Developmental:* Abilities emerge with brain maturation; failure of the brain to mature arrests mental development.
> *Clinical:* Brain damage from accidental, toxic, or infectious sources, or from deprivation of nutrition or stimulation during brain development, results in predictable and largely irreversible losses of mental function.
> *Experimental:* Mental operations correlate with electrical, biochemical, biomagnetic, and anatomical changes in the brain. When the human brain is stimulated electrically or chemically during neurosurgery, movements, percepts, memories, and appetites are produced that are like those arising from ordinary activation of the same cells.
> *Experiential:* Numerous natural and synthetic substances interact chemically with brain cells. Were these neural modifiers unable to affect consciousness pleasurably and predictably, the recreational value of nicotine, alcohol, caffeine, LSD, cocaine, and marijuana would roughly be equal to that of blowing soap bubbles.
>
> Despite their abundance, diversity, and mutual reinforcement, the foregoing data cannot, by themselves, entail the truth of PNI [the psychoneural identity theory]. Nevertheless, the theory's parsimony [simplicity] and research productivity [fruitfulness], the range of phenomena it accounts for [scope], and the lack of credible counter-evidence [conservativism] are persuasive to virtually all neuroscientists.[58]

The view that we think with our brains, then, is not merely an assumption of psychology and neuroscience—it's one of their most well-confirmed theories. What makes it the best explanation of these data is that it's simpler, more fruitful, has a wider scope, and is more conservative than any competitor, including the theory that the mind is separate from the body. It's simpler because it doesn't assume the existence of an immaterial substance. It's more fruitful because it has successfully predicted a number of novel phenomena, such as the production of mental states through electronic stimulation of the brain. It has greater scope because it can explain all of the foregoing phenomena without making any ad hoc assumptions. And it's more conservative because it doesn't conflict with any reliable data.

NDE researchers argue, on the contrary, that it does conflict with reliable data, namely, that some experiencers accurately perceive things while their brain is no longer working. If perception can take place in the absence of brain function, then the mind doesn't depend on the brain. The two cases that many consider to be the best evidence of such disembodied cognition are those of Maria[59] and Pam Reynolds.[60]

Maria was a migrant worker in Washington State who, in 1977, suffered a heart attack and was admitted to Seattle's Harborview Medical Center. While at the Center, her heart stopped beating and she was quickly resuscitated. When she met with her social worker, Kimberly Clark, however, she recounted a most remarkable experience: "The strangest thing happened when the doctors and nurses were working on me: I found myself looking down from the ceiling at them working on my body."[61] Maria had a classic out-of-body experience. But even more remarkably, while she was apparently out of her body, she claims to have "thought her way" over to the north side of the building and saw a tennis shoe on a third-floor window ledge. She asked Kimberly Clark to find the shoe, but when Clark walked outside the building, she couldn't see anything on the ledge. So she looked out the windows on the third floor, but to see the ledge, she had to press her face to the glass. After a diligent search, she eventually found the shoe.

At first glance, it appears that Maria knew something that she couldn't possibly have known unless she really was out of her body. According to Clark, the shoe couldn't be seen from outside the building, and it couldn't be seen from inside the building without pressing one's face to the glass, which supposedly Maria didn't do. But as we have seen, appearances can be deceiving, especially in the case of anecdotal reports, because we can never be sure that they have not been influenced by cognitive or perceptual biases, memory errors, or other confounding factors.

In 1994, seventeen years after the incident and ten years after Kimberly Clark published her account of it, Hayden Ebbern and Sean Mulligan tried to verify Maria's story. After interviewing Clark and learning where on the third-floor ledge the tennis shoe was located, they placed another one there to determine just how difficult it was to see. To their surprise, they found that it wasn't difficult at all. They "were astonished at the ease with which they could see and identify the shoe."[62] They also found that it wasn't difficult to see the shoe from inside the room. "There was no need whatsoever for anyone to press his or her face against the glass to see the shoe," they report. "In fact, one needed only to take a few steps into the room to see it clearly."[63] So there is no need to invoke a paranormal or supernatural explanation to account for Maria's encounter with the shoe. She may have seen it during her stay there, or she may have overheard someone talking about it.

In most near-death experiences, it's difficult to tell whether the subjects' brains have truly ceased to function because there's no time or opportunity to hook them up to an electroencephalogram, or EEG, which records electrical activity in the outermost portion of the brain known as the neocortex. If a heart stops beating during an operation, for example, resuscitation efforts start immediately, and the subsequent flurry of activity makes it difficult to attach an EEG. After the heart stops beating, it takes about 10 seconds for the EEG pattern to begin to change and about 20 seconds for the EEG to flatline—to record no electrical activity in the neocortex.[64] A flat EEG doesn't mean that the entire brain has stopped working, however, because structures deeper in the brain that are not monitored by an EEG, like the brain stem, take longer to shut down. And even in those rare cases where an EEG is present, and the patient has "flatlined," it's difficult to tell whether the experience occurred during that period. It could have happened before the patient flatlined or as the patient was regaining consciousness. There is one remarkable case, however, where the patient was hooked up to an EEG, had no detectable brain activity for over half an hour, and yet had a vivid near-death experience.

In 1991, Pam Reynolds had an aneurysm (a bulging artery) removed from her brain following an unusual medical procedure known as "deep hypothermic circulatory arrest" in which her body was cooled down to 60 degrees Fahrenheit, her heartbeat and breathing were stopped, and the blood was drained from her head. This procedure is used to minimize the risk of brain damage during delicate brain operations. While in this state, known as "stillness," the patient has no detectable brain activity. Nevertheless, when Reynolds was revived, she reported having a near-death experience in which she seemed to float out of her body, witness the medical personnel involved in the operation, and hear one of the surgeons remark that her arteries were too small.[65] Her description of these events, while brief, was relatively accurate.[66] If they happened while she was in a state of stillness, it would be strong evidence for disembodied cognition.

But the events she recounts did not happen during that time. A detailed analysis of the timeline of the operation by Keith Augustine reveals that Reynolds had her near-death experience well before her body was cooled down.

> As Sabom's own account reveals, her standstill condition had absolutely nothing to do with the time we know that her near-death OBE began: a full two hours and five minutes before medical staff began to cool her blood, during perfectly normal body temperature.[67]

The anesthesiologist Dr. Gerald Woerlee hypothesizes that Reynolds's brain was still functioning at the time her near-death experience took place, and that she was able to recall details of the operation because she experienced "anesthetic awareness": a condition in which a patient becomes conscious while still under the influence of an anesthetic.[68]

General anesthesia involves the administration of three types of drugs: sedatives to induce sleep, muscle relaxants to prevent movement, and anesthetics to alleviate pain. If the sedatives wear off before the other drugs, the patient may experience anesthetic awareness. During deep hypothermic circulatory arrest, sedatives are no longer administered after cooldown begins because the deep hypothermia is sufficient to keep the patient unconscious. So, Woerlee suggests, "Pam Reynolds could have undergone periods of anesthetic awareness which would explain her veridical experiences."[69] Since her accurate perceptions can be given a natural explanation, there is no need to invoke a supernatural one.

If it could be proved beyond a reasonable doubt that someone acquired knowledge during a period of stillness—or even while he or she was flatlined—the existence of disembodied cognition would be difficult to deny. But there are no such cases. As neuropsychologist Sebastian Dieguez reveals, "the embarrassing failure to find even one irrefutable case of 'veridical perceptions' during brain inactivity (or simply unconsciousness)" casts doubt on the existence of disembodied cognition.[70]

To show that we can acquire knowledge of the world around us without using our brains, near-death researchers need more than anecdotal reports—they need clinical evidence gathered under controlled conditions where the possibility of ordinary cognition is ruled out. A recently completed study tried to gather just that kind of evidence. As part of this study, known as AWARE (AWAreness during REsuscitation), over 1,000 images were placed on shelves in operating rooms that were visible only from the ceiling.[71] An accurate identification of one of these images by a cardiac patient would be strong evidence for the existence of disembodied cognition. Over a four-year period, 2,060 cases of cardiac arrest from 15 hospitals in the United Kingdom, United States, and Australia were analyzed. None of the patients were able to accurately identify an image. One patient accurately described aspects of his resuscitation, but there is no direct evidence that he was unconscious at the time.[72] So reliable evidence of disembodied cognition remains elusive.

One way to study near-death experiences under controlled conditions would be to artificially induce death (as was done in the movie *Flatliners*), have the subjects try to identify specific objects chosen through a double-blind procedure, and then revive them. Ethical considerations, however, prevent us from performing such experiments.

Fortunately, it's not necessary to kill people to check the veracity of out-of-body perception, for out-of-body experiences can be induced by other means. Meditation, stress, drugs, and exhaustion, for example, are known to produce out-of-body experiences. There are even people who claim to be able to produce them at will. Studies of these people by parapsychologists have produced equivocal results, however, leaving no solid evidence that accurate out-of-body perception occurs. After reviewing all the major studies, psychologist Susan Blackmore concludes:

> All these experiments were aimed at finding out whether subjects could see a distant target during an OBE [out-of-body experience]. At best there are a very few properly controlled experiments (some critics would say, none) which have provided unequivocal evidence that a subject could detect anything by other than normal means. Although the experimental OBE may differ from the spontaneous kind, a simple conclusion is possible from the experimental studies. That is, OBE vision, if it occurs, is extremely poor.[73]

The experimental evidence, then, does not establish beyond a reasonable doubt that a person can acquire knowledge of the physical world during an out-of-body or near-death experience.

The soul hypothesis also raises a number of difficult questions. If we think with our souls rather than our brains, then what does the brain do? Is it merely a relay station, sending messages back and forth between the soul and the body? If so, then brain damage doesn't really affect our ability to think; just our ability to convey our thoughts. On this view, people with Alzheimer's, dementia, severe mental retardation, and so on are just as lucid as you or me, it's just that the cell tower to their soul is damaged. Is that plausible? And if the soul doesn't need the brain to see, why is its vision limited to the spectrum of light that affects our eyes? Why can't it see infrared or ultraviolet light?[74] Furthermore, if the soul creates and stores its own memories independently of the brain, why can't we recall what happened to us when we are under the influence of anesthetics?[75] A credible soul theory would have to answer all these questions.

And that's not all. A plausible soul theory should tell us what sort of thing the soul is. Apparently, it has a location in space because people report that it can float around rooms and travel through walls. It also apparently has a shape because people describe it as a body with arms, legs, and so on. So it can't be totally nonphysical. What, then, is it made of? Since it has some physical properties, you would expect that it would be detectable. All attempts to detect it, however, have failed. Investigators have used ultraviolet and infrared devices, magnetometers, thermometers, and thermistors in the attempt to register the presence of the soul. No attempts, however, have been successful.

If the soul can acquire knowledge about our world while it is out of the body, it must interact with that world. But if it interacts with the world, it must be observable. Psychologist William Rushton explains:

> We know that all information coming to us normally from the outside is caught by the sense organs and encoded by their nerves. And that a tiny damage to the retina (for instance) or its nerves to the brain produces such characteristic deficiencies in the visual sensation that the site of the damage may usually be correctly inferred. What is this OOB [out-of-body] eye that can encode the visual scene exactly as does the real eye, with its hundred million photoreceptors and its million signaling optic nerves? Can you imagine anything but a replica of the real eye that could manage to do this? But if this floating replica is to see, it must catch light, and hence cannot be transparent, and so must be visible to people in the vicinity.
>
> In fact, floating eyes are not observed, nor would this be expected, for they only exist in fantasy.[76]

Since the soul is not observable, it's doubtful that it can acquire knowledge while out of the body. The problem is this: If the soul is physical, it should be detectable. The fact that we haven't detected it casts doubt on its physicality. If it's nonphysical, however, it's unclear how it could have a shape and a position in space or acquire knowledge of our world. Without more information about the nature of the soul and its commerce with the physical world, there is no good reason to take the nonphysical soul hypothesis seriously. For in the absence of such information, all that this hypothesis tells us is that something, we know not what, acquires information, we know not how, and goes someplace, we know not where. Needless to say, this hypothesis is not very enlightening.

One of the most popular hypotheses regarding near-death experiences was championed by astronomer Carl Sagan in his book *Broca's Brain*.[77] First proposed by the psychologists Stanislov Grof and Joan Halifax, this hypothesis claims that near-death experiences are vivid recollections of the birth experience.[78] This explanation can apparently account for the universality of near-death experiences, for being born is an experience that all humans share. It can also apparently account for the experience of traveling through a tunnel (entering the darkness) and seeing the light, for that is what many imagine the birth experience to be like. As a result, it deserves a closer examination.

Hypothesis 2: *Near-death experiences are vivid recollections of the birth experience.* This hypothesis assumes that we can remember our birth and that what we remember is traveling down a long tunnel. Studies of infant cognition, however, indicate that their brains are not fully enough developed to remember specific details of their birth.[79] And even if they could, it's doubtful that they would remember the experience as traveling down a long tunnel, for during birth their faces are pressed against the walls of the birth canal. Fetuses don't see anything until they've emerged from the uterus.

Moreover, if near-death experiences were based on birth memories, then those who were born by caesarean section (C-section) should not have tunnel experiences. Susan Blackmore tested this prediction by sending a questionnaire to 254 people, 36 of whom had been born by C-section. She found that people born by C-section were just as likely to have tunnel experiences as those who weren't. So the best test we have so far of the birth memory hypothesis has turned out negative.[80]

To fully explain the near-death experience, the birth memory hypothesis would have to tell us why only birth in particular is relived at death and not some other experience. One suggestion is that because our physiological condition at death is similar to that at birth, it triggers memories of it, in much the same way that smells trigger memories associated with them. But are the physiological conditions of birth and death really that similar? Can these conditions be produced under any other circumstances? If so, why aren't those situations recalled? Until these questions are answered, the birth memory explanation can't be considered a satisfactory one.

Hypothesis 3: *Near-Death experiences are the result of abnormal neuron firing patterns in the brain.* Near-death experiences are had in many different kinds of situations, not all of which involve a close brush with death. Drugs, fainting, and direct stimulation of the brain as well as cardiac arrest, car accidents, and falling can generate near-death experiences. So it's doubtful that one explanation can account for all aspects of the experience. Nevertheless, neuroscientists have discovered "neurophysiological correlates" (patterns of neuron firing in the brain) that correspond to all the main features of a near-death experience. Dean Mobbs and Caroline Watt explain:

> The vivid pleasure frequently experienced in near-death experiences may be the result of fear-elicited opioid release, while the life review and REM components of the near-death experience could be attributed to the action of the locus coeruleus-noradrenaline system. Out-of-body experiences and feelings of disconnection with the physical body could arise because of a breakdown in multisensory processes, and the bright lights and tunneling could be the result of a peripheral to fovea breakdown of the visual system through oxygen deprivation. A priori expectations, where the individual makes sense of the situation by believing they will experience the archetypal near-death experience package, may also play a crucial role.[81]

Feelings of peace and well-being can be caused by dopamine and opioids produced by the brain during times of stress; life reviews can be caused by stimulation of the amygdala or hippocampus which are involved in emotion and memory; out-of-body experiences, can be caused by stimulating the temporoparietal junction which is responsible for integrating sensory information, and the tunnel effect can be caused by lack of oxygen to the visual system. Mobbs and Watt conclude: "Taken together, the scientific evidence suggests that all aspects of the near-death experience have a neurophysiological or psychological basis."[82] Note that this is just a suggestion because detailed neurological data regarding what is happening deep within the brain during a near-death experience are not available. But these neurological correlates make the view that the near-death experience is a brain-based phenomenon hard to dismiss.

There remains the problem of why near-death experiences seem so real, even "more real than real," as some experiencers put it.[83] Part of the explanation may be that many of these experiences are triggered by hypoxia (lack of oxygen), which often produces vivid sensations:

> Hypoxia (oxygen starvation) quickly affects the higher centers, causing a blunting of the finer sensibilities and a loss of the sense of judgement and of self-criticism. The subject feels, however, that his mind is not only clear but unusually keen.[84]

Susan Blackmore offers another explanation. Our brains, she tells us, are information-processing mechanisms that try to make sense out of the information they receive by constructing models of reality. The model we take to be real at any one time is the one that is the most stable, that is, the one that fits best with the available information. As she puts it:

> Our brains have no trouble distinguishing "reality" from "imagination." But this distinction is not given. It is one the brain has to make for itself by deciding which of its own models represents the world "out here." I suggest it does this by comparing all the models it has at any time and choosing the most stable one as "reality."[85]

When our normal sources of information are disrupted, as when we are under severe stress or near death, our models of reality will become unstable. In that case, the brain will try to construct a stable model by using the only information available to it, namely, memory. Remembered events, however, have a peculiar characteristic: They are almost always seen from a bird's-eye point of view. Try to remember the last time you walked down the beach or through the woods, for example. If you're like most of us, you'll see yourself from above. This aspect of our memories, she claims, helps explain out-of-body experiences. These experiences are simply the result of a memory model of reality taking over from a sensory model.[86]

One advantage of Blackmore's hypothesis is that it can account for the perceived reality of the out-of-body experience. Since reality is whatever our most stable model says it is, if a memory model becomes the most stable, then it will be taken to be real. Extraordinary events can have a profound effect on us, especially if they are considered to be real. The events that occur during an NDE are, to say the least, extraordinary, and since they're part of an NDEer's most stable model of reality at the time, they seem real. It's no wonder, then, that people often come away from an NDE with a radically altered view of the world.

The hypothesis that near-death experiences are caused by abnormal neuron firing patterns does an admirable job of accounting for the major features of the near-death experience. Is it the best hypothesis? Let's review the bidding. Hypothesis 1 (the soul hypothesis) has not borne any epistemological fruit, for it has not predicted any heretofore unknown phenomena. It is also less simple and less conservative than any of the other hypotheses considered, for it postulates more entities than they do, and the entities postulated are not recognized by our current best theories. The scope of this theory is also questionable, for it raises more questions than it answers. Hypothesis 2 (the birth-memory hypothesis) is inconsistent

Spontaneous Human Combustion

There is a phenomenon known as "spontaneous human combustion" (SHC), which seems to involve people bursting into flames and burning so completely that nothing remains of them but ashes. Charles Dickens was well acquainted with this phenomenon and provides the following description of it in his novel, *Bleak House.*

> there is a smouldering, suffocating vapour in the room, and a dark greasy coating on the walls and ceiling. The chairs and table, and the bottle so rarely absent from the table, all stand as usual. . . . Here is a small burnt patch of flooring: . . . and here is—is it the cinder of a small charred and broken log of wood sprinkled with white ashes, or is it coal? O Horror, he is here! . . . Call the death by any name Your Highness will . . . it is the same death eternally—inborn, inbred, engendered in the corrupted humours of the vicious body itself, and that only—Spontaneous Combustion, and none other of all the deaths that can be died.[87]

After Dickens published this account of SHC, philosopher George Lewes chided him in print for promoting an uneducated superstition. Dickens responded to Lewes by revealing in the preface of the second edition of *Bleak House* that he had thoroughly researched the subject and was aware of at least thirty well-documented cases of SHC. Since then, many more cases have been documented. So there is no doubt that people burn to death in the manner described by Dickens. The question is whether their combustion is truly spontaneous.

Cases of alleged spontaneous human combustion share a number of common features: (1) The body, except for the extremities, is sometimes completely reduced to ashes; (2) objects in the room, except those that are in contact with the body, are usually not burned; and (3) a greasy coating of soot covers the ceiling and part of the walls, usually stopping a few feet from the floor. What makes cases of SHC so mysterious is that it takes a temperature of about 1,600 degrees Fahrenheit for approximately two hours to cremate a body, and even then the bones are not completely reduced to ash. (Crematoriums destroy the remaining bone fragments by crushing them with a mortar and pestle.) A fire that hot should destroy much more than just the individual involved. Since it doesn't, spontaneous human combustion seems physically impossible.

Given the seeming impossibility of these fires, some have invoked the supernatural to explain them. They view SHC as a form of divine retribution. Many victims of SHC are alcoholic and overweight, but those

with what we know about the nature of the birth experience and has not lived up to its predictions. Hypothesis 3 (the brain-based theory), on the other hand, has the greatest scope and remains the simplest, most fruitful, and most conservative of the bunch. With what we know now, it remains the most plausible.

GHOSTS

In 1575, Gilles Delacre of Tours, France, sued his landlord on the grounds that the house he was renting was haunted. The lawyer for the landlord tried to get the case dismissed on the grounds that indiscretions don't seem deserving of such dramatic (and painful) death. Others have speculated that the intensity of the fire is due to the amount of alcohol consumed by the victims. Experiments conducted in 1850 by Justus von Leibig, however, showed that even flesh soaked in alcohol will not burn to ashes by itself.[88] Some have even gone so far as to postulate a new subatomic particle—a "pyroton"—which can initiate an internal chain reaction similar to that which occurs in an atomic bomb.[89]

There is no need to invoke the supernatural or amend the laws of physics to explain SHC, however, because the phenomenon can be accounted for in much more conventional terms. Forensic biologists now believe that the victims of SHC have essentially become human candles. A human with clothes on is like a candle turned inside out; clothes serve as the wick, and body fat serves as the wax. What happens in cases of SHC is that the victim's clothing catches on fire, melting their subcutaneous fat. The fat then melts onto the clothing, or onto the chair upon which the victim is sitting, providing additional fuel for the fire. In a closed room, most of the oxygen is quickly used up, reducing the flames to a slow smolder and generating a great deal of greasy smoke. The grease in the smoke coats the ceilings and walls. Objects not in contact with the burning body do not burn because there is not enough oxygen to support their combustion. Objects engulfed in the hot smoke, however, may show signs of heat damage such as cracking or melting. Alcohol does play a role, but not the one traditionally assumed. It doesn't fuel the fire; it simply impairs the victim's ability to respond to it.

A human candle doesn't burn at 1,600 degrees Fahrenheit. But provided it burns long enough, it doesn't have to burn that hot to completely reduce bone to ash. Douglas Drysdale explains:

> In a crematorium you need high temperatures about 1300°C or even higher to reduce the body to ash in a relatively short period of time. But it's a misconception to think you need those temperatures within a living room to reduce a body to ash in this way. You can produce local, high temperatures by means of the wick effect and a combination of smouldering and flaming to reduce even bones to ash. At relatively low temperatures of 500°C—and, if given enough time—the bone will transform into something approaching a powder in composition.[90]

So you don't need to worry about bursting into flames while you're walking down the street. But it is not a good idea to sit in a closed room and have a smoke after you've had a lot to drink.

ghosts didn't exist. In rebuttal, Delacre's lawyer cited a number of authorities, including Origen, Seneca, Livy, Cicero, Plutarch, and Pliny, attesting to the existence of ghosts. The judge found this testimony convincing and decided in favor of Delacre.[91]

In 1990, Jeffrey Stambovsky of Nyack, New York, sued Helen Ackley and Ellis Reality to void his purchase agreement on the grounds that the house he was about to buy was haunted. Stambovsky had already paid Ackley $32,500 of the $650,000 asking price for the old Victorian mansion, which bore a resemblance to the house inhabited by the television family, the Munsters. For years, Ackley had been telling her friends and neighbors that the house was haunted.

In a 1977 *Reader's Digest* article, she claimed that one of the ghosts was "a cheerful apple-faced man" who looked like Santa Claus. A 1989 newspaper article on Nyack real estate described the house as a "riverfront Victorian—with ghost." All this was news to the Strombovskys, who found out about the house's haunted history only after they had made their down payment. A lower court initially denied their petition, but the Strombovskys persevered, and in 1991, the appellate division of the state supreme court ruled in their favor, finding Ackley guilty of fraudulently concealing information from them. In his decision, Judge Rubin wrote:

> Not being a "local," plaintiff could not readily learn that the home he had contracted to purchase is haunted. Whether the source of the spectral apparition seen by defendant seller are parapsychic or psychogenic having reported their presence in both a national publication and the local press, defendant is estopped to deny their existence and, as a matter of law, the house is haunted. . . . Finally, if the language of the contract is to be construed as broadly as defendant urges to encompass the presence of poltergeists in the house, it cannot be said that she has delivered the premises "vacant" in accordance with her obligation under the provisions of the contract rider.[92]

So the legal recognition of the existence of haunted houses is not something relegated to fifteenth-century Europe. It can be found in twentieth-century America as well.

It's unclear whether Justice Rubin believes in the existence of ghosts. But according to a recent Gallup poll, 38 percent of Americans do. Ghosts are traditionally defined as the spirits or souls of people who have died, and many claim to have experienced them. These experiences may range from full-form apparitions to sudden changes in temperature, unnatural odors, and a feeling of presence. These experiences are undoubtedly real. The question is, were they caused by disembodied spirits? To answer this question we'll have to determine whether the claim that they were provides the best explanation of the evidence.

While ghost experiences are many and varied, they can usefully be divided into two basic categories: hauntings and apparitions. Hauntings are characterized by ghosts that appear repeatedly at the same place and go through the same motions time and time again. Apparitions, on the other hand, are ghosts that appear to interact with the people around them. Some appear only once in an attempt to impart some information or complete some business. Others appear many times. Let's see if there are such things.

Hypothesis 1: *Ghost experiences are caused by disembodied spirits.* The easiest way to explain ghost experiences is to take them at face value: What we seem to see is what we do see, namely, a disembodied spirit. But if ghosts are truly immaterial, it's difficult to understand how we could see them.

Those who believe in the existence of souls or spirits are traditionally known as *dualists* because they believe that there are two different types of things in the world: physical and nonphysical. The most influential modern dualist was René Descartes (1566–1627), who argues that the mind or soul must be a nonphysical thing because physical things can't think, feel, or desire. (Many people remain skeptical of the prospect for artificial intelligence for just this reason.) The soul, he claims, has no physical properties whatsoever: no mass, no charge, no extension in space. But without any of these properties, sensing souls is a problem. They can't be seen because photons can't bounce off of them; they can't be touched because they have no mass; they can't be smelled because they don't emit any molecules. How we would ever be aware of such entities is a mystery. If ghost experiences are caused by disembodied spirits, they cannot be of the Cartesian variety.

Maybe ghosts are not as immaterial as Descartes thought. The Hindus claim that human beings are composed of a number of different bodies, including the physical body, the astral body, and the causal body. The *astral body,* like the physical body, is supposedly made up of atoms, but of a more ethereal kind than those that make up the physical world. The Hindu mystic Paramahansa Yogananda refers to these atoms as "lifetrons" and claims that they are "finer than atomic energies."[93] But what could this mean? What makes one sort of energy "finer" than another? Are lifetrons made out of protons, neutrons, and electrons like ordinary atoms? Or are they made out of some totally different kind of matter? Are there different types of lifetrons like there are different types of ordinary atoms? Do lifetrons combine in different ways to form different substances like ordinary atoms do? Why can't we detect them with our current instruments? The stuff out of which ghosts are made is a mysterious thing.

Professor Charles Richet former president of the Society for Psychical Research, coined another name for ghost substance: *ectoplasm.* It is derived from the Greek word *ektos* (interiorization) and *plasm* (substance). Ghosts supposedly not only leave some of this substance behind (as in the movie *Ghostbusters*), but mediums also can excrete this substance when they contact a spirit. Whenever any of the ectoplasm produced during a seance was analyzed, however, it turned out to be decidedly nonmysterious. Egg white, cheesecloth, and wood pulp were the most common constituents of ectoplasm.

If ghost substance does have physical properties, it should be detectable with modern measuring apparatus. That's why present-day ghostbusters take along equipment like electromagnetic sensors. Sometimes these paranormal investigators will find anamolous readings at haunted sites. But as we will see, the existence of these readings does not necessarily indicate the presence of a ghost.

Most people who see ghosts see them with clothes on, but where do these clothes come from? Are there ghost clothes stores? Do they carry all styles from ancient Greek to modern hip-hop? Why do ghosts only wear clothes of their period? Do ghosts ever get makeovers? These are serious questions, and the ghost theory needs to answer them if we are to take it seriously.

In addition to the foregoing objective explanations of ghost experiences, which attribute them to the actual perception of a ghost, there are also a number of subjective explanations, which attribute them to unusual states of mind caused by various environmental factors. One such theory is the "stone tape theory."

Hypothesis 2: *Ghost experiences are caused by sounds and images stored in the stones of buildings or outcroppings.* The idea is that emotionally charged events of the sort associated with ghosts get impressed upon the stones in the vicinity. Somehow, during a ghost experience, the event recorded in the stone is played back. The analogy here is that of a tape player to a tape: the stones are the tape and the mind is the tape player.

The problem is that we know of no mechanism that could record such information in a stone or play it back. Chunks of stone just do not have the same properties as reels of tape. Even magnetic tape can't record sound or video without a special recording head. Speaking to a magnetic tape will not record anything. Nor can one hear what's recorded on a magnetic tape by putting it up to one's ear. In both cases, a special device like a read/write head is needed, and the stone tape theory provides no clue as to what such a device would be.

Many ghost sightings happen at night right before one goes to sleep or in the morning, right after one wakes up. The ghosts reported at these times often appear as faces in the dark that move through the room and may even call out the sleeper's name. The sleeper, though, is usually paralyzed and not able to respond. We have encountered the phenomenon of sleep paralysis before as an explanation for the experience of alien abduction. It may also account for a number of ghost sightings.

Hypothesis 3: *Ghost experiences are the result of sleep paralysis.* During periods of REM (rapid eye movement) sleep when most dreams occur, the body is paralyzed to prevent people from acting out their dreams and possibly hurting themselves. If you fall asleep too quickly, however, you may slip into REM sleep while still conscious.

The result may be night terrors or waking dreams where conscious experiences mix with dream imagery, producing vivid hallucinations.

Narcoleptics are more prone to night terrors than others because they can fall asleep almost instantly anytime during the day. Traditional therapy has involved taking various pep pills and stimulants to keep them awake until it is time to go to sleep. A new drug—modafinal—promises to reduce the experience of night terrors without the side effects of stimulants. In clinical trials, modafinal helped narcoleptics stay awake 50 percent longer than those in the control group.[94] Since it serves to lessen the frequency of night terrors, some are touting modafinal as a chemical ghostbuster.

Houses and structures that acquire the reputation of being haunted often have a history of producing ghost experiences, and those experiences often occur in particular parts of the house or structure. Psychologist and parapsychological investigator Richard Wiseman of the University of Hertfordshire wondered whether there might be something in the environment of those haunted places that produces the ghost experiences. To test this hypothesis, he decided to investigate two of the most haunted places in Great Britain: Hampton Court Palace in England and the South Bridge Vaults in Edinburgh, Scotland.

Hampton Court Palace served as the residence for British monarchs for over 500 years. Legend has it that it is haunted by the ghost of the fifth wife of Henry VIII, Catherine Howard, who was accused of adultery and sentenced to death. When she learned of her fate, she supposedly ran to the king to plead for her life, but was dragged away screaming through a part of the palace known as the "haunted gallery." This is not the only haunted area of the palace, however. Ghost experiences have also been reported in other parts of the palace, including one known as the "Georgian rooms."

The Edinburgh vaults are a series of small chambers and corridors that were built under South Bridge when it was erected in the late eighteenth century. Originally they served as workshops, storage, and housing for the poor. By the mid-nineteenth century, however, leaks and overcrowding had made them a public health hazard, so they were abandoned and forgotten. The vaults were rediscovered in the late twentieth century, and in 1996 they were opened to the public for tours. Since then, many people have reported ghost experiences in particular areas of the vaults.

To see whether ghost experiences are correlated with environmental cues, Wiseman and his colleagues had over 600 people walk through these structures and make note of any unusual phenomena they experienced. At Hampton Court, Wiseman's team placed electromagnetic sensors at various places throughout the palace to monitor the magnetic fields. At South Bridge, they monitored air temperature, air movement, and light levels as well as magnetic fields. What they found was that even when people had no prior knowledge of what parts of these edifices were haunted, they consistently reported unusual experiences in those places with the highest fluctuations in the magnetic field or other environmental variables. Wiseman concludes that "the data strongly support the notion that people consistently report unusual experiences in 'haunted' areas because of environmental factors, which may differ across locations. . . . Taken together, these findings strongly suggest that these alleged hauntings do not represent evidence for 'ghostly' activity, but are instead the result of people responding—perhaps unwittingly—to 'normal' factors in their surroundings."[95]

Hypothesis 4: *Ghost experiences are the result of environmental factors interacting with the senses and brain.* Wiseman's research corroborates that of Michael Persinger who has found that changes in magnetic fields can generate all sorts of paranormal experiences, including alien abductions, out-of-body experiences, and religious experiences. Other researchers have noted similar correlations. In an article published in the *Journal of Psychical Research,* for example, Wilkinson and Gauld found a link between ghost sightings and sunspot cycles, which create fluctuations in the Earth's magnetic field.[96] William Roll of the State University of West Georgia has also discovered hauntings that are associated with fluctuating magnetic fields.[97] The brain is an electrochemical device. It makes sense that it could be affected by changes in the electromagnetic field around it.

Another environmental factor that may be involved is infrasound. *Infrasound* is the name given to sound waves whose frequency is below the limit of human hearing, usually 20 cycles per second or less. Computer specialist Vic Tandy discovered that infrasound could generate ghost experiences quite by accident. One night, while working in his laboratory, he broke into a cold sweat and had the distinct feeling that he was being watched. Then he saw a gray shape materialize and move across the room. Sometime later, he brought his rapier to the lab in preparation for a fencing tournament. As he held it in his hand, it began to vibrate as if it were being shaken by some unknown entity. Tandy knew that sound waves could create those sorts of vibrations, so he decided to measure the sound waves in his laboratory. He found that the air in his laboratory was vibrating at 19 cycles per second, which is the frequency at which eyeballs start to vibrate. He also found that when he turned off a newly installed extractor fan, the vibrations ceased. Fans are not the only things that create such low-frequency vibrations. Earthquakes, thunder, and winds blowing down chimneys or through long corridors can also produce infrasound. Maybe that's why ghosts are often associated with howling winds or thunderstorms.

To study the effects of infrasound under more controlled conditions, Richard Wiseman and Richard Lord of England's National Physical Laboratory had people record their feelings during a concert at London's Metropolitan Cathedral. At various points throughout the show, they secretly generated infrasound by playing a bass speaker through a 21-foot-long sewer pipe. The people at the concert did seem to notice when the infrasound was being generated. At those times they jotted down comments like "a tingly feeling in the back of my neck," "something in my stomach," and "a sense of presence."[98] A house equipped with fluctuating magnetic fields, light levels, air currents, and infrasound could prove to be much scarier than those encountered at amusement parks.[99]

An alleged ghost photographed by a surveillance camera at Hampton Court Palace.

What should we believe about the cause of ghost experiences? Let's examine the relative plausibility of the various hypotheses. The soul hypothesis is the least simple of the bunch because it postulates the existence of an unknown substance. And while it may seem to explain most aspects of ghost experiences, its scope is questionable because it raises more questions than it answers: What is the soul made of? How does it get around? Does it possess muscles, nerves, or a brain? How is it able to interact with the world? Why aren't we able to detect it? Where does it get its clothes? Until these questions are answered, the soul hypothesis leaves us with as big a mystery as we started.

The stone tape theory doesn't postulate any unknown entities, but it does postulate unknown processes. We know of no way for sounds or images to be stored in stone. What's more, even if such a mechanism were found, it would only explain hauntings, not apparitions that seem to interact with humans. So its scope is somewhat limited.

The sleep paralysis and environmental factors hypotheses have the advantage of simplicity over the others because they do not assume the existence of any unknown entities or forces. They have more scope than the others because, taken together, they can explain all aspects of the ghost experience from a feeling of presence to full-form apparitions. They can also explain why ghosts are so often seen wearing clothes: Ghosts are mental constructions, not external existents.

CONSPIRACY THEORIES

Have you heard that the world is controlled by reptilian creatures from the fourth dimension who must consume human blood to maintain their human appearance? That the Apollo 11 moon landings were faked by NASA? That a secret society known as the Bavarian Illuminati has been at work since 1776 to destroy all religions, topple all governments, and establish a new world order? If so, you have been exposed to a conspiracy theory, which attempts to explain events by attributing them to the actions of a small but powerful group of people working under cover behind the scenes. Usually there is no direct evidence linking any of the alleged conspirators to their nefarious deeds. Nonetheless, conspiracy theorists claim that the circumstantial evidence can best be explained on the assumption that a secret group of conspirators is at work.

Senator Joe McCarthy, for example, thought that America's loss of global power and prestige in the years immediately following World War II could only be explained on the assumption that communists had conspired to destroy America. In a speech before Congress, he asks:

> How can we account for our present situation unless we believe that men high in this government are concerting to deliver us to disaster? This must be the product of a great conspiracy on a scale so immense as to dwarf any previous such venture in the history of man. A conspiracy of infamy so black that, when it is finally exposed, its principals shall be forever deserving of the malediction of all honest men.[100]

To root out these conspirators, McCarthy conducted open hearings in the Senate, the infamous McCarthy hearings. His accusations tarnished or ruined the careers of many otherwise reputable people. But ultimately McCarthy himself turned out to be the only one deserving the malediction of all honest men.

McCarthy's attitude toward the communists, however, is representative of many conspiracy theorists' view of the alleged conspirators. They are often seen as extremely evil, exceedingly powerful, and exceptionally well organized. The events attributed to them are of such magnitude, the conspiracy theorists argue, that only a group possessing great powers could accomplish them. We have encountered this style of reasoning before. It's a version of the representativeness heuristic: Like causes like. Big events require big causes. Psychologist Patrick Leman of the Royal Holloway University of London believes that this cognitive bias lies behind the psychological appeal of many conspiracy theories.[101]

To test this hypothesis, Leman had sixty-four students read one of four fictional—yet seemingly authentic—newspaper accounts of an attempted assassination. In the first, a gunman shot and killed the president of a foreign country. In the second, a gunman wounded the president, but he survived. In the third, the gunman wounded the president, but he later died of an unrelated cause. In the fourth, the gunman shot at but missed the president. When the students were asked how likely it was that the assassination attempt was the result of a conspiracy, the students who read the first account found it much more likely than those who read the others. Why? Dr. Leman suggests that it is our tendency to associate big effects (like the killing of a president) with big causes (like a conspiracy). This may go some way toward explaining why so many people believe that the assassinations of President John Fitzgerald Kennedy, Attorney General Bobby Kennedy, and Reverend Martin Luther King were not the work of a lone gunman.

Once one has bought into the belief system associated with a conspiracy theory, another cognitive error—confirmation bias—often helps reinforce those beliefs. Buying into a conspiracy theory, especially one that views the conspirators as being bent on global domination, gives one a particular set of rose-colored glasses through which to view the world. As sociologist Donna Kossy observes:

Three photo features that have inspired conspiracy theorists (and provoked explanations from anti-hoaxers): A "waving" flag; a starless sky; and, on the lunar module, a flag decal that is well lit though seemingly in shadow.

©Corbis Historical/Getty Images

> Conspiracy theories are like black holes—they suck in everything that comes their way, regardless of content or origin; conspiracies are portals to other universes that paradoxically reside within our own. Everything you've ever known or experienced, no matter how "meaningless," once it contacts the conspiratorial universe, is enveloped by and cloaked in sinister significance. Once inside, the vortex gains in size and strength, sucking in everything you touch.[102]

Events that seem to confirm one's beliefs are noticed and remembered; those that conflict with them are ignored and forgotten. In this way, conspiracy theorists can fool themselves into thinking that a massive amount of evidence supports their view when, in reality, the totality of evidence may be better explained in a more mundane way.

Other psychological factors undoubtedly lie behind the acceptance of many conspiracy theories. In a world of accelerating change and senseless suffering, viewing major social upheavals as the work of a powerful yet clandestine group may seem to make sense of it all. No longer is the world so dense, opaque, and unintelligible. Events that formerly seemed random and unconnected are now seen as part of a master plan. The question of why bad things happen to good people can now be answered: because the conspirators did it. Having such an answer can also give one a sense of power and superiority—power because one has identified the enemy and superiority because one possesses knowledge that others don't.

But even if you derive some psychological benefit from believing in a conspiracy theory, that doesn't mean that it's true. Even though you may think you're in the know, you may not be, because as we've seen, believing something to be true doesn't make it true. Only if a conspiracy theory actually provides the best explanation of something are you justified in believing it to be true.

Part of the cognitive appeal of conspiracy theories is that they seem to explain so much with so little. In other words, they seem to have wide scope while being remarkably simple. For example, the world's oldest conspiracy theory—that the Freemasons did it—has been used to explain everything from the French Revolution to the slayings of Jack the Ripper. (Freemasonry is the world's oldest and largest fraternal organization whose meetings, like those of all fraternities, are restricted to members only.) Scope and simplicity are indeed hallmarks of a good theory. But in the case of many conspiracy theories, their scope and simplicity are more apparent than real.

The simplicity of a theory is measured not by its ease of comprehension but by the number of independent assumptions it makes. Most conspiracy theories, while easy to comprehend, make a bewildering array of assumptions. The Masonic conspiracy theory, for example, assumes that Freemasons are out to control the world; that a central governing body coordinates the activities of individual Masons; that individual Masons—no matter what their social standing—will do the bidding of their Masonic masters—no matter how immoral, and so on. All of these assumptions are demonstrably false and yet must be taken for granted if the Masonic conspiracy theory is to get off the ground.

The scope of a theory is determined by the amount of diverse phenomena it explains, and conspiracy theories seem to have almost unlimited scope. The claim, "the Freemasons (the communists, the CIA, the Bavarian Illuminati, the Jews, the Reptilians, and so on) did it" can be invoked to explain almost anything. But unless the conspiracy theorists have sufficient evidence to indicate that their group (rather than some other) did it, and some idea of how their group did it, their conspiracy theory explains very little. Recall the gremlin theory of the bridge collapse discussed in Chapter 6. The claim that the bridge collapse was caused by a gun-toting gremlin is not one that any rational person would take seriously because there is no evidence

The Apollo Conspiracy: Did We Land on the Moon?

Most people take the moon landings by NASA astronauts to be historical fact—but some don't buy it. Through books, websites, and a 2001 Fox television program called "Conspiracy Theory: Did We Land on the Moon?" doubters have insisted that the lunar landings never happened and were actually staged in a movie studio. They claim that the well-known lunar feats—Neil Armstrong's famous "one small step," the flag-planting, astronaut golf, moon buggy maneuvers, and all the rest—were cleverly concocted on Earth because NASA didn't have the technology to pull off the real thing. In other words, the Apollo program's six moon landings of 1969–1972 were the result of a massive and highly successful conspiracy. The point of this elaborate scam, the doubters say, was to win the space race against the Soviet Union—even if winning involved faking it.

The evidence thought to support the conspiracy idea consists mostly of apparent discrepancies in the videos and photographs said to have been taken on the moon. Conspiracy theorists point to many photographic details that seem to suggest that the pictures were not taken on the moon but were shot in a studio or faked by technicians. Some examples:

- In the lunar pictures, there are no stars in the sky, which you would expect to see in the blackness of space if the pictures were genuine.
- The video of the astronauts planting an American flag shows the flag fluttering as if blown by the wind, but there is no wind on the moon.
- The shadows cast by objects on the lunar surface should be parallel because the sun's light rays are parallel. But in many pictures, the shadows of the astronauts and other objects fall at nonparallel angles, just as you would expect in a studio using multiple light sources.
- In a photo of an astronaut standing next to the moon buggy, the letter *C* is clearly visible on a nearby rock—probably a marking made by the props department.

The list of such discrepancies is long, but how strong are they as evidence of a conspiracy? They are actually fairly weak because the support they offer is, at best, equivocal. In each case, the discrepancy could be due to a hoax, or it could simply be an anomaly arising from the conditions in which the lunar pictures were taken. No corroborating evidence shows that the discrepancy must be the result of conspiracy or deception.

that a gremlin (rather than something else) did it, and the nature of the gremlin's ray gun is left completely unspecified. So to claim that a particular group of conspirators did something is no better than saying a gremlin did it unless the evidence can best be explained on the assumption that the specified group did it by means at their disposal.

What conspiracy theories seem to have going for them in terms of simplicity and scope they usually lack in terms of conservatism. Conservatism is fit with existing knowledge. The more knowledge a claim conflicts with, the less conservative it is, and thus the less likely it is. Conspiracy theories often conflict with all sorts of knowledge we have about human nature and the natural world. One thing we know about humans, for example, is that their powers of discipline

On the other hand, experts have provided plausible explanations for many of the photographic oddities, including most of those that doubters focus on. For example, they point out that stars aren't visible in the pictures because camera exposures were set for brightly lit lunar scenes—camera settings that would prevent faint objects like stars from showing on the film. The flag flutters because the astronauts pushed and twisted the flagpole into the lunar soil, causing the horizontally supported flag to wave back and forth and, because of the lack of wind resistance on the moon, to continue waving. Because of the nature of visual perspective, shadows appear not to be parallel even though there was only one source of light—a common phenomenon both on the moon and on Earth. And the letter *C* that seems to appear on a lunar rock is an effect of photographic print-making—the *C* (a hair, perhaps) does not appear on the original image.

A major difficulty for the hoax theory is its lack of simplicity, for it's built on several dubious assumptions. It assumes, for example, that hundreds of thousands of people could work on the Apollo project without one of them revealing that the whole thing was a hoax; that such a massive and complex conspiracy could be orchestrated without being exposed by whistle-blowers, disgruntled employees, or conspirators; that the thousands of contractors who worked for NASA would never come forward to cry foul; that after more than thirty-five years no definitive evidence—no genuine documents, files, recordings, or anything else—would surface to reveal the truth; that of all the scientists and engineers from all over the world who have had access to staggering amounts of Apollo data, none would suspect fraud and tell all; that the Soviet Union was not able or willing to expose the United States' most elaborate con job of the cold war; and that many other countries with advanced technology could not figure out that the Apollo radio signals were not coming from the moon.

The hoax theory also conflicts with strong evidence suggesting that the Apollo missions actually happened. Among other things, there are images taken by Earth-based telescopes of Apollo spacecraft soaring to the moon, data gathered from scientific experiments on the lunar surface, the testimony of the Apollo astronauts and countless technicians and scientists, and 841 pounds of moon rocks, which are unique to the moon and cannot be faked by Earth technology.

and organization are limited. Yet conspiracy theorists would have us believe that members of certain organizations, like the Masons, are so disciplined and organized that they can keep secrets for centuries, even though thousands of people know those secrets.

Not even the most powerful group is immune from leaks, however. One of the most famous of these alleged leaks—one that many consider to be the basis of all modern conspiracy literature—turns out to be a fraud and a hoax. Known as the "Protocols of the Elders of Zion," it first appeared in print in Russia in 1903. It purports to be an instruction manual given to new elders (members of an elite council of Jewish leaders) on how to bring about world domination. In reality, it's a fictional document created by the Okhrana—the Tsarist secret police—that plagiarizes a political satire written by Maurice Joly in 1864 titled "Dialogues in Hell between Machiavelli and Montesquieu." Joly's "Dialogues," however, makes no mention of Jews. That aspect of the "Protocols" was borrowed from the novel *Biarritz* written by the German anti-Semite Herman Goedsche. The Okhrana apparently produced the "Protocols," not to justify the persecution of Jews, but to suggest that the then minister of finance, Sergey Witte, was under the control of the Jews, thus undermining his authority. It's been known since 1921, when *The Times* of London published an exposé revealing its fictional sources, that the "Protocols" are a fraud. Nevertheless, it continues to be a best-seller in certain Arab countries to this day. Other conspiracy theorists have used the "Protocols" to bolster their own pet theories claiming that the mention of Jews is code for their conspirators of choice, be it Masons, Illuminati, or Reptilians.

Besides their discipline, conspirators are also often said to have other remarkable powers such as the ability to use black magic or advanced technology to promote their cause. Some conspiracy theorists, for example, claim that Masons have known for centuries how to make antigravity devices but have kept that knowledge from us in an attempt to keep us under their control. The claim that someone has developed an antigravity device—like the claim that someone can walk through walls without using a door—conflicts with our background knowledge of how the world works. As a result, its credibility is low. The more such claims a conspiracy theory makes, the less reason we have to accept it.

CLIMATE CHANGE

To the dismay of many and the disbelief of some, scientists have been issuing some disturbing reports about changes in Earth's climate. The gist is that the planet's global average temperature has been rising—by more than 1.4 degrees Fahrenheit over the last century, a seemingly tiny amount that is producing enormous, potentially catastrophic effects worldwide. Earth naturally cycles through eras of warming and cooling, but experts say this hotter trend is a recent abnormality that threatens global warming and creates calamitous patterns that cannot be reversed. Moreover these changes are claimed to be caused not by nature gone wrong but mostly by human behavior—behavior that humans can modify to avert or minimize planetary disaster.

Climate scientists say this global warming happens through the Earth's *greenhouse effect*, the bottling up of the sun's radiation (and thus its heat) in our lower atmosphere. When solar radiation strikes the Earth, some of it bounces back into space, but much of it enters Earth's atmosphere where the heat is trapped by gases (called *greenhouse gases* because, like a greenhouse, they let in radiation but prevent its heat from leaving). Greenhouse gases include water vapor, carbon dioxide, methane, and others. Carbon dioxide is the most worrisome; it has been on the rise for the past 200 years and has surged dramatically in the last 50. Some of this increase comes from deforestation and volcanic eruptions, but most is due to the combustion of fossil fuels—coal, oil, and gas. And the result, say scientists, is rising global temperatures.

Climatologists insist that the planet has been feeling the dire effects of global warming for some time and is certain to feel even more in the future. According to a report by the United States Global Change Research Program, climate-related changes have already been observed globally and in the United States. These include increases in air and water temperatures, reduced frost days, increased frequency and intensity of heavy downpours, a rise in sea level, and reduced snow cover, glaciers, permafrost, and sea ice. A longer ice-free period on lakes and rivers, lengthening of the growing season, and increased water vapor in the atmosphere have also been observed.

These climate-related changes are expected to continue while new ones develop. Likely future changes for the United States and surrounding coastal waters include more intense hurricanes with related increases in wind, rain, and storm surges (but not necessarily an increase in the number of these storms that make landfall), as well as drier conditions in the Southwest and Caribbean. These changes will affect human health, water supply, agriculture, coastal areas, and many other aspects of society and the natural environment.[103]

In some quarters the notion of human-made global warming is controversial, largely because of its political implications. Many argue that if the planet as a whole really is becoming dangerously warm, and if the main cause is the burning of fossil fuels, then we should try to stop or at least drastically reduce the burning. Doing so would radically reshape every economic, social, and governmental system that now depends on fossil fuels—and to some people, these are fighting words. There is nothing inherently wrong with holding either position, but partisans in this debate err when they let their political views dictate their evaluation of the evidence. Too many fall prey to confirmation bias, evidence denial, availability error, and fallacious appeals to authority. These distractions can lead to satisfying conclusions—which are usually unfounded.

So let's see if we can do better. The question is, what is the best theory to explain the climate-change data? A common view is Hypothesis 1: *Global climate change is due to natural variations in the Earth's warming and cooling and has little to do with human activities*. As evidence for this view, some point to Earth's glacial episodes—the Ice Ages (and the warming periods between them). In the last 3.5 million years, twenty-four such warming and cooling eras have occurred, and scientists now know why. In regular phases (called Milankovitch cycles), slight variations in Earth's orbit move the planet nearer and farther away from the sun, bringing long-lasting cold phases and warming trends.

In the last 10,000 years, the planet has also undergone some less pronounced climate cycles that seem to undermine the idea of an Earth gradually warmed by human activity. For example, between 950 and AD 1250, during what's called the Medieval Warm Period, there was a slight rise in temperatures—*before* the Industrial Revolution began to pump carbon dioxide into the atmosphere. And more recently, from 1998 to 2000, the world went into a mild cooling period (cool relative to other years).

How strong is this evidence? The support for Hypothesis 1 is weaker than it seems at first glance. Earth's climate has indeed fluctuated through the centuries in predictable ways; Ice Ages and warming spikes have come and gone. But these variations, scientists say, cannot explain the relatively recent jump in Earth's surface temperature. Over the next 1,000 years or so, the planet should be easing into another Ice Age, but it's already warmer than in any earlier warming phase. According to the prestigious Intergovernmental Panel on Climate Change (IPCC),

> Eleven of the last twelve years (1995–2006) rank among the twelve warmest years in the instrumental record of global surface temperature (since 1850). . . . The temperature increase is widespread over the globe and is greater at higher northern latitudes. Land regions have warmed faster than the oceans.[104]

A report issued by the National Academy of Sciences takes a similar view:

> It can be said with a high level of confidence that global mean surface temperature was higher during the last few decades of the 20th century than during any comparable period during the preceding four centuries. This statement is justified by the consistency of the evidence from a wide variety of geographically diverse proxies [indirect evidence from tree rings, corals, ocean and lake sediments, cave deposits, ice cores, boreholes, and glaciers].[105]

Another explanation is Hypothesis 2: *Global climate change is caused by variations in the sun's energy output, not by human activity.* There is no question that Earth's climate system is basically propelled by the sun and that changes in the sun's energy can affect our climate.

In fact, scientists have documented an eleven- and twenty-two-year cycle of fluctuations in solar radiation related to sunspots. Some take these facts as evidence that global warming is a solar phenomenon, not a human one.

But NASA scientists (and many others) reject this claim:

> [S]everal lines of evidence show that current global warming cannot be explained by changes in energy from the sun:
>
> - Since 1750, the average amount of energy coming from the sun either remained constant or increased slightly.
> - If the warming were caused by a more active sun, then scientists would expect to see warmer temperatures in all layers of the atmosphere. Instead, they have observed a cooling in the upper atmosphere, and a warming at the surface and in the lower parts of the atmosphere. That's because greenhouse gasses are trapping heat in the lower atmosphere.
> - Climate models that include solar irradiance changes can't reproduce the observed temperature trend over the past century or more without including a rise in greenhouse gases.[106]

Now we come to Hypothesis 3: *There is no worldwide climate change; the notion of human-made global warming is a fraud perpetuated by a conspiracy of scientists.* Like most conspiracy theories, Hypothesis 3 has only circumstantial evidence in its favor; direct evidence is scarce. And attempts to marshal evidence often involve the twin blunders of confirmation error and denying the evidence.

The hypothesis also has three strikes against it: it fails the criteria of scope, simplicity, and conservatism. It has little or no scope because it comes with no evidence showing who the conspirators are and how they accomplished their ends. So it explains nothing. It lacks simplicity because it makes countless assumptions: that there are in fact conspirators (some scientists), that they can follow a partisan agenda to promote the idea of global warming without raising suspicion, that they can coordinate their activities, that they all can keep the conspiracy secret, that they would risk their careers to perpetrate a lie, that the scientific community would not discover the deception, and so on. The hypothesis is not conservative, conflicting as it does with what we know about human nature, the conduct and attitudes of scientists, and the standards and procedures used in scientific research. It also doesn't fit with existing knowledge about climate, for it diverges sharply from what virtually all climate scientists take to be established fact—that human-made global warming is a reality.

Now here's Hypothesis 4: *Global warming is taking place, and the main cause is people's use of fossil fuels.* A multitude of climate studies show that Earth is indeed getting warmer. Global temperatures are not only rising, but they are rising faster than ever. Scientists have predicted that if the world is getting hotter, certain global events should occur—warming oceans, loss of sea ice, rising sea levels, increasing global surface temperatures, shrinking icebergs, decreased mass of Greenland and Antarctic ice sheets, retreating glaciers (in the Alps, the Himalayas, Alaska, the Andes, and elsewhere), and more extremely high temperatures in the United States. And all these changes are occurring as predicted. The consensus of scientific opinion is summed up in an IPCC report:

> Warming of the climate system is unequivocal, as is now evident from observations of increases in global average air and ocean temperatures, widespread melting of snow and ice and rising global average sea level.[107]

A great deal of evidence also supports the conclusion that global warming is caused mostly by carbon dioxide generated from the burning of fossil fuels. Levels of carbon dioxide in our atmosphere are higher now than at any other time in the past 650,000 years. Before the Industrial Revolution, the atmospheric level of this greenhouse gas was about 280 parts per million by volume; now the levels are over 380 parts per million. And as carbon dioxide has sharply increased, so has global surface temperature.

By using sophisticated mathematical models, climate scientists have found that natural processes alone (volcanic activity, solar radiation, Earth's orbit, etc.) cannot account for Earth's warming trend in the last hundred years. But people-generated greenhouse gases (principally carbon dioxide) *can* explain it.

Major scientific organizations around the world—including the National Academies of Science, the IPCC, NASA, and the National Oceanic and Atmospheric Administration—have examined the climate-change evidence and come to the same conclusion: global warming is happening, and the human addiction to fossil fuels is to blame.

Hypothesis 4 seems to be the clear winner here, but let's review all the hypotheses to see why. Hypothesis 1 (natural variability) is testable and simple, and it has some scope, since natural variations in Earth's climate can also explain some climatic eras such as the Little Ice Age of the eighteenth and nineteenth centuries. But it is not fruitful; it has predicted no previously unknown phenomena. Worst of all, it falls short in conservatism: it conflicts with established facts about the magnitude and pattern of global warming. Variations in the Earth's normal cycles of heating and cooling simply do not match the scientific data regarding Earth's extraordinary warming trend.

Hypothesis 2 (solar energy output) is also testable and simple. Like Hypothesis 1, it may earn points for scope by explaining phenomena related to the sun's eleven-year cycle of radiation. But it isn't fruitful, and it fails the criterion of conservatism for the same reason that Hypothesis 1 does: the cycles of solar radiation don't match the known patterns of global warming.

As mentioned earlier, Hypothesis 3 (conspiracy of scientists) fails the criteria of scope, simplicity, and conservatism. It also gets no credit for being fruitful. It is the worst of the competing hypotheses.

Hypothesis 4 wins this competition because it is testable, simple, fruitful, and conservative. It's fruitful because it has successfully predicted some previously unknown phenomena—everything from rising sea levels to retreating glaciers to cooling and warming of the atmosphere. And it is conservative because it is consistent with scientific laws, well supported theories, and established facts.

Science is a search for the truth. It's an attempt to ascertain the way the world is. But there are those who claim that such a search is misguided, for we each create our own reality. What's true for you is not true for me, they say. For them, objective truth is not only an unattainable goal but an outmoded myth. In the next chapter, we'll try to discover the truth about truth.

SUMMARY

Weird things are events or objects that seem impossible, given what we know about the world. To explain these things, people often postulate powers or properties that are just as weird. We're justified in believing in these powers or properties, however, only if they provide the best explanation of the phenomena in question. We can evaluate how good competing explanations are in relation to each other by determining how much understanding they produce. The amount of understanding produced by an explanation is determined by the extent to which it systematizes and unifies our knowledge, and that is determined by how well it meets the criteria of adequacy: simplicity, conservatism, scope, and fruitfulness. The SEARCH method highlights the steps that should be taken when evaluating an explanation: *S*tate the claim, examine the *E*vidence for it, consider *A*lternative explanations, and *R*ate, according to the Criteria of adequacy, each *H*ypothesis.

These considerations should not be taken as the final word on the matters investigated in this book. We've simply tried to present our best thinking about them. You may disagree—but if you do, we trust that it's on the basis of good reasons.

Now that you know the difference between good and bad reasons, you have the basic intellectual tools necessary to evaluate all sorts of claims, weird and otherwise. We hope that you use these tools, for the quality of your life is determined by the quality of your decisions, and the quality of your decisions is determined by the quality of your reasoning.

STUDY QUESTIONS

1. What is the SEARCH formula?
2. What are the criteria of adequacy?
3. Hundreds of thousands of people use homeopathic remedies. Does this fact alone show that homeopathy works?
4. How much weight would you give to the evidence for UFO abductions and why?
5. The UFO-abduction hypothesis is not a very simple explanation because it involves some unsupported assumptions. What are these assumptions?
6. In what ways is the communication with the dead hypothesis much less conservative than the competing hypotheses?
7. What is the best explanation for near-death experiences? Why is it best?

EVALUATE THESE CLAIMS BY USING THE SEARCH METHOD

1. There is a phenomenon known as "spontaneous human combustion" in which most of the victim's body, as well as the chair the person was sitting in, is found burned to ashes but the rest of the objects in the room are relatively unaffected. This phenomenon suggests that there is a new type of subatomic particle—a "pyroton"—that interacts with cells and causes the victim to burst into flame.—L. Arnold, *Ablaze!* (New York: M. Evans, 1995).
2. Many reported ghost sightings involve reenactments of battles, deaths, or murders. This finding suggests that certain physical objects, such as stones, can record emotions and events like a video recorder.—Nigel Kneale, "The Stone Tape," broadcast on BBC, December 25, 1972.
3. No one has ever actually been abducted by aliens. Instead, the experience of being abducted has been beamed into the minds of abductees by an intelligence somewhere in the universe that is symbiotically linked to life on this planet.—D. Scott Rogo, *Beyond Reality* (Wellingborough, England: Aquarian Press, 1990).
4. People often know when others are staring at them. This shows that perception involves not only receiving light rays from an object but also projecting some sort of image onto the object.—Rubert Sheldrake, *Seven Experiments That Could Change the World: A Do-It-Yourself Guide to Revolutionary Science* (London: Fourth Estate, 1994).
5. Dreams often seem as real as waking experiences because humans are composed of two bodies: a physical body and an astral body. When we

dream, our astral body leaves the physical body and travels to the astral plane where the dream actually takes place.—T. Lobsang Rampa, *You Forever* (York Beach, ME: Samuel Weiser, 1990).

6. Food kept inside a structure with the shape of Cheops's pyramid stays fresher longer than food kept outside the structure. The pyramid must serve as a lens that focuses some sort of cosmic energy onto the food.—Max Toth and Greg Nielson, *Pyramid Power* (Rochester, VT: Destiny Books, 1990).
7. Peggy awoke one morning and remembered having an odd dream. She dreamed that space aliens came into her bedroom while she was sleeping and abducted her. The dream was vivid and realistic. Later in the day, she noticed a bruise on her left knee that she couldn't account for. The dream must have been more than just a dream. She had to have been abducted by aliens.

FIELD PROBLEM

Assignment: Recall an experience that you had that you regard as mysterious and weird. (If you have never experienced anything that fits this description, recall a weird experience told to you by a friend or family member.) List at least three possible explanations for the experience, including at least one paranormal or supernatural explanation. Now apply the SEARCH formula to these hypotheses. If necessary, do research on the internet to get the facts on each one. State your conclusion: According to your analysis, which explanation is best?

CRITICAL READING AND WRITING

I. Read the passage below and answer the following questions:
   1. What is the phenomenon being explained in the passage?
   2. What are the theories proposed to explain the phenomenon?
   3. Are any of the proposed theories logically impossible?
   4. What are the natural explanations offered?
   5. What other natural theories could be proposed?

II. In a 250-word paper, evaluate the theory that the Shadow People are ghosts. Compare the theory to this naturalistic one: The Shadow People phenomenon is the result of natural anomalies in visual perception such as "floaters," spots that drift in front of the eye due to debris in the vitreous fluid. Use the SEARCH formula.

Passage 6

You're sitting at your computer late at night—only the dim glow of your screen lights the room. Your cat is happily sitting on the small table beside your desk. It's quiet, you're comfortable, and lost in your work. Suddenly, your work is disturbed as you spy a black figure racing at the edge of your vision. You jump and look around. Nothing is there.

How many times has this happened to you? If you're honest with yourself, I'm sure you'll answer that it's happened more times than you can count. Generally, you would laugh it off as a bit of paranoia or perhaps you were tired. If you're part of a growing group of people, you might claim it was the Shadow People.

Who are the Shadow People? Not much is known at this time. Maybe it is indeed our imagination or mythology gone astray. Maybe we're all seeing exactly what we think we're seeing—creatures moving through the shadows. I've heard numerous stories and claims about the true identity of the Shadow People. Are they ghosts? Aliens? Extradimensionals? (From the website shadowers.com.)

NOTES

1. Mahlon W. Wagner, "Is Homeopathy 'New Science' or 'New Age'?" *Scientific Review of Alternative Medicine* (Fall–Winter 1997): 7–12.
2. E. Ernst, "A Systematic Review of Systematic Reviews of Homeopathy," *British Journal of Clinical Pharmacology* 54, no. 6 (2002): 577–82.
3. Australian National Health and Medical Research Council, "NHMRC Information Paper: Evidence on the Effectiveness of Homeopathy for Treating Health Conditions," Canberra: National Health and Medical Research Council, 2015, pp. 5–6.
4. Rick Warren, "God Debate: Sam Harris vs. Rick Warren," *Newsweek*, April 9, 2007.
5. Andrew Neher, *The Psychology of Transcendence* (Englewood Cliffs, NJ: Prentice-Hall, 1980), pp. 182–83.
6. Whitley Strieber, *Communion* (New York: William Morrow, 1987).
7. Budd Hopkins, *Intruders* (New York: Random House, 1987).
8. Martin T. Orne, "The Use and Misuse of Hypnosis in Court," *International Journal of Clinical and Experimental Hypnosis* 27, no. 4 (October 1979): 311–41.
9. Ibid.
10. H. Cooper, R. Blumenthal, and L. Kean, "Glowing Auras and 'Black Money': The Pentagon's Mysterious U.F.O. Program," *New York Times*, December 16, 2017, accessed June 27, 2018, https://www.nytimes.com/2017/12/16/us/politics/pentagon-program-ufo-harry-reid.html.
11. Maj. Audricia Harris, official communication to John Greenewald regarding AATIP program information, accessed June 27, 2018, http://www.theblackvault.com/casefiles/to-the-stars-academy-of-arts-science-tom-delonge-and-the-secret-dod-ufo-research-program/#.
12. Luis Elizondo quoted in Sarah Scoles, "What's Up with Those Pentagon UFO Videos?" *Wired*, February 17, 2018, accessed June 27, 2018, https://www.wired.com/story/what-is-up-with-those-pentagon-ufo-videos/.
13. Luis Elizondo quoted in Tom Embury-Davis, "Existence of Advanced UFOs beyond Reasonable Doubt,' Says Ex-Pentagon Official Who Ran

Secret US Government Programme," *The Independent*, December 25, 2017, accessed June 27, 2018, https://www.independent.co.uk/news/world/americas/ufo-pentagon-beyond-reasonable-doubt-video-us-navy-tracking-pilots-footage-unidentified-flying-a8127881.html.

14. Maj. Audricia Harris, official communication to John Greenewald.
15. Scoles, "What's Up with Those Pentagon UFO Videos?"
16. Ibid.
17. Mick West, "NYT: GIMBAL Video of U.S. Navy Jet Encounter with Unknown Object," Metabunk.org, accessed June 27, 2018, https://www.metabunk.org/nyt-gimbal-video-of-u-s-navy-jet-encounter-with-unknown-object.t9333/; see also Mick West, "2004 USS Nimitz Tic Tac UFO FLIR Footage," Metabunk.org, accessed June 27, 2018, https://www.metabunk.org/2004-uss-nimitz-tic-tac-ufo-flir-footage.t9190/.
18. Emma Parry, "How the Blink 182 Rocker Who Outed the Pentagon's Secret UFO Unit Claims He Can Prove Existence of Alien Civilisations," *The Sun*, December 21, 2017, accessed June 27, 2018, https://www.thesun.co.uk/uncategorized/5186074/how-the-blink-182-rocker-who-outed-pentagons-secret-ufo-unit-claims-he-can-prove-existence-of-alien-civilisations/.
19. A. H. Lawson and W. C. McCall, "What Can We Learn from the Hypnosis of Imaginary Attackers?" *MUFON UFO Symposium Proceedings* (Seguin, TX: Mutual UFO Network, 1977), pp. 107–35.
20. Terence Hines, *Pseudoscience and the Paranormal* (Buffalo: Prometheus Books, 1988), p. 195.
21. Robert Allen Baker, *They Call It Hypnosis* (Buffalo: Prometheus Books, 1990), p. 247.
22. Ibid., p. 252.
23. Philip J. Klass, *UFO Abductions: A Dangerous Game,* updated edition (Buffalo: Prometheus Books, 1989).
24. U.S. Office of Technology Assessment, *Scientific Validity of Polygraph Testing: A Research Review and Evaluation* (Washington, DC: Office of Technology Assessment, 1993, November) (OTA-TM-H-15); D. Lykken, *A Tremor in the Blood* (New York: McGraw-Hill, 1981).
25. Phil Patton, "UFO Myths: A Special Investigation into Stephenville and Other Major Sightings," *Popular Mechanics,* December 18, 2009, http://www.popularmechanics.com/technology/aviation/ufo/4304170.
26. Jeffrey Weiss, "Military says fighter jets were in area; witnesses don't buy explanation", *The Dallas Morning News*, January 24, 2008.
27. "The Stephenville Lights: What Actually Happened," *Skeptical Inquirer* 33, no. 1 (January/February 2009), http://www.csicop.org/si/show/stephenville_lights_what_actually_happened/.
28. Charles H. Bennett, Gilles Brassard, Claude Crepeau, Richard Jozsa, Ashes Peres, and William K. Wootters, "Teleporting an Unknown Quantum State via Dual Classical and EPR Channels," *Physical Review Letters* 70 (March 29, 1993): 1895–99.

29. Samuel L. Braunstein, *A Fun Talk on Teleportation* (University of York), accessed June 2018, http://www-users.cs.york.ac.uk/schmuel/tport.html.
30. Elizabeth Slater, "Conclusions on Nine Psychologies" in *Final Report on the Psychological Testing of UFO "Abductees"* (Fund for UFO Research, 1985), pp. 17–31.
31. Ibid.
32. Klass, *UFO Abductions,* pp. 25–37.
33. Anees A. Sheikh, *Imagery: Current Theory, Research, and Application* (John Wiley & Sons, 1983), 340.
34. Ibid., p. 210.
35. K. Basterfield and R. Bartholomew, "Abductions: The Fantasy-Prone Personality Hypothesis," *International UFO Review* 13, no. 3 (May/June 1988): 9–11.
36. Baker, *They Call It Hypnosis,* pp. 247–51.
37. Ibid., p. 250.
38. Hines, *Pseudoscience and the Paranormal,* p. 203.
39. Susan Blackmore, "Alien Abduction," *New Scientist* (November 19, 1994): 29–31.
40. "Harassed Rancher who located 'Saucer' sorry he told about it," *Roswell Daily Record* (July 9 1947).
41. *Report of Air Force Research Regarding the "Roswell Incident," Skeptical Inquirer* 19 (July 1994).
42. Dave Thomas, "The Roswell Incident and Project MOGUL," *Skeptical Inquirer* 19, no. 4 (July/August 1995).
43. Ray Hyman, "How *Not* to Test Mediums: Critiquing the Afterlife Experiments," *Skeptical Inquirer* 27, no. 1 (January/February 2003).
44. Raymond A. Moody Jr., *Life After Life: And Reflections on Life After Life* (Guideposts, 1975), pp. 16–17.
45. Raymond A. Moody Jr., *The Light Beyond* (New York: Bantam Books, 1988), p. 7.
46. Ibid., pp. 4–5.
47. Fred Schoonmaker, "Denver Cardiologist Discloses Findings after Eighteen Years of Near-Death Research," *Anabiosis* 1 (1979): 1–2.
48. Michael Sabom, *Recollections of Death* (New York: Harper and Row, 1982).
49. Susan Blackmore, "Near-Death Experiences: In or Out of the Body?" *Skeptical Inquirer* 16 (1991): 36.
50. Kenneth Ring, *Life at Death* (New York: Coward, McCann and Geoghegan, 1980), p. 32.
51. Ibid., p. 40.
52. Lynn A. Silva, *The Problem of the Self in Buddhism and Christianity* (Springer, 1979).
53. Ibid., p. 184.
54. Karlis Osis and Erlendur Haraldsson, "OBE's in Indian Swamis: Sathya Sai Baba and Dadaji," in *Research in Parapsychology 1976,* ed. J. D. Morris, W. G. Roll, and R. L. Morris (Metuchen, NJ: Scarecrow Press, 1980), pp. 142–45.

55. Pim van Lommel et al., "Near Death Experience in Survivors of Cardiac Arrest: A Prospective Study in the Netherlands," *Lancet* 358 (December 15, 2001): 2039–45.
56. Moody, *Light Beyond*, pp. 196–97.
57. Ibid., p. 197.
58. Barry Beyerstein, *The Hundredth Monkey and Other Paradigms of the Paranormal,* ed. Kendrick Frazier (Amherst, NY: Prometheus Books, 1991), p. 45.
59. K. Ring and M. Lawrence, "Further Evidence for Veridical Perception during Near-Death Experiences," *Journal of Near-Death Studies* 11 (1993): 223–22; J. Long, *Evidence of the Afterlife: The Science of Near-Death Experiences* (New York: HarperCollins e-books, 2010); I. Wilson, *The After-Death Experience* (New York: William Morrow, 1987); D. S. Rogo, *The Return from Silence* (Northamptonshire: Aquarian Press, 1989).
60. B. Greyson, "Near-Death Experiences," in *Varieties of Anomalous Experience: Examining the Scientific Evidence*, ed. E. Cardena, S. J. Lynn, and S. Krippner (Washington, DC: American Psychological Association, 2000), pp. 339–40; M. Beauregard et al., "Conscious Mental Activity during a Deep Hypothermic Cardiocirculatory Arrest?" *Resuscitation* 83: e19; P. Van Lommel et al., "Near-Death Experience in Survivors of Cardiac Arrest: A Prospective Study in the Netherlands," *Lancet* 358 (2001): 2043.
61. Maria, quoted in K. Clark, "Clinical Interventions with Near-Death Experiencers," in *The Near-Death Experience: Problems, Prospects, Prospectives,* ed. B. Greyson and C. P. Flynn (Springfield, IL: Charles C Thomas, 1984), pp. 242–55.
62. H. Ebbern, S. Mulligan, and B. Beyerstein, "Maria's Near-Death Experience: Waiting for the Other Shoe to Drop," *Skeptical Inquirer* 20 (1996): 32.
63. Ibid.
64. Mark Crislip, "Near-Death Experiences and the Medical Literature," *eSkeptic*, June 18, 2008, accessed June 10, 2017, https://www.skeptic.com/eskeptic/08-06-18/.
65. K. Augustine, "Hallucinatory Near-Death Experiences," 2008, p. 22, accessed June 10, 2017, https://infidels.org/library/modern/keith_augustine/HNDEs.html.
66. G. M. Woerlee, "Pam Reynolds Near-Death Experience," n.d., accessed June 10, 2017, http://neardth.com/pamreynolds-near-death-experience.php.
67. Augustine, "Hallucinatory Near-Death Experiences," p. 22.
68. Woerlee, "Pam Reynolds Near-Death Experience," p. 6.
69. Ibid.
70. Sebastian Dieguez, "NDEs Redux," *eSkeptic*, August 13, 2008, accessed June 10, 2017, https://www.skeptic.com/eskeptic/08-08-13/. See also "Leaving Body and Life Behind: Out-of-Body and Near-Death Experience," *The Neurology of Consciousness,* ed. S. Laureys and G. Tononi (New York: Academic Press, 2009), pp. 303–25.

71. S. Parnia et al., "AWARE—AWAreness during Resuscitation—A Prospective Study," *Resuscitation* 85 (2014): 1799–805.
72. P. F. Craffert, "Do Out-of-Body and Near-Death Experiences Point Towards the Reality of Nonlocal Consciousness? A Critical Evaluation," *Journal for Transdisciplinary Research in Southern Africa* 11 (2015): 1–20.
73. Susan J. Blackmore, *Beyond the Body* (Chicago: Academy Chicago, 1992), p. 199.
74. M. Potts, "The Evidential Value of Near-Death Experiences for Belief in Life after Death," *Journal of Near-Death Studies* 20 (2002): 248.
75. G. M. Woerlee, "NDEs and OOBEs Are Hallucinations: The Soul Has No Memory," n.d., accessed June 10, 2018, http://neardth.com/hallucination.php.
76. William Rushton, "Letter to the Editor," *Journal of the Society for Psychical Research* 48 (1976): 412, cited in Blackmore, *Beyond the Body,* pp. 227–28.
77. Carl Sagan, *Broca's Brain* (New York: Ballantine Books, 1979), p. 356ff.
78. S. Grof and J. Halifax, *The Human Encounter with Death* (New York: E. P. Dutton, 1977).
79. C. B. Becker, "The Failure of Saganomics: Why Birth Models Cannot Explain Near-Death Phenomena," *Anabiosis* 2 (1982): 102–09.
80. Susan Blackmore, "Birth and the OBE: An Unhelpful Analogy," *Journal of the American Society for Psychical Research* 77 (1983): 229–38.
81. Dean Mobbs and Caroline Watt, "There Is Nothing Paranormal about Near-Death Experiences: How Neuroscience Can Explain Seeing Bright Lights, Meeting the Dead, or Being Convinced You Are One of Them," *Trends in Cognitive Sciences* 16 (2012): 449.
82. Ibid.
83. Ben Brumfield, "'Afterlife' Feels 'Even More Real Than Real,' Researcher Says," CNN, April 10, 2013, accessed June 10, 2018, https://www.cnn.com/2013/04/09/health/belgium-near-death-experiences/index.html.
84. E. J. Vam Liere and J. C. Stickney, *Hypoxia* (Chicago: University of Chicago Press, 1963), p. 3000.
85. Blackmore, "Near-Death Experiences," p. 42.
86. Ibid.
87. Charles Dickens, *Bleak House* (Chapman and Hall, 1873), p. 228.
88. Justus von Liebig, *Familiar Letters on Chemistry* (London: Taylor, Walton, and Maberly, 1851), letter 22.
89. Larry E. Arnold, *Ablaze! The Mysterious Fires of Spontaneous Human Combustion* (New York: M. Evans, 1995).
90. Jenny Randles, *Spontaneous Human Combustion* (London: Robert Hale, July 30, 2013).
91. F. W. H. Myers, *Human Personality,* vol. 2 (London: Longmans, Green, 1903), p. 19.
92. Stambovsky v. Ackley, Supreme Court, Appellate Division, First Department, July 18, 1991.

93. Paramahansa Yogananda, *Autobiography of a Yogi* (Los Angeles: Self-Realization Fellowship, 2001), p. 56.
94. R. J. Broughton et al., "Randomized, Double-Blind, Placebo-Controlled Crossover Trial of Modafinal in the Treatment of Excessive Daytime Sleepiness in Narcolepsy," *Neurology* 49 (1997): 444–51.
95. Richard Wiseman, Caroline Watt, Paul Stevens, Emma Greening, and Ciaran O'Keeffe, "An Investigation into Alleged 'Hauntings,'" *British Journal of Psychology* 94 (2003): 209.
96. H. P. Wilkinson and Alan Gauld, "Geomagnetism and Anomalous Experiences, 1868–1980," *Proceedings of the Society for Psychical Research* 57 (1993).
97. Andy Coghlan, "Midnight Watch," *New Scientist* 160 (December 19, 1998): 42.
98. Mick Hamer, "Silent Fright," *New Scientist* 176 (December 21, 2002): 50.
99. Andy Coghlan, "Little House of Horrors," *New Scientist* 179 (July 26, 2003): 30.
100. *Congressional Record,* 82d Cong. 1st sess. vol. 97 (U.S. Goverment Publishing Office, June 14, 1951): p. 6602.
101. Patrick Leman, "Who Shot the President? A Possible Explanation for Conspiracy Theories," *Economist* 20 (March 2003): 74.
102. Donna Kossy, *Kooks: A Guide to the Outer Limits of Human Belief* (Portland, OR: Feral House, 1994), p. 191.
103. Global Climate Change Impacts in the U.S.,"United States Global Change Research Program, 2009," accessed August 8, 2018, https://nca2014.globalchange.gov/highlights/overview/overview.
104. *Climate Change 2007 Synthesis Report* (The Intergovernmental Panel on Climate Change, 2007), p. 30.
105. *Surface Temperature Reconstructions for the Last 2,000 Years* (National Academy of Sciences, 2006).
106. National Aeronautics and Space Administration, "A Blanket Around the Earth," accessed December 3, 2012, http://climate.nasa.gov/causes/.
107. *Climate Change 2007 Synthesis Report* (The Intergovernmental Panel on Climate Change, 2007), p. 02.

EIGHT

Relativism, Truth, and Reality

There is nothing so powerful as truth, and often nothing so strange.
—DANIEL WEBSTER

WE GIVE YOU A PARABLE:

Four men came upon a duck—or what seemed a duck.

"It quacks like a duck. It waddles like a duck. It's a duck," said the first man.

"To you it's a duck, but to me it's not a duck, for we each create our own reality," said the second man.

"In your society it may be a duck, but in mine it's not; reality is socially constructed," said the third man.

"Your conceptual scheme may classify it as a duck, but mine doesn't; reality is constituted by conceptual schemes," said the fourth.

This discussion may seem to be a strange one, but you may have engaged in such a discussion yourself. Have you ever been told, "What's true for you isn't true for me"? If so, you have come face-to-face with the problem of relativism. The problem is this: Does reality exist independently of our ways of representing it, or do individuals, societies, or conceptual schemes create their own realities? Those who accept the first alternative are called "external realists," or "realists" for short, because they do not believe that reality depends on our thoughts about it. Those who accept the second alternative are called "relativists" because they believe that the way the world is depends on what we think about it.

To say that reality exists independently of how we represent it to ourselves is not to say that there is one correct way to represent it. Reality can be represented in many different ways, just as a territory can be mapped in many different ways. Consider, for example, road maps, topographical maps, and relief maps. These maps use different symbols to represent different aspects of the terrain, and the symbols that appear on one map may not appear on another. Nevertheless, it makes no sense to say that one of these maps is the correct map. Each can provide an accurate representation of the territory.

As scarce as truth is, the supply has always been in excess of the demand.

—JOSH BILLINGS

Relativism is appealing to many people because they incorrectly assume that realism entails absolutism—the view that there is only one correct way to represent reality. As Allan Bloom reveals:

> There is one thing a professor can be absolutely certain of: almost every student entering the university believes that truth is relative. . . . The relativity of truth is not a theoretical insight but a moral postulate, the condition of a free society, or so they see it. . . . That it is a moral issue for students is revealed by the character of their response when challenged—a combination of disbelief and indignation: "Are you an absolutist?" the only alternative they know, uttered in the same tone as "Are you a monarchist?" or "Do you really believe in witches?"[1]

Absolutism is considered morally objectionable because it leads to intolerance. After all, weren't all persecutions in history perpetrated by those who believed in objective reality and knew that their view of it was the correct one? Relativism, on the other hand, is supposed to foster tolerance, implying that different views are entitled to equal respect because they're equally true.

We have seen that relativists are wrong in assuming that realism implies absolutism. From the fact that reality exists independently of our representations of it, it doesn't follow that there is one correct way to represent reality. It remains to be seen whether they are correct in assuming that relativism fosters tolerance. To evaluate that claim, we'll have to take a closer look at the various types of relativism.

WE EACH CREATE OUR OWN REALITY

The view of the second man is that we each create our own reality. Many people, past and present, have embraced this idea and thought it both liberating and profound. Actress Shirley MacLaine, for example, declared in the introduction to her book *Out on a Limb:*

> If my search for inner truth helps give you, the reader, the gift of insight, then I am rewarded. But my first reward has been the journey through myself, the only journey worth taking. Through it all I have learned one deep and meaningful lesson: LIFE, LIVES, and REALITY are only what we each perceive them to be. Life doesn't happen to us. We make it happen. Reality isn't separate from us. We are creating our reality every moment of the day. For me that truth is the ultimate freedom and the ultimate responsibility.[2]

The mind does not create what it perceives, any more than the eye creates the rose.
—RALPH WALDO EMERSON

Later, to the amazement of her friends, she followed this claim to its logical conclusion—to solipsism, the idea that "I alone exist" and create all of reality. In *It's All in the Playing,* she tells how she scandalized guests at a New Year's Eve party when she expressed solipsistic sentiments:

> I began by saying that since I realized I created my own reality in every way, I must therefore admit that, in essence, *I was the only person alive in my universe.* I could feel the instant shock waves undulate around the table. I went on to express my feeling of total responsibility *and power* for all events that occur in the world because the world is happening only in my reality. *And* human beings feeling pain, terror, depression, panic, and so forth, were really only aspects of pain, terror, depression, panic and so on, in *me*! . . . I knew I had created the reality of the evening news at night. It was my reality. But whether anyone else was experiencing the news *separately* from me was unclear, because *they* existed in my reality too. And if they reacted to world events, then I was creating them to react so I would have someone to interact with, thereby enabling myself to know me better.[3]

In 1970, long before MacLaine spoke of creating reality, a book called *The Seth Material* was published. It was to be one of many bestsellers based on the words of a putative entity named Seth (a personality "no longer focused in physical reality") and "channeled" by novelist Jane Roberts. A major theme of the book is that physical reality is our own creation:

> Seth says that we form the physical universe as unselfconsciously as we breathe. We aren't to think of it as a prison from which we will one day escape, or as an execution chamber from which all escape is impossible. Instead *we form matter* in order to operate in three-dimensional reality,

> develop our abilities and help others. . . . Without realizing it we project our ideas outward to form physical reality. Our bodies are the materialization of what we think we are. We are all creators, then, and this world is our creation.[4]

So do we each make physical reality? At one time, biologist Ted Schultz was attracted to this idea but soon came to have doubts about it.

> I began to wonder about the logical extensions of "consensus reality," "personal reality," and the power of belief. Supposing a schizophrenic was totally convinced that he could fly. Could he? If so, why weren't there frequent reports from mental institutions of miracles performed by the inmates? What about large groups of people like the Jehovah's Witnesses, who devoutly believed that Jesus would return on a particular day? Hadn't he failed to appear twice in that religion's history (in 1914 and 1975), forcing the faithful to reset the dates? What if the inhabitants of some other solar system believed astronomical physics to work differently than we believe they do on earth? Could both be true at the same time? If not, which would the universe align itself with? Does the large number of Catholics on earth make the Catholic God and saints a reality? Should I worry about the consequences of denying the Catholic faith? Before Columbus, was the earth really flat because everyone believed it to be? Did it only "become" round after the consensus opinion changed?[5]

The truth is not only stranger than you imagine, it is stranger than you can imagine.

—J. B. S. HALDANE

What could be more appealing than the notion that if we just believe in something, it will become true? Just the same, as Schultz indicates, there are serious problems with the idea that belief alone can transfigure reality. For one thing, it involves a logical contradiction. If it's true that our beliefs can alter reality, then what happens when different people have opposing beliefs? Let's say that person A believes *p* (a statement about reality), and *p* therefore becomes true. Person B, however, believes not-*p,* and it becomes true. We would then have the same state of affairs both existing and not existing simultaneously—a logical impossibility. What if A believes that all known terrorists are dead, and B believes that they're not dead? What if A believes that the Earth is round, and B believes it's flat? Since the supposition that our beliefs create reality leads to a logical contradiction, we must conclude that reality is independent of our beliefs.

Solipsists can avoid this problem because, in their view, there is only one person in the world and hence only one person doing the believing. But is it reasonable to believe that there is only one person in the world and that person creates everything there is by merely thinking about it? Consider your own experience.

You have a leaking faucet. You position a bucket to catch the drops. You leave the room. When you return, the bucket is full of water, the sink is overflowing, and the carpet is soaked. Simple events like this—and billions of other experiences—lead us to believe that causal sequences continue whether we're experiencing them or not, as though they were independent of our minds.

You open a closet door, and—surprise!—books fall on your head. The last thing on your mind was falling books. It's as though such events were causally connected to something outside our minds.

You fall asleep on your bed. When you awaken the next day, everything in the room is just as it was before you drifted off. It's as though your room continued to exist whether you were thinking about it or not.

You hold a rose in your hand. You see it, feel it, smell it. Your senses converge to give you a unified picture of this flower—as though it existed independently. If it's solely a product of your mind, this convergence is more difficult to account for.

Every day of your life, you're aware of a distinction between experiences that you yourself create (such as daydreams, thoughts, imaginings) and those that seem forced on you by an external reality (such as unpleasant smells, loud noises, cold wind). If there is an independent world, this distinction makes sense. If there isn't and you create your own reality, the distinction is mysterious.

The point is that the existence of an independent world explains our experiences better than any known alternative. We have good reason to believe that the world—which seems independent of our minds—really is. We have little if any reason to believe that the world is our mind's own creation. Science writer Martin Gardner, in an essay on solipsism, puts the point like this:

> We, who of course are not solipsists, all believe that other people exist. Is it not an astonishing set of coincidences—astonishing, that is, to anyone who doubts an external world—that everybody sees essentially the same phaneron [phenomena]? We walk the same streets of the same cities. We find the same buildings at the same locations. Two people can see the same spiral galaxy through a telescope. Not only that, they see the same spiral structure. The hypothesis that there is an external world, not dependent on human minds, made of *something,* is so obviously useful and so strongly confirmed by experience down through the ages that we can say without exaggerating that it is better confirmed than any other empirical hypothesis. So useful is the posit that it is almost impossible for anyone except a madman or a professional metaphysician to comprehend a reason for doubting it.[6]

The belief that there is an external reality is more than just a convenient fiction or a dogmatic assumption—it is the best explanation of our experience.

While it's ludicrous to believe that our minds create external reality, it's perfectly reasonable to believe that our minds create our beliefs about external reality. As we have seen, the mind is not merely a passive receiver of information but an active manipulator of it. In our attempt to understand and cope with the world, each of us forms many different beliefs about it. This diversity of belief can be expressed by saying that what's true for me may not be true for you. Different people take different things to be true. But taking something to be true doesn't make it true.

I never know how much of what I say is true.

—BETTE MIDLER

The view that each of us creates our own reality is known as subjectivism. This view is not unique to the twenty-first century, however. It flourished in ancient Greece over 2,500 years ago. The ancient champions of subjectivism are known as Sophists. They were professors of rhetoric who earned their living by teaching wealthy Athenians how to win friends and influence people. Because they did not believe in objective truth, however, they taught their pupils to argue both sides of any case, which created quite a scandal at the time. (The words *sophistic* and *sophistical* are used to describe arguments that appear sound but are actually fallacious.) The greatest of the Sophists—Protagoras—famously expressed his subjectivism thus: "Man is the measure of all things, of existing things that they exist, and of non-existing things that they do not exist."[7] Reality does not exist independently of human minds but is created by our thoughts. Consequently, whatever anyone believes is true.

Plato (ca. 427–347 BCE) saw clearly the implications of such a view. If whatever anyone believes is true, then everyone's belief is as true as everyone else's. And if everyone's belief is as true as everyone else's, then the belief that subjectivism is false is as true as the belief that subjectivism is true. Plato put it this way: "Protagoras, for his part, admitting as he does that everybody's opinion is true, must acknowledge the truth of his opponents' belief about his own belief, where they think he is wrong."[8] Protagorean subjectivism, then, is self-refuting. If it's true, it's false. Any claim whose truth implies its falsehood cannot possibly be true.

It's ironic that Protagoras taught argumentation, because in a Protagorean world, there shouldn't be any arguments. Arguments arise when there is some reason to believe that someone is mistaken. If believing something to be true made it true, however, no one could ever be mistaken; everyone would be infallible. It would be impossible

Whoever tells the truth is chased out of nine villages.

—TURKISH PROVERB

for anyone to have a false belief because the mere fact that he or she believed something would make it true. So if Protagoras's customers took his philosophy seriously, he would be out of a job. If no one can lose an argument, there's no need to learn how to argue.

You may not be coming from where I'm coming from, but I know that relativism isn't true for me.
—ALAN GARFINKEL

That subjectivism renders disagreement futile often goes unnoticed. As Ted Schultz observes:

> Paradoxically, many New Agers, having demonstrated to their satisfaction that objective truth is the unattainable bugaboo of thick-headed rationalists, often become extremely dogmatic about the minutiae of their own favorite belief systems. After all, if what is "true for you" isn't necessarily "true for me," should I really worry about the exact dates and locations of the upcoming geological upheavals predicted by Ramtha or the coming of the "space brothers" in 2012 predicted by Jose Argüelles?[9]

If the New Agers are right, no one should worry about such things, for if everyone manufactures their own truth, no one could ever be in error.

Much as we might like to be infallible, we know that we aren't. Even the most fervently relativistic New Ager must confess that he or she dials a wrong number, bets on a losing racehorse, or forgets a friend's birthday. These admissions reveal that reality is not constituted by our beliefs. The operative principle here is:

Just because you believe something to be true doesn't mean that it is.

If believing something to be so made it so, the world would contain a lot fewer unfulfilled desires, unrealized ambitions, and unsuccessful projects than it does.

REALITY IS SOCIALLY CONSTRUCTED

The basic idea behind the third man's claim in our parable is that if enough people believe that something is true, it literally becomes true for everyone. We don't each create our own separate realities—we all live in one reality, but we can radically alter this reality for everybody if a sufficient number of us believe. If within our group we can reach a kind of consensus, a critical mass of belief, then we can change the world.

Facts do not cease to exist because they are ignored.
—ALDOUS HUXLEY

Probably the most influential articulation of this idea was a book called *The Crack in the Cosmic Egg* by Joseph Chilton Pearce.[10] In it, Pearce asserted that people have a hand in shaping physical reality—even the laws of physics. We can transform the physical world, or parts of it, if enough of us believe in a new reality. If we attain a group consensus, we can change the world any way we want—for everyone.

On Good Myth and Bad Myth

Psychologist Maureen O'Hara was the first to publish a skeptical analysis of Lyall Watson's hundredth-monkey story of a paranormal critical mass of consciousness. She's aware that many people have embraced the tale as a significant myth. She acknowledges the importance of myth in our lives but contends that, as a myth, the Watson story is "profoundly nonhumanistic" and a "betrayal of the whole idea of human empowerment":

> There are major contradictions in the present idealization of critical mass—seen not only in the Hundredth Monkey story, but in the ideologies of such organizations as est, Bhagwan Rajneesh, and the "Aquarian conspirators." In promoting the idea that, although our ideas are shared by only an enlightened few (for the time being), if we really believe them, in some magical way what we hold to be true becomes true for everyone, proponents of the critical mass ideal ignore the principles of both humanism and democratic open society. The basis for openness in our kind of society is the belief that, for good or ill, each of us holds his or her own beliefs as a responsible participant in a pluralistic culture. Are we really willing to give up on this ideal and promote instead a monolithic ideology in which what is true for a "critical mass" of people becomes true for everyone? The idea gives me the willies. . . .
>
> My objection to the Hundredth Monkey Phenomenon, then, is not that it is a myth, but that it is bad myth, and that it draws its force not from the collective imagination, but by masquerading as science. It leads us (as I have tried to show) in the direction of propaganda, manipulation, totalitarianism, and a worldview dominated by the powerful and persuasive—in other words, business as usual. . . .
>
> . . . This is not a transformation myth impelling us toward the fullest development of our capacities, but one that reduces us instead to quite literally nothing more than a mindless herd at the mercy of the "Great Communicators." The myth of the Hundredth Monkey Phenomenon is more chillingly Orwellian than Aquarian.

Source: Maureen O'Hara, "Of Myths and Monkeys: A Critical Look at Critical Mass," in *The Fringes of Reason: A Whole Earth Catalog* (1989), pp. 182–85.

In recent years, this extraordinary thesis—that if enough people believe in something, it suddenly becomes true for everyone—has been enormously influential. It got its single biggest boost from the hundredth-monkey phenomenon (mentioned in Chapter 1), a story told by Lyall Watson in his book *Lifetide*. This tale has been told and retold in a best-selling book by Ken Keyes called *The Hundredth Monkey*, in a film with the same name, and in several articles.

Here's the story: Watson tells of reports coming from scientists in the 1950s about wild Japanese monkeys on the island of Koshima. After the monkeys were given raw sweet potatoes for the first time, one of the monkeys, named Imo, learned to wash the sand and grit off the potatoes by dunking them in a stream. In the next few years, Imo taught this skill to other monkeys in the colony. "Then something extraordinary took place," says Watson.

It is proof of a base and low mind for one to wish to think with the masses or majority merely because the majority is the majority. Truth does not change because it is, or is not, believed by a majority of the people.
—GIORDANO BRUNO

> The details up to this point in the study are clear, but one has to gather the rest of the story from personal anecdotes and bits of folklore among primate researchers, because most of them are still not quite sure what happened. And those who do suspect the truth are reluctant to publish it for fear of ridicule. So I am forced to improvise the details, but as near as I can tell, this is what seems to have happened.
>
> In the autumn of that year [1958] an unspecified number of monkeys on Koshima were washing sweet potatoes in the sea, because Imo had made the further discovery that salt water not only cleaned the food but also gave it an interesting new flavor. Let us say, for argument's sake, that the number was ninety-nine and that at eleven o'clock on a Tuesday morning, one further convert was added to the fold in the usual way. But the addition of the hundredth monkey apparently carried the number across some sort of threshold, pushing it through a kind of critical mass, because by the evening almost everyone in the colony was doing it. Not only that, but the habit seems to have jumped natural barriers and to have appeared spontaneously, like glycerin crystals in sealed laboratory jars, in colonies on other islands and on the mainland in a troop at Takasakiyama.[11]

Watson uses the story to support the consensus-truth thesis. But you might ask at this point, "Is the story true? Did these events really happen?" (Many people who retold the story in books and articles never bothered to ask this question.)

If it did happen, it would be of enormous scientific interest. But it still wouldn't constitute proof of the thesis that a critical mass of humans can make something true for everyone else. For one thing, the evidence could easily support alternative hypotheses—perhaps the potato-washing habit wasn't really spread, but resulted from independent experimentation and learning by different monkeys (in other words, other monkeys learned it the way Imo did).

On the other hand, if the story didn't happen, this wouldn't prove that the consensus-truth thesis was false, either. It would simply mean that one potential piece of empirical evidence that would justify our believing in the thesis was not valid.

As it turns out, *the story didn't happen,* at least not as told by Watson and others. Regardless of the literal truth of Watson's story, though, we can still scrutinize his thesis. In *Lifetide* he says, "When enough of us hold something to be true, it becomes true for everyone."[12] If by this he means that consensus belief by groups of people can literally alter physical reality (Pearce's notion), he's mistaken.

It's just as implausible to believe that the thoughts of a group of people (or monkeys) create external reality as it is to believe that the thoughts of an individual person create external reality. But it is not at all implausible to believe that social forces influence individual thoughts. What we believe is largely a function of the society in which we were brought up. For example, if we were raised in a Hindu society, we may believe that God is an impersonal force. If we were raised in a Buddhist society, we may believe that there is no God. And if we were raised in a Christian society, we may believe that God is an immaterial person. But the fact that society believes something to be true doesn't make it true. If it did, societies would be infallible, and we know that's not the case. Societies used to believe that the Earth was flat, that the sun orbited the Earth, and that storms were caused by angry gods. In each case, society was wrong. We must conclude, then, that:

Most men live like raisins in a cake of custom.

—BRAND BLANSHARD

Just because a group of people believe that something is true doesn't mean that it is.

Groups are just as prone to error as individuals are—perhaps more so. We can't justify our beliefs by claiming that everyone shares them, for everyone may be mistaken. To attempt to do so is to commit the fallacy of appeal to the masses.

What's more, if society were infallible, it would be impossible to disagree with society and be correct. Since truth is whatever society says it is, any claim that society is wrong would have to be false. Thus social reformers could never justifiably claim that truth is on their side.

According to social constructivism, then, scientists are deluded in believing that there are truths that apply universally to all people regardless of what society they belong to—truths like $f = ma$ (force equals mass times acceleration) and $E = mc^2$ (energy equals mass times the velocity of light squared). If truth is relative to society, no such universal truths exist. Whatever society says, goes. Here's tyranny of the majority with a vengeance.

The exact contrary of what is generally believed is often the truth.

—JEAN DE LA BRUYÈRE

But suppose (as may well be the case) that our society agrees with scientists that not all truth is socially constructed. Does this conclusion mean that social constructivism is false? According to the constructivist doctrine, it does. You see, social constructivism faces the same problem that subjectivism does: If every society's belief is as true as every other's, then a society's belief that reality is not socially constructed is also true. Just as a subjectivist must recognize the truth of another individual's opposing view, so a social constructivist must recognize the truth of another society's opposing view.

Social constructivists would have us believe that no one can legitimately criticize another society. As long as a society is acting on what it believes to be true, no one can defensibly claim that what it's

Let's Resonate Together

Related to the hundredth-monkey idea is the extraordinary theory of *morphic resonance* put forth by biologist and author Rupert Sheldrake. His notion is that all organisms and structures in the universe have the form (morph) that they do because they exist in "morphic fields" that shape them. These energy fields contain the form or pattern of objects, with every type of object being determined by its own field. The fields "have a kind of built-in memory derived from previous forms of a similar kind," Sheldrake says. "The liver field is shaped by the forms of previous livers and the oak tree field by the forms and organization of previous oak trees."[13] The liver forms and the oak-leaf forms resonate, or communicate, with each other to create their respective fields. Morphic fields impose patterns on both animate and inanimate objects—cells, crystals, protein molecules, atoms, and everything else.

According to Sheldrake, the behavior of animals and people also creates morphic fields, which in turn shape future behavior. Thus if you teach mice in London to navigate a maze, the morphic field for the species changes, and suddenly mice in Paris can navigate the same maze much easier.

Sheldrake cites several phenomena that he says are best explained by his theory of morphic resonance. These include alleged instances of spontaneous animal learning (similar to the hundredth-monkey phenomenon), cases in which humans seem to learn something faster after other humans learn it first, and the ability of some organisms (such as flatworms) to regenerate parts and repair physical damage. Scientists question whether some of Sheldrake's phenomena have even occurred, and much of the relevant research is controversial.

Nevertheless, we can ask, is it reasonable to accept Sheldrake's theory of morphic resonance? Well, not yet. Scientists judge the worth of theories according to certain key criteria, and Sheldrake's theory falls short on at least two of them. One criterion is simplicity, the number of unproven assumptions a theory makes. The more assumptions, the less likely the theory is to be true. Sheldrake's theory assumes both unknown entities and unknown processes—morphic fields and their vast influence on just about everything. These assumptions alone render the theory suspect. The other criterion is conservatism, how well a theory fits with what we already know. Theories that conflict with our well-founded beliefs are less likely to be true. Other things being equal, the theory most consistent with the entire corpus of our knowledge is the best. Sheldrake's theory is not conservative. It conflicts with a massive amount of scientific evidence regarding fields, energy, biochemistry, genetics, human behavior, and much more. There simply is no good evidence that morphic fields exist and exert an influence on the world. This lack of conservatism renders the theory unlikely.

We should accept an extraordinary theory only if no ordinary one will do. And in this case we have no good reason to believe that no ordinary one will do. In the history of science, scientists have often been confronted with astonishing phenomena that they could not explain in natural terms at the time. But they didn't assume that the phenomena must be paranormal or supernatural. They simply kept investigating, and they eventually found natural explanations.

doing is wrong. Suppose, for example, that during World War II the German people agreed with the Nazis that the Jews were a plague on humankind and needed to be eradicated. If so, then according to social constructivism, the Holocaust was justified. Since the Nazis were acting on what their society believed to be true, they were doing the right thing. Like Protagoras, social constructivists have to consider the Nazis' view as true as everyone else's.

If you disagree—if you believe that the Nazis were wrong about the Jews even if they had the support of the German people—then you can't be a social constructivist, for you have admitted that society can be mistaken. Given the history of civilization, such a conclusion seems unavoidable. Society has been wrong about many things: that kings have a divine right to rule, that letting blood cures disease, or that women are inferior to men, just to name a few. So the doctrine of social constructivism has little to recommend it.

Since social constructivism holds that what makes a proposition true is that society believes it to be true, it follows that whenever individuals disagree about the truth of a proposition, what they must really disagree about is whether their society believes it or not. But are all our disputes really about what society believes? Suppose we disagree about whether the universe contains black holes. Can we really resolve this dispute by simply polling the members of our society? Of course not. Even disagreements about the truth of various moral principles can't be settled by opinion surveys. Whether abortion is morally justified, for example, can't be determined by simply canvassing the populace. So truth must be more than just social consensus.

The idea of cultural relativism is nothing but an excuse to violate human rights.

—SHIRIN EBADI

Even if truth were manufactured by society, it wouldn't be any easier to find, for there is no single society to which each of us clearly belongs. Suppose, for example, that you were a black Jewish communist living in Bavaria during the 1940s. Which would be your real society? The blacks? The Jews? The communists? The Bavarians? Unfortunately, there is no way to answer this question because we all belong to a number of different societies, none of which can claim to be our real society. So not only is social constructivism not a very reasonable theory, it's not a very useful one either.

REALITY IS CONSTITUTED BY CONCEPTUAL SCHEMES

Common sense tells us that neither individuals nor societies are infallible. Both can believe things that are false, and something can be true even if no individual or society has ever believed it. To preserve these insights, some relativists, like the fourth man in our parable, have claimed that truth is relative not to individuals or societies but

Truth has no special time of its own. Its hour is now—always.

—ALBERT SCHWEITZER

to conceptual schemes. A conceptual scheme is a set of concepts for classifying objects. These concepts provide categories into which the items of our experience can be placed. Just as the post office uses pigeonholes to sort mail into deliverable piles, so we use conceptual schemes to sort things into meaningful groups. Different people may sort things differently, however. One person may believe that an item falls under one concept, while someone else may believe that it falls under another. So even though two people share the same concepts, they may apply them differently.[14]

To account for individual and social fallibility, the conceptual relativist must maintain that simply believing something to fall under a certain concept isn't enough to make it so. There must be a fact of the matter as to how it should be classified, and that fact can't be determined solely by belief. What, then, is it determined by? According to the conceptual relativist, it is determined, at least in part, by the world. So the conceptual relativist must admit that the world plays a role in determining what's true.[15]

Although the world constrains the truth, conceptual relativists do not believe that the world uniquely determines the truth, for, in their view, there is no one way that the world is. Rather, different conceptual schemes create different worlds.

For the conceptual relativist, the relationship between conceptual schemes and the world is analogous to that of a cookie cutter and cookie dough. Just as cookie dough takes on whatever shape is imparted to it by a cookie cutter, so the world takes on whatever properties are imputed to it by a conceptual scheme. The world has some properties that are not affected by the conceptual scheme, just as the dough has some properties that are not affected by the cookie cutter. These properties allow the conceptual relativist to account for mistaken classifications. Nevertheless, in an important sense, the world is a product of a conceptual scheme. As philosopher Nelson Goodman puts it, conceptual schemes are ways of making worlds.[16] So people with different conceptual schemes live in different worlds.

One of the most influential proponents of this view is philosopher and historian Thomas Kuhn. His preferred term for a conceptual scheme is paradigm. In his book, *The Structure of Scientific Revolutions* (see Chapter 2), Kuhn uses the word *paradigm* to refer to particular scientific theories as well as the concepts, methods, and standards used to arrive at those theories. Paradigms tell scientists what's real and how to go about investigating reality. They indicate what sorts of puzzles are worth solving and what sorts of methods will solve them.

Normal science, says Kuhn, involves trying to solve the puzzles generated by a paradigm. Good theories make predictions that go beyond the data they were intended to explain. Scientists investigate these predictions to see if they are borne out by the facts. If not, they have a puzzle on their hands. Scientists try to solve these puzzles by using the conceptual resources provided by the paradigm. But sometimes no solution can be found. In that case, the scientific community enters a state of crisis and begins to look for a new paradigm that would explain the anomaly. When such a paradigm is found, the scientific community undergoes what Kuhn calls a paradigm shift. Since paradigms define reality, undergoing a paradigm shift is like being transported to an alien universe. Kuhn describes it this way:

> Examining the record of past research from the vantage of contemporary historiography, the historian of science may be tempted to exclaim that when paradigms change, the world itself changes with them. Led by a new paradigm, scientists adopt new instruments and look in new places. Even more important, during revolutions scientists see new and different things when looking with familiar instruments in places they have looked before. It is rather as if the professional community had been suddenly transported to another planet where familiar objects are seen in a different light and are joined by unfamiliar ones as well. Of course, nothing of quite that sort does occur: there is no geographical transplantation; outside the laboratory everyday affairs usually continue as before. Nevertheless, paradigm changes do cause scientists to see the world of their research engagement differently. In so far as their only recourse to that world is through what they see and do, we may want to say that after a revolution scientists are responding to a different world.[17]

Although Kuhn's statements here are highly qualified, he seems to be saying that people who accept different paradigms effectively live in different worlds.

A harmful truth is better than a useful lie.

—Thomas Mann

But why talk this way? Why say that those who accept different paradigms live in different worlds instead of simply saying that they have different beliefs about the world? Apparently because Kuhn believes that your world is made up of your experiences, and insofar as each paradigm produces its own experiences, those who accept different paradigms live in different worlds. After discussing some of the differences between Aristotle's and Galileo's theory of motion, he remarks: "the immediate content of Galileo's experience with falling stones was not what Aristotle's had been."[18] Because Galileo had a different theory of motion than Aristotle, Kuhn claims that what Galileo saw when he looked at a moving body was different from what Aristotle saw.

The assumption behind the view that different paradigms create different worlds is that all observation is theory-laden. What we observe is determined by the theory we accept. For example, those who believe that the Earth is the center of the solar system see a sunrise very differently from those who believe that the sun is the center of the solar system. Because each paradigm manufactures its own data, there are no neutral data that can be used to make objective comparisons between paradigms. As a result, no paradigm can be considered to be objectively better than any other.

Even if we grant that all observation is theory laden, however, it doesn't follow that there are no paradigm-neutral data because two paradigms may share some theories in common. For example, proponents of the geocentric (Earth-centered) view of the solar system as well as those of the heliocentric (sun-centered) view could agree that, during a sunrise, the perceived distance between the sun and the horizon gets larger. They could also agree on other observationally relevant theories like the theory of the telescope, the compass, and the sextant. So the dependence of data on theory doesn't rule out objective comparisons between paradigms.

Facts are facts and will not disappear on account of your likes.
—Jawaharlal Nehru

What's more, there is reason to believe that at least some observations are not theory laden. If our paradigm determined everything that we observed, then it would be impossible to observe anything that didn't fit our paradigm. But if we never observed anything that didn't fit our paradigm—if we never perceived any anomalies—there would never be any need to undergo a paradigm shift. So Kuhn's theory undermines itself—if we accept his theory of observation, we must reject his history of science.

Neurophysiological research into the nature of perception provides further reason for believing that not all observation is theory laden. Psychologist Edward Hundert explains:

> If someone loses the primary visual cortex (say, because of a tumor), they lose their vision; they go almost totally blind. But if they just lose the secondary or tertiary visual cortex, they manifest an unusual condition called visual agnosia. In this condition, visual acuity is normal (the person could correctly identify the orientation of the "E's" on the eye chart). But they lose the ability to identify, name, or match even simple objects in any part of their visual field. . . . This model can be translated into psychological terms as endorsing a functional distinction between "perception" (input analysis) and "cognition" (central processing). . . .
>
> It is easy to see the evolutionary advantage of this whole scheme, with its "upward" input analysis: if our transducers were hooked directly to our central systems, we would spend most of our time seeing (hearing, etc.) the world the way we remember, believe, or expect the world to be. The recognition of novelty—of unexpected stimuli—has extremely obvious evolutionary advantage, and is made possible only by the separation of transducers and central systems by "dumb" input analyzers.[19]

If all observations were theory laden, we would never be able to observe anything new. Since we can observe new things, some observations must be theory free. Hundert suggests that there are two types of observation: recognition and discrimination. Recognition may involve the use of theory, but discrimination does not. By keeping these two functions separate, the brain allows us to deal with the unexpected. Access to an objective reality, then, seems to be a necessary condition of survival.

It also seems to be a necessary condition of communication. If the world really was constituted by conceptual schemes, it would be difficult to account for the fact that people with different conceptual schemes can understand and communicate with one another. Philosopher Roger Trigg explains:

> The result of granting that "the world" or "reality" cannot be conceived as independent of all conceptual schemes is that there is no reason to suppose that what the peoples of very different communities see as the world is similar in any way. Unfortunately, however, this supposition is absolutely necessary before any translation or comparison between languages of different societies can take place. Without it, the situation would be like one where the inhabitants of two planets which differed fundamentally in their nature met each other and tried to communicate. So few things (if any) would be matters of common experience that their respective languages would hardly ever run parallel.[20]

Because translation is possible among all the different conceptual schemes we know of, the world must not be constituted by conceptual schemes.

Translation requires a common point of reference. Consequently, some people argue that the very notion of an alternate conceptual scheme makes no sense. Philosopher Donald Davidson, for example, claims that if we can translate an alien's utterances into our own, our conceptual schemes must be essentially the same. And if we can't translate their utterances, we have no reason to suppose that they even have a conceptual scheme.[21]

Reality is that which, when you stop believing in it, doesn't go away.

—PHILIP K. DICK

As long as we don't consider truth to be relative to conceptual schemes, however, we do not need to reject the notion of alternate conceptual schemes. Without getting too technical, we can say that people who use different concepts have different conceptual schemes. We can even say that people with different conceptual schemes experience the world in different ways. What we can't say is that people with different conceptual schemes live in different worlds, because that statement generates all the problems already discussed. Different conceptual schemes represent the world differently; they don't create different worlds.

Instead of viewing conceptual schemes as cookie cutters, we can view them as maps. A territory, as mentioned earlier, can be mapped in many different ways, and each map, provided that it is an accurate one, can be considered true. Each science, for example, can be considered a different map of reality. The map provided by biology may contain very few of the concepts contained in the map provided by physics, just as a topographical map may contain very few of the symbols contained in a road map. But both biology and physics can be considered to be maps of the same reality just as topographical and road maps can be considered maps of the same territory, and both can be considered to be true. Whether you consult a biologist or a physicist will depend on what you want to do, just as whether you consult a topographical or a road map will depend on where you want to go. Different theories, like different maps, are good for different things. So there is no one best theory just as there is no one best map. What we must not forget is that, as mathematician Alfred Korzybski famously noted, "the map is not the territory."[22] People using different maps are not necessarily traversing different territories, and, contrary to what Kuhn seems to suggest, changing the map we're using doesn't change the territory we're traversing. The territory is what it is and is not affected by our representations of it.

THE RELATIVIST'S PETARD

All generalizations are dangerous, even this one.

—ALEXANDRE DUMAS FILS

The considerations presented in this chapter weigh heavily against relativism. But the most serious flaw of relativism in all its forms is a purely logical one: It's self-refuting because its truth implies its falsity.

According to the relativist—whether a subjectivist, a social constructivist, or a conceptual relativist—everything is relative. To say that everything is relative is to say that no unrestricted universal generalizations are true (an unrestricted universal generalization is a statement to the effect that something holds for all individuals, societies, or conceptual schemes). But the statement "No unrestricted universal generalizations are true" is itself an unrestricted universal generalization. So if relativism in any of its forms is true, it's false. As a result, it cannot possibly be true.

To avoid such self-contradiction, the relativist may try to claim that the statement "Everything is relative" is only relatively true. But this claim won't help, because it just says that relativists (or their society or their conceptual scheme) take relativism to be true. Such a claim should not give the nonrelativist pause, for the fact that relativists take relativism to be true is not in question. The question is whether a nonrelativist should take relativism to be true. Only if relativists can provide objective evidence that relativism is true should a nonrelativist believe that it's true. But this evidence is precisely the kind that relativists can't provide, for, in their view, there is no objective evidence.

Relativists, then, face a dilemma: If they interpret their theory objectively, they defeat themselves by providing evidence against it. If they interpret their theory relativistically, they defeat themselves by failing to provide any evidence for it. Either way, relativists defeat themselves.

Philosopher Harvey Siegel describes the dilemma this way:

> First the framework relativist must, in order to join the issue with the nonrelativist, defend framework relativism non-relativistically. To "defend" framework relativism relativistically (i.e., "according to my framework, framework relativism is true (correct, warranted, etc.)") is to fail to defend it, since the nonrelativist is appropriately unimpressed with such framework-bound claims. But to defend framework relativism non-relativistically is to give it up, since to defend it in this way is to acknowledge the legitimacy of framework-neutral criteria of assessment of claims, which is precisely what the framework relativist must deny. Thus to defend framework relativism relativistically is to fail to defend it; to defend it non-relativistically is to give it up. Thus framework relativism is self-defeating.[23]

And anything that is self-defeating cannot be true.

The problem with relativists is that they want to have their cake and eat it too. On the one hand, they want to say that they or their society or conceptual scheme is the supreme authority on matters of truth. But, on the other hand, they want to say that other individuals, societies, or conceptual schemes are equally authoritative. Relativists can't have it both ways. As philosopher W. V. O. Quine explains:

> Truth, says the cultural relativist, is culture-bound. But if it were, then he, within his own culture, ought to see his own culture-bound truth as absolute. He cannot proclaim cultural relativism without rising above it, and he cannot rise above it without giving it up.[24]

If individual, social, or conceptual relativism were true, there would be no standpoint outside yourself, your society, or your conceptual scheme from which to make valid judgments. But if there were no such standpoint, you would have no grounds for thinking that relativism is true. In proclaiming that truth is relative, then, relativists hoist themselves on their own petard; they blow themselves up, so to speak.

One must accept the truth from whatever source it comes.
—MAIMONIDES

FACING REALITY

The arguments presented in the previous section indicate that truth isn't relative to individuals, societies, or conceptual schemes. Belief can be relative because different individuals, societies, and conceptual schemes often have different beliefs. But the existence of relative beliefs doesn't mean that truth is relative, for, as we've seen, you can't make something true by simply believing it to be true. The upshot, then, is that:

There is an external reality that is independent of our representations of it.

In other words, there is a way that the world is. We can represent the world to ourselves in many different ways, but that which is being represented is the same for all of us.

The concept of objective reality is not optional, something we can take or leave. Each time we assert that something is the case or we think that something is a certain way, we assume that there is objective reality. Each time relativists deny objective reality, they entangle themselves in self-refutation and contradictions. In the very argument over the existence of objective reality, both those who accept it and those who deny it must assume it or the argument would never get off the ground.

The truth may not be helpful, but the concealment of it cannot be.
—MELVIN KONNER

"But wait," you say. "Still, there must be some things that are 'true for me' and 'not true for you.' If I say that I hate opera, isn't that statement true for me? If I love Bart Simpson, have a pain in my left leg, or am bored silly by discussions of politics, aren't these assertions true for me?"

Clearly there are things about ourselves that are relative—that are a certain way to us and a different way to others. Personal characteristics—peculiarities of psychology and physiology—are relative to persons (Jane likes pizza, but Jack doesn't; Jane has a mole on her nose and Jack doesn't). The effects that anything might have on a person are also relative to that person (Jane is intrigued by quantum mechanics, but Jack isn't; loud music gives Jane a headache, but not Jack). Certain states of affairs, then, may be relative to individuals.

But the truth about those states of affairs isn't relative. Let's say that Jane loves white wine and Jack doesn't. On their first dinner date, Jane says, "I love white wine." Is Jane's statement true for her but not true for Jack? No. Her statement reports a fact about herself, and because she does love white wine, her statement is true. It's not true for her and false for Jack; it's just true. If Jack says, "I don't love white wine," his statement refers to a fact about himself and is also true for both of them. In each statement, the "I" refers to a different person, and so the statements correctly report on different states of affairs.

Now we can consider the question raised at the beginning of this chapter: Does realism lead to intolerance and arrogance? The answer is no. The realist believes that when there's disagreement, it's theoretically possible to determine the truth through rational argument. After all, if there is a way that things are, then the only way to resolve disputes is by appeal to the way things are. But, as Trigg points out,

> there is no reason why someone who believes that basic disagreement *can* admit of solution firstly should arrogantly assume that he himself has a monopoly of truth, and secondly should then make others accept his views by force. The mere fact that a disagreement is capable of solution does not of itself suggest which side is right. When two sides contradict each other, whether in the fields of morality, religion or any other area, each will recognize (if they are objectivists) that at least one side must be mistaken. There need be no contradiction between strongly believing that one is right and yet realizing that one could be wrong. Arrogance is not entailed by any objectivist theory.[25]

True, realists might indeed be tempted to force their views on others. But so might relativists. Relativists might use force to get a person to agree with them because they have no other recourse. After all, relativists can't persuade anyone by appealing to objective standards or using rational argument. Since relativists don't believe that's possible, if they want to persuade someone, what is left besides force and manipulation?

Truth is a great flirt.
—Franz Liszt

Certainly, dogmatism isn't ruled out by relativism. It crops up among relativists just as it does among some realists. It's apparent, for example, among some people who have espoused New Age subjectivism. So relativism doesn't entail tolerance any more than realism entails intolerance.

Also, relativists who do embrace the virtue of tolerance once again get themselves stuck in contradictions. Is their statement that tolerance of other views is a good thing an objectively true statement or not? If it's objectively true, the relativists are denying their relativism because they regard something as objectively true. If their statement means that it's only relatively true that tolerance is a good thing, then they must admit that the opposite view could be equally justified. Consequently, relativists can't consistently claim that everyone should be tolerant.

Truth does not do so much good in the world as the appearance of it does evil.
—Duc François de La Rochefoucauld

There's no contradiction at all for the realist who says all of the following: Statements are objectively true or false; it's often difficult to tell whether statements are true or false; we may be mistaken about their truth or falsity; and because of our fallibility, we must be tolerant of those who have opposing views and uphold their right to disagree.

Understand this as well: Just because there is an objective reality (and thus objective truth) doesn't mean that people can't view this objective reality differently. In fact, some people are tempted by relativism precisely because they are aware that there are different perspectives on reality—and plenty of disagreements about those perspectives. But it doesn't follow from the existence of differing perspectives and disagreements that there is no objective reality or objective truth.

SUMMARY

Relativists believe that reality does not exist independently of our ways of representing it, that individuals, societies, or conceptual schemes create their own realities by representing it in different ways. Many people have embraced the idea that we each create our own reality, and they have welcomed the implication that if we just believe something, it will come true. But this notion involves us in contradictions, with people's beliefs causing something to exist and not exist at the same time. Solipsists can try to avoid this problem, but only by ignoring the fact that the best explanation of our experiences is that there is an independently existing world.

If reality is created by one's thoughts (the view known as subjectivism), then whatever anyone believes is true. But if whatever anyone believes is true, then everyone's belief is as true as everyone else's. And if everyone's belief is as true as everyone else's, then the belief that subjectivism is false is as true as the belief that subjectivism is true. Subjectivism, then, is self-refuting.

Some believe that if enough people believe that something is true, it literally becomes true for everyone—truth is socially constructed. But just because a group of people believe that something is true doesn't mean that it is. If this social constructivism were true, society would be infallible, an implausible result. The doctrine is also self-refuting in the same way that subjectivism is.

A related view is that reality is constituted by conceptual schemes. An assumption often lurking behind it is that all observation is theory laden. But there are reasons to believe that at least some observations are not theory laden. If all observation were theory laden, we would never be able to observe anything new. Access to an objective reality seems to be a necessary condition of survival and of communication.

According to the relativist—whether a subjectivist, a social constructivist, or a conceptual relativist—everything is relative. To say that everything is relative is to say that no unrestricted universal generalizations are true. But the statement "No unrestricted universal generalizations are true" is itself an unrestricted universal generalization. So if relativism in any of its forms is true, it's false. So it cannot possibly be true.

STUDY QUESTIONS

1. Can an individual make a statement true simply by believing it to be true? Why or why not?
2. Can a society make a statement true simply by believing it to be true? Why or why not?
3. Can a statement be true in one conceptual scheme and false in another? Why or why not?
4. Consider this statement: No universal generalizations are true. Can this statement be true? Why or why not?
5. Is it reasonable to believe that everything we experience (including the people we meet) is a creation of our own minds? Why or why not?

EVALUATE THESE CLAIMS. ARE THEY REASONABLE? WHY OR WHY NOT?

1. Don't pick up that toad. Toads cause warts. Everyone knows that.
2. Recent polls indicate that 90 percent of Americans believe in angels. Therefore, angels must exist.
3. Millions of people use psychic hotlines. So there must be something to them.
4. The tax system in this country is unfair and ridiculous. Just ask anyone.
5. The people of Ireland have believed in leprechauns for centuries. Leprechauns must be real.
6. Sightings of ghosts and spirits have been reported many times in history by countless societies. The descriptions of the ghosts vary in every era, but the disembodied nature of the phenomena does not. Even without any physical proof, we can say that ghosts are definitely real.

DISCUSSION QUESTIONS

1. A person can't make something true by simply believing it to be true. Can a person make something morally right by simply believing it to be right? Can a culture or society make something right by simply believing it to be right? Evaluate your answers to these questions by examining their implications.
2. Identify as many as possible of the different cultural or societal groups that you belong to. Is there any objective way to determine which of these groups is your real group? If so, which group is it? If not, what are the implications for social constructivism?
3. Suppose that two people have different beliefs about something they are looking at. Does it follow that they perceive it differently? Does it follow that they are perceiving different things? Is there any way to tell which, if either, of these alternatives is correct? Explain your answers by means of specific examples.

FIELD PROBLEM

In June 1989, the prodemocracy movement in China had captured the attention of people all over the world. Thousands of students gathered in the famed Tiananmen Square to demand greater freedom and democratic reforms in the Chinese government. The government responded with a massive military crackdown on the dissidents in the square, wounding and killing several of them. People who believed in universal human rights (ethical objectivists) condemned the killings as a tragic, immoral act. People in the Chinese government who rejected the notion of universal human rights (ethical relativists) said that, according to the values of Chinese society, the crackdown was morally right.

Assignment: Pretend for a moment that you are a Chinese official who uses moral relativism to defend the crackdown. In one paragraph, state your case. Then take the other side and pretend that you are a citizen of a Western nation who uses the concept of universal moral rights to condemn the crackdown. In one paragraph, present your argument. Compare the arguments. Which do you think is strongest?

CRITICAL READING AND WRITING

I. Read the passage below and answer the following questions:
   1. What is the claim being made in this passage?
   2. Are any reasons offered to support the claim?
   3. Are morphic fields physically possible? Why or why not?
   4. Would the existence of morphic fields lend support to the notion that reality is socially constructed? Why or why not?
   5. What kind of evidence would convince you that morphic fields exist?

II. Write a 200-word critique of this passage, focusing on how well its claim is supported by good reasons and why you think accepting the claim would be reasonable (or unreasonable).

Passage 7

Related to the hundredth-monkey idea is the extraordinary theory of "morphic resonance" put forth by biologist and author Rupert Sheldrake. His notion is that all organisms and structures in the universe have the form (morph) that they do because they exist in "morphic fields" that shape them. These energy fields contain the form or pattern of objects, with every type of object being determined by its own field.

According to Sheldrake, the behavior of animals and people also creates morphic fields, which in turn shape future behavior. Thus if you teach mice in London to navigate a maze, the morphic field for the species changes, and suddenly mice in Paris can navigate the same maze much easier. "Within the present century," he says, "it should have become progressively easier to learn to ride a bicycle, drive a car, play the piano, to use a typewriter, owing to the cumulative morphic resonance from the large number of people who have already acquired these skills."

Sheldrake cites several phenomena that he says are best explained by his theory of morphic resonance. These include alleged instances of spontaneous animal learning (similar to the hundredth-monkey phenomenon), cases in which humans seem to learn something faster after other humans learn it first, and the ability of some organisms (such as flatworms) to regenerate parts and repair physical damage.

NOTES

1. Allan Bloom, *The Closing of the American Mind* (New York: Simon and Schuster, 1987), p. 25.
2. Shirley MacLaine, *Out on a Limb* (New York: Bantam Books, 1986).
3. Shirley MacLaine, *It's All in the Playing* (New York: Bantam Books, 1987), p. 174.
4. Jane Roberts, *The Seth Material* (New York: Bantam Books, 1970), p. 124.
5. Ted Schultz, "A Personal Odyssey through the New Age," in *Not Necessarily the New Age* (New York: Bantam Books, 1976).
6. Martin Gardner, *The Whys of a Philosophical Scrivener* (St. Martin's Press, 1999), p. 15.
7. John Owen, *Evenings with the Skeptics: Or, Free Discussion on Free Thinkers* (Pearson, 1881), p. 157.
8. Plato, "Theaetetus," 171 a, trans. F. M. Cornford, in *The Collected Dialogues of Plato,* ed. Edith Hamilton and Huntington Cairns (Princeton: Princeton University Press, 1961), p. 876.
9. Robert Basil, "A Personal Odyssey Through the New Age" in *Not Necessarily the New Age: Critical Essays* (Prometheus Books, 1988), p. 342.
10. Joseph Chilton Pearce, *The Crack in the Cosmic Egg* (New York: Julian Press, 1971).
11. Lyall Watson, *Lifetide: the Biology of the Unconscious* (Simon and Schuste, 1979), p. 148.
12. Ibid., pp. 148–49.
13. Rupert Sheldrake, "Part I – Mind, Memory, and Archetype Morphic Resonance and the Collective Unconscious," *Psychological Perspectives* 18, no. 1 (1987): 9–25.
14. Israel Scheffler, *Science and Subjectivity* (Indianapolis: Bobbs-Merrill, 1967), p. 36ff.
15. Chris Swoyer, "True For," in *Relativism: Cognitive and Moral,* ed. Jack W. Meiland and Michael Krausz (Notre Dame, IN: University of Notre Dame Press, 1982), p. 97.
16. Nelson Goodman, *Ways of World Making* (Indianapolis: Hackett, 1978).
17. Thomas S. Kuhn, *The Structure of Scientific Revolutions* (Chicago: University of Chicago Press, 1970).
18. Kuhn, *The Structure of Scientific Revolutions*, 125.
19. Edward Hundert, "Can Neuroscience Contribute to Philosophy?" in *Mindwaves: Thoughts on Intelligence, Identity and Consciousness* (Basil Blackwell, 1987), pp. 413, 420–21.

20. Roger Trigg, *Reason and Commitment* (London: Cambridge University Press, 1973), pp. 15–16.
21. Donald Davidson, "Presidential Address" (speech made to the seventieth annual eastern meeting of the American Philosophical Association, Atlanta, December 28, 1973).
22. Alfred Korzybski, *Science and Sanity,* 4th ed. (Lakeville, CT: International Non-Aristotelian Library, 1933), p. 58.
23. Harvey Siegel, Relativism Refuted: A Critique of Contemporary Epistemological Relativism (Springer Science & Business Media, 2013), pp. 43–44.
24. Willard V. Quine, "On Empirically Equivalent Systems of the World," *Erkenntnis* 9, no. 3 (November 1975): 327–28.
25. Trigg, *Reason and Commitment,* pp. 135–36.

Index